↣ *Forging Ties, Forging Passports* ↢

Stanford Studies in Jewish History and Culture
Edited by David Biale and Sarah Abrevaya Stein

FORGING TIES, FORGING PASSPORTS

Migration and the Modern Sephardi Diaspora

DEVI MAYS

STANFORD UNIVERSITY PRESS
Stanford, California

STANFORD UNIVERSITY PRESS
Stanford, California

©2020 by the Board of Trustees of the Leland Stanford Junior University. All rights reserved.

No part of this book may be reproduced or transmitted in any form or by any means, electronic or mechanical, including photocopying and recording, or in any information storage or retrieval system without the prior written permission of Stanford University Press.

Printed in the United States of America on acid-free, archival-quality paper

Library of Congress Cataloging-in-Publication Data

Names: Mays, Devi, author.

Title: Forging ties, forging passports : migration and the modern sephardi diaspora / Devi Mays.

Description: Stanford : Stanford University Press, 2020. | Includes bibliographical references and index.

Identifiers: LCCN 2019050117 (print) | LCCN 2019050118 (ebook) | ISBN 9781503613201 (cloth) | ISBN 9781503613218 (paperback) | ISBN 9781503613225 (ebook)

Subjects: LCSH: Sephardim—Mexico—History—20th century. | Jews, Turkish—Mexico—History—20th century. | Jews—Mexico—History—20th century. | Citizenship—Mexico—History—20th century. | Emigration and immigration law—Mexico—History—20th century. | Mexico—Politics and government—1910-1946.

Classification: LCC F1392.J4 M39 2020 (print) | LCC F1392.J4 (ebook) | DDC 909/.04924—dc23

LC record available at https://lccn.loc.gov/2019050117

LC ebook record available at https://lccn.loc.gov/2019050118

Cover photos: (above) Sephardi Synagogue, Yehuda Halevi, in Mexico City. (below) Crowd inauguration in front of the Synagogue, Yehuda Halevi. Mexico City, 1942. Courtesy of Comunidad Sefaradí, AC de México.

Cover design: Rob Ehle

Typeset by Kevin Barrett Kane in 10.25/15 Adobe Caslon Pro

CONTENTS

Acknowledgments vii

A Note on Transliteration xi

INTRODUCTION 1

1 Fabricating the Foreign 21

2 Patriot Games 53

3 Uncertain Futures 97

4 "They Are Entirely Equal to the Spanish" 138

5 The Sephardi Connection 180

6 Forge Your Own Passport 215

CONCLUSION 239

Notes 247

Works Cited 309

Index 331

ACKNOWLEDGMENTS

In researching and writing a transnational history of migrants and their networks, I have forged many networks of my own. This book would not have been possible without the assistance, encouragement, support, and questions of many individuals and institutions, too many to list exhaustively here, but every one deeply appreciated.

Matthias Lehmann has consistently shown me what an ideal scholar is—constructively incisive, always supportive, a generous thinker, mentor, and colleague. Peter Guardino, Mark Roseman, Kaya Şahin, and Sara Scalenghe contributed to shaping the framework of this study and inspired avenues forward. Richard Menkis saw potential in an undergraduate student, and has always encouraged me.

Over the years, I have shared my work at various institutions and workshops. While I was a postdoctoral fellow at the Jewish Theological Seminary, Alan Cooper, Barbara Mann, and Shuly Rubin Schwartz propelled me to think more deeply about what is Jewish about this story and all that Jewishness can encompass. Hasia Diner and Derek Penslar asked probing questions about intersections between modern Sephardi migrants and capitalism in the working group on Jews and the economy at the Center for Jewish History, and the fellows for the theme year on Jews and empire of the Frankel Institute for Advanced Judaic Studies at the University of Michigan encouraged me to explore how Sephardim negotiated the end of empire. The National Endowment for the Humanities summer seminar on World War I in the Middle East, under the thoughtful guidance of Mustafa Aksakal and Elizabeth Thompson, enabled me to put Sephardi experiences into a larger regional context and allowed me to begin conversations with Dominique Reill and Ipek Yosmaoğlu that have transformed my thinking. I was fortunate to participate in the Instituto Tepoztlán's stimulating discussions of theory and action on Colonial Complexes and Migrations and Diasporas, and Gerry Cadava, Heather Vrana, and Elliott Young encouraged me to link Jewish and Latin American histories. The Khayrallah Center for Lebanese Diaspora Studies under Akram Khater has shown me that there is also a home for Sephardi Jews within *Mahjar* studies, and I am particularly grateful to Lily Ballofet, Steven Hyland, and Camila Pastor for sharing their expertise. Stacy Fahrenthold is an inspiration as a scholar and friend. Adriana Brodsky and Rebecca Kobrin pushed me to reconsider the broader implications of my research in critiquing an earlier draft of the full manuscript, and Tobias Brinkmann and Libby Garland have provided crucial guidance in questions about the narratives of migration. Alexander Kaye, Shira Kohn, and Joshua Teplitsky offered invaluable critiques. Julia Phillips Cohen and Devin Naar have been generous with their time, sources, and intellect.

I owe much to scholars and archivists who have welcomed me into their networks of knowledge. Rıfat Bali in Turkey and Daniela Gleizer and Liz Hamui in Mexico have been critical in shaping my research questions. Magy Sommer at the Centro de Documentación e Investigación de la Comunidad Ashkenazí in Mexico City was an engaging interlocutor. Ricardo at the Archivo Histórico del Distrito Federal shared his love of Oaxacan music. Rose Levyne at the Alliance Israélite Universelle in Paris was always patient with my French-for-reading-knowledge-only. Dana Herman and Gary Zola made the American Jewish Archives my most comfortable archival experience.

At the University of Michigan, I have benefited greatly from supportive colleagues and friends. Deborah Dash Moore has offered detailed feedback and mentorship. Melanie Tanielian and Jeffrey Veidlinger have provided critical eyes and compassionate hearts. Paroma Chatterjee, Mayte Green-Mercado, Michèle Hannoosh, Karla Mallette, Ryan Szpiech, and Ruth Tsoffar have pushed me to consider Mediterranean Jews from global perspectives. Yasmin Moll and the Writing Wizards have provided discipline and encouragement. I am grateful for the friendship and intellectual camaraderie of Mai Hassan, Harry Kashdan, R. R. Neis, Bryan Roby, Sasha de Vogel, and Rebecca Wollenberg.

A special thanks is owed to Sarah Abrevaya Stein and David Biale for seeing the value in this project, and to Margo Irvin and Stanford University Press for ushering it along. The anonymous peer reviewers pushed me to strengthen my thoughts, and Marie Deer was an astute copyeditor. Any errors are mine alone.

I owe a deep debt of gratitude to supportive family and friends, particularly my parents, Bhavani Mair and Dick Mays, and my cousin, Beth Zilberman, who is the only person with whom I can enthusiastically discuss immigration law. Jessica Carr, Erin Corber, and Evelyn Dean-Olmsted are the best of friends and intellectual interlocuters. And finally, I acknowledge those past migrants whose histories I convey herein and whose experiences resound today in the lives of millions of others.

A NOTE ON TRANSLITERATION

Ottoman Turkish has been transliterated according to the simplified system employed by the *International Journal of Middle East Studies*. Judeo-Spanish, called many different things by its speakers, is called "Ladino" herein for simplicity's sake and has been transliterated according to a modified version of the *Aki Yerushalayim* transcription system. For Ladino originally written in Latin script, the author's spelling has been preserved.

Names of individuals and places changed, sometimes dramatically, over the course of the early twentieth century, often depending on who was speaking and whom they were addressing. I preserve this historical transition—thus, Salonica becomes Thessaloniki in later chapters, and Constantinople becomes Istanbul—unless directly quoting a source. Individual migrants' names likewise changed across geography and time, a process that I note by putting new names in parentheses; similarly, the new surnames of Turkish officials are noted in parentheses.

Forging Ties, Forging Passports

INTRODUCTION

IN THE SPRING OF 1949, a man by the name of Mauricio Fresco living in Mexico City wrote a letter in French to the renowned Turkish Jewish historian Abraham Galanté in Istanbul, Turkey. "I doubt you will remember me," penned Mauricio, since they had last met at least twenty-nine years earlier, when Mauricio was but a youth. Mauricio reminded Galanté that the latter had regularly visited the office where David Fresco, Mauricio's father, struggled to publish his newspaper, the Ladino-language *El Tiempo* that circulated widely among Sephardi Jews in the Ottoman capital and beyond.[1] And it was information about his father that Mauricio sought, since he had been "unfortunately too young and naïve to be able to inquire or know much about my father's past" before his father died in France in 1933. "Although much time has passed, I still have fond memories of those who collaborated with and loved my father, because I must confess I am proud to be his son."[2]

Mauricio sketched a brief portrait for Galanté of his life since leaving the Ottoman Empire as a young man. He had worked "in America" as a journalist, publishing many books and articles in various languages, and had spent time in Russia and China. And perhaps David Fresco had told his old friend that his youngest son, Mauricio, had involved himself "in the world of diplomacy?" Protected by his diplomatic post, he had witnessed both the occupation and liberation of Paris. Though Mauricio did not tell Galanté that it was in the Mexican diplomatic corps that he had worked for eighteen years, he shared that his experiences had compelled him to prepare a new book, titled *Forge Your Own Passport*. This book, Mauricio noted, would "prove the stupidity of passports, visas, nationalities, races, etc."

Fresco's letter—and particularly his disdain for passports, visas, nationalities, and races as means that enabled, in his words, the exploitation of humanity—hints at the central tension this volume aims to explore: states constitute their status as states, in part, through distinguishing between citizens or subjects and possible interlopers and controlling the ingress and egress of both populations. This is enabled by documentation such as passports and visas and often refracted through the categorization of certain races or nationalities as more desirable than others. Over the course of his own life, Fresco and thousands of his Sephardi coreligionists migrated from areas in the Ottoman Empire to Western Europe, the Americas, and beyond. For these individuals, migration was often the most effective form of removing themselves from violence or oppression, employing their education, and exploring opportunities for economic advancement and social mobility. If states attempt to categorize, make stable, and fix populations, the individuals and groups this book examines often thrived in motion, in blurring categories that were not as rigid as consular and border officials liked to believe, or at least to portray in their interactions with higher-ups. Sometimes the officials themselves, like Fresco, had a vested interest in allowing for ambiguity, since that very ambiguity enabled their own mobility and even, in Fresco's own case, forged documentation.

Over the course of the early twentieth century, advances in technology and transportation made the world ever smaller. Journeys from the eastern Mediterranean to Atlantic port cities in the Americas that had previously taken months were shortened to weeks, and expanded railroad networks hastened inland travel. Telegrams, though prohibitively expensive, enabled almost instantaneous communication across vast distances. Photography, increasingly ubiquitous, provided a means of sharing new landscapes, identifying possible future spouses, and keeping friends and relatives abreast of changes in personal and professional fortunes. They also enabled authorities to fix images to documentation assigned to people in motion. By 1920, newspapers published in Ladino in New York boasted of agents as far afield as Seattle, Havana,

Mexico City, Rio de Janeiro, and Skopje and readers throughout the Americas, Europe, and Asia; Ladino periodicals in Izmir, Istanbul, and elsewhere regularly published pieces drawn from the American Ladino press and from Jewish and non-Jewish publications in Europe and the Americas.[3] Ladino novels exposed readers to the possibilities of migration within Europe and across the Atlantic—emphasizing for dramatic effect the changes in clothing, names, behaviors, and wealth that ensued—and of married women abandoned by husbands and pregnant women unable to wed for lack of documentation.[4] Music and food, too, increasingly linked the world. The quintessential song of the Mexican Revolution, "La Cucaracha," made its way to interwar Salonica. There, it was adapted into Ladino and the reference to marijuana removed.[5] Bananas, meanwhile, were expensive in the Ottoman Empire, yet one new arrival to Mexico noted that because he was familiar with them from before he migrated, he knew to purchase them as his only food for the train journey from the port of Veracruz to Mexico City. They were quite cheap in Mexico.[6] Accelerated flows of people, goods, and knowledge helped to bind together individuals separated by mountains, seas, and borders and to increase familiarity between distant lands and peoples.

Language, too, allowed for a certain type of understanding. Ladino-speaking migrants from the Mediterranean expressed the strange familiarity they experienced upon hearing Spanish in their ports of entry into the Americas—whether in Havana, Veracruz, or Buenos Aires. This marked their migratory experience as dramatically different from that of Jewish and Ottoman migrants whose mother tongue was Arabic, Armenian, Yiddish, or Greek. "Some time ago, a Sephardi established in Havana sent for his elderly mother to come, an old woman who had never left Salonica. Upon stepping upon Cuban soil, the good woman exclaimed with surprise: "Listen, my son, are they all Jews here . . . that they speak like us?" wrote a Sephardi migrant in a book published in Havana in 1958.[7] Rarer were the stories of the incommensurability of Ladino and Spanish, of women who went to the market to purchase food only to find that they could not communicate their desires to the Mexican sellers; *muestro espanyol*, "our Spanish," was actually quite distinct from Mexican Spanish. But the shared heritage of Ladino and Spanish was sometimes understood, by Sephardi migrants and Mexican officials alike, as a manifestation of cultural and even biological commonalities between their speakers, regardless of whether their birthplace was in the eastern Mediterranean or the Americas.

Even as new technologies brought the world together, the collapse of long-standing empires created new states and borders that grew more difficult to cross as states increasingly regulated migration. The proliferation of passports and other forms of state-issued documentation in the years after World War I aided monitoring. The regulation and control of documentation and movement was essential to the institutionalization of postwar nationalizing states, which were often idealized as being culturally and ethnically homogenous.[8] Though passports and visas existed in some countries prior to World War I, that war is often seen as the harbinger of the Passport Age, in which passports, visas, and other forms of documentation of identity and travel became ubiquitous and often the sole basis upon which legal movement was decided. New countries engaged in intensive processes of nation-building that often resulted in the marginalization of ethnic and religious minorities, if not the tacit or active encouragement of their emigration. Nationality was a key factor in the transition from empire to nation-state, holding a particular character in each postwar state.[9] Regulating the movements of people and goods across their borders became a means by which states established their legitimacy and power. This required the establishment of normative classifications of religion, language, nationality, and race and the ability of officials to easily fit migrants within these categories.

Individuals could and did confound states' attempts to classify them and thereby regulate and restrict their movement. It was precisely characteristics that defied confinement within externally discernible categories that at times enabled individuals to cross boundaries and borders effectively. Migratory laws and restrictions were not all-powerful. The individuals explored in this volume drew on all tools at their disposal in response to or subversion of such legal regimes, thereby prompting state responses in an ongoing dialectic on the desirability of certain types of immigrants or emigrations.

For states invested in creating a coherent national vision, individuals who possessed characteristics that defied confinement posed a problem, if not a direct threat. Successful enforcement of the state policies that shaped nationalizing projects depended on state actors being able to properly identify individuals. As this book will show, officials were often not equipped to do so, particularly with individuals deeply embedded within transnational networks.

Histories of migration are often told from the perspective of one particular country, as narratives of immigrant assimilation or the lack thereof, or they analyze migration as linear, whether unidirectionally or, in the case of return migration, bidirectionally so.[10] As the philosopher Thomas Nail asserts, "place-bound membership in a society is assumed as primary."[11] The terminology of "emigrant" and "immigrant" emphasizes the state-centered perspective and the implied normalcy of stasis over movement. However, migration is often far more complex than that. Centering the practices of mobile individuals highlights the complexities of migration and the limits of the ability of state-centered terminologies and perspectives to effectively encapsulate their experiences. I therefore use the term "migrant" and its derivatives—except when reflecting the usage of specific sources or highlighting the state perspective—in order to center individuals' experiences of migration and to challenge the presumed primacy of state understandings of people on the move.

The individuals explored in this book lived in a state of hypermobility—sustained, long-term, nonlinear migrations lacking a clear teleology. These individuals, like Mauricio Fresco, moved frequently, whether those moves took the form of relocations intended to be permanent or of prolonged business trips between destinations throughout the Mediterranean, Caribbean, and Atlantic.[12] Nation-states and national laws mattered even for such transnational individuals, but we should not blindly accept nationalizing states as the norm and transnational individuals as exceptions.[13] Even those ostensibly "settled" in one country moved frequently within its borders. Such hypermobility necessitated acquiring and maintaining the tools—linguistic, monetary, legal, and extralegal—that enabled continued mobility. This mobility was often aided by others of the same religious and linguistic background, who shared strategies, capital and goods, homes, and even documentation.

Hypermobility, which entailed the sustained movements of peoples, knowledge, and goods, connected Sephardi individuals from similar origins in the northeastern Mediterranean who were now spread across oceans and continents. In doing so, it enabled the creation and perpetuation of a diaspora. The historian Matthias Lehmann has argued for understanding diaspora as "something that *happens* rather than something that *is*."[14] The "continuous circulation of people, money, goods, and information" creates networks of individuals and communities in communication. These networks, sustained through constant interaction, transform separate places into one community.[15] Hypermobility, and the networks of communication and exchange that it maintained across continents, transformed dispersed Sephardi individuals into a modern Sephardi diaspora.

This book is not one of simple stories and trajectories. Even in stasis and stability, lives traverse obstacles and triumphs. This is all the more true when an individual is on the move and must acquire and employ new skills to survive, and even more so to thrive, in new contexts, or when changing political and economic circumstances change the familiar into the unfamiliar. When we explore the stories of thousands of individuals who contended with profound transformations in politics and laws on local, national, and international scales, who crossed or were crossed by borders, all the while maintaining strong bonds to others across oceans and seas, we must delve into the complexities behind their decisions, actions, and trajectories.

Understanding their histories requires teasing out threads of class, race, gender, legal codes, and nation-building, exploring how these threads themselves changed over time and how together they wove the fabric through which individuals embroidered their lives. This book cobbles together the history of individual actors: how people bound together by religion, language, and a shared regional origin in an empire that ceased to exist in their lifetime navigated these profound changes and made a space for themselves. Their story cannot be told, nor understood, without simultaneously exploring how states became states in the tumultuous years of the early twentieth century and how this was inextricably connected to the process of creating nations, often through the deliberate inclusion or exclusion of certain populations.[16] Tracing the complex histories of several thousand Sephardi migrants and how they intersected with those in other locations, including those who never left their places of origin, enables us to explore questions of nation- and state-building from the vantage point of those whose religion, language, perceived race, and origins often—but not always—cast them to the margins of the new nations forged in the twentieth century.

While migration histories like this one reveal how individuals on the move encountered and countered attempts by various states to fix them in space and their identities in paperwork, this does not mean that migrants operated beyond the reach of coercive networks. Migrants created their own transnational networks, linking places of origin and diasporic nodes that monitored and controlled the behaviors of those on the move, at times reinforcing preexisting hierarchies of authority and at times creating new ones. Migration might afford women the freedom to choose their own husbands, for example, but they were nevertheless constrained by social and familial pressure to marry someone within their own community or class, or by the threat of exclusion should they decide not to marry a man with whom they had only exchanged letters and photographs and whom they had crossed the Atlantic to marry, only to find that he had lied about his appearance.[17] Migrant women in particular turned to the Ottoman chief rabbi for information on the character of potential husbands they met abroad, to which the informal networks of communication on lineage and reputation did not extend.[18] Migrants threatened to report others to their family members in their places of origin should they behave inappropriately, while Ladino periodicals reported on, shamed, and sought to track down migrant men who had abandoned wives, dodged the draft, or committed murder. These internal coercive networks perpetuated gendered modes of behavior even in diaspora and offer a corrective to understandings of migration as a means of escaping social, cultural, or political controls.

"The migrant is the political figure of our time," writes the philosopher Thomas Nail, positing the migrant as a social position that "people move into and out of under certain social conditions of mobility."[19] This presumes that having once been a migrant—or, in the case of Jews in Turkey, simply having descended from those who had crossed seas centuries earlier—one can never hope to be understood as anything other than a migrant. Many of the individuals whose histories this book brings to light were of a generation whose adolescence or young adulthood was framed by a world war, the dissolution of the empire into which they were born, and the creation of new states in its wake. They contended with migration in an age where passports and visas came to be of utmost importance but were not yet regularized and where ideas of citizenship, nationality, and the nation were omnipresent but what these concepts defined or conveyed, when and how they mattered, and to whom was not clearly understood or agreed upon by all parties involved. For this generation of men and women, "migrant" was not a temporary status but rather a semipermanent or permanent condition that was shaped by, and shaped, the historical benchmarks their lives traversed. For those of a generation that one migrant described as "arrived from the other side," their experiences of dislocation differentiated them from those born in the Americas; their being migrants meant that "the form of thinking was totally different" from that of Sephardi coreligionists without such experiences.[20] The migrant may be the political figure of our time, but if we look at the experiences of migrants from a century before, we see that the migrant has been a central political figure for more than our moment and that the social position of the migrant is a condition that not all want to move out of or are even capable of doing so.

This is not to claim that the individuals whose stories we explore in the following pages did not try to belong—and often succeed. The Sephardi migrants whose histories this book weaves within the broader historical framework of state- and nation-building often proved adept at understanding and adapting to legal, social, economic, linguistic, racial, and cultural norms within the countries in which they moved. Tobias Brinkmann has described early-twentieth-century Jewish migrants in general as "supranationals in a world of nation-states," who often lacked state protection and occupied marginal and transitory spaces as they accommodated the transition from empire to nationalizing states.[21] At times, those who occupy culturally or socially marginal positions have deep familiarity not only with their own positionality but also with the norms of the non-marginalized and the mainstream. Sephardi Jews, whether in migration or stasis, often shifted their performances of self, family, and community in ways that enabled them to blur the boundaries of belonging. Doing this successfully required migrants to quickly learn the local or national expectations for who fit in and how to mold themselves to these expectations. As we will see, at times, certain forms of explicit otherness or the performance of specific types of foreignness that did not necessarily correspond to migrants' origins or the documents they possessed served as the most effective way for these migrants to claim a space for themselves. Sometimes visibility—on the pages of newspapers, in the marketplaces or on the street, in the eyes of state officials who at times deliberately looked the other way—aided belonging, often when linked to particular performances of class status and raced and gendered behavioral expectations. At other moments, it was invisibility to the same audiences, walking down the street as a stranger but not a foreigner, that indicated belonging.[22] But success was never guaranteed, and full belonging remained tantalizingly elusive for many individuals.

The possibility of using migration as a strategy for transforming cultural capital into economic capital was both aided and hindered, in various periods, by the ways in which migrants were racialized in new locales, and how their skin color, accent, and religion marked them.[23] Throughout Latin America, migrants from regions that had once formed part of the Ottoman Empire, as well as areas as far afield as Morocco, were popularly grouped together, regardless of their religion, nationality, native language, or ethnicity, as *"turcos,"* a term that carried economically desirable and socially undesirable connotations.[24] In the United States, meanwhile, while Syrians repeatedly adjudicated their racial status in order to be declared white by law and entitled to the protections and privileges that whiteness conferred, socially and culturally they were "not quite white."[25] Concurrently, American Jews also grappled with their racialization, negotiating Jewishness, whiteness, and blackness within a framework that did not easily fit Jews, whose patterns of endogamy, urbanness, and specific trades marked them as something other than white to many white Americans.[26] And in Brazil, French West Africa, Southeast Asia, and elsewhere, Ottoman migrants negotiated local and imperial racialized hierarchies that were intimately linked with class and capitalism, transforming these migrants into what one historian called "interlopers of empire" or, in the less generous view of another, empire's "ugly tools."[27] As the anthropologist Camila Pastor argues in regard to elite *Mahjari* migrants in Mexico, largely Christian and from areas that had come under French mandate after the dissolution of the Ottoman Empire, French patronage enabled the reading of these migrants, when they claimed to be French, as being equivalent to the Spanish and thereby racialized as white, with the attendant privilege that afforded.[28] Social and economic ascent might be hindered by the negative associations of the *turco* label, but deep familiarity with Mexican racial norms and the skilled use of language, gendered performance of class, and even clothing at times enabled Sephardi migrants and others to be read as something other than *turco*.

Precarity undergirded all aspects of these individuals' lives. Although histories of Jewish migration often emphasize upward mobility—a pitfall into which, admittedly, this book too sometimes falls—for every success story there was likely a less-well-documented story of failure. For every migrant man who moved from peddling to having his own shop, there was likely a peddler who, having acquired a shop, lost it when governmental regulations changed, or whose ill health forced his young children to peddle in his stead.[29] And it is all too easy to overlook the migrant women—Sephardi and *Mahjari* alike—who appear as "homemakers" on all official documentation but who often worked late into the night sewing the clothing that their husbands, fathers, or they themselves peddled, or who owned their own businesses or ran those of their husbands when the latter were traveling for extended periods of time, but who often concealed this.[30]

Migration narratives are often told as linear and direct, with one set of push factors propelling emigration and another set of pull factors that drew migrants to their destination. In the Age of Migration, when millions of people crossed borders and oceans, there are certain set narratives—the primary motivation behind the emigration of Jews is often described as flight from persecution, the primary pull factor the opportunity to live unoppressed as Jews. But history is neither monocausal nor simple. The decision to leave was informed by multiple factors. While persecution did, at times, play an important role, other key factors ranged from the desire for economic advancement, sometimes with the intent to return home wealthier; the search for a social mobility that was often not available within the rigid structures of Ottoman Jewish society; capitalizing on the linguistic and other tools that widespread education among this generation had provided; a desire for adventure, to escape overbearing families, or to join an unknown spouse whose photograph had been sent across the Atlantic; or even just the happenstance that a cousin with the same name had received exit papers and a passport and was then unable to travel. Likewise, the choice of destination depended on a number of factors that changed over time. These ranged from the personal—the cost of a ticket and what an individual or family could afford, where one had friends or relatives who might ease the transition into a new place, and what languages one spoke—to the logistical and legal: the routes of trains or ships; the ease with which one could acquire an exit permit; what country was accepting individuals of which ages, nationalities, races, religions, genders, or financial status; and how to acquire the necessary documentation should one not fit into the desired immigrant profile. Staying put was a choice that likewise entailed repeated decisions as circumstances changed. As these factors evolved over time, the same individual might relocate again, and again, and again. Migration was often multi-staged, involving several new countries and many new cities, and the initial final destination might, over months or years, transform into a place of prolonged transit.

Migration involved not just the migrating individual but also family, friends, and community. It was an act with profound repercussions for all involved. Migration stretched apart family units, created new obstacles for Jewish institutions, and challenged what it meant to belong to a community, whether that was desirable, and what such a community might look like amidst all the other changes. As more people relocated, local Jewish communities and institutions found themselves stressed and stretched, whether by the lack of financial support because of their shrinking base, the pressing need to aid Jewish refugees and internal or external migrants, or the desire to establish Jewish cemeteries in cities or countries that had never before contended with the Jewish dead. In adopting the lens of the migrant, this book attempts to weave together all those connected to and affected by migration.

Individuals drive the book's narrative and analysis. Many historical studies of migrants focus on the organizations and institutions that combated, aided, and relocated them or on state and local responses to and control of people on the move. In such narratives, the lives, voices, and choices of individuals are relegated to the sidelines, if not altogether absent. But migrants, particularly hypermobile individuals, were fully constrained neither by states nor institutions. Even as this book contends with the rhetoric and actions of state actors surrounding the monitoring, controlling, and restricting of migrants, it shifts focus to individual migrants as they contended with and crossed the borders of many states. It draws on a wide array of archival research, conducted in multiple archives across seven countries—immigration and naturalization records, ship manifests, civil and criminal court cases, confidential investigations, international treaties and correspondence—as well as press sources, memoirs, and oral histories. It moves beyond focusing on how one or two states sought to make sense or use of Sephardi migrants. Rather, in tracing the movement of individuals across time and space—and through various archives and periodicals—I explore how these migrants played with the ways that their religious, national, ethnic, racial, gender, and class taxonomies were read across different legal and national regimes. These subversive practices, indicative of the ability to speedily recognize and react to political and legal shifts in various national contexts, enabled the migrants' transoceanic hypermobility even as states increasingly sought to circumscribe ingress and egress.

This focus on individuals and their movements, actions, and connections disrupts categories like "Sephardi," "Jewish," "Ottoman," "Mexican," or "Salonican" that historians and others sometimes unquestioningly employ. The use of such categories fixes attendant meanings and boundaries onto individuals and communities who may never have understood themselves in such terms, or for whom the concepts bore a very different valence. Focusing on the networks that these hypermobile individuals forged and maintained over the course of their complex trajectories gives us insight into the precise ways in which such individuals conceived of their world and ensured space for themselves and others within them. This book pays close attention to such questions as: to whom did these migrants turn when choosing a spouse or a business partner? who served as claimants, defendants, and witnesses in criminal and civil court cases and for marriages and on birth certificates? from whom did they borrow money or merchandise? who attested for them in naturalization petitions? and whom did they list as contacts on overseas trips? These dense individual connections shed light on broader patterns of association that, in turn, enable us to grasp which networks were meaningful in which contexts, blurring the bounded categories that scholars often affix to historical subjects. Categories like nationality and citizenship mattered little to these individuals in their associations with certain others, even though it is through such categories that their records are preserved in archives and these categories certainly affected when and how they moved through the world. Unlike in places like New York, Seattle, or Paris, whether one was *Selanikli* or *Izmirli* did not play a critical role for the division or connection of the migrants this book examines.[31]

Jewishness often mattered, but most of the migrants at the center of this book's analysis did not socialize or conduct business with or marry Jews who came from Eastern Europe, or Aleppo, or Damascus. Sometimes men, in particular those who had migrated to Mexico early or who lived in relatively remote areas of the Yucatán or Oaxaca, married non-Jewish women, and many migrant men had non-Jewish mistresses in addition to their Jewish wives; others not only married non-Jewish women but were also cremated upon death; and yet many of their social and familial connections remained within a common sphere. And while the individuals examined here would come to be grouped together in Mexico as part of an eventual *comunidad sefardita*, some of them would not have belonged to a Sephardi community within their places of origin, but were *francos* of Italian Jewish extraction or Ottoman subjects of Central European origins.[32] Class distinctions remained critical, with those coming from elite families in their cities of origin often retaining such a status in new surroundings and marrying others from similar class but not geographical origins. Social and economic mobility for others could be possible through recourse to patronage from these elites. Hypermobility was a strategy employed by women and men alike, from peddlers and homemakers to diplomats and communal elites.

Nonetheless, most of these individuals not only originated in and traveled to and from, but also married, socialized with, relied upon, testified for, and fought with others who came from what Aron Rodrigue and Esther Benbassa have referred to as a Sephardi *Kulturbereich*, or Ladino-language cultural sphere that encompassed the Aegean littoral and parts of the Balkans and extended to Alexandria in Egypt.[33] They formed extensive networks of communication and interaction, in the form of transnationally shared Ladino periodicals that maintained both imagined and real communities, marriages, commercial relationships, patronage and kinship networks, and continued recourse to the Ottoman chief rabbi. In other historical and geographical contexts, "Sephardi" might be applied as a blanket term in contrast to "Ashkenazi," or might be deliberately adopted by migrants from origins as disparate as Morocco, Syria, and Yugoslavia, as a means of uniting to amplify their voice among the cacophony created by the much larger Ashkenazi contingents.[34] In Mexico, in contrast, by the early 1920s, large numbers of Ottoman Jews of Aleppan and Damascene origins, as well as

Ashkenazi Jews, each formed their own distinct communities, and the term "Sephardi" came to be used in reference only to those of specifically Ladino-speaking origins, who embraced the term themselves. While these various Jewish subgroups often lived and worked in similar locations, a focus on the networks created through individual interactions highlights the discreteness of these groups, which rarely intersected; Aleppan Jews, as the sociologist Liz Hamui has shown, rarely married Jews of other geographical origins, and deliberately reproduced through marriage and familial relations the patterns of informal association and collective identity that had characterized Jewish life in Aleppo.[35] The specific networks that migrants created through their interactions created meaning and transformed space into place.[36] Common geographical spaces were shared by a diverse array of Jews who maintained their own networks, but common nodes did not mean that these discrete networks intersected.[37] This book's attention to individuals' networks of association, commerce, and marriage establishes the contours of my analysis and reveals few points of interaction between Ladino-speaking Sephardi Jews and other Jews of Ottoman provenance, and even fewer between Sephardi Jews and non-Jews of Ottoman origins. Even as borders increasingly divided the region in which Ladino speakers lived and from which they migrated, individual relationships highlight the maintenance of shared networks of communication, marriage, commerce, patronage, and religious authority. Migration expanded the boundaries of a Ladino cultural sphere to include the Americas and beyond.

Originating in the same empire or sharing the same religious ascription did not mean that all those of Ottoman or even Ottoman Jewish provenance saw themselves as belonging to the same diaspora, despite Ottoman attempts to create a shared identification. Rather, they might best be understood as belonging to a series of overlapping diasporas that intersected at key moments and diverged at others, and who often drew on similar tactics to sustain networks and facilitate geographical and social mobility.[38] These tactics included hypermobility, multilinguality, transnational connections, variegated citizenship, engagement with extralegal practices to secure geographical and social mobility, strong familial ties shored up through marriage, and distinct patronage networks.[39] However, the various subgroups also drew on distinct traits that they might employ to their advantage. Maronite Christian migrants from what would become Lebanon played up their shared Catholicism to be included in Mexico and to make claims on French patronage.[40] After the dissolution of the Ottoman Empire and the establishment of mandate systems, Arabic-speaking Jews from Syria and Lebanon could access French protection in a way not available to Ladino-speaking Jews from the new Republic of Turkey, Greece, Bulgaria, or Yugoslavia, as discussed in chapter 4. Arabic-speaking migrants in Mexico, often but not always Christian, drew on their ostensible connections to the Holy Land to peddle religious artifacts to Mexico's Catholic population, playing up their purported regional and religious origins in order to ease their economic and social integration.[41] Later, they opened commercial establishments with names such as "La Perla de Oriente," "La Mariposa de Oriente," or "El Arca de Noé," highlighting an Oriental or biblical connection.[42] Sephardi Jews, in contrast, often emphasized the ambiguity of their foreignness by highlighting French connections and language, including, as analyzed in chapters 1 and 2, through naming their commercial establishments "La Ciudad de Paris," "La Ciudad de Lyon," or "Paris-Bijou." Sephardi Jews also drew on ancestral ties to Spain and the similarities between Ladino and Spanish to highlight their ability to belong in a post-revolutionary Mexico taken with the idea of creating a mestizo nation that combined indigenous and Spanish elements. This distinguished them from others of Ottoman provenance, as well as Ashkenazi Jews, who did not have the same linguistic and ancestral heritage.

Sephardi Jews were only one out of the multiplicity of Ottoman and Jewish diasporas who navigated the transformation from the world of empires to a world of mandates and nationalizing states. Yet exploring how they drew on strategies shared by those of Ottoman origins along with how they diverged from others who might have made similar claims on French culture and commerce in Mexico and yet did not, as well as how they drew on linguistic and ancestral heritage unique to them, highlights the diversity of Ottoman and post-Ottoman migrations. It allows us to see in sharp relief the active forging of a twentieth-century Sephardi diaspora through networked liminalities, which were similar in broad strokes to other diasporic communities of Ottoman origins but whose details emphasize the resourcefulness of migrants who quickly learned how their specificities of religion, language, or citizenship could become a pretext for inclusion or exclusion.

Nonetheless, this book avoids making claims about the identity of these individuals beyond what can be gleaned from their patterns of interactions. While there were intellectuals and religious leaders who thought deeply and published about Sephardi, Jewish, Ottoman, or Turkish Jewish identity throughout the period in question, few of the migrants—many of whom were peddlers, or pieceworkers, or owned dry goods and novelty stores—left behind historical traces of how they viewed themselves. This is not to say that they did not think of their own identity or place within the world—in personal correspondence they sometimes referred to *nuestra colonia*, "our colony," suggesting a shared understanding of the community to which they belonged. But what these parameters were is rarely explicitly articulated by these individuals in the types of materials that have left archival traces.

And it is nigh impossible to glean a sense of individual identity from external sources. In the chaotic period that accompanied and followed the end of the Ottoman Empire and the attendant rise of nationalizing states, categories became destabilized and boundaries blurred. How accurately did categories of nationality, citizenship, or even religion fit a woman like Rebecca Mitrani, born in 1881 in Kirkkilise, then a part of the Ottoman Empire, but who claimed on entry paperwork into Mexico in 1930 that Kirkkilise was part of Greece, not Turkey? Prior to moving to Mexico, she had lived in Cuba, where she gave birth to several children who migrated to Mexico with her. And though she signed her name in *soletreo*, the Sephardi cursive script, she declared that her religion was Greek Orthodox. From these sources, should we surmise that Mitrani felt Greek? Or Cuban? Or Greek Orthodox? Or Jewish? Or did she simply provide Mexican authorities with paperwork attesting to a specific nationality and religious affiliation because of immigration restrictions in Mexico that prohibited the entry of Turkish nationals and did not look favorably upon Jews? Does not the paperwork that bears her photograph and signature—preserved in Mexico's national archive—tell us far more about how clearly she grasped the stakes of her appearing to fit into certain categories over others in her attempt to relocate than it does about how she conceived of herself?

But questioner and answerer learned from each other, producing mutually constituted statuses.[43] For bureaucratic institutions, documents helped to standardize and fix social identity and significance.[44] However, understanding migrants primarily from the perspective of states and institutions obscures the meanings that individuals assigned to these social identities. That is to say, the values and significance that bureaucratic institutions and state assigned to identity categories may not have held the same meaning for the individuals to whom those categories were assigned, even if those individuals used that same language to express themselves.

Any historical analysis is a story of archives and the sources they contain. Writing a transnational history requires research in a wide array of archival and other historical materials. But even on the level of state archives, different countries value, preserve, reveal, and conceal different types of sources. In Mexico, the archives of the *Secretaría de Relaciones Exteriores* (secretariat of foreign relations) are available to any researcher willing to use the paper card catalogue that holds the location information for the files; in Turkey, the archives of the *Dışişleri Bakanlığı* (ministry of foreign affairs) were, at the time this book was researched, not available to historians at all. The Sephardi community in Mexico did not keep records from its early history, and the Turkish Jewish community does not allow access to its records. When tracing an individual across borders and over time, names themselves might change, and their spelling or the conventions for identifying people certainly did—one migrant was born Yohanan in Ottoman Izmir, became Jean in France, and died as Juan in Mexico; and while Mexican, American, or French sources might identify an individual by surname, Ottoman and some Jewish sources, in the absence of patronyms, used the person's father's first name, making it nigh impossible to trace such people. The history written here is, like most histories, woven together from scraps and fragments. Unlike in many histories, however, because this book draws on materials from over a dozen archives in many countries, here the scraps do not always match in color and texture. The narrative is sometimes uneven, with different types of histories being conveyed depending on whether it is focusing on developments in one country versus another, much less on stories that weave multiple countries together. In spite of its unevenness, however, I hope that I have made a successful claim for the value of this approach. It reveals much about how migrants themselves moved in the world and navigated obstacles and opportunities, and it sheds light on the similar and divergent ways in which the figure of the migrant was critical to processes of nation-building across the world.

This book is divided into six chronological chapters that span the first half of the twentieth century. Laws built on or demolished previous laws as empires transformed into nationalizing states and the rule of dictator or sultan was supplanted by ostensibly democratic one-party rule. An individual who departed from Constantinople to arrive in Mexico City in 1907 contended with drastically different political and migratory regimes than did an individual following the same trajectory several decades later. To grasp the motives, decisions, and movements that a person made, we must understand the specific geographical, legal, and political contexts in which that person acted. We follow a roughly chronological approach, exploring how persistent questions of belonging, nationality, citizenship, gender, class, race, and even Judaism were transformed in the face of marked changes in political, legal, and social norms in the places through which migrants traversed.

The first chapter argues that Ottoman Sephardi migrants in Mexico were caught up in a process of defining citizenship and national belonging. They resisted classification as either Ottoman expatriates or unequivocal Mexicans simply by maintaining a diasporic consciousness and connectedness with Sephardim in the Ottoman homeland, France, Cuba, and the United States. Drawing on these transnational financial and familial networks, Sephardi migrants were able to acquire and sell wares from the United States and Europe (specifically France). In doing so, they capitalized on Mexican Francophilia and their ambiguous national backgrounds to market themselves and their products as "desirable."

Chapter 2 explores the period of prolonged war that accompanied the end of the Ottoman Empire and the Mexican Revolution. This chapter argues that in spite of Ottoman and Jewish communal leaders' demands that Sephardi subjects actively manifest their loyalty to the Ottoman war effort by serving in the armed forces, many Sephardim migrated instead. Some desired to avoid military service altogether, while others were eager to serve in the armed forces of the new states in which they resided and with which they identified. Mexico-based émigrés subverted Ottoman and American attempts to regulate them by acquiring or performing alternative nationalities. This allowed them to bypass American restrictions on the entrance and commercial transactions of enemy nationals, facilitating their continued mobility in the face of the increasing surveillance of movement that accompanied World War I.

The exploration of how migrants and others made sense of the upheaval, chaos, and possibility that came in the wake of World War I and the Mexican Revolution undergirds the third chapter. Migrants and those who remained navigated transforming and unfamiliar layers of bureaucracy and authority as borders and powers changed around them. This required imagining and implementing new social and communal realities in light of divergent futures, of fitting oneself, one's family, and one's community into what seemed the most plausible future at any given point in an era of many possible futures. In this period of chaos and possibility, borders were redrawn and new authorities imposed themselves; critically, too, meanings ascribed to nationality, class, race, and gender were in flux. Countless Sephardi individuals made calculated choices based on their reading of the present in light of what they believed the future likely to hold, where they envisioned that they might belong, and how they shaped themselves to belong and shaped belonging to fit them.

The fourth chapter assumes a world that was divided along new borders and therefore required building nations to fit. It demonstrates that, in the face of the United States' implementation of quotas on immigration, an increasing number of Sephardim migrated to Mexico, which initially remained relatively open to Jewish immigration. Mexico was particularly receptive to Sephardi Jewish migrants, who were perceived, as a result of their distant Iberian origins, to be "equally Spanish and Jewish" and assimilable. Sephardi migrants sustained active transnational commercial, familial, and even policing networks between the United States, Cuba, and Mexico, facilitating movement and acclimation in these states. Many had migrated as a result of Turkish policies discriminating against religious minorities that were designed to encourage emigration and the religious and ethnic homogenization of the newly-formed Turkish Republic. The very Iberian linguistic and cultural heritage that in Mexico forged a bond perceived by both Mexican officials and Sephardi migrants, marking Sephardi Jews as potentially assimilable, was held up in Turkey as proof of the lack of Sephardi integration.

As the 1920s moved into the 1930s, the deportation, denaturalization, and prohibition of certain types of migrants became increasingly common strategies states used to enforce their sovereignty and their national designs. Chapter 5 examines how Sephardi migrants adapted when the goods they dealt in, and they themselves, became undesirable and sometimes illegal. It explores how Sephardi migrants mobilized extensive transnational patronage, familial, and commercial networks that traversed the Mediterranean and Atlantic to circumvent prohibitions on trade and migration.

The book's final chapter follows the life and career of Mauricio Fresco, the youngest son of Constantinople's most prominent Ladino-language newspaper editor, as he transformed himself from a Turkish Jewish migrant in Mexico to a prominent Mexican diplomat, stationed first in Shanghai in the 1930s and later in Bordeaux, Lisbon, and Nazi-occupied Paris. It traces the narrative of transnational Sephardi networks in the face of state control on mobility into a period in which they began to break down, just as they became most crucial.

This book explores the lived experiences of these individuals as a conversation with state policies, providing a history of migration and nation-building from the vantage point of those who lived among and between states. It is not a story of entrance or exit, of assimilation or perpetual outsider status. Rather, it is a story of individuals encountering and countering flux and transformation in borders, nationality practices, mobility regimes, and personal relationships; of their ability to traverse gray areas and blurred boundaries by forging ties with others even as they forged their own passports.

(CHAPTER 1)

FABRICATING THE FOREIGN

MAURICIO ASSAEL HAD A FLAIR FOR THE DRAMATIC. One of five brothers of Sephardi extraction born in the cosmopolitan Ottoman port city of Izmir in the later decades of the 1800s who made their way to Mexico at the beginning of the twentieth century, he arrived in Mexico with his wife in 1903. Two pictures exist of Mauricio at the turn of the century, displaying his colorful personality and full mustache and offering alternative images of how this individual self-fashioned. In the first, Mauricio poses in the garb of a wealthy Ottoman Turk, alluding to his prosperous economic background; this outfit would not have been the usual vestments of a Westernized Sephardi Jew in the Aegean port city of his birth. Seated on a low stool embroidered in a typical Turkish floral motif and resting on an intricate oriental rug, he wears loose pants, a silk vest, and a wide sash. Atop his head is a fez, that quintessential Ottoman head covering of Moroccan origin, which had replaced the turban in a gesture to Westernization and by the time the photo was taken was a concrete marker of progressive Ottomanism.[1] The fez would itself be banned in 1925 as part of Mustafa Kemal's modernization program.

The second photograph displays a very different vision of Mauricio Assael. In it, he stands with his wife, Rachel Corri, also from Izmir, having just arrived in the Mexican port city of Veracruz. In contrast to the earlier photo of Mauricio, he and his wife are dressed in European garb in this photo. Although maintaining the same mustache, Mauricio here wears matching dark pants and jacket, a tie, and a wide-rimmed, beribboned hat. Rachel wears a matching long skirt and jacket, a belt buckle shining at her waist, her blouse buttoned high around her throat in spite of the heat and humidity of the port, her hair gathered atop her head in an Edwardian pompadour, her fair skin protected from the sun by a white hat. They stand in front of a thatched hut, her hand resting on his shoulder, his hand, in a pose reminiscent of a Western gunslinger, resting in his left pocket, from which the chain of a pocket watch hangs. Flanking Assael and Corri stand three indigenous Mexicans. Next to Rachel, a young man in tailored clothing holds a bag monogrammed with the letter M, probably belonging to Mauricio, while next to Mauricio stand an older man, barefoot in a straw hat and clothing made of raw muslin, holding a ceramic pitcher, and a bareheaded woman squinting at the camera, her hair in a braid, wearing a long canvas dress, an infant tied on her back with a shawl.

Both photographs are clearly staged. In the first photograph, Mauricio fashions himself as a wealthy Ottoman. In the second, there is nothing Ottoman about either his or his wife's appearance. While the intended audience of the first is unclear, though it is clear that it was taken before departure from the Ottoman Empire, in the second, Assael and his wife have deliberately assembled the indigenous Mexican individuals next to them and posed in front of a hut with a palm-frond roof. A photo like this may have been sent back to family members who had not yet migrated, as if to offer them a sense of the "authentic" Mexico in terms of population, clothing, and habitation. This photograph remained in the family of the last Assael brother to migrate to Mexico: Isaco, who arrived three years after Mauricio. Simultaneously, this photograph distinguished Assael and Corri from their surroundings. Mauricio Assael, though not a tall man, barely reaching five foot six, towers over the Mexicans next to the couple. The Assaels' clothing and skin mark them as white, perhaps European, and certainly not poor; in other words, they were the type of immigrants that were desirable in Porfirio Díaz's Mexico. There is nothing in either photo that would identify either Rachel or Mauricio as Jewish.

This chapter examines the earliest phase of Sephardi migration between the Ottoman Empire and Mexico, from the turn to the twentieth century until the outbreak of the Balkan Wars and the Mexican Revolution. In an age in which individual identification became increasingly predicated on national belonging and being a citizen of a particular state, Ottoman Sephardi migrants were caught in processes of defining citizenship and national belonging.[2] They resisted easy classification as either Ottoman expatriates or unambiguous Mexicans by maintaining active commercial and familial connections with Sephardi Jews in France, Cuba, the United States, the Ottoman homeland, and elsewhere. As the borders of empires and states were torn apart by war and revolution, often to resolidify along new national boundaries, Sephardim capitalized on disjunctures between the new national and older imperial systems. They adeptly cultivated transnational connections and identities, manipulating their affiliations to negotiate spaces for themselves and to succeed in new economic and social orders. For these migrants, transnational networks, geographic mobility, and ambiguous foreignness provided the means for economic and social mobility in new locations.

The Assaels' sartorial practice of "clothes-switching" was not unique to Ottoman Jews but was common practice for nineteenth-century Ottoman diplomats and travelers, who would trade their fezzes for top hats as soon as their train crossed the border of Bulgaria or Serbia.[3] Likewise, many migrants to the United States bore with them apocryphal tales of Americanizing their names upon arrival at Ellis Island, mirroring the adaptations of the names of the five Assael brothers as they made their way between Izmir, Paris, New York, Mexico City, and Havana—Johanan became Jean, then Juan; Isaco adopted Francisco before shortening his name to Ico; Israel became Isidoro; Albert became Alberto; and Mauricio occasionally went by Maurice.[4] And Mauricio's transmission of the photograph of him and his wife to his brother was a link in a chain of migration that bridged the Mediterranean and Atlantic worlds, not unlike the chains of migration formed by individuals of countless other national, racial, and religious backgrounds who relocated in an era marked by unprecedented mobility.

And yet, unlike their Ottoman coreligionists in the United States who cast themselves, or found themselves cast, as Orientals, or Ottoman Christians from the Arab provinces in Latin America who played up their Levantine origins to mark themselves and their goods as coming from the Holy Land, the Assael brothers and countless other Ottoman Jews adopted an ambiguously European persona upon their arrival in Mexico.[5] It was their ability to fluidly transform that enabled Mauricio Assael and numerous other Sephardi migrants to successfully navigate the turbulence of the early twentieth century. Dissimulation, self-fashioning, and improvisation had long been critical elements in the experience of individuals who lived their lives on a global stage.[6] However, the preoccupation of fin-de-siècle states with citizenship, monitoring movement, and positivist ideas of the economic and genetic value of certain peoples created an additional urgency. Self-fashioning as unproblematically European, white, and modern—whether through their sartorial choices, naming practices for themselves and their businesses, and their commercial endeavors and advertising—was a deliberate strategy that Mauricio Assael and countless other Sephardi migrants employed to mark their desirability as migrants.

In Search of a Future, but Where?

"It is to hide certain defects from their surroundings and to appear better," lamented one Doctor Joseph A. Schemonti, an Ottoman Christian subject from a region that would later form Lebanon (in a 1909 booklet entitled *États des Ottomans au Méxique, Devoirs de l'Empire à leur Égard, Remèdes*),

> some of them call themselves Turks and Syrians in Mexico, Egyptians in Veracruz, Lebanese in Oaxaca, Arabs almost everywhere, Armenians and Greeks in the northern states, the young schoolgirl is French; there are even some who, speaking a little English, call themselves Americans or Englishmen, and others who, never having been in any South American republic, say that they are Chilean, Argentine, Brazilian, but they never pronounce the word: **Ottoman**, a sacred word which alone should resonate in their hearts without concourse to any other.[7]

Schemonti's pamphlet was published on the eve of events that would transform the Ottoman Empire and Mexico and propel an increasing number of Sephardi Jews and others to seek new shores. Mexico was writhing in the shade of the *Pax Porfiriana*, on the eve of the centennial of independence from Spain; the revolution that was to end the three-decade rule of the dictator Porfirio Díaz would erupt two years later. The Ottoman Empire, meanwhile, was basking in the glow of the hopeful optimism that accompanied the Young Turk Revolution of 1908 and the reinstatement of the constitution, allowing Schemonti to claim that "We are in the era of human fraternization, holy democracy, where the powers should unite ... to organize a just end and to arrive at a common goal: the perfection of humanity and universal peace."[8] Both states clung to the tenets of positivism, seeking order and progress in the name of inexorable forward development.

Addressing himself to Ahmed Rıza Bey, the president of the Ottoman Chamber of Deputies, Schemonti encouraged the Ottoman Empire to intervene directly in favor of Ottoman subjects living in Mexico. By establishing an Ottoman diplomatic mission, Schemonti proposed, the Ottoman Empire, under its new Young Turk leaders, could overcome former Sultan Abdülhamid II's autocratic legacy of ruling by dividing and uniting, under a common Ottoman identity, the purported eighty thousand Ottoman expatriates in Mexico. Ottoman diplomats, Schemonti asserted, could advocate for their polyglot subjects abroad engaged in commercial activity, encouraging them to move beyond their ubiquitous ambulatory peddling and petty commerce in dry goods, hardware, hosiery, and clothing into unspecified other commercial endeavors. Although Schemonti did not mention it explicitly, the establishment of an Ottoman diplomatic presence would also be positioned to counter the efforts of France to serve as unofficial protectors of certain segments of Ottoman migrant populations and thereby to coopt these individuals as agents of the global French civilizing mission.[9] Schemonti's pamphlet was reviewed in Mexico and in Ottoman newspapers in Paris and read by Ottoman and Mexican officials, who took to heart Schemonti's suggestion that establishing Ottoman diplomatic representation in Mexico would encourage Ottoman subjects to identify as Ottomans.[10] In advocating this agenda, Schemonti sought to promote Ottomanism, the doctrine of a shared Ottoman affiliation regardless of religious, ethnic, or linguistic background. Ottomanism, in Schemonti's estimation, could only be maintained through the oversight of the Ottoman state. This project took on an added urgency once subjects were distant from Ottoman territories and therefore experienced less external pressure to affiliate as Ottomans.

In the face of increasingly violent and successful separatist nationalist movements based on ethnic and religious difference, the Ottomanism that the elites of the empire had espoused in varying forms for decades, and which large swaths of the population had seemed to embrace fervently in the immediate aftermath of the 1908 revolution, provided an ideology of cohesion that transcended the empire's diversity. Efforts to institute further equality between Muslims and religious minorities involved removing certain privileges that the latter enjoyed, for instance by introducing mandatory military service in lieu of the exemption tax (the *bedel-i askeri*) that they had been paying since the Tanzimat reforms of 1839 removed the *zimmet*, or poll tax for non-Muslims. Additional steps centered on education, including the institution of mandatory instruction in the Turkish language in minority schools in an attempt to create a basic level of linguistic commonality as well as the opening of Ottoman schools to religious minorities.[11] Prior to the Young Turk Revolution, some Ottoman Jews had encouraged the adoption of Ottoman Turkish, particularly among children, as a means of expressing thanks and taking part in progress, profiting like all the other subjects (*bütün tebaa*) around them. Learning Ottoman Turkish became seen as increasingly critical in the face of the erasure of legal distinctions between Muslim and non-Muslim Ottomans.[12] Such changes ostensibly allowed minorities to enter professions that had been reserved for Muslims, particularly military leadership positions.[13] "Later, when you leave school, I see that you can render service to the homeland. I will not let you use [your skills] commercially, I will engage you in administration," explained the *vali* of Edirne to Jewish students at the city's Alliance Israélite Universelle school at an assembly in 1910.[14] Non-Muslims and Muslims alike were now expected to contribute to the betterment of the empire by filling the roles that the government assigned to them. Previous professions that had dominated among Jews, particularly in trade, were no longer seen as beneficial to the empire, and the skills that Jews had employed in commerce were now to be channeled into directions more productive for the empire's progress. As Schemonti's pamphlet suggests, governmental involvement extended to promoting a common Ottoman identity and monitoring subjects abroad regardless of their linguistic, religious, or ethnic affiliation.

The Ottoman Empire had an ambivalent attitude toward the emigration of Ottoman subjects. This was not unique among Europe's empires; the Russian Empire sought to stem emigration because of its fear of population loss and refused to recognize the naturalization of Russian subjects in other locales, and the Habsburgs had similar concerns over maintaining their population, or at least maintaining populations deemed desirable.[15] Throughout much of Central Europe, governments required people to obtain work papers, visas, or passports of various kinds to travel beyond their home provinces.[16] Monitoring and restricting movement, in part through the implementation of internal and external passports for Ottoman subjects, proved a means by which the Ottoman state, like other empires and states, sought to render its diverse and rapidly changing population more legible.[17]

The *Tanzimat* reforms of the nineteenth century sought to strengthen the central authority of the Ottoman state and reconfigure the relationship between the state and male Ottomans by eliminating legal distinctions among Ottomans, regardless of their religious origins.[18] Included in these reforms was the 1841 *Men'-i Müru Nizamnamesi* (regulations pursuant to the restriction of movement), which remained in place until 1910. This stipulated that travel beyond the boundaries of the township required an internal passport (*mürur tezkeresi*). By the end of the nineteenth century, an individual had to submit a certificate signed by a local religious official to the local registrar, who then issued an internal passport valid for travel to a specified final destination. Upon arrival at that destination, the *mürur tezkeresi*—which noted the bearer's physical characteristics and his or her ethnic and religious background—was to be submitted to local authorities for registration.[19] Some civil registrars, the officials responsible for granting internal passports, did so only after receiving substantial bribes; by the late 1890s, these registrars could receive payments of hundreds of times the legally stipulated price for a *mürur tezkeresi*.[20] The *Tabiiyet-i Osmaniye Kanunnamesi* (law of Ottoman citizenship) of 1869, modeled after the 1851 French code, declared all those born in the Ottoman Empire, regardless of religion, to be Ottoman citizens unless they provided proof to the contrary.[21] Recognizing the correlation between the monitoring of mobility and citizenship as state-building practices, this law required an Ottoman passport to be used for all external travel. Many Ottoman migrants circumvented these external passport requirements, using their *mürur tezkeresi* to clear Ottoman port authorities on the pretense of traveling to another Ottoman port city, only to transfer to a ship leaving the empire.[22] Regulating and monitoring internal and external migration and the activities of migrants abroad became a means of centralizing Ottoman authority, even as a growing number of Ottomans, Jews and otherwise, sought new shores and developed strategies for evading Ottoman control.

In addition to concerns over population maintenance, Ottoman authorities were preoccupied with how emigrants could undermine Ottoman political and economic structures. As thousands of Ottoman subjects migrated to Western Europe and the Americas during the final decades of the nineteenth century, Ottoman authorities increasingly regulated their movement and monitored their behavior abroad. Shortly after the beginning of large-scale migration from the empire in the late 1880s, the Ottoman Empire imposed restrictions on overseas migration, which were lightly enforced for movement from the Levant and the Balkans but heavily so for migration from eastern Anatolia. These restrictions were driven, in part, by the Ottoman state's belief in a relationship between North American migration and a growing transnational Armenian revolutionary movement.[23] Fear of emigrants' fomenting of political opposition led to an 1896 ban on the traveling of political actors, particularly aimed at Armenians who had settled in the United States before returning to the empire as American citizens, sometimes under false names, to foment Armenian nationalist causes. Ottoman consular officials in the United States were charged with monitoring the activities of Ottoman Armenians, few of whom registered with Ottoman consulates in spite of the government's encouragement for them to do so.[24] An 1898 decree required all Ottoman travelers to foreign lands to pledge to retain their Ottoman citizenship and included a rule, not always enforced, that those who changed their nationality and received a passport would be prohibited from reentering Ottoman territory.[25] Several years earlier, a handful of Ottoman Armenian migrants had been arrested following their return to the empire when they were discovered with American passports. Ottoman officials feared that these individuals would use their American citizenship, given the empire's Capitulation agreement with the United States and certain other foreign powers, to claim exemption from prosecution under Ottoman law.[26] American consular officials stationed in Constantinople warned Ottoman subjects who had naturalized as Americans, many of whom were Armenian, that Ottoman authorities would not recognize the validity of their new nationality, that they might face punishment for having acquired a new nationality, and that the American government would be unable to intervene on their behalf should they run afoul of Ottoman laws.[27]

Economic concerns undergirded Ottoman ambivalence toward emigration. On the one hand, remittances from emigrants abroad could help support family members within the empire. Places like Mount Lebanon, where many migrants originated, bore striking houses built by returning migrants with the money they had accrued abroad.[28] Tropes of migrants making their fortunes in Europe or elsewhere before returning to the empire appeared in Ladino literature; the novella *La Novia Aguna* (The Grasswidow Bride) described migrants returning from Europe, freely spending the money they had acquired there, clean-shaven, dressed in riding coats as opposed to traditional robes, and wearing tall *chapeaux ala moda*.[29]

On the other hand, the government feared the infamy that indigent Ottomans abroad could bring upon the Ottoman state, as well as the costs of their repatriation.[30] In 1893, Ottoman authorities had sought to clear the way for Ottoman subjects wanting to travel for trade purposes to the United States, Mexico, and Cuba.[31] A few months later, however, Ottoman officials sought to prevent migration to Cuba because of the "displeasing behavior" of earlier migrants to the island.[32] Further draining the state coffers was the practice by Ottoman subjects traveling abroad of acquiring new nationalities and then returning to the Ottoman Empire to capitalize on the commercial benefits granted to the nationals of certain states under the Ottoman Capitulations.[33]

In his picaresque autobiography, the Ladino *literatus* Elia Karmona recounts the need to acquire travel documentation from the Ottoman government and letters of introduction from Sephardi rabbis and prominent merchants as he moved among Constantinople, Salonica, Izmir, Alexandria, and Cairo in hopes of earning a living through Ladino publications.[34] Such travel within and beyond Ottoman realms of the eastern Mediterranean was not uncommon for Ottoman Sephardim across class divides, marking the centrality of Sephardi ties and geographic mobility in Sephardi life. Like Karmona, the noted Ottoman Jewish intellectual Abraham Galanté also temporarily relocated to Alexandria to bypass Ottoman press censorship, participating in a world of Ladino letters that radiated from the Ottoman port cities of Salonica, Izmir, and Istanbul to Jerusalem, Vienna, Cairo, and

Livorno.³⁵ On the lower end of the socioeconomic spectrum, men living in towns in Thrace and Anatolia often traveled from village to village, peddling wares to Greek Orthodox and Muslim inhabitants.³⁶ Young girls from the same towns who needed dowry money worked for Jewish families in larger cities who desired "robust serving girls." Ninety-five percent of these girls returned to their natal towns to marry; there, they tatted lace in their homes for between 25 and 30 *centimes* per day and sold it to Jewish middlemen, who exported it to Europe at great profit.³⁷ Likewise, the growing tobacco industry in Ottoman Thrace and Macedonia drew indigent Jews from as far away as Sofia in hopes that the Ottoman *Régie de Tabac*'s well-known preference for child and female employees would offer the possibility of increased family income.³⁸

Families like the Assael brothers and many of the other first Sephardi migrants in Mexico maintained extensive familial networks that bridged Ottoman port cities. Such ties often cemented economic relations between dispersed branches of the extended family. This practice would come to stretch across the world as members of these families migrated to places as disparate as India, Rhodesia, and Venezuela.³⁹ While there is no documentary evidence of Mauricio Assael or his brothers traveling from Izmir to Salonica, the Assaels would later be joined in Mexico by a cousin from Salonica, Manuel Modiano, the son of Sunhula Assael, a relative of the *Izmirli* Assaels; the Assaels' father, meanwhile, had been born in the Adriatic Habsburg port city of Trieste.⁴⁰ When Ico Assael, one of Mauricio's brothers, declared bankruptcy in 1935, Modiano and Jacques Benuzillo Assael, another cousin of Salonican origins, were listed among his creditors.⁴¹ The presence of numerous members of the extended Assael family in Mexico attests to the power of affective ties and economic success in drawing chain migration to Mexico, the complexity of intra-Sephardi financial transactions, and marriage practices that united families across empires prior to migration.

Ladino periodicals in the Ottoman Empire and beyond were crucial means by which readers and others learned of current events, histories, and old and new Jewish communities around the world. These publications had a flexible understanding of intellectual property and accuracy in reporting, liberally borrowing, altering, and even inventing stories. But they attempted to shape readers' knowledge by offering articles deemed "useful."⁴² This included informing readers about current events and about the unique Jewish histories of areas of the world distant from Ottoman lands. Mexico was not often featured until the upheaval of its revolution, and particularly the American invasion of Veracruz, catapulted it onto the pages of the foreign events section of the newspapers. But even before that, articles like the 1908 "The Inquisition in Mexico" occasionally alerted readers to Mexico, its complex colonial history, and its participation in a history that had transformed Sephardi Jewry. Published correspondence from writers in Argentina or reports on Jewish colonization in Canada, in conjunction with letters that migrants sent home, meant that Sephardim had some awareness of geographical differences and distances in the Americas and the challenges that faced them in various locales, and chose their destinations accordingly.[43]

"The idea of immigration is a sickness that is materializing in the minds of many," opined Moses Ben Ghiat, a contributor to and sometime editor of the Ladino newspaper *El Meseret* of Izmir, in 1908.[44] While geographic mobility, familial and commercial ties, and the Sephardi press across the Ottoman Empire, Bulgaria, and Egypt sustained broad Sephardi affiliation in the eastern Mediterranean, during the final decades of the nineteenth century and early years of the twentieth, Sephardi Jews increasing looked west, whether to Vienna, Berlin, or Paris or even further afield, to the United States, Canada, or Latin America and the Caribbean.[45] As early as 1904, *La Epoka* of Salonica published a letter from a reader noting that the journal had begun to advise Jewish youth of the city against migrating to Paris and other great cities of Europe, suggesting instead that they go to "America or other distant countries where it is possible to make a good situation more quickly." This reader wrote that his young nephew, "who was not very well-educated ... but has a grand passion and a will of iron to labor and make a future for himself" had done quite well in the interior of China, working for a train company and earning a good salary.[46]

Ben Ghiat noted that countries of destination ran in trends, though he did not explain why: "for a time, it was Paris; then it was London; then Buenos Aires; then New York; then Egypt; and recently here, immigration to Mexico has erupted."[47] Within Ottoman lands, the interest in foreign places manifested even in the names of restaurants and businesses—Buenos Aires was the name of a kosher restaurant near the heavily Jewish neighborhood of Karataş in Izmir; this paralleled the names of cafés in New York and elsewhere that were heavily frequented by Sephardi migrant males, names like *Café Constantinople*, *Café Oriental*, and *Café Smyrna*.[48]

Ben Ghiat's characterization of the fervor for migration as a "sickness" among Ottoman Jews in the early years of the twentieth century highlights his negative assessment of migration, a view that others shared. "You well remember that as soon as Buenos Aires began to be named in Izmir, everyone went crazy, young men and married men alike, selling their clothing and leaving their women and children without protection, they left for Buenos Aires," wrote an *Izmirli* migrant from Argentina.[49] An individual in England, who signed his piece "*un Selanikli*," responded to a letter describing migration in positive terms. That author, the *Selanikli* wrote, had certainly never migrated himself and had therefore not experienced the days of anxiety, anguish, and hopelessness that faced new migrants, experiences that such individuals might not desire to share with relatives and friends who remained behind. It was only upon receiving a good position and salary that people chose to write back to relatives.[50]

Although the drive to migrate was, in part, propelled by those who sent back letters painting the possibilities in glowing terms and by spendthrift migrants returning in stylish clothing, Ladino periodicals cautioned against migration. By 1908, *La Epoka* of Salonica reported large numbers of Jews returning from America, having been unable to earn a living (a report that was then picked up by *El Meseret*). It cautioned that "those who advise emigration should do so with much prudence and make sure that the emigrants know what awaits them," a much more circumspect perspective than was on evidence in pieces the same periodical published in favor of migration scant years before.[51] *El Meseret*, meanwhile, published a long piece on the difficulties for urbanites of earning a good living in the United States, asserting that those who were successful were provincial villagers, not Jews from the cities. Villagers were not affected by poor weather and long hours of work. For them, a few slices of bread with salt and an onion would seem like a feast, and they could therefore save their meager earnings. Jews of the cities, in contrast, were accustomed to better living conditions, and long hours of work in factories or selling postcards on the street for little recompense would seem shameful. "Better to be poor here than a beggar in foreign lands," the article concluded.[52]

Ladino periodicals published letters from readers who had migrated abroad, challenging the perception that migrants acquired wealth with ease. Some of these letters addressed how it was that individuals who, in Izmir, had seemed incapable of earning even a *metallik* returned to Izmir from the Americas "with a bag of liras."[53] One submission from Buenos Aires tackled those individuals who had been accustomed, prior to emigration, to gambling in cafés and living by swindling others but then returned, after a short time abroad, seemingly flush with money. "None of them turned their face," the letter cautioned. They had, through false promises and entreaties, acquired loans of clothing from other migrants, supposedly to be peddled on their account, but took the money from the sales themselves rather than repaying their creditors and disappeared from Buenos Aires, "returning [to Izmir] lacking in nothing, full of liras." *El Meseret*'s editor added a brief note that it had pained them to read the names of those that the letter had identified, and that they had chosen not to republish the names "in consideration of some of our friends." However, they wanted those individuals to be aware that "we are informed of their ill deeds."[54]

Still other articles focused on the difficult conditions that awaited migrants upon arrival in the Americas, challenging the rosy picture of migrant life. Ben Ghiat published an interview in *El Meseret* with Isaac Algranati, recently returned to Izmir from Mexico after three or four months, "alive and healthy, but with nothing remaining of the significant sum of money that he had brought with him." In confiding his story to *El Meseret*, Algranati hoped to convince "those who are thinking of going forward in emigrating to this country to renounce" their plan. He explained that those who migrated with the idea of making a fortune would be sorely disappointed. "I arrived in Mexico and I became a peddler, as are all the other *turkinos* there. Selling takes this form: a client calls you and buys from you, for example, 20 francs of clothing. She gives you 2 francs immediately and the rest at 2 francs per week." At that rate, a large number of clients and a substantial amount of capital or loans of goods to sell were required in order to be able to meet the daily costs of life. Algranati had not possessed that capital and had been unable to acquire it on credit, and therefore decided to repatriate before he became reliant on alms like others there, including the man with whom he had traveled from Izmir, who remained in Mexico. "The only wealth of the place," he concluded, was yellow fever.⁵⁵ And yet, while such interviews and letters from migrants were clearly intended to dissuade Ottoman Jews from migrating, there is no indication that they were effective.

Beyond informing potential and actual migrants and the broader Ottoman Jewish public about the histories of and current events in countries where Sephardi populations were growing, Ladino periodicals offered readers concrete guidance for the migration process. By the early years of the twentieth century, periodicals in Ottoman lands were publishing advertisements for agencies offering ship tickets to the United States, elsewhere in North and South America, and even as far afield as Africa and Australia, in addition to train tickets for interior travel upon arrival.⁵⁶ They also offered cautionary tales about migrants who, uninformed of immigration regulations, found themselves detained and deported.

Soon after its establishment in 1910, *La Amerika*, the first Ladino periodical in the United States, published several articles about "our Jews of Turkey" who faced detainment on Ellis Island, or even deportation, because they were unaware of American immigration laws. One woman, traveling to Seattle to join her husband with her own six-year old son and her ten-year old nephew, found herself and the two boys returned, at great personal suffering and expense, because American law forbade the entrance of those under sixteen traveling without their parents. Another individual, a 53-year-old rabbi, kosher butcher, and mohel who had intended to stay in New York, was sent back after the commission at Ellis Island could not contact his grandson in Seattle and feared he would become a public charge. Two youths from Edirne were returned to the Ottoman Empire after the *turkino* café worker they had listed as their acquaintance refused to come to Ellis Island, while another youth took money from the two young men with the false promise that he would assist them.⁵⁷

Stories like that of Gabriel Kapitulo, from Bodrum in the Ottoman Empire, who arrived at Ellis Island from Buenos Aires intending to join his brother-in-law in Atlanta, also served as cautionary tales for future migrants of what might happen if they were unfamiliar with the immigration regulations. Kapitulo, when asked by American officials to what nation he belonged, responded that he was Turkish and then acknowledged that Turks believed in polygamy. Unbeknownst to him, this disqualified him from entering the United States, and he was detained at Ellis Island for two weeks while awaiting deportation. *La Amerika*'s editors intervened in Washington on his behalf, assuring American officials that Kapitulo himself was Jewish and that the Law of Moses did not permit polygamy, thereby securing his freedom. The editors promised that they would soon publish a booklet of American immigration laws translated into Ladino to prevent such occurrences in the future.[58] Less than one month later, this article was republished word-for-word in *El Meseret* in Izmir, attesting to the connected nature of Ladino publishing and Sephardi access to knowledge across a growing diasporic world.[59] It also indicates the divergence between how migrants might have seen themselves and how American systems of classifications of nationalities saw them. Successful migration, these articles suggested, depended on knowledge of American laws and norms.

Ladino journal editors, and presumably their readers, saw value in this shared sphere of knowledge that spanned the expanding Sephardi world. In time, it could be boasted that subscribers were able to read Ladino newspapers on five continents.[60] This shared reading public was built up through the reprinting of stories from and advertisements for other periodicals. Not only did *El Meseret* reprint articles from *La Amerika*, for example, but it also printed advertisements for the latter. One such advertisement for *La Amerika*, described as "the only Judeo-Spanish journal edited in the United States," highlighted that it was written in "*espanyol*" and the "Yiddish jargon" and therefore able to keep the "Ashkenazi *puevlo*" and the "Sephardi *puevlo*" abreast of current events. The journal periodically published inserts about American immigration laws and English and Yiddish vocabularies, "languages of absolute necessity on this continent." This approach was "entirely indispensable for every Sephardi Jew in America and in the Orient" and of even greater importance for those who considered immigrating to the United States.[61] These laws and languages were not inherently part of the legal and linguistic repertoire of Sephardi Jews in the eastern Mediterranean, but American-based Ladino periodicals could rectify this and could attract subscribers and agents abroad by publishing in other Ladino periodicals. In doing so, they aided the exchange of information and the maintenance of a shared reading public spanning the Mediterranean, Atlantic, and beyond.

Dynamics within the Ottoman Jewish world encouraged migration, even as some returned from abroad browbeaten and discouraged. The educational institutions of the French Jewish Alliance Israélite Universelle (AIU), numbering some 108 in the Ottoman Empire by the eve of World War I, exposed a broad swath of Ottoman Jewry to the French language and modern education.[62] The AIU transformed France, in the eyes of many Sephardim, into a paragon of liberty, civilization, and culture; made French into the lingua franca of upwardly mobile segments of Jewish society; and contributed to the widespread gallicization of names among the Jewish populace. This "galloping Gallomania" encouraged an unbridled taste for all things "made in France" or "made in Paris" and propelled migration to France.[63]

"For some time, the movements of expatriation for the countries of the future have taken on considerable proportions in our city," noted two AIU alumni from the Anatolian city of Bursa in a letter requesting funds from the AIU to join friends who had already migrated to the United States. The AIU had a duty to encourage the migration of young people "with a certain level of intelligence who were without a future like their parents."[64] The AIU offered Ottoman Jewish youth the foreign-language training necessary for the import trade into the empire and for travel abroad, and broadened their horizons through modern education. It occasionally financed the migration of individuals desirous of a future elsewhere, contributing to the creation of a widely cast net of educated Sephardi youth throughout Europe and the Americas. Graduates of the AIU agricultural school Or Yehouda, just outside of Akhisar in Anatolia, set out for Manitoba, Canada, where they could acquire land and put their education into practice; the Canadian government wanted to populate the western plains with farmers.[65] Teachers in the AIU system sought employment with the Jewish Colonization Association (JCA) in Argentina, whether to take advantage of higher wages to aid their elderly and indigent parents who remained behind or to bring over and support their spouses and parents.[66] Some of these individuals drew on connections with family members to acquire the requisite exit papers: Jacques Taranto, for example, having been offered a teaching position with the JCA in Argentina, declined the position following his new wife's refusal to leave Izmir, but only after he had secured his Ottoman passport; he then gave his passport to a cousin of the same name, who migrated in his place.[67] A new country offered migrants the opportunity and space to use their skills and create a future for themselves that was not circumscribed by the paths of their parents or social and governmental intervention.

Migration was not always voluntary. During the 1911 Italo-Turkish War, the Ottoman government mandated the expulsion of those in Ottoman territory who possessed Italian citizenship, propelling some to renounce that status in favor of Ottoman nationality.[68] Though not all *franco* Jews living in Ottoman territory were Italian nationals, many had retained Italian nationality to capitalize on the tax advantages that the Ottoman Capitulations granted to nationals or subjects of certain European states. Scions of prominent *franco* families, together with their Armenian, Maronite, and Greek Orthodox counterparts, maintained Italian, Austrian, British, or French nationalities or protégé status, occasionally serving as the representatives of these states within various Ottoman cities.[69] Beyond the prestige and financial benefits of non-Ottoman nationality, being the subject of European powers granted benefits of extraterritoriality, removing these individuals from the mandate of the Ottoman and Jewish legal systems.[70] Edgar Morin recounts that his father's family in Salonica opted for Italian nationality in the wake of the Russo-Turkish War of 1877–1878, while other families in the same city chose Spanish nationality for the financial and legal benefits this entailed.[71] The presence of Sephardi Italians in Alexandria transformed the city into one where individuals, after identifying their shared Italian nationality, then switched into speaking their Ladino mother tongue.[72] The threat of expulsion of Italian nationals from Ottoman territory during the 1911 war, however, propelled a number of these individuals to follow shipping lines to the port cities of Trieste, Naples, and Marseille, with some of these travelers continuing further inland, to Verona or Paris.[73] At times, these expulsions divided families and caused difficulties for those who, despite bearing Italian nationality, did not speak a word of Italian.[74] Though some returned after the cessation of hostilities, others remained in France or Italy, sometimes involved in exporting goods to their coreligionists in their places of origin.[75]

Compelled by the perception that France in particular offered paths for upward mobility, by a rudimentary knowledge of French among large segments of the Ottoman Sephardi world, and by relatively lax immigration laws, a growing stream of Ottoman Sephardim flowed into France. At the beginning of the twentieth century, some eight thousand Ottomans, many of them Jewish, lived in France, predominantly in Paris, Marseille, and Lyon.[76] This community grew in the years leading up to World War I. The Roquette area in Paris's eleventh *arrondissement* came to be known as the "quarter of the Oriental Jews."[77] There, Jews of Ottoman origins gathered in cafés that advertised their kosher, "Oriental" foods in Ladino publications throughout the Ottoman Empire.[78] Poorer Ottoman Jewish migrants, established in the textile and hosiery trade or as street vendors, populated the Roquette, many helping in family businesses or working for fellow Sephardi migrants.[79] Wealthier migrants, often carpet merchants or exporters, settled in Faubourg-Montmartre and the Sentier in the ninth *arrondissement*, the heart of the Parisian textile district.[80] In 1909, an *Istanbullu* jewelry merchant, Nissim Rozanes, founded the *Association cultuelle orientale Israélite de Paris*, which established a synagogue for the Roquette's growing Sephardi population.[81] In 1910, he hosted visiting Ottoman officials, demonstrating the sort of attachment to the Ottoman Empire that Schemonti sought to promote in Mexico.[82] The growing Sephardi presence in France proved crucial for Sephardi migrants in Mexico like the Assaels, who drew on their facility with the French language and their commercial connections with fellow Sephardim in France to emphasize their Europeanness.

"Will the Judaism of Mexico Come from the Orient?"

In 1889, Francisco Rivas Puigcever, a Mexican professor of the Hebrew language who claimed to be the descendent of conversos, published a Ladino periodical, *El Sábado Secreto*, in the Ottoman Empire and the Balkans. In it, he advocated for the immigration to Mexico of Jews who lived in "antiliberal" countries where a "suspiciously religious fanaticism for the hatred of race" hounded them. Mexico and the other countries of the Americas would welcome them, needing honest citizens to develop its riches and foment commerce.[83] Although there is no indication that Rivas's efforts directly resulted in Sephardi migration to Mexico, by the turn to the twentieth century, Sephardim had begun trickling into Mexico.[84]

Among these early Sephardi migrants in Mexico were the Assael brothers, all coming to Mexico after extended stays in France. Albert arrived first. At the time, he spelled his surname Assaël, with a diaeresis, in a gesture to gallicism. Departing from the Atlantic port of Cherbourg in France, he passed through New York City on January 25, 1901. He was 22 years old, single, and literate. He claimed Ottoman nationality, though he had last lived in Paris. He was a "merchant" and had already purchased the ticket to his final destination. Although he had never been to the United States before, he had been to South America.[85] Albert was traveling at almost the same time as his 23-year-old brother, Johanan, who passed through New York on January 28, 1901, having departed from Boulogne-sur-Mer, France, with his 21-year-old wife of French origin, improbably named Marie Antoinette. Marie Antoinette, due to the law that wives acquired their husbands' nationality, was also listed as being of Turkish nationality.[86] Johanan, like Albert, had last lived in Paris and was also a merchant—his wife was a "wife." He was going to stay with unspecified friends in Mexico City.[87] Next, Mauricio Assael and his wife Rachel Corri arrived, in 1903, as did the fourth brother, 20-year-old Isaco (Ico), who came from Boulogne to join his brothers. Ico soon married a fellow *Izmirli* Jew, Esther Matalon, who relocated to Mexico to join him. The final brother to arrive was 26-year-old Israel, who became "Isidoro" within several years of arrival and who would be murdered on the grounds of the Mexican presidential residence in 1919 as a result of soured business dealings.[88]

All five Assael brothers quickly established commercial establishments selling novelties, notions, and jewelry, partnering in a store called "La Turquesa." Ico and his wife moved south to the city of Puebla to establish a jewelry business there. La Turquesa was located just off the Zócalo, the central plaza in Mexico City, on Plateros Street, which was renamed "San Francisco" in 1908 and renamed again, following the Mexican Revolution, as "Francisco I. Madero" in honor of the assassinated revolutionary leader. The area around the Zócalo attracted most of Mexico City's Jewish and Middle Eastern migrant populations, offering ample stomping grounds for peddlers and shopkeepers. While wealthier merchants, including several of the Assaels, moved their families to the neighboring districts of Colonia Roma and Condesa along the expanding tram routes, old colonial buildings in the city center provided crowded tenement housing for poor migrant families and individuals. Foreign merchants established businesses aimed at an elite clientele on the streets to the west of the Zócalo and Avenida Juárez along the

Alameda Park, while the streets to the east and south of the plaza were populated by wholesale stores and shops aimed at lower classes of customers.

Although the Assael brothers were among the earliest Sephardi migrants to Mexico, Jewish immigration, particularly by single men from Germany, France, and Alsace, began in the 1880s. While Baron de Hirsch and others had explored Mexico as a possible alternative to Argentina for Jewish colonization, such plans went unrealized, in part due to poor agricultural conditions and in part due to the opposition of the Catholic Church. The Alsatian, French, and German Jews who first came to Mexico publicly identified not as Jews, but as citizens of their countries of origin. They married Mexican Catholic women, blending into the general Mexican population as Porfirian intellectuals hoped they would. Rabbi Martin Zielonka from El Paso, Texas noted in his 1908 visit to ascertain whether Mexico was a suitable location for Jewish colonization:

> Some of these having married native women, have adopted the faith of their wives and are lost to Judaism; others hide their identity behind the name of the land from which they came and are known as Frenchmen, Germans, Alsatians, Spaniards and Americans.... We are told that a Jew is a Jew at all times, and looked upon as such under all conditions, yet here are any number of men and women who are reckoned as representatives of different lands and not as Jews.[89]

While Sephardi migrants, unlike their Alsatian brethren, rarely forwent their Jewish identity and would several years later be at the forefront of establishing the Monte Sinaí Jewish cemetery, many nevertheless sought to be reckoned as representatives of different lands. These lands, however, were not the lands from which they came, in contrast to what was the case for their Ashkenazi coreligionists and their non-Jewish Ottoman fellow subjects. Instead, they drew on transnational connections with fellow Sephardi Jews in France to self-fashion as Europeans, most often of French origin.

Many of the early Jews in Mexico—whether of Western European or Ottoman origins—capitalized on the Francophilia of Díaz's reign to secure their economic place in Mexican society.[90] Among the Latin American upwardly mobile, the foreign—particularly the European—held great allure, representing the "progress" that positivist elites eagerly sought out. The consumption of imported products, such as clothing, wine, education, and travel, became a material expression of claims to cosmopolitan identity, status markers whose often-French origins conveyed social cachet. The late-nineteenth-century boom in imported products offered upwardly mobile Mexicans the possibility of addressing or altering divisions along the lines of class, region, gender, and race.[91] Porfirian elites enthusiastically adopted bicycles and other forms of imported recreation and sought to imitate French cooking in their kitchens.[92] This embrace of foreign—particularly French—products and language offered Sephardi Jews, as well as Maronite elites and others, many of whom had commercial and familial connections in France, a means of marketing their wares and themselves as desirable.[93]

Mexican officials viewed immigration as a means of infusing perceived positive European economic and racial attributes into Mexico. The first *Ley de Migración* (1909), while restricting entrance to include only healthy non-anarchists, called for "the most complete equality of all the countries and all the races, not establishing a single special precept for citizens of any nation, nor for individuals of a determined race."[94] Despite the *Ley de Migración* decreeing that race would not be a factor in welcoming immigrants, scholars have noted that Díaz was driven by an ideology of racial determinism, seeking out the immigration of white, European foreigners with the idea that these individuals would propel commercial and industrial development in Mexico, while simultaneously contributing to the whitening of the Mexican race. For Porfirians, whitening did not necessarily entail the biological "improvement" of racial stock but was a sort of *mission civilisatrice*, infusing European money, customs, and education into an indigenous population supposedly lacking those qualities.[95] Jews were included in this categorization of useful foreigners to further this positivist agenda. By Porfirian standards, Jews were considered to be racially white and to possess a developed degree of culture and civilization that could positively transform Mexico; Díaz hoped that Jewish immigrants could "teach the Mexican people to work" and induce them to save.[96] Mauricio Assael and Rachel Corri's clothing choice and self-fashioning, and even Mauricio's monogrammed bag, would seem to be deliberate choices used to convey themselves as cultured and European, separating them from the indigenous people posed in the picture with them and from their own questionable status as authentic Europeans, given their Ottoman origins.

Scholars focusing on the migration of Middle Easterners, including Jews, to Mexico have suggested that these individuals intended to immigrate to the United States but were redirected to Mexico as a result of conniving ship agents, conflation of "the Americas" with "the United States of America," or because the 1891 passage of the Disease Act prevented entrance into the United States of would-be immigrants with trachoma or other infectious diseases.[97] And in fact some migrants from the Syrian provinces, like the Chinese who were barred from immigrating to the United States after 1882, did go to Mexico in hopes of crossing the northern border, often posing as Mexican nationals and relying on networks of compatriots throughout their endeavor.[98] However, the itineraries of individual Sephardi migrants to Mexico make clear the intentionality of their choice of destination, though for many, choosing to settle in Mexico did not entail permanent immobility. Frequent journeys, whether for business or personal reasons, remained a salient aspect of their lives.

An exploration of the trajectories of early Sephardi migrants to Mexico suggests that Mexico was a deliberate destination and not merely a poor alternative to the United States. Some, like 23-year-old Saul Carasso from Salonica, spent several years living in New York, Los Angeles, and San Francisco prior to migrating to Mexico in 1907. When Carasso entered Mexico, he did so as a Spanish national. He would go on to become a prominent businessman in Mexico City and listed his profession as "merchant" and "peddler" in the manifests of his travels between the United States, Mexico, Canada, Cuba, and France.[99] Carasso's business partner, Isaac Capon of Salonica (a driving force behind the establishment of a Jewish community in Mexico several years later), was detained for one day at Ellis Island, for having previously been in prison, when he traveled from Hamburg to New York. He was eventually permitted entry.[100] The paths taken by others, such as Clement Gabai, who lived in New York for seven years before moving to Torreón, Coahuila in 1909, or Albert Salem, who lived in the United States from 1902 to 1911, visiting Mexico before going to South Africa and later returning to settle in Mexico City, highlight that Mexico was a deliberate destination through which migrants passed and in which they sometimes stayed.[101] These men could enter the United States and other countries freely, and often did, even living there for a period of time before choosing to relocate to Mexico.

Early, albeit unsuccessful, attempts at naturalization attest to the attachment that Sephardi migrants felt to Mexico and provide some clues as to what drew them there. In 1905 and 1907, Juan (no longer Johanan) and Marie Antoinette Assael made return trips from Veracruz to Paris.[102] Three of the other Assael brothers, Alberto (no longer Albert), Mauricio, and Israel (not yet Isidoro), applied for Mexican naturalization, in direct contradiction of Ottoman policy prohibiting subjects from acquiring another nationality without permission.[103] The naturalization petitions of two other Jewish brothers, from Constantinople but of German nationality, preceded those of the brothers Assael by a year. The Assaels petitioned on the same day as three other Jews from Izmir, presumably together. Leon Alazraki, Salomon Castro, and Isaac Benveniste were all in their early twenties, from prominent families in the Izmir region, had spent several years in Mexico, and were friends and commercial partners with the Assael brothers and the Salonicans Capon and Carasso.[104] Their wives did not attempt to naturalize. While Israel offered no reason for his desire to acquire Mexican citizenship, and Alberto linked his to a profound gratitude as a result of his business' prosperity, Mauricio was, characteristically, more profuse. In flowery prose that harkened back to the typical Ottoman writing style, Mauricio also attributed his desire to become Mexican to his financial success, which was due to "the benevolent welcome that is dispensed to foreigners in this hospitable country, which, guided by the wise direction of its leaders has fully succeeded in entering the road of progress, figuring fittingly into the concert of the civilized nations."[105] The trope of a state's hospitality and benevolent welcome accorded to foreigners was not a new Sephardi expression; it was often used by Turks and Sephardim in explaining Sephardi presence in, and loyalty to, Turkey, and later became a central motif in the castigation of Jews in the Turkish Republic for *not* being more loyal in spite of Turkey's past and continued hospitality.[106] It did not appear to be incongruous for Assael to appeal to the same language of gratitude and hospitality, so prevalent among Sephardim in the Ottoman Empire, in his attempt to attain Mexican nationality, removing the name of one hospitable country and replacing it with another.

The success of early Sephardi migrants was partly due to their ability to draw on discursive and economic semiotic systems from the Ottoman Empire and employ them in the Mexican context. In Mexico, foreigners—whether

Spanish, French, Chinese, or of other geographic origin—traditionally filled the role of "middleman minorities" or "immigrant entrepreneurs," falling into those positions because abundant native labor meant that there was little to offer immigrant urban workers. The historian Robert Weis notes that "[a]s ethnic or religious outsiders subject to hostility or distrust, immigrant entrepreneurs tend to concentrate in lines that are undesirable for local elites and inaccessible for local poor, but that provide vital services for both."[107] These migrants, largely an urban phenomenon, often created unassimilated expatriate communities, *colonias*, forming clubs and casinos to socialize along national lines, often remaining endogamous when marrying, and enjoying a degree of power and wealth precisely because of their status as outsiders.[108] Occasionally, their wealth allowed them to marry into the Porfirian elite, as was the case with Antonio Letayf, an Ottoman Maronite from Mount Lebanon, giving them access to political power that would allow them to serve as intermediaries between the government and less-connected compatriots.[109]

The mass consumption market so well established in the United States was less entrenched in Mexico. This allowed Sephardi migrants and others of Ottoman origins the possibility of creating and filling key niches in this developing market. Peddling, obsolete in much of the United States by the turn of the century, offered early Middle Eastern migrants a potentially lucrative economic path.[110] While Rabbi Zielonka noted that much of Mexico was too poor to support peddlers, a small collective of Syrian Jewish men, though "undergoing the hardships that come to the pioneer," was prospering, sending remittances back to their relatives and friends in their natal lands.[111] For Sephardi Jews, transitioning to the Mexican economic structure did not provide a significant challenge. Although the business was distasteful to Mexican elites, migrants willingly peddled products, utilizing the *abono* (installment) system to bring mass-market dry goods to segments of the Mexican population that had previously been financially unable to acquire them.[112] And while some migrants decried the precarity of peddling, by the 1920s peddlers earned an average of three to four pesos daily, while laborers earned only five *centavos*.[113] The greater opportunity for Sephardim to acquire capital through peddling, or to open clothing, jewelry, or novelty stores and accrue financial success quickly, as noted in the naturalization petitions, may have been a reason why these men chose to come to and remain in Mexico.

Meanwhile, both the economic success of some of the early migrants and the risks of entering into economic endeavors in Mexico can be seen in insurance reimbursements for Ico Assael's jewelry store in Puebla: a 34,000-peso reimbursement after the store was destroyed by a fire and another reimbursement several months later when one of his employees robbed his store of 104 rings of different value, 48 silver watches, and 35 pairs of gold-plated earrings.[114] Ico Assael's success in achieving economic and social upward mobility was evidenced through notifications in the society pages of English- and Spanish-language Mexico City periodicals when he traveled from Puebla to Mexico City, while announcements of weddings, dances, or other fetes hosted by or featuring Sephardi migrants attest to broader patterns of financial and social success.[115]

Early migrants capitalized on their local and transnational connections, often but not exclusively with other Sephardim, and on their familiarity with travel to acquire and market goods. In doing so, they served as transnational entrepreneurs, participating in multiple polities and utilizing cross-border social networks to find new paths of economic mobility.[116] While the Assaels kept their domicile in Mexico, where in 1908 Alberto would be voted first the Spanish-language secretary and then the vice president of the nascent Jewish Relief Society of Mexico, the brothers continued to journey between Mexico and France.[117] Alberto traveled from France to Mexico via New York in 1908 as a Mexican national, even though his petition for naturalization was never approved, and Ico traveled in 1909 as an Ottoman, noting that he had previously been in the United States in 1903, 1907, and 1908.[118] When Alberto died in 1909, he left behind creditors in Bordeaux, France, pointing to the international nature of the Assaels' business dealings. Paul Dubois y Cía. filed two civil proceedings in Mexico to receive recompense from Alberto Assael's estate in the amount of 286.40 francs (a little over a hundred pesos), which he still owed for merchandise he had acquired.[119]

These international ties, particularly with France, allowed the Assaels and other Sephardi merchants to market their wares as originating in the home of modern fashion, making their products more appealing to upwardly mobile Mexicans for whom French goods represented a visible form of social cachet. Some migrants, like Carasso and Capon, gave their commercial establishments names such as "La Ciudad de Paris" to attest to a French connection. This naming practice grew increasing common during the years of the Mexican Revolution.

Such practices of appealing to the desire for French goods and culture that upwardly mobile Mexicans displayed became apparent in a 1908 advertisement for the Assael jewelry store, "La Turquesa." This advertisement prominently noted that La Turquesa had houses in Mexico and Paris, in an effort to entice clientele by appealing to a desirable type of foreignness. A 1912 half-page spread for La Turquesa employed a similar tactic, asserting that La Turquesa was "the only house in Mexico that has its factory of jewelry of all classes in Paris, on 43 *Rue de Trevise*."[120] By noting that La Turquesa's goods came from Paris, and making a point of supplying the physical address in Paris where the Assaels' factory was located, the Assaels offered Mexican consumers a concrete link to Paris, something that, according to the advertisement, only La Turquesa could supply. Although the advertisement did not mention this, *Rue de Trevise* lay at the center of the ninth *arrondissement* in Paris, where wealthier Ottoman Sephardi Jews lived.[121] On travel manifests between the United States and France of Sephardi Jews who had settled in Mexico, a number of these migrants listed their contacts in France as Sephardi friends and relatives living on the *Rue de Trevise*.[122] The Assaels' Parisian business suppliers, therefore, were likely fellow Sephardi Jewish migrants who had settled in Paris. These transnational Sephardi financial networks allowed the Assaels and other Sephardim in Mexico to market their goods and themselves as a desirable, cultured, and "civilizing" presence in Mexico, providing Sephardi migrants with a proven path of social and economic upward mobility.

Early Sephardi migrants also established ties with coreligionists throughout Latin America. In 1909, Isaac Capon and three other Sephardi salesmen traveled to Venezuela, while in 1910, four Sephardim living in Mexico City, from Athens and Constantinople and of Greek and Turkish nationality, traveled to Lima, Peru via New York.[123] In 1910, Capon again went to Venezuela, returning on the same steamer as Leon Alazraki, who had gone to Venezuela through Havana. Alazraki traveled as an Ottoman national to Venezuela and as a Mexican national on his return, though he later reverted to Italian nationality before permanently acquiring Mexican citizenship in 1926.[124] These frequent transnational, transatlantic, and transcontinental voyages were a key component of Sephardi life in Mexico, attesting to the creation and perpetuation of an active familial and financial diaspora that stretched from the Ottoman Empire and France to the United States, Mexico, Cuba, and South America.

That these Sephardim living in Mexico traveled, mingled, and entered into financial dealings together regardless of their city of origin or current nationality suggests that, while Sephardim in the United States may have organized and socialized in accordance with their city of origin, such was not the case in Mexico.[125] Although Syrian Jews quickly fractured along city lines, creating separate communities for Jews originating in Aleppo and Damascus, Sephardi Jews, perhaps because of the small size of their community in comparison to the much larger Sephardi communities in New York or Paris, retained cohesion across disparate geographic origins.

The early interactions among Sephardim were not always cordial, however, and the potential for family disapprobation despite distance could sway migrant behavior, as a 1907 slander case between Isaac Abuof and Marcos E. Habif, both young, single Ottoman merchants, demonstrates. Abuof alleged that he was walking past the Portal de Mercaderes, a large commercial complex on the western edge of the Zócalo, when Habif insulted him, calling him a *puto*. In addition, Abuof alleged, Habif had written back to their natal land, alleging to Abuof's family there that Abuof was a "young man of very bad conduct" who lived in bordellos. Habif, denying Abuof's charge, asserted that several days earlier, Abuof had shown up outside of his domicile, calling him a *desgraciado padrotón*, and that that very day, when Habif was in a friend's shop in the Portal de Mercaderes, Abuof hurled insults at him, calling him a *puto cabrón*. The case was eventually resolved with both men agreeing never to get involved with each other again.[126] Both apparently felt secure enough of their status in Mexico to resort to the Mexican court system for vindication. *Padrotón* (pimp), *puto* (homosexual), and *cabrón* (colloquially "bastard") were all words with overtly sexual connotations, as was Habif's assertion that Abuof frequently visited bordellos. Both allegedly referred to the other as *puto*, suggesting that each was a receptive partner in male same-sex sexual relations, which their Ottoman Jewish context marked as unsuitable for an adult man.[127]

This exchange exposed the internal coercive networks of migrant life, where a young man like Abuof, removed from the parental gaze, had the opportunity to act in ways his family and society of origin would have censured. Nonetheless, familial disapprobation still held power, which Habif knew and deliberately capitalized on to modify Abuof's behavior. Transnational networks of information and monitoring perpetuated the control of familial and social norms from the Ottoman Empire over migrants across the Atlantic.

Contacts, Context, and Conclusion

When Joseph Schemonti wrote as an "Ottoman subject living in Mexico" to the Ottoman minister of foreign affairs in 1909, he noted that "if the Empire wants to ... strengthen the attachment of this populous Ottoman colony, it will act in favor of its subjects in Mexico in honoring them with the next national representation, that is to say, a consular official."[128] This would uplift Ottoman subjects and compel them to identify as Ottomans. Although Schemonti presented his ideas as innovative, something that was only possible after the overthrow of the "despotic" Sultan Abdülhamid II, the Ottoman Empire had in fact been trying unsuccessfully to enter into diplomatic relations with Mexico since 1904, compelled by the presence of the growing number of Ottoman migrants in Mexico. The negotiations that this process entailed simultaneously cast light onto the processes of positioning and attempts at dominance between the two states and highlighted the increasing presence of Ottoman subjects in Mexico.

In July of 1904, the Mexican ambassador to Rome, Gonzalo Esteva, met his Ottoman counterpart, Mustapha Rechid Bey, by chance in the waiting room of the Italian ministry of foreign trade. In a formal letter that Rechid sent to Esteva several days later, requesting the establishment of a consular accord between the two states, Rechid explained that "this understanding, which would have the effect of strengthening the commercial and friendly relations between these states [Mexico and Colombia] and Turkey, would only be necessary because of the numerous Ottoman subjects who want to conduct commerce there." He requested that Mexico serve as an intermediary in establishing diplomatic ties with Colombia.[129] The Secretaría de Relaciones Exteriores responded that a treaty with the Ottoman Empire "would not be exempt from inconvenience" and declined to facilitate relations between Colombia and the Ottoman Empire. The Ottoman ambassador to Rome again approached the Mexican legation in 1905, insisting upon an agreement "with the aim of establishing Ottoman consulates in Mexico and Mexican ones in Turkey, for the protection of commerce between both states and of the respective subjects." The presence of Ottoman subjects in Mexico propelled the need for an Ottoman consular presence. The SRE again demurred, noting that reaching an agreement was not possible, "especially since the foundation of interest is from the side of Turkey and not of Mexico."[130] Esteva again attempted to advocate for the establishment of consular relations following a meeting with İbrahim Hakkı Bey, the new ambassador of Turkey in Rome, in which the latter reiterated the need because of the "number of Ottoman subjects resident in Mexico." Esteva noted that "the conditions of the Ottoman Empire have changed with their recent evolution, and perhaps our government will now consider convenient that which in the past it esteemed differently," alluding to the political changes wrought by the Young Turk Revolution.[131] This time, the SRE assented, leading to the commencement of a process of negotiation over the language of the treaty that would last for several years.

In an agreement modeled after the one between the Ottoman Empire and Argentina, the content of the treaty was not contested.[132] Both countries would establish consular posts in port cities and other metropolitan areas to represent the interests of commerce and their respective subjects. The Ottoman Empire, wary of granting Capitulations and not seeing Mexico as being on the same level as European powers, stipulated that Mexico was to receive no Capitulations. The conflicts came over the language of the treaty, and where to sign it, with both states endeavoring to position themselves as the more powerful party.

Initially, Hakkı proposed that the agreement should be written "conforming to the rules of public European law," perhaps in an attempt to cast the Ottoman state as European or, at least, as a way to indicate which entities the Ottoman government looked to as models. The SRE objected, saying that the clause should read "conforming to that which our consular law dictates." Further, the Mexican government insisted that the accords be signed in Mexico City.[133] This posturing placed Mexico as more powerful and would require the Ottoman government to recognize the supremacy of Mexican consular law and make the long journey to Mexico City. Unsurprisingly, Hakkı Pasha (no longer "Bey" after his promotion to grand vizier) declined, because the language referred only to the law of Mexico, "not the law of both signatory states." The empire would send diplomatic representatives to Mexico only after the ratification of the accord. He proffered "conforming to the rules of international public law" as a more universal alternative to Mexico's exclusivist language.[134] Although the SRE accepted that language, they noted that "the Government of the Republic has particular interest in it being signed in America and chooses for this act the city of Washington, where there are representatives of Mexico and the Sublime Porte."[135] However, when the agreement was finally signed in December 1910 after approval by the Ottoman parliament, it was done in Rome.[136] Mexico's attempt to push the Ottoman Empire into recognizing the former's superiority had failed.

That same year marked the centenary of Mexican independence. For Mexico, the *centenario* provided elite and popular constructions of collective memory, reflecting a popular trend in Western Europe, with an audience not only of Mexico City residents and visitors from the provinces but also foreign dignitaries and the international press.[137] The Ottoman Empire, though it was invited to the festivities by the Mexican ambassador to the United States, who noted that "this homage of a distant country, with no political or commercial relations with ours and worthy of estimation for the firmness with which it has entered the road of progress, would satisfy our self-love," was unable to send a diplomatic envoy to the event.[138] The ambassador's statement highlighted the mutual path of positivism on the road to progress and the interest that these two states shared in promoting mutual relations.

The centenary also provided Ottoman subjects in Mexico with the opportunity to inscribe their place in this national celebration. The Assael brothers recognized the centenary by marketing a "souvenir of the centenary," featuring artistic portraits of Miguel Hidalgo, Benito Juárez, and Porfirio Díaz in gold plate, at a reduced price. Again, they noted their Mexican and Parisian connections, pointing out that their "new art" was "unique in Paris, unique in Mexico."[139]

Some Ottoman subjects who had united to form a *Comité Patriótico Otomano* wanted to offer a token of their gratitude for their hospitable reception in Mexico. In keeping with the *centenario*'s documenting of Mexico's achievement of progress and modernity, they wanted the clock tower they offered to "simultaneously serve as an ornament and also lend utility to the metropolis." It should be raised in a central, obvious point, ostensibly for utility, but also to make visible the *colonia otomana* and this manifestation of gratitude. They selected a site to the southwest of the Zócalo, near many of their businesses.[140] The organizers were all from Ottoman Arab provinces, while the clock tower itself had a mechanism from Istanbul and was decorated with tiles that simultaneously recalled Mexican *azulejos*, the Iznik tiles of Anatolia, and the tiles decorating the Umayyad Mosque in Damascus.[141] In choosing a clock tower as their symbol of gratitude, these Ottoman migrants drew on shared Mexican and Ottoman understandings of clock towers as symbols of modernity and progress.[142]

Although the amalgamation of different motifs might suggest that Schemonti's call for Ottoman subjects in Mexico to proudly identify as Ottomans had been taken to heart, such a conclusion would be premature. The *colonia otomana* represented by the *Comité Patriotico Otomano* was composed solely of Syrio-Lebanese Christian Ottomans, a population divided by allegations of corruption and nepotism in the selection of the Ottoman representative in Mexico.[143] Meanwhile, in 1911, the *Casino Otomano* was formed in the Zócalo to be a recreational society to "augment the union that exists between the Ottomans resident in Mexico, and to form a pleasant center of reunion that will permit them ... to affirm their sentiments in all questions that must augment the development of the Ottoman influence in Mexico." The constituent members again were all Syrio-Lebanese. That same year, a group of Syrian Jews inaugurated the *Casino Turco*.[144] The small Sephardi community neither formed its own recreational or social organizations nor participated in those of their fellow Ottomans of disparate linguistic and religious origins. While Ottoman officials and intellectuals like Schemonti aimed to gloss over differences in encouraging all Ottoman subjects abroad to proclaim themselves "Ottomans," the lack of cohesiveness and the persistence of ethnic, linguistic, and religious divides among Ottoman subjects in Mexico point to the failure of this attempt. This mirrors the inability to unite disparate communities within the Ottoman Empire in a common Ottoman identity, in spite of the optimism that accompanied the Young Turk Revolution of 1908.

Sephardim who migrated to Mexico in the first decade of the twentieth century left one state that viewed itself ensconced on the road to order, progress, and civilization for another that conceived of itself in the same way. The Ottoman Empire sought to incorporate religious minorities by erasing divisions between them and the Muslim populace, such as exemption from military service and lack of access to governmental schools and careers. Officials attempted to overcome the inherent "foreignness" of Sephardim by encouraging them to learn the Ottoman language, which would allow them to render service to the homeland through employment in administration. For many Sephardim, however, Ottoman was not perceived as useful for the spheres of commerce that they frequented, nor was administration a popular career alternative to commerce. Mexico, meanwhile, sought out foreigners, particularly Europeans, in an effort to "whiten" its population, bring in civilization and modernity, and transform commerce and industry.

Propelled to leave by the appeal of economic mobility and a future different from that of those around them and unswayed by the promises of equality that the Young Turk Revolution ushered in, some Sephardi émigrés deliberately sought out Mexico. There, the developing economy and the propensity of foreigners to establish themselves in trade allowed Sephardim to capitalize on their prior experience as peddlers and merchants. Drawing on their economic background in local and international trade, comfort with frequent mobility, multilingual education, and ambiguous and varied national affiliations, they used their indeterminate foreignness and connections to Western European countries perceived as models of culture to increase their social and economic capital. Entering into business relations with each other and with Sephardim and others in Latin America and beyond, they socialized beyond the confines of their cities of origin, yet predominantly among themselves. In doing so, they formed the basis of a Sephardi community that expanded exponentially in the following decades, establishing patterns of economic and social engagement that remained in force well into the 1930s.

(CHAPTER 2)

PATRIOT GAMES

SÁLOMON LEVY WAS BORN in the early 1890s in Sofia, the capital of the recently constituted Bulgarian state, and grew up in Constantinople before moving to Kavala with his family. Having previously studied in a *meldar* and then in an Alliance Israélite Universelle (AIU) school, he attended a Turkish secondary school after the Young Turk Revolution opened Turkish schools to minority students. According to his later recounting, he and four Jewish friends sought to enter a Turkish military school after graduating from secondary school. But Levy and his friends quickly encountered the glass ceiling that existed in the Ottoman military for religious minorities who actively wanted to serve the empire, turned away with the answer that Jews could not become officers, since "how could a Jewish officer give orders to or punish a Turk?" Levy and his Jewish companions therefore decided to emigrate to America. However, as he told it, the mandatory military service that had been newly instituted for religious minorities in the place of the *bedel-i askeri* (military exemption tax) prevented these young men of draftable age from leaving the country. In the aftermath of the Turco-Italian War and with the Balkan hostilities brewing, the Ottoman Empire was reluctant to allow young male subjects to leave. They only granted permission in cases where young men could provide birth certificates proving that they had not yet reached the age of draft eligibility along with other documents detailing the purpose of their travels and their intent to return.

Although Levy and his friends were of the prime age for military service and had the intention to emigrate permanently, however, this official policy and the documentation required for exit permits proved to be surmountable obstacles after all. In the Ottoman Empire, record-keeping duties were carried out in each neighborhood by individual *muhtars*, representing the members of their *millet* who lived in that neighborhood; the *muhtars* were obligated to report births, deaths, and marriages to the government. Levy went to the Jewish representative of his neighborhood and offered him a gold coin worth about five dollars. In exchange, he acquired a birth certificate saying that he had been born three years later than he actually was, putting him under the age of conscription.[1] Levy and his friends, who were all proficient in French as a result of their AIU education, showed their new doctored birth certificates and informed the Ottoman officials that they were traveling to France to continue their education there; they were all granted permission to leave.[2] Once arrived in France, they continued across the Atlantic, heading for New York in steerage class, sleeping on planks with their shoes as pillows, both in an attempt at comfort and to prevent the theft of the shoes.

Although Sálomon's friends were admitted at Ellis Island, Sálomon's new birth certificate, which had allowed him to leave the Ottoman Empire, proved his undoing at this next threshold. He was now officially fifteen, too young to enter the United States unaccompanied by a parent. While his friends entered the United States, never to see Sálomon again, U.S. officials put Sálomon on a ship destined for Trieste. The local Ashkenazi Jewish community there paid half of the price for a ticket back to the Ottoman Empire for him, with the local Ottoman consulate covering the rest. He worked as an assistant cook on a boat that retrieved Ottoman subjects fleeing Greek-occupied Salonica, depositing them, together with Sálomon, in the Dardanelles. When Sálomon presented himself as a refugee from the Balkan Wars, the Jewish community of the Dardanelles provided him with passage on a Russian ship heading to Constantinople. However, he was still intent on emigration. Upon reaching the Ottoman capital, he borrowed $30 from his father to purchase a ticket to Havana, where an uncle lived; Havana was experiencing unparalleled economic prosperity due to the success of the sugar industry.[3] Finally, now, Sálomon left the Ottoman Empire permanently. From Cuba, he went on to Mexico in 1917, returning again to Cuba, then back to Mexico, back to Cuba again, and on to Colombia before permanently settling in Mexico with his extended family in 1927. Once he was in Cuba, he, like many other Sephardi migrants and others from the Middle East, began to peddle. In both Cuba and Mexico, he acquired wares from other Sephardi migrants, allowing him to slowly accumulate the capital necessary to bring over the rest of his family.[4]

This chapter explores how years of war altered Sephardi life and how Sephardi Jews accommodated and manipulated these changes. The Ottoman Empire contended with the Turco-Italian War of 1911, in which it lost its final holdings in North Africa; the Balkan Wars of 1912 and 1913, which vastly reduced its Balkan territories; and then its ultimately disastrous involvement in World War I, from 1914 to 1918. Mexico, meanwhile, was torn asunder by the violence of competing parties that followed the ousting of the dictator Porfirio Díaz in 1910, violence that lasted for close to a decade. These periods of prolonged fighting were accompanied by economic and social instability, violence, famine, and general upheaval.

In the Ottoman Empire and Mexico, these wars catalyzed rearticulations of citizenship and belonging. They created and perpetuated new physical and psychological borders between those who belonged and those did not. Meanwhile, the increasing presence of Sephardi Jews outside of Ottoman territory, whether due to intentional migration or to the redrawing of borders based on the outcome of war, led to the exhibition of multiple and conflicting identities and loyalties among the Sephardi populace. Some intellectual and religious Sephardi leaders loudly proclaimed Sephardi patriotism toward the Ottoman state and demanded its active manifestation, whether through military service or donations. However, individuals like Sálomon Levy subverted such calls by emigrating, while the same intellectual and communal leaders who advocated Sephardi loyalty to the Ottoman cause simultaneously promoted Sephardi ties that stretched beyond the Ottoman borders, often extending to Sephardim resident in enemy states or far away across the Atlantic. Although Sephardim beyond the Ottoman Empire sometimes relinquished ties to the Ottoman state, they still maintained attachment to other Sephardi Jews, undergirding a growing diasporic world. For these individuals, neither a state nor a territorial entity was the linchpin of affiliation. Instead, transnational familial and economic connections propelled the creation and perpetuation of a Sephardi, and at times, a broader Jewish collective that transcended borders.

This multivalent Sephardi affiliation had its roots in the mobility that continued despite the increased scrutiny of international travel and of potentially subversive foreigners that accompanied World War I. Migration created new challenges for political, communal, familial, and gender continuity and control as Ottoman and Jewish leaders sought to contain and accommodate the presence of new individuals and the loss of old ones. Sephardi migrants traveling internationally encountered increased state regulation that complicated or prohibited their entry into countries that were enemies or allies of the Ottoman Empire. For some of these migrants living in Mexico, the problem posed by Ottoman origins could be overcome by obfuscating their place of birth, either by illicitly acquiring documentation of another nationality or by relying on their inheritance of non-Ottoman nationality. For others, their Ottoman nationality made movement more difficult, even when they were traveling in the employ of the Mexican government.

States at War, States of War

On February 2, 1913, the office of the chief rabbinate of the Ottoman Empire issued "A Call to Our Brothers," published on the third page of *El Tiempo*, the most widely circulated Ladino periodical, which was issued three times a week from Constantinople.[5] This article, which appeared in the midst of the Balkan Wars, was placed just after articles calling for "patriotic" donations to the Ottoman war effort and describing a meeting of the "Women of the National Defense" at a conference hall in the *Darülfünun* (the Ottoman Empire's only university) that had been convened to discuss means of increasing patriotism among Turkish women. Rabbi Haim Nahum, the recently elected, AIU-educated, *Hahambaşı* (chief rabbi) who had been chosen in part for his political acumen,[6] issued the following call to his "dear brothers":

> Our well-loved *patria* is in danger. The enemies who descend on our state, the war with all its calamities, they now want to tear out its heart and its honor! Because of this circumstance, the Ottoman nation, without difference of race and religion, arises like a single man to defend our holy *patria*, its honor, its family. A committee of national defense was formed in our city,

others are being formed in the different cities of the empire. This committee, in which are some of our brothers, will issue a call in the coming days so that every Ottoman will take part in the salvation of this land, which opened its arms to us when we were in anguish, without shelter, without protection.

Dear brothers! In these difficult moments through which our well-loved *patria* traverses, it is for us, particularly, an imperative duty to show to our tolerant government our gratitude and our unlimited attachment, that each and every one of us does something to contribute to the salvation of the honor of the nation and its patrimony. Let us think that thousands of our compatriots, our own sons, give their lives on the battlefields, causing their blood to run to accomplish their sacred duty and to protect our families and our goods against the enemies.[7]

Rabbi Nahum's call, invoking the language of the defense of the honor of the "mother *patria*"[8] and the gratitude that Ottoman Jews owed to the Ottoman state for welcoming them with open arms upon their expulsion from Spain roughly four hundred years earlier, paints Ottoman Jews as staunch believers in Ottomanism, clinging to the hope that they could remain an integral part of an inclusive Ottoman Empire, while other groups—most notably Greeks and Armenians—and even the government itself were shifting toward an exclusive nationalism.[9] Ottoman Jews, according to Nahum's plea, were part of the Ottoman family; the blood of Jewish sons and the sons of other Ottoman families, whether Muslim or Christian, blended together on the battlefield as if it was the blood of one man, inseparable in the performance of the sacred duty of patriotism. Ottoman Jews were the quintessential patriotic citizens, loyal to the bloody end.

The article immediately following Rabbi Nahum's call, entitled "Jewish Prisoners in Bulgaria," offered an alternative view of Ottoman Jewish affiliation. *El Tiempo* reprinted a letter from *La Luz*, a Ladino periodical from Sofia, penned by eight Ottoman Jewish prisoners of war from Çanakkale, Constantinople, and Monastir. They had been captured by the enemy Bulgarian army at Kırklareli and held in Bulgaria. These Ottoman Jews expressed their "profoundest thanks" to the Jews of Yambol for "all the care that *our* Jews of Bulgaria have done and do for us."[10] They described arriving in the city on the night of Shabbat and knocking on the first Jewish house they saw, noting that "it is impossible to describe the joy on the face of the man who received us," where they were treated "with the care that a mother has for her sons." These eight Ottoman Jewish soldiers, part of the Ottoman family to which Nahum referred, positioned themselves as part of a different collective. In the midst of the Balkan Wars, these supposed enemies, Ottoman and Bulgarian Jews, were members of the same family. As the tension between the two articles suggests, Ottoman Jewish identification, on a popular and elite level, manifested in terms of affiliation with the Ottoman state and its other denizens regardless of religion, on the one hand, as well as with coreligionists in other, often enemy, states, on the other.

The territorial division of the Ottoman Empire before and during the Balkan Wars and World War I transformed the empire writ large and had vast repercussions for the Ladino-speaking world concentrated around the Aegean littoral and up the Balkan peninsula. The annexation of Sarajevo by the Austro-Hungarian Empire in 1908 and the losses of Salonica, Monastir, and other cities with significant Sephardi populations during the Balkan Wars divided the Sephardi *Kulturbereich* along new state borders. As a result of territorial transformations, flows of refugees in all directions, and Ottoman policies targeting Armenian, Assyrian, and Orthodox populations for destruction, the demographic profile of the remaining Ottoman territory changed dramatically. As the European provinces with their large Christian populations were divided among Serbia, Macedonia, Bulgaria, and Greece, the Ottoman Empire became increasingly Muslim. State discourse and policies reflected and sought to harness these transforming demographics.[11]

The conflicts exacerbated sectarian and ethnic tensions between the different collectives that composed the Ottoman Empire and the Balkan states, while the perceived disloyalty of Armenian and Greek Orthodox subjects during hostilities changed Ottoman policy toward the military service of religious minorities, moving them away from the front, where they had served during the Balkan Wars, to labor battalions, or even deliberate extermination, during World War I. The loss of territory propelled the ideological transformation from Ottomanism into a Turkish nationalism centered upon Anatolia rather than the newly ceded Balkans. The Balkan nations' success against the Ottomans during the Balkan Wars provided the Committee of Union and Progress (CUP), which officially took power between December 1912 and January 1913, with a model that attributed Balkan victory to racial consciousness, leading to the proliferation of a racialized Turkishness as the determinative identity for Ottoman citizens. The official journal of the CUP and the government in 1913, *Türk Yurdu*, represented itself as a "real Turkish nationalist journal," while the Turkish Hearths organization, *Türk Ocakları*, also founded in 1913, aimed at glorifying the Turkish race through public lectures and articles. Only Turks were permitted to become members.[12]

"We have been betrayed by the Greeks and Armenians . . . and you have suffered as much from their treason," announced the First Inspector of the *Viyalet* of Edirne to the Jewish population of the Thracian town of Çorlu in 1914. Loyal residents of the area should frequent stores owned by Turks and, if those were lacking, the stores of Jews, but never Armenian- or Greek-owned establishments, he went on. His views reflected a new era of economic policy that sought to increase Muslim participation in trade while challenging the perceived centrality of religious minorities—particularly Christians—in Ottoman commerce.[13] In September 1914, the government unilaterally abrogated the Capitulations. This, in turn, precipitated the "nationalization" or "Turkification" of the state by requiring the use of Turkish exclusively in the post offices and communications with the ministry of finance.[14] These policies built upon Hamidian preferences for patronizing Ottoman stores and purchasing Ottoman Muslim products. Together with CUP monopolies on sugar, petrol, and other products, which the government distributed to Muslim merchants of their choosing, these new policies encouraged commercial and industrial activity while attempting to create a Turkish Muslim bourgeoisie to challenge the economic dominance of the religious minorities.[15]

As the wars raged, many Jewish population centers were caught in the midst of hostilities. Jewish residents were among the refugees streaming toward Constantinople and Izmir from the fronts. Concurrently, the increasing costs of living made migration an attractive option for city dwellers.[16] While Jewish religious and intellectual leaders advocated for Jews to manifest their patriotism as Ottoman subjects by contributing to the Ottoman military cause, whether by willingly completing their military service or by donating money to the war effort, young men like Sálomon Levy resisted their call by emigrating. Others openly challenged the terms of conscription, indicating that not all Ottoman Jews enthusiastically embraced the Ottoman military's call or were loyal exclusively to the Ottoman cause.

Under Siege

The hostilities of the Balkan Wars and World War I affected Sephardi populations in different ways, depending on the region in which they lived. Cities and villages in Thrace, Macedonia, and the Dardenelles were at the center of hostilities, first during the Balkan Wars and then during World War I.[17] Salonica, the "Jerusalem of the Balkans," was lost to Ottoman forces in 1912, incorporated into the expanding Greek state. Many Salonican Jews opposed Greek annexation, fearing economic disruption, loss of trade with the Macedonian hinterland, and the supplanting of Salonica's key role as a port city by the Hellenic ports of Volos and Piraeus. They advocated for an Austrian plan that would make Salonica an international city. Following Greek entry into Salonica, Greek soldiers and the Salonican Christian populace unleashed a series of violent attacks against Jews, raping fifty women, pillaging Jewish shops and houses, and murdering several who resisted.[18] The Greek government enacted an aggressive plan to Hellenize the Salonican economy, supplanting Jewish merchants, agents, peddlers, and bankers with Orthodox Greeks, many of whom were refugees fleeing areas under Bulgarian and Ottoman control.[19]

For many of Salonica's Jews, particularly the city's elite, a solution to this upheaval lay in looking abroad. In the six months after the city was annexed, some twenty-five hundred Salonican Jews—roughly five percent of the urban Jewish population—rushed to acquire protégé status from Spanish, Portuguese, and Austro-Hungarian consuls, hopeful that this would afford them some level of political security.[20] Others fled to Constantinople to remain under Ottoman rule.[21] Still others decided to leave altogether, whether as a response to the new Greek governance over the city, in flight from the mandatory Greek conscription put in place after 1916, or because of the massive 1917 fire that displaced seventy thousand people, including fifty thousand Jews, and destroyed hundreds of Jewish-owned businesses. This fire also provided the Greek government with the opportunity to rebuild the city in a way that effaced its multicultural heritage.[22] Even before the fire, many Jews had left, via Dedeagaç and Constantinople, for New York—where *La Amerika* reported that all find work and are content, other than those turned away because of trachoma—and elsewhere. Because of Jewish emigration, Salonica now appeared, according to this article, to be a city "in which the only sounds heard are sad songs and the disagreements of the Greek soldiers and gendarmes in the cabarets."[23] Many of the Jews leaving Salonica in the recent aftermath of the city's Hellenization had little sense of themselves as Greek, although they bore newly acquired Greek nationality.[24] As Devin Naar notes, in going to the Americas they were choosing not between an "old world" and a new but rather which "new world" they preferred. Their old world had disappeared when the Ottoman state relinquished its control of their city.[25]

While Salonican Jews found themselves permanently within the Greek state, towns within Thrace flip-flopped between Ottoman and Bulgarian control as the front moved and Ottoman forces barely prevented Bulgarian entry into Constantinople. The city of Edirne was under siege for five months before being ceded to Bulgarian troops in March of 1913. Angèle Guéron, an AIU instructor, remained in Edirne throughout the siege, recording her experiences in a diary after train service to Constantinople was cut on October 30, 1912, which effectively ended postal service. Disinformation prevailed, as the Ottoman government tried to boost morale by preventing the transmission of news recounting its successive losses against Bulgarian forces. Many of the city's wealthy residents fled to Constantinople, and Muslim subjects of surrounding villages sought protection within Edirne's walls. Although basic supplies like salt, sugar, and flour ran out or could only be obtained at exorbitant prices on the black market or by exchanging sexual favors with millers and shopkeepers, meat remained relatively plentiful, as the refugee farmers sold their animals for a pittance; there was nowhere to pasture the animals.[26] In contrast to the situation in Salonica, Ottoman forces recaptured Edirne during the second Balkan War, which meant that for Jewish residents who remained in Edirne or returned following the cessation of hostilities, there was no need to undergo a permanent reidentification. Many Jewish residents of Edirne, however, particularly the wealthy, remained in Constantinople or migrated, lessening the income that Edirne's Jewish community received through taxes and donations and complicating its efforts to assist members of the community made indigent or widowed by war.[27]

The Sephardi residents of smaller towns in Thrace also fled the clashing armies that destroyed their homes and livelihoods. Many Jewish residents of Mustafapaşa, Kırklareli, Rodosto (Tekirdağ), Silivri, Çorlu, Vize, Demotica, and Lüleburgaz sought refuge in Constantinople as the battlefields grew nearer during the Balkan hostilities of 1912–1913. Those who returned found their properties destroyed, whether by fighting forces, Bulgarian vandalism, or Christian residents targeting Jewish properties as a result of perceived Jewish alignment with Ottoman forces.[28] During the early years of World War I, the several thousand Jews living in the Dardanelles (Çanakkale) and Gallipoli (Gelibolu) were displaced as Ottoman and Allied forces engaged in prolonged trench warfare. Individual Jewish families were also relocated from Thracian towns by the Ottoman government.[29] Displacement often entailed the loss of livelihood and home, necessitating either later rebuilding or permanent relocation elsewhere. Many set their sights on locations in Latin America; Cuba and Mexico attracted a disproportional share of migrants from Thrace.[30]

Constantinople drew thousands of Jewish refugees during the Balkan Wars and World War I, requiring a response from the local Jewish communities now tasked with their housing and care. Refugees were distributed throughout the city, initially placed in synagogues and AIU schools, while the infirm were sheltered in the Or-Ahayim Jewish National Hospital.[31] Istanbul's Jewish community struggled to raise funds, with local and international appeals to fund soup kitchens for indigent local and refugee populations and to support the families of soldiers.[32] Although the Ottoman government offered a small monthly pension of 30 piastres to the families of soldiers in active service, these payments were often delayed. The widows and orphans of soldiers who had died elsewhere than on the battlefield received nothing.[33] The wives and widows of soldiers or deserters often therefore faced eviction and were forced to work at menial cleaning and peddling jobs to provide for their children.[34] The need to attend to them and to Ottoman Jews fleeing war zones added to the financial strain on the Jewish communities of Constantinople. The high rate of inflation and soaring prices for basic foodstuffs further confounded the effort to provide for the burgeoning number of poor.[35] The economic hardships imposed by a decade of continual war, the strain that demographic loss put on families and communal tax revenues, and the prospect of rebuilding homes and livelihoods propelled many to look for new, friendlier shores.

"The Terror of Our Dreams": Military Service and Emigration

In the midst of the Balkan Wars, Judith Russo, a contributor to *El Tiempo*, noted with pride that Salonican Jews had resisted Hellenic forces during the first Balkan War and exhorted Ottoman Jews to serve, claiming:

> For us, Ottoman Jews, the duty of fidelity to the state is most sacred.... Think of it! They left behind them the Inquisition and its fires.... How could we possibly forget the noble and generous protection that the sultans accorded us every time the calumny of blood libel arose, over and over, causing in them the horror and terror of the Turk, our brother.... Brother Muslim, our tears are more numerous, maybe more bitter than yours. The hearts of the Jews fall sadly together with yours. Whatever is your fate, we will share it. Your suffering is our suffering and your pain is our pain, where you die, we will die, because your God is also our God.[36]

Russo's impassioned call to Ottoman Jews to unite with their Muslim brothers in defense of the state that had so long protected them built upon an Ottoman Jewish strategy of emphasizing their Ottoman belonging through overt reference to a special alliance with Ottoman Muslims.[37] In Russo's formulation, Ottoman Jewish ties to the empire were deeper even than those of Ottoman Muslims, since Ottoman Jews had the protection of the empire to thank for their very existence. Ottoman Muslims and Jews were of the same family in life, underscored by sharing the same death. Though Ottoman Jews had been transplanted from Spain, they flourished and withered in Ottoman soil, intertwining their roots with those of the empire's other residents.

In the aftermath of the Young Turk Revolution, Ottoman leaders briefly increased their rhetoric of eliminating differences between ethnic and religious groups in the empire and inculcating a shared Ottoman identity among the empire's subjects. By 1909, there was already concern that the inability of different ethno-religious groups to look beyond their particular nationalist tendencies would produce frictions that would exacerbate divisions and suspicions among the different subjects of the state, eclipsing the outpouring of optimism that had come in the wake of the revolution. Universal military conscription became a potential means of erasing differences of class and religion and addressed the need for a larger base from which to draw troops. This legislated equality did not always translate into transformed practice, however, as religious minorities encountered obstacles in achieving officer ranks and, with World War I, were removed from the front and stripped of their arms to form labor battalions instead.

"Soldiers of every nation, and Jews as well," proclaimed the headline of an August 1908 article in the Izmir-based Ladino periodical *El Meseret*. This article, coming only weeks after the July 1908 restoration of the Ottoman constitution, broached the possibility that Jews would now be obliged to serve in the Ottoman army rather than pay an exemption tax, as had been established practice.[38] But the imposition of changes in military service did not proceed as smoothly as Ottoman officials may have hoped, as Ottoman authorities struggled to draft and implement a host of changes to preexisting conscription and mobilization practices that had, up until the Balkan Wars, contained provisions for exemption from service, sometimes in exchange for a fee, for religious minorities and others. An AIU instructor in Edirne sent a letter to AIU officials in 1910 complaining that "the law of military service is still not completely defined and well thought-out, each functionary giving it the interpretation that to him appears the most just."[39] And although teachers and rabbinic scholars were to be exempt from the service, these young men often required intervention by the chief rabbi or AIU officials to end government harassment.[40]

The Balkan Wars exacted a heavy toll on the Ottoman army, and as World War I commenced and continued, Ottoman authorities grappled with balancing the need for income that exemption fees could provide with the need for manpower that necessitated expanding the pool of those eligible to serve. The May 1914 Law of Military Obligation (Mükellefiyet-i Askeriye Kanun-i Muvakkatı) required all male Ottomans over the age of twenty-one to perform military service; during wartime, this age limit could be lowered to include nineteen- and twenty-year-olds. Exemptions for sole breadwinners were abolished; waivers for governmental officials, religious functionaries, and students in high schools and universities were heavily restricted; and the waiving of active service for a fee was limited to peacetime.[41] As the war continued, the ages at which soldiers could be conscripted were extended both up and down—by May 1917, boys aged seventeen could be conscripted and, in an effort to counter falsified documentation and the unreliability of population records, those who were not eligible for conscription according to their registered age could nevertheless be conscripted based on physical appearance alone. In response, parents dressed their teenaged sons in children's clothes to make them appear younger, while men with white facial hair grew out their beards to look older.[42] Those who had purchased exemption were mobilized anyway; they were promised, but not always delivered, the return of their exemption fee.

The changing regulations regarding conscription and exemption from conscription prompted confusion and consternation among Jewish communal leaders and laypeople. In 1914, Jews under the age of thirty-two were to be conscripted, but there was uncertainty as to whether earlier decrees were still applicable that exempted those between thirty-two and forty-five if they paid the *bedel-i askeri*.[43] Others, having paid the *bedel* believing that it would exempt them, were then placed in companies that did not bear arms.[44] Though non-Muslims had served as officers and soldiers during the Balkan Wars, distrust and mounting Turkish nationalism meant that by World War I, most non-Muslim conscripts were disarmed and serving in labor battalions (*amele taburları*) building roads away from the fronts, often in treacherous conditions.[45] Complaints about the hard labor and difficult conditions were common in the immediate postwar years.[46]

Meanwhile, military service caused social disruptions. These ranged from the poor widow of a Jewish soldier in Salonica setting her house on fire in an attempt to kill herself and her six children because she could not afford medicine[47] to uproar over the raising of the maximum draft age to forty-five during the Balkan Wars, among the Jews in Salonica and Izmir, who asserted that "the commerce of the country would suffer greatly" if the "fathers and heads of families ... [were] obliged to leave their families and their work."[48]

Although Ottoman Jews enlisted in the Ottoman armed forces, they did not always do so enthusiastically. Many sought to evade military service, with the elite paying exemption fees if possible while others hid in attics or bribed doctors to give them a writ of reprieve.[49] Still others attempted to capitalize on the possibility of exemption for religious figures by drawing on connections within the Jewish community to be declared religious leaders. In his diary of the war from Izmir, Alexandre Ben Ghiat distinguished these individuals—whom he designated *chobeleros*—from genuine religious figures, or *chobelis*, both names referring to the *chobe*, or long robe, of the Ottoman rabbinate. The former, alleged Ben Ghiat, had bribed one of Izmir's rabbis to be exempted from military service and to profit from the war.[50]

Those who did serve faced the possibility of death or being held as prisoners of war. During the Balkan Wars, of 340 thousand Ottoman soldiers, some 125 thousand died in battle or from disease, 100 thousand were wounded, and 115 thousand ended up in captivity.[51] Allowing for overlaps in categories, this nonetheless highlights the peril of military service. Although the extent of Jewish war casualties is unknown, the impact of military service made its way into the Ladino musical repertoire through the refrain "Mi ermano el grande/ era soldado/ el fue matado/ en Lüleburgaz" [My older brother/ was a soldier/ he was killed/ in Lüleburgaz].[52] With Salonica's capture by Greek forces and territorial loss to the Bulgarian army, some Ottoman Sephardim became prisoners of war, while Ottoman forces captured Sephardim serving in the Bulgarian army.[53] And yet, although the Ottoman Empire was at war with Bulgaria, Bulgarian and Ottoman Jewish officials protected and advocated for their captured enemy coreligionists. As a result of Haim Nahum's efforts, for instance, the Ottoman ministry of war released at least fifty-three Bulgarian Jewish prisoners of war who had been held in Izmit.[54] Meanwhile, the chief rabbinates of the Ottoman Empire and of Bulgaria communicated frequently over the status and well-being of Ottoman Jewish prisoners of war as well as of those living in territories, like Edirne, that were newly under Bulgarian control; the two chief rabbinates exchanged money to care for the prisoners.[55] *El Tiempo* reprinted letters of thanks from Ottoman Jewish prisoners of war to their Bulgarian coreligionists.[56] While these letters reassured readers on the home front that their sons and husbands were being cared for, the sentiments these articles expressed countered notions of Jewish exclusive affiliation with the Ottoman Empire and its war effort. Ottoman Jewish soldiers were not only sons of the Ottoman *patria*, brothers with their Muslim and Christian compatriots. Bulgarian Jewish soldiers, ostensibly enemies, were part of the Sephardi family too.[57] A common Sephardi identification transcended war between states, transforming enemies into brothers.

Emigration compounded the challenges posed by military service. In 1909, lists of Jewish youth called to serve were posted in the public squares of

Izmir, but *El Meseret* noted that "the majority of them are in Buenos Aires, New York, Egypt, and other places."[58] Although some Sephardi migrants to the United States may have used the threat of Ottoman military service simply as a ploy to present a shared experience with the much larger number of eastern European Jewish migrants bearing the psychological scars of Czar Nicholas I's conscription policies, the stories of individuals like Sálomon Levy suggest that young Sephardi men did in fact leave precisely for that reason.[59] Even before the Balkan Wars, the Italo-Turkish war of 1911 prompted numerous Jewish youth from Izmir and its environs to flee to Egypt, sometimes accompanied by their whole families, to avoid mobilization.[60] The head of the AIU school in Tire, near Izmir, complained that over one hundred of the most active and vigorous men of the community had left because of the threat of military service. "For every one hundred people," he elaborated, "forty are found under the flag and the sixty others have emigrated. Our forty soldiers depict their service in very somber colors, and all around, one sees only preparations for emigration for the two Americas." Although he had organized conferences trying to persuade young people to stay and complete their military service, presenting the issue from the point of view of honor, duty, and hygiene, that did little to stop the emigration. Young men were leaving en masse because the military service in Turkey was much harder than in other countries, the food "too greasy for the taste of our young people accustomed to the very refined cuisine of Spanish importation," the barracks unhealthy and full of insects, the hospitals suffering from poor hygiene and a complete lack of medicine. Young men were unaccustomed to long marches and succumbed to fatigue and pain in their feet. "Thus, without there being any persecution, Turkey, which has always been for us the most hospitable country, is becoming from one day to the next the terror of our dreams."[61] This continual emigration, combined with the fact that those men who did stay were away serving in the military, meant that the revenue the community received sank progressively lower, diminishing the community's ability to provide services to the increasing number of indigents.[62]

Such levels of migration were not exclusive to the Jewish populations of Anatolia; Anatolia as a whole, in fact, was less directly affected by the Balkan Wars than Thrace. Because of the war, seventeen families from the small Jewish community of Çorlu had departed for Constantinople, while twelve more families and fifty young people had left for South America, leaving a hundred and thirty or a hundred and forty families missing at least one family member and twenty families without any kind of support.[63] At times, individuals left hurriedly and without money to support themselves, appealing to local Jewish communities in transit cities like Marseille for aid. This practice propelled the *Société de Bienfaisance Israélite de Marseille* to declare that the organization would "no longer usefully occupy itself with anyone who voyages to Marseille or in transit," specifically naming Jews from Tunisia, Algeria, and the Levant.[64] Appeals to honor and duty, which the chief rabbinate also employed, may have had less success than *El Tiempo* portrayed, as some young Jewish men fled the draft. For some, as was the case for the many in Çorlu who had survived day to day as peddlers before the war, the destruction of the surrounding villages eliminated their only source of income and may have contributed to their desire to leave. There was a parallel increase in Jewish migration from Salonica in the wake of the Greek government's instatement of mandatory conscription in 1916, a trend that the local Ladino press tried to stem by publishing the names of draft dodgers as a form of public shaming.[65]

As hostilities progressed, the exigencies of war propelled the Ottoman government to take measures to stem the flow of young men, Jewish and otherwise, fleeing the draft. Ottoman and Austro-Hungarian authorities agreed to monitor and restrict the movements of their respective subjects within and between their empires, even as the Entente's naval blockade ended most passenger traffic in the eastern Mediterranean.[66] An AIU instructor assigned to move from Monastir to Buenos Aires could not leave to take up his new post. While Salonica was the obvious port of exit, he informed the AIU that the train between Salonica and Monastir was no longer transporting travelers. All wagons had been requisitioned to transport soldiers and munitions. And while he could have tried to go from Salonica to Edirne, then to Sofia, Vienna, and finally Paris, there no longer existed lines of communications between the Ottoman Empire and Bulgaria. Although letters still traveled from Constantinople through Constanța, Vienna, and on to Paris, men could not: "from Constantinople, like Salonica, and the other ports of Turkey, no Ottoman subject is allowed to board a ship unless he has passed the age of forty-five."[67] These policies were designed to aid the Ottoman war effort by preventing the emigration of Ottoman deserters, who, by 1917, counted over three hundred thousand men, many of whom roamed the countryside in robber bands.⁶⁸

Restrictions on emigration and even internal travel intensified with the beginning of World War I. A 1919 report on the Jewish community of Kırklareli noted that it had shrunk drastically, partially as a result of refugees fleeing to Constantinople and partially due to emigration. The author explained that "our compatriots have a horror of military service, applied to non-Muslims a dozen years ago, not solely for the pains and fatigue that it entails, and to which they are not habituated, but also for the ways in which they are treated, and above all, the necessity to cease all sorts of affairs for a long lapse of time." The coming of the Balkan Wars, he explained, precipitated emigration to America, with young men being summoned by those who had migrated before them. "For the people here, AMERICA has become a second PALESTINE," he went on, noting that Cuba was a particularly popular destination for those from Kırklareli. The outbreak of World War I, however, made it impossible to expatriate. Many people who had already purchased tickets had to remain in the Ottoman Empire.⁶⁹

The Ottoman government began to regulate travel within the empire more stringently, requiring that Ottoman and foreign subjects acquire a certificate of travel (*seyahat varakası*) prior to traveling outside of their province. This could be obtained from the local police chief, or *kaymakam* [prefect] in areas without police, and was to be turned over to the equivalent upon arrival in their destination. Traveling from certain regions, like from Urla to Izmir or from Mandıra in the Kırklareli province to Istanbul, could only be done with a passport, a *seyahat varakası* necessary for any further travel in the empire. Additionally, traveling by train into Istanbul from Thrace was prohibited, presumably because the train was needed for military purposes. Even after all required documentation had been acquired, permission to depart could be revoked for military or political reasons.⁷⁰

While *El Tiempo* frequently lauded the enthusiasm with which Ottoman Jews served their *patria*, at times, Ottoman Jews, like other Ottoman émigrés, were far more willing to serve other states, particularly France and the United States.⁷¹ For many Ottoman Jews, due in great part to the influence of the AIU, France had come to be viewed as the paragon of culture and civilization. In 1914, Nissim Rozanes, an Ottoman Jewish merchant living in France who had founded the *Association cultuelle orientale Israélite de Paris*, made an effort to organize a league for those who wanted to volunteer for the French army. While the Ottoman government denied his request to form such a league, they did respond to press reports of a number of Ottoman Jews living in France who had volunteered, explaining that if such subjects wanted to register for service in the French army, they would have to appear before the Ottoman consular representative in Paris. Serving in a foreign military would mean that these subjects were prohibited from returning to Ottoman lands.[72] Still, as many as two thousand Ottoman Jews served France, a substantial portion of an Ottoman Jewish expatriate community that only numbered between six and seven thousand.[73]

José Estrugo, a self-described "Spanish Jew" living in Los Angeles in 1918, contrasted France's acceptance of Ottoman Jews into the army, even though the Ottoman Empire was France's enemy, with the United States' treatment of Sephardi Jews. Estrugo wrote on behalf of "nearly fifty thousand Sephardim or Spanish Hebrews in the United States, who are unfortunately, like the Armenians, Turkish Subjects, but not Turks, and who unfortunately also, in the midst of the stormy times are being sunk into oblivion and made to suffer for the mistakes and crimes of others." Estrugo asserted that his attempts to naturalize, as well as his applications to serve in the Marines, Navy, and Air Force, were all denied "as I had the misfortune of being born in Turkey."[74] Stories like those of Rozanes and Estrugo indicate that while some Sephardim served in the Ottoman military, others allied themselves with the Entente. Britain and France, meanwhile, created fictitious categories such as "Ottoman [Spanish] Jew" or "a Foreigner of the Israelite Nationality of the Levant" in order to distinguish Ottoman Jews from Ottoman Turks and permit Ottoman Jews to remain in their territory.[75] As Estrugo explained, though born in Turkey, he was not a Turk. His loyalties lay with his new home, the United States, and this was the power that he wanted to serve. The Ottoman Jews who volunteered for the French army, such as Rozanes, were eager to serve their new place of residence and may even have already identified as French prior to emigration due to the realignment of cultural, social, and linguistic preferences resulting from the education offered by the AIU.[76] Although the Ottoman and later Turkish governments would view individuals who emigrated to avoid Ottoman conscription as "draft dodgers" and restrict their return, examples like those of Rozanes, Estrugo, and other Ottoman Sephardim who willingly served in the French or American armed forces suggest that avoiding military service itself was not the impetus behind their emigration. Rather, these men identified with the *tricolore* or the Stars and Stripes, but not with their Ottoman *patria*, and they wanted their service to reflect their personal affiliation. Although some Ottoman subjects abroad remained loyal to the government of their natal lands, this was not universally the case. While they continued to identify with other Sephardi Jews, their bonds of loyalty to the Ottoman Empire diminished with geographical and temporal distance.

"The Grave Crime of Being Foreigners and Having Blue Eyes"

Sálomon Levy was just one of many Ottoman Jewish subjects escaping the chaos of the Balkan Wars and World War I and searching for increased economic opportunity who were drawn to Latin America. While those who initially settled in countries like Cuba found themselves in relatively peaceful and prosperous circumstances, new Sephardi migrants who joined the Assael brothers, Isaac Capon, and other Ottoman Jews in Mexico found themselves substituting one war-torn state for another. For many of the Sephardim in Mexico, the Mexican Revolution provided the opportunity to create economic niches for themselves or to insert themselves into positions left vacant by other foreigners fleeing the violence. For these Sephardi migrants, the upheaval and hostilities of the Mexican Revolution were not necessarily cause to leave. Besides, where could they go?

The Mexican Revolution was ignited when Porfirio Díaz, challenged by Francisco I. Madero's Anti-Reelection Campaign, fled to France. The revolution divided the population into a multitude of factions, each following a revolutionary leader with his own agenda, and many of those leaders trying to address the vast inequality of a society where seventy percent of the population directly depended on agriculture for survival while land ownership was in the hands of only two percent.[77] Madero briefly claimed the presidency while trying to neutralize Emiliano Zapata's peasant-based uprising in Morelos, centered on land rights and agrarian reform and advocating the expropriation of the wealthy *hacendados* who forced large segments of the population into debt peonage. Madero, however, failed to defeat Zapata, and was killed by General Victoriano Huerta in 1913; Huerta then took over the government. Huerta's control was challenged by Venustiano Carranza from Coahuila in the latter's 1913 Plan of Guadalupe, which presented Carranza as the head of the Constitutionalist army. Huerta fled as the United States Marines, under the command of President Woodrow Wilson, occupied Veracruz in 1914, news that was deemed worthy of being reported in the Ladino press in Constantinople and the developments of which the American embassy in Constantinople kept the Sublime Porte abreast.[78] Zapata then allied himself with Pancho Villa, based in the north of Mexico, fighting Carranza's Constitutionalists for power for several years, until Carranza finally gained control of the government and propelled the creation of a new constitution. The constitution of 1917 contained provisions regulating the purchase of land by foreigners, requiring them to relinquish any recourse to foreign governments. It also reinforced Article 33 of the constitution of 1857, which had allowed for the expulsion of foreigners deemed "pernicious" for moral, social, or economic reasons. The 1917 constitution's version of Article 33, however, went one step further, making foreign involvement in Mexican politics a basis for expulsion.[79] 1917 saw the regulation of laws of Mexican citizenship, specifying how Mexican citizenship could be acquired through birth or naturalization and, in the case of the latter, the requisites for successful naturalization.[80] During the years of fighting, hundreds of thousands of Mexicans and others were killed. Newspapers bore headlines describing people burned alive for holding opposing political views or shot on the suspicion of being spies. At least two of those shot by revolutionary forces were Arabic-speaking Jews.[81]

The violence of the revolution compelled many foreigners established in Mexico to leave, their consulates arranging safe travel to regions of Mexico less affected by violence or facilitating their repatriation.[82] Much of the original anti-Porfirian sentiment that propelled the instigators of the revolution was a response to Díaz's economic policies, which were held to favor foreign investors and merchants in Mexico over the interests of the Mexican people. The rallying cry of the anti-Porfirian newspaper *El Hijo de Ahuizote*, "México para los Mexicanos," expressed the desire to wrest control of Mexican land and economy from foreigners. They wanted to form and protect an autochthonous middle class, similar to the CUP attempts to Turkify the economy by supplanting foreign and minority merchants with a Turkish Muslim bourgeoisie. In Mexico, this anti-foreigner sentiment manifested itself particularly against Spanish and American citizens, the anti-Spanish sentiment being clearest among the Zapatistas.[83] Denunciations were levied against and investigations launched into foreigners accused of being "pernicious," with Americans and Spaniards the most frequent targets of attempts at expulsion; Villa decreed the expulsion of all Spaniards from the state of Chihuahua in December 1913, and Spanish-owned shops were sacked when the Conventionalist forces entered Mexico City in November 1914.[84] Chinese residents were targeted as "dangerous competitors for the common people of Mexico," and over two hundred and fifty of them killed in a massacre in Torreón in 1911.[85]

And yet, in spite of the anti-foreigner rhetoric, some Middle Eastern migrants, Jewish and otherwise, were able to exploit gaps in the chain of supply. They drew on transnational networks to buy and distribute goods, sometimes to opposing revolutionary forces.[86] Lacking the desire to return to their places of origin because of the state of war there and, in some cases, lacking the means to return even if they had wanted to, they capitalized on the economic niches left vacant by Europeans who had repatriated.[87] As discussed below, some Sephardi merchants manipulated their citizenship or national identity to aid their travel for trade purposes. The transnational connections that these individuals fostered also provided them with opportunities to circumvent trade prohibitions, helping them to accrue more capital and to establish themselves more firmly in Mexico.

As the calls of "Mexico for the Mexicans" rang out with increasing frequency, the perceived "whiteness" of Middle Eastern migrants in Mexico made them targets of attention. In 1914, *La Opinión* of Veracruz reported a pamphlet being distributed in the Jáuregui market in Xalapa that attacked "comerciantes árabes." This pamphlet alleged "that these Turkish men [señores turcos] have taken possession of the plaza of the market only because they have blue eyes, and although from the *ESTRANJA* [sic], they have much more money to gift and to be wherever they please." The writer for *La Opinión* taunted those who held that the *señores turcos* had committed the "grave crime of being foreigners and of having blue eyes," adding that the distributors of the pamphlet were ignoramuses.[88] According to the pamphlet's authors, Turkish merchants formed an undue presence in the market, displacing Mexican vendors, particularly Mexican woman who sold produce and footstuffs, a sentiment echoed elsewhere in the Mexican press.[89] Their blue eyes were a synecdoche for their whiteness, which when combined with their foreignness, allowed them to accumulate undue wealth. That Middle Eastern and Jewish merchants exploited the poorer elements of Mexican society—those unlikely to have blue eyes—and particularly women became a common trope in anti-immigrant propaganda in the later 1920s and 1930s. Mexico's long colonial history and the legacy of Porfirian economic policies favorable to Europeans and Americans made the individuals protesting Turkish merchants in the market sensitive to the complex legacy of exploitation in which blue-eyed foreigners were implicated.

It was not only Mexicans who perceived a connection between white skin or blue eyes and foreignness. Denise Benbassat, the daughter of Miguel Palacci, born in 1914 in a village north of Mexico City, described how her mother felt very foreign "because her skin color was different, very fair [*muy güerito*]." In what was likely a constructed tale of her experience as an infant during the revolution, Benbassat described an encounter between her mother, Sara Levy, and the revolutionary forces of Pancho Villa:

> My mother was walking with me in her arms, because I was one or two months old and then he [Pancho Villa] saw her and he said to one of his assistants "Tell that women to lend me that doll." He thought I was a doll, because of the colors. And then he went with my mother and said "My General says for you to lend him the doll." "Tell him that it isn't a doll, that it's my daughter." He went and told the General that it was not a doll, but her daughter. "I want to see her." So my mother approached him and handed him the girl, and he saw me and he gave my mother a gold coin to buy me a doll.[90]

It is unlikely that this story occurred the way that Benbassat describes it, although Villa and Zapata did enter Mexico City in November of 1914, remaining for several months, after Carranza had left the city to establish his government in Veracruz. The scene is still striking.[91] It was a situation fraught with danger, as Sara Levy could have had her infant daughter snatched away from her by Pancho Villa, a man not known for his empathy toward foreigners. Instead, when seeing that the blond "doll" was in fact a child, Villa was moved to sympathy. Although a male *turco* might have been associated with exploitation of the poor, particularly women, Sara Levy in her position as a mother, though obviously foreign, garnered sympathetic interest.

In spite of the violence of the revolution, in which Sephardi and other Jews were at times targeted or caught in the crossfire, during this period Jews of different origins decided to formally organize a community. Under the leadership of the Salonican Isaac Capon and the Habsburg Jacobo Granat, Jews living in Mexico formed the *Sociedad de Beneficencia Alianza Monte Sinaí* in 1912. In August of that year, several Jewish men sent a circular to "all the Jews of Mexico" inviting them to a general assembly to be held in the Masonic Temple in the Zócalo in hopes of forming an organization in the interest of "our brothers of Mexico" and to purchase a cemetery.[92] Granat's connections with Francisco I. Madero, briefly Mexico's president, would ease this process.[93] As in Cuba and Argentina, opening a Jewish cemetery was of primary importance to new migrants; unlike in certain cities in Argentina, however, this cemetery interred Jews of all origins.[94] The following year, land was purchased in the municipality of Tacuba for a Jewish cemetery. Permission to use the cemetery—requiring that Capon, who served as the intermediary between *Monte Sinaí* and Mexico City's municipality, communicate with various governmental agencies—was not acquired until 1916.[95] In 1917, the Young Men's Hebrew Association social club was formed, catering to all Jews, though it predominantly served Ashkenazim and the wealthier Sephardi and Syrian Jews. The formation of such groups indicates the existence of a number of migrants who intended to put down roots in Mexico.[96] *La Amerika* reported that all men older than fifteen could become members of the *Sociedad de Beneficencia Alianza Monte Sinaí* and that annual membership fees assessed according to the income of each member were dedicated to "aiding needy members in case of their illness and in other questions of the moral and material development of the members of their community."[97]

The establishment of the Monte Sinaí society entailed interethnic Jewish cooperation and was designed to gather all the Jews of Mexico, "without distinction of Sephardim and Ashkenazi"—the president, Isaac Capon, was Sephardi; the vice president, Theofilo Sacal, was Halebi; the secretary Miguel Vidal Schmill, Ashkenazi from Constantinople. However, when

Capon sought to find a rabbi, ritual slaughterer, and cantor for Monte Sinaí, he advertised in the New York Ladino press and described the organization as a "*hevra sefardita*," a Sephardi society.[98] Although the society did not have any religious leaders yet, Marcos Reinah, newly arrived from New York, organized music for the High Holiday festivities of 1917, which included a celebration in Granat's Salon Rojo cinema attended by five thousand people and songs in English, Hebrew, Arabic, and Ladino. This was remarkable, noted *La Amerika*, "because although they are from different countries, there are not separate groups as there are in New York; all work in union as equal brothers."[99]

Meanwhile, the new cemetery enabled deceased Jews in Mexico to be buried in accordance with Jewish law.[100] This was so important that once the Monte Sinaí cemetery was functioning, several Jews who had died prior to its opening and been buried in other cemeteries were disinterred and their remains reburied in Monte Sinaí, free of cost when the families of the deceased did not have the requisite funds.[101] Although the Jewish community of Mexico soon fractured along linguistic and geographical lines, the establishment of the basic communal infrastructure by financially and socially established migrants demonstrated the permanency of the Jewish presence in Mexico and laid the foundation for the later, larger waves of migration.

"Mercantilism Stronger than Patriotism"

For the Ottoman government, regulating and protecting its subjects abroad became increasingly difficult as the Balkan Wars and World War I progressed and as the governments in which these subjects now lived resisted Ottoman attempts at control. When, in 1911, the Ottoman ambassador in Argentina requested that Argentina prohibit Ottoman subjects from changing or Hispanicizing their names (which allowed migrants to avoid Ottoman conscription and taxes), the Argentine government refused. Firstly, the Argentine respondent noted, there was nothing in the Argentine civil code that regulated the changing of names, and that this could be achieved either in a court or informally, by informing acquaintances that one wanted to be known by another appellation. Secondly, there was no distinction between foreigner and national in this regard.[102] Argentina would not change its policies to accommodate Ottoman requests.

As World War I continued, the Ottoman Empire first contracted with the United States to represent Ottoman subjects in areas without a strong Ottoman diplomatic presence. The Ladino press in New York alerted Ottoman subjects in Mexico that representatives of the United States and Germany were now in charge of Ottoman interests, which was particularly important given that Ottoman subjects were being caught up in the violence of the revolution.[103] Following the United States' declaration of war against Ottoman allies, although not against the Ottoman Empire itself, it was Germany that represented and monitored Ottoman subjects in Mexico, Cuba, and elsewhere. The German ambassador to Washington, DC transmitted a report to the Ottoman government in 1916 alerting it to the disloyal behavior of some subjects of Syrian origin living in Cuba. After Syrians in Havana had allegedly killed three Cuban butchers, prompting an outbreak of anti-Syrian sentiment in the Cuban press, the editor of the local biweekly Arabic newspaper *Al Ettehad* wrote a response in the name of the *colonie syrienne* that it was "under the protection of France." And to make matters worse, in direct contrast to the Ottoman Empire's promotion of a shared Ottoman identity, when asked if the president was doing anything to help the large number of indigent Ottomans in Cuba, he responded that his society "was only occupied with Syrian interests and he refused to have anything to do with Turks." The German minister went on to note that many Ottoman subjects thought the attitude of their compatriots was treasonous. The Ottoman chargé d'affaires in Washington suggested that an investigation be undertaken and considered this behavior treasonous.[104]

The *millet* system's legacy of communal autonomy designated the figure of the *Hahambaşı*, rather than Ottoman consular representatives, as the default authority figure for Ottoman Jews. While in Cuba, the Sephardi mutual aid society *Chevet Ahim*, founded in 1914, was charged with representing the interests of Ottoman Jewish subjects on the island, Sephardim within the Ottoman Empire, throughout Europe, the Americas, and even as far away as the Philippines contacted Haim Nahum in hopes that he could address a variety of woes.[105] For Ottoman Jewish émigrés and family members in the empire, contact through the Ottoman chief rabbi became increasingly critical as the Ottoman Empire censored mail and communications began to break down.[106] While some questions regarded religious practice, like a

1914 query from Buenos Aires about the proper time of year to recite seasonal blessings in the southern hemisphere, many others were about family matters.[107] Some were attempts to notify family members remaining in the Ottoman Empire that a relative abroad had died.[108] Others correspondents were trying to track down spouses who had abandoned their significant others upon migration.[109] The spouses being abandoned, though they were most often women, also included some men.[110] Numerous other letters document divorces between Ottoman Jewish subjects abroad or the return of Ottoman Jewish girls, alone abroad and potential prey for sex traffickers, to the empire.[111] Still others contacted Rabbi Nahum in hopes that he could mediate financial disputes between family members stretched over several continents. Simon Lahana, who would arrive in Mexico in the early 1920s with his wife and four children, requested the *Hahambaşı*'s intervention through the American consulate in Ambos Camarines, Philippines, arguing that he had sent his sister-in-law money on behalf of his wife's brother, Joseph Halfon. His brother-in-law, Lahana explained, could not accede to his wife's request that he return to Constantinople "because, in view of the European war, it would be impossible for him to render himself to Constantinople without risking his life."[112]

The spate of personal communication directed toward Chief Rabbi Nahum suggests that Sephardim abroad still looked to the Ottoman Jewish institutional apparatus to intervene on their behalf. The correspondence, featuring many divorce and abandonment cases, emphasizes that migration challenged the stability of existing familial structures and gender roles, which were also transforming as women were forced to work to sustain their families in the absence of their husbands at the front.[113] That Sephardim abroad turned to rabbinic authorities as intermediaries in transnational financial disputes or to disburse the earnings of deceased emigrants indicates that they trusted the rabbinate to represent their interests, more so than they trusted the Ottoman diplomatic apparatus, which had a diluted reach in many areas of new Ottoman settlement. Sephardi Jews abroad still had personal, commercial, and religious ties to their homeland.

The death of Ottoman Sephardi subjects abroad made clear the limit of the reach of Ottoman jurisdiction, providing an opportunity for the states in which the subjects resided to exert their sovereignty. In 1913, Juan Assael died in Mexico. In 1914 the *Ministerio Público* recognized his wife, French-born Marie Antoinette, as the executor of his will and granted her the right to La Turquesa, the jewelry shop that Juan owned with his brothers. Although Mauricio Assael returned to Mexico from France to contest the ruling, his failure to prevail emphasizes how international migration complicated inheritance issues and how migrants could not assume that the laws of their places of origin would be followed elsewhere.[114]

The Assael brothers challenged the *Ministerio Público*'s granting of executor status to Marie Antoinette based on the invalidity of her marriage to their brother, arguing that the marriage did not conform to laws in the place of Juan's birth—Izmir, Turkey.[115] Although they did not specify any reasons why the marriage was not valid, a clue is found in Ottoman legal precedent. That year, the Ottoman foreign ministry was queried about whether a marriage between a German Protestant woman and an Ottoman Jewish man would be valid. Following Ottoman policy, which dictated that the government allow non-Muslims autonomy in civil issues, the foreign ministry sought the opinions of Protestant and Jewish religious officials. Though the Protestants ruled that the marriage would be valid as long as the children were raised as Protestants, the chief rabbinate asserted that the marriage would not be valid or recognized unless both were Jewish.[116] Marie Antoinette presented the civil registration of the marriage in the Mexican *Registro Civil*, which the Assaels contested on the grounds that it was not sufficiently legalized. The Mexican court, however, disregarded the Assaels' claim. Although civil marriages did not exist in the Ottoman Empire and this interreligious marriage would not have been valid in Ottoman courts, the Assaels' attempt to force the Mexican government to conform to Ottoman legal standards failed.[117] This case was complicated by the fact that the Assael brothers still maintained foreign citizenship, in spite of their earlier attempts to become naturalized Mexicans, and that Marie Antoinette Gaillard de Assael, contrary to international policy, retained French nationality following her marriage.[118] The Mexican government disregarded foreign legal systems and competing sites of allegiance for the parties involved. The claimants may have had different nationalities, but Mexican law reigned on Mexican soil.

The decision of the Mexican government regarding the fate of Juan Assael's estate did not resolve the bad blood between his widow and his brothers.

Emotions between Marie Antoinette Vda. de Assael and Mauricio Assael erupted in violence in April 1915, leaving both injured. The parties agreed that Marie Antoinette had summoned Mauricio to La Turquesa. According to Marie Antoinette, they argued and an altercation ensured. Mauricio, in contrast, asserted that everything had been cordial until they began to talk of the European war (*la Guerra europea*). When he said that he thought England was responsible for the declaration of war, Marie Antoinette attacked him. Mauricio defended his actions, saying that, when faced with an odious attack by Sra. Assael, who called him to her house, insulted him, and injured him, he had only tried to free himself from "that Fury." Had he wanted to hurt her, he argued, she would have had far more injuries. Those she had, she had perpetrated on herself: "Women scratch themselves to harm the men." He should be absolved of all guilt.[119] Meanwhile, two Mexican shop assistants testified that Mauricio had asked Marie Antoinette to return a silver placard with the name "Assael" engraved upon it, which she refused to do, since it was her name as well.

In the end, the court sided against Mauricio. Although his injuries were worse, she had had a reason to fight him, while he had not given a probable explanation, and he had entered her property and provoked her. The granting of executorial rights to Marie Antoinette forced them to have continued business relationships with each other. Mauricio's initial contestation of these rights was based on his contention that her marriage to his brother was invalid, an understanding bolstered by his request that she return a plaque with the family's name on it. Marie Antoinette's claim to belong to the Assael family was repeatedly recognized by the Mexican government, in terms of her right to the estate of her deceased spouse and in the validity of her attack on Mauricio Assael to defend her claim to her husband's name. Though the judge did not believe Assael's account that the fight had broken out after a heated discussion of politics, Assael's explanation indicates the extent to which political developments in the "European war" provoked conflicts between migrants in Mexico or the extent to which migrants used the war as a pretext to manifest preexisting animosity.

Debates about loyalty and the cause of war were not confined to those, like Marie Antoinette and Mauricio Assael, whose places of origin were declared enemies, but also manifested among Ottoman subjects themselves, whether in Mexico, Argentina, or the United States.[120] *Al-Jawater*, a biweekly newspaper published by José Helú in Mexico City, railed against the Syrio-Lebanese in Mexico who allied themselves with France. Many of those men, Helú noted, were "Germanophiles when it suits and Francophiles when commercial circumstances thus require." He accused certain individuals of "mercantilism stronger than patriotism," espousing their immense love of the Entente Powers immediately after the United States declared war on the Central Powers. "I am sure," he concluded, "that upon the termination of the war and when the German bankers can resume their work and the German factories export their articles, then all those rabid Allied-lovers will forget their love of France and go back to proclaiming themselves Ottoman."[121]

But while some Ottomans professed continued support for Ottoman allies, others sought to strengthen ties with France and the Entente. The famed poet Ameen Rihani, for example, traveled to Mérida to open a new chapter of the Syria-Mount Lebanon League of Liberation to promote an alliance between Syria, France, and the United States.[122] In Mexico City and Veracruz, some Ottoman subjects formed pro-French Lebanese nationalist groups like the Union Libanaise and the Syrio-Lebanese movement.[123] Internal dissension within the Syrio-Lebanese community in Mexico over whom to support in the war also led to a stabbing in the *Casino Árabe* social club.[124]

The United States government, which in 1914 agreed to protect Ottoman subjects and their relatives against the looting and violence of the Mexican Revolution, relinquished that responsibility to Germany upon American alliance with the Entente on April 6, 1917.[125] German representatives tried to advocate for the return of money allegedly confiscated from the *Casino Turco* by a major in the Constitutionalist army, only to become frustrated by the large number of Ottoman subjects in Mexico falsely claiming German nationality and cards of protection to travel freely. This, the representatives held, showed the perfidy of those Ottomans who sought to make claims to a nationality that was not legally theirs. The German representatives ended up canceling all but three of the German cards of protection.[126]

American officials continued to monitor Ottoman subjects, prohibiting their passage between Progresso and Havana.[127] In September of 1917, a U.S. immigration official at the border crossing between Laredo, Texas and Nuevo Laredo, Tamaulipas noticed something that disturbed him. Citing an article published the month before in a Spanish-language magazine from New York entitled "The Spanish Jew," this official noted that "there are some fifty thousand of these [Spanish Jews] residing in New York, and that they are beginning to leave the United States for fear of possible service," propelled by the rallying cry that "we want nothing to do with wars." One month earlier, only two or three such individuals had sought to cross into Mexico, but within the previous month, "there [had] been fully one hundred passing through this port." When questioned, they initially claimed to be traveling to visit "some parent or friend in Mexico," but then admitted that they did not want to fight. Expressing some frustrating, the official concluded by noting: "These are peculiar people inasmuch as they are Jewish in blood and religion, are Turkish citizens and speak Spanish. They do their writing with Hebraic characters but write in the Arabic language."[128]

The official's concerns were deemed irrelevant, as higher authorities noted that "as all these persons"—described now as Turkish Jews—"are aliens, they are of course exempt from military service."[129] This confidence belied the actual lack of clear policy exempting Ottoman subjects from American military service.[130] But as American officials turned their attention away from those Turkish Jews who migrated south across the border during the period of hostilities, American consular officials in Mexico and elsewhere closely monitored the activities and movements of any such individuals whose words or personal histories betrayed sympathy for the Central Powers. They, like their Allied partners, sought to stem the granting of visas to and limit the transnational trade of those suspected of harboring anti-Entente views.

In a 1917 investigation into the political identification of the "Turks" residing in Veracruz, the American consul in Veracruz elaborated:

> Generally they consider themselves French protégés when they needed some help from the Consuls of the allied nations, but they never show papers proving their identity and they find all sorts of pretexts to explain the want of identification papers, saying, e.g. that they left their country when they were very young, etc., and adding that they have a great love and admiration for France, their second mother, and they are Christian Syrians or Jews and hate the Turks. When they want to go to the United States to buy goods, they apply to the Allied Consulates for a pass (which is never granted) and profess

pro-Ally feelings. In my opinion, although it is very difficult to prove it, it is very likely that these Turks buy in the United States for the account of the enemy firms in Veracruz and that they favor the latter in having merchandise, with the exception of textiles, sent from the United States to the address of a Syrian or Jewish firm here to deliver it later to the Germans. However, one can say frankly that these people have only one love and that is to make money.[131]

Some Sephardim, including Mauricio Assael, his partner Isaac Benveniste, the company of Israel Roffe in Tampico, and Roberto Mechulam in Saltillo earned spots on the Enemy Trading List for being "Pro-German and intimate with the German Legation," their manifested loyalty to the allies of the Ottoman state negatively impacting their financial concerns.[132] This list, shared among Britain, France, and the United States, specified individuals with loyalty to enemy powers and who should therefore not be permitted to conduct business of any type with entities in the Entente. More extensive investigations were conducted into the Sephardi businessman Jacobo Elnecave and the Mexico City dry goods store "Paris-Bijou," owned by two Sephardi merchants, Corkidhi and Palacci. Elnecave was placed on the Cloak List, which indicated that he did business as a "cloak" for German companies, while the latter was accused of doing business with a firm on the Enemy Trading List.

The ability to capitalize on transnational networks in order to trade with the United States provided some Middle Eastern and Sephardi Jews with merchandise that allowed them to accumulate capital and reinforce their ties to Mexico.[133] Being banned from entering the United States or from trading with France, a hub of Sephardi transatlantic commercial activity, had dire implications for these merchants. A closer examination of the cases of Elnecave, Corkidhi, and Palacci sheds light on how the American government sought to control physical and economic access to its territory and goods and the ways in which Ottoman nationality proved to be costly for certain Sephardi merchants in Mexico. It illustrates the transnational ties of Sephardi Jews and how Sephardim in various countries advocated for the physical and economic well-being of their coreligionists.

Jacobo Elnecave owned a clothing store called "La Moda Americana" in Veracruz, where he had come from Cuba with his brother Victor. In Cuba,

Jacobo sought employment in 1914 as an interpreter, since he knew several languages; but he and his brother had both migrated to Veracruz by 1916.[134] Their third brother, David, who remained in Constantinople, was the director of the Zionist periodical *El Djudio*, a member of the Jewish *Meclis-i Umumi* (General Assembly), and president of the local committee of the Hasköy soup kitchen. David, a noted Zionist, translated Hebrew plays into Ladino for performance in Constantinople.[135] Ten months before Jacobo and his brother Victor were investigated by the United States Consulate in Veracruz and deemed to have a bad moral and financial reputation, and three days before the United States Congress declared war, David met with the American ambassador, Abram Elkus, in Constantinople to thank him on behalf of the fifteen thousand Jewish residents of Hasköy who "would have literally died of starvation" without the assistance of "our American brethren."[136]

Months prior to the release of the American investigative report into the Elnecave brothers in Mexico, Jacobo and Victor traveled to New York, where they listed a cousin as their contact; both had been in the United States in 1916 as well. On each trip, they were accompanied by other Sephardi merchants, and all declared their race as "Hebrew" and their place of origin as Constantinople.[137] On their last trip to New York, one of the brothers spoke to the Oriental Jewish Federation of America, presenting himself as a native of Constantinople and informing this organization that a number of Jews that were Turkish subjects living in Veracruz had been mistreated and persecuted by various political parties in Mexico. General Villa, Elnecave explained, had shot *djidios orientales*[138] under various pretexts, while several weeks earlier, an Ottoman Jew was falsely accused of being a Zapatista and would have been killed if a local notable had not intervened. The Federation attributed the suffering of these *djidios turkinos* in Veracruz to the lack of Ottoman diplomatic representation and contacted the American Jewish Committee and the State Department of the United States to advocate for their coreligionists in Veracruz.[139] The State Department sent a response, published in *La Boz del Pueblo*, that the consulate in Veracruz had been informed and would act, unofficially, in favor of the *djidios otomanos*.[140]

United States intervention on behalf of Ottoman Jews in Veracruz was not entirely altruistic. In addition to the June 1918 report that questioned the loyalty of Ottomans resident in Veracruz to any state, the local consulate released a report on Jacobo Elnecave. The report noted that he was born in Salonica to Turkish parents and that he was in business with his brother Victor, who operated out of Mexico City and had been jailed in Nuevo Laredo on smuggling charges; Jacobo had also been jailed, for fraud.[141] The Elnecave brothers' dissimulating character was not confined to economic transactions. The consular official noted that: "Just before the entrance of the US into the war, Jacobo was overheard making very pro-German statements while on an ocean voyage from New York to Veracruz and until he found it to be to his disadvantage recently, always asserted that he was a Turk and not, as he now claims, a Greek."[142] This report indicates that the United States government did extensive research into the background of merchants potentially holding enemy loyalties. It also suggests that Elnecave sought to circumvent possible questions into his loyalty by asserting that he held Greek, rather than Turkish, nationality. In this case, publicly manifesting Greek nationality did not prevent Elnecave's being placed on the Cloak List. His earlier declarations of Turkishness and pro-German sentiments came back to haunt him.[143]

The other Sephardi target in Mexico of a State Department investigation was the Paris-Bijou dry goods store in Mexico City, owned by the *Izmirli* Miguel/Michel Palacci and Benjamin (Beno) Corkidhi. Palacci, the grandson of the chief rabbi of Izmir, came to Mexico in 1911 or 1912 and claimed to have migrated to avoid military service, having been told that there were many possibilities for business in Mexico. He arrived single; Sara Levy married him by proxy in Izmir before embarking on the transatlantic voyage herself. Palacci and Levy eventually married in Mexico under the same chuppah as another Sephardi couple of *Izmirli* origins, the Alazrakis, because the Sephardi community in the early 1910s was so small that gathering a minyan was difficult.[144] By 1913, Corkidhi and Palacci had entered into business together.[145] In 1914, Palacci and his wife had a daughter, Dionisia Palacci y Levy, her birth certificate witnessed by A. B. Salvo and Isaac Capon, both Sephardim, the first *Izmirli*, the second *Selanikli*. Palacci stipulated that Dionisia maintain Ottoman nationality.[146] Corkidhi, meanwhile, arrived in Mexico in 1912 as a French national and traveled between Paris and Mexico for business.[147] As it had been during the Porfiriato, during the revolution as well having a commercial connection with France was key for acquiring and marketing wares in spite of anti-foreigner sentiment. In addition to the name of the store, the French connection could be seen in a 1917 advertisement for "Paris-Bijou," describing its goods as being of Parisian origin, at "excessively low" prices.[148]

For Corkidhi and Palacci, being placed on the Enemy Trading List and being unable to continue traveling to France and the United States would have negative economic implications. But they had contingency plans in place. The investigation by the American embassy of Mexico into Paris-Bijou revealed that Corkidhi and Palacci had been selling silks, lace, and women's clothing to a firm, "La Gran Sedería," that was on the Enemy Trading List. Corkidhi had traveled to Spain early in the war and, from there, throughout South America "to advise his countrymen to make preparations for having large stocks of goods on hand and to establish connections to ensure future shipments reaching them in case the United States entered the war." Corkidhi traveled under a French passport bearing the notation "Turkish born, but under French protection," and while Corkidhi and Palacci had been refused visas to the United States, they allegedly used unknown agents, capitalizing on their connections, to purchase and ship large quantities of goods from the United States even while under the State Department's gaze.[149] A 1919 investigation into Palacci's approved American visa application revealed that Harry Mazal, who had previously lived in Mexico and whose brother, Ruben, owned a prominent optical store on Francisco I. Madero, was one of Palacci's contacts during the war years. Mazal testified that "[Palacci] had formerly purchased his stock from Paris, but after the war, informant [Mazal] succeeded in getting him to try goods purchased in New York and he has for the last two or three years purchased his entire supply in New York City."[150] Transnational economic and familial connections—in another document, Palacci lists Mazal as his cousin—provided Sephardi merchants in Mexico and elsewhere with the tools to circumvent American and French attempts to stifle their trade, facilitating their accrual of capital in spite of the wars.[151]

Some Sephardi merchants circumvented the impediments that Ottoman nationality posed for international travel by taking on a new national identity, as Jacobo Elnecave had attempted unsuccessfully to do. Nissim Roffe was a prominent merchant who first established himself in Veracruz in 1916. Later, in the early 1920s, he moved to the neighborhood of Santa María de la Ribera in Mexico City and established his business in the Zócalo. Roffe traveled several times from Veracruz to the United States prior to the United States' declaration of war on the Central Powers. In his 1915 and 1916 travels into the United States, Roffe listed his place of birth as "Silivri" and his nationality as "Turkish," of the Hebrew race.[152] However, when traveling in May 1917, he was now a Greek from Salonica, a city of origin he then continued to claim throughout his life and a nationality he maintained until acquiring Mexican citizenship in 1928 (in 1922, he had made an unsuccessful application for Mexican citizenship, in which he listed his religion as "Slavic").[153] Others, like Maurice Asher, who possessed French nationality, avoided observation by the United States by describing his city of origin as "Smyrna, Syria."[154] Since many Syrians abroad expressed their loyalty to France and their desire to be French subjects, having Syrian, rather than Turkish, origins could potentially be advantageous; some Syrians obtained a French safe-conduct that named them as temporary French clients able to travel under French protection.[155] Meanwhile, Asher's friend, Jacques (Jack) Couriel, a merchant who traveled extensively between New York City and Mérida, Yucatán, in 1916 declared his nationality as "French," born in the city of Nancy, while in 1917 he traveled under "Greek nationality" and declared his place of birth to be the city of Salonica on his American Draft Registration card.[156] In his travels to New York from 1923 onward, his place of birth was listed as "Smyrna."[157] Such discrepancies on entry paperwork went unnoted by American officials, attesting to the undeveloped state of migrant tracking at that time.

It was not only wealthy Sephardi migrants who employed such tactics to bypass anti-Ottoman restrictions. David Barsimantov, who had come to Mexico in 1912 to try to make his fortune, was the eldest of six children born to parents who were domestic servants in the household of a *franco* family in Izmir.[158] In September of 1917, when crossing the border from Mexico into Texas, Barsimantov claimed that he had been born in Marseille and bore French nationality.[159] By 1923, however, Barsimantov's documentation attested that he was a Greek national born in Salonica, a status he also maintained on a 1925 business trip.[160] Playing with documentation and the performance of origin and nationality was not the exclusive purview of the elite.

Sálomon Levy, too, acquired a different nationality during this period, compelled by his desire to travel for economic reasons rather than by a sense of patriotism or national identification. Although Levy had lived for several years in Cuba, peddling towels, sheets, and other textile-related goods, in 1917 he decided to try his luck in Mexico. Mexico at the time did not require travel documents for those entering the country, nor did it keep records of entries and exits. Briefly settling in Santa María de la Ribera in Mexico City, where he acquired merchandise on credit from the firm "Capon y Carasso," he then moved to the Yucatán, where he first approached an Ottoman of Arab Christian origins in hopes of attaining credit. Rebuffed, Levy encountered Jacques Couriel, who provided him with silk lingerie that Couriel had brought from New York and who told Levy where the nearest brothel was, where he could sell the goods. When Levy decided to return to Cuba, the agent of the shipping line informed him that because of the war, Bulgarians were not allowed to enter Cuba. Levy bribed a Greek migrant selling popcorn in a central plaza to testify before the Greek ambassador that he had known Levy from Kavala and that Levy was Greek. A telegram from overseas reported that a Sálomon Levy had lived in Kavala. From that point on, Levy was Greek. He returned to the shipping agent the following day, this time as a Greek, and acquired immediate passage to Havana. All his relatives who later joined him in Cuba before following him to Mexico bore documentation attesting to their birth in Kavala and their Greek citizenship.[161]

For such individuals, questions of citizenship, patriotism, and national identity seemed not to play a significant role in shaping their lives. As the United States, England, and France sought to limit who could enter and conduct trade within their borders and beyond, publicizing an Ottoman identity became detrimental to personal financial growth. While during the late 1920s and 1930s, as Mexico tightened its control over who had legal access to its borders, Sephardi migrants adopted non-Turkish nationalities in a ploy to overcome restrictions against Turkish migrants, Mexican entry requirements had little to do with why Sephardi merchants in Mexico acquired other citizenships during the years of World War I. At that time Mexico did not yet require travelers to bear passports as a requisite for entry, nor did it record their comings and goings beyond customs checks that occasionally worked to the detriment of those engaged in smuggling. For these Sephardi migrants, then, the acquisition of new national identities did not necessarily reflect their personal patriotic affiliations but was a tactic to continue to be able to travel and conduct business freely. Many of these migrants altered their nationality as a direct result of the American entrance into the war as an enemy of Ottoman allies and the concomitant increase in monitoring of Ottoman subjects attempting to enter or do business with the United States. Although the Ottoman government attempted to stem the flow of emigrants and to perpetuate its view of a shared identity among Ottoman subjects, it had little direct ability to prevent those abroad from altering their cities of birth to territories no longer under Ottoman control or obtaining new nationalities by other means.

Mauricio Assael: Ottoman Subject, Mexican Patriot?

Although many Sephardi migrants in Mexico willingly acquired new nationalities during the war years to facilitate their ability to travel for trade, none, except for Mauricio Assael, applied for Mexican citizenship. However, like the other changes of nationality, Assael's decision to take on Mexican nationality was one shaped by the need to travel internationally, though in this case that need was provoked by governmental duty rather than individual gain.

Mauricio Assael's reputation in the Mexican business world propelled him into the world of international politics, demonstrating the utility that the Mexican government saw in its Sephardi migrants and the ways that Sephardi Jews accommodated challenges posed by the increasing regulation of movement and identity documents in the midst of World War I. A May 9, 1916 letter sent to the Secretary of State explained that Assael "[was] one of the most respected foreign merchants of this city [Mexico City], completely identified in spirit with our Cause and our Government." It recommended that Assael be named the honorary consul of Mexico to the city of Izmir.[162] On the same day, Mauricio Assael received the official nomination to the post. He would be responsible for representing Mexico's business interests in Izmir and the interests of Mexican citizens in that city. Assael would receive no recompense for his position, but could claim up to twenty-four hundred pesos per year and the expenses of installation and of the office of the consulate. Several days later, the Mexico City press announced Assael's nomination and acceptance of the position.[163] This news was received with great joy by Mexico's Jewish community, and more than a hundred pesos was donated to the *Sociedad de Beneficencia Alianza Monte Sinaí* in his honor.[164]

In order to take up his new post, Assael had to take an oath before the Secretary of Foreign Relations and the Director General of Consulates, in which he promised to loyally and patriotically fulfill the duty that the First Chief of the Constitutional Army, Venustiano Carranza, had conferred upon him, in accordance with the Plan of Guadalupe of March 26, 1913. The wording of this oath reflected the revolutionary chaos that still reigned in Mexico and Carranza's still-unofficialized control of Mexico. Although Assael swore an oath to behave loyally and patriotically toward Mexico, no mention was made of the fact that he was still an Ottoman subject and that he would be representing the interests of his adopted country in the country and city of his birth.[165] The Mexican government did not view Assael's holding Ottoman nationality as contradicting his ability to intervene on behalf of Mexican interests with the Ottoman state.[166]

Although Assael represented Mexico in an official capacity, his Ottoman nationality complicated his realization of his duties. On June 15, 1916, now in Madrid, he sent a letter to the Minister of Mexico in Madrid complaining of "the injustices and barbarities committed by the French authorities." He had arrived in the Spanish city of San Sebastián, twenty kilometers from the French border, on June 2, 1916, and had immediately gone to the French consulate to receive a visa for France, from where he was to travel to Izmir to take possession of his post. He was forced to wait first before meeting with the vice consul, and then to receive authorization from Paris. This delay, Assael complained, indicated that the French government "naturally lacked the courtesy of reciprocity in treating me as a member of the public."[167] As a representative of the Mexican government, regardless of his nationality, he felt he deserved to be treated with respect.

Assael's troubles were not yet over. Having received his visa, he went to the border, where he was asked for all of the gold that he was carrying with him to cover the cost of travel and the establishment of the consulate in Izmir. The gold was exchanged for 6,200 francs, not including a portion that the border agents kept. Assael was also required to register his belongings, and the customs agent confiscated his Colt pistol. His frustration was apparent in the heavily underlined sentence in Spanish accented by Ladino: "Imagine my surprise, Mr. Minister, that after taking the gold from me, they obliged me to return to Spanish territory and refused me entrance into France."

When Juan Sánchez, the Mexican ambassador to Spain, attempted to intercede on Assael's behalf, the French embassy responded that "in regards to a Turkish subject, he cannot be permitted to pass through France, a nation that is at war with Turkey." They reprimanded the Mexican government for having conferred the position of honorary consul on a Turk. Although Sánchez noted that Assael's passing was permitted by consular authorities, "as we are currently in a time of war, there are military authorities who have special instructions, he was notified by them that he could not enter France, and that in consideration, not of his nationality, but of the honorary post with which he was invested, instead of being held, he was permitted to return to Spain."[168]

In spite of Assael's earlier residence in France, the tolerant attitude of French authorities toward Ottoman Jews as "Israélites du Levant" entitled to French protection, and the fact that Ottoman Jews served in the French military, as the war proceeded, the French government became wary about letting any potentially subversive elements into its borders. While France continued to behave with "great humanity" to the majority of "Spanish Jews, who are Turkish subjects," by 1917 there were reports of a number of such individuals that the French government had placed in internment camps. Some of these people had been held for up to two years, "victims of denunciation, inspired by personal malice, unfair competition, base envy or suspicions which ... are unfounded in almost every case."[169] Governmental recourse exhausted, Assael was forced to return to Mexico, unable to take command of his post in Izmir.[170]

Having foreign nationality in Mexico had hitherto not posed a significant problem for Assael, who had established a jewelry business together with another Jew from Izmir, Isaac Benveniste; availed himself of the Mexican legal system in his interactions over the estate of his deceased brother; and been named as a representative of the Mexican government. Upon his return from the debacle at the French border, Assael temporarily relinquished his Ottoman nationality in order to purchase a large house at 73 Córdoba in accordance with the newly instated law, a byproduct of constitutional reforms, that forbade foreigners from owning property without renouncing their right to appeal to their own courts in disputes.[171] This house was located just off the fashionable plaza Río de Janeiro in the neighborhood of Roma Norte, an area that began to be developed in the 1890s and that had a tram connecting it to businesses in the Zócalo. Roma Norte and the neighboring districts of Condesa, Juárez, and

Cuauhtemoc were increasingly attractive options for upwardly mobile migrants and Mexican elites eager to move out of the crowded colonial quarters in the city center into single-family dwellings with fenced-in yards.[172]

Mauricio Assael had not given up on the post of Mexican honorary consul to Izmir, however. The Mexican government renewed his nomination for the position in July of 1917, and on October 2, Assael made another declaration. While his earlier declaration had been made to the First Chief of the Constitutional Army, in accordance with the Plan of Guadalupe, his second declaration reflected the political changes that had occurred in Mexico in the intervening years. He now swore an oath to the Subsecretary of the State of the Exterior, that he would "Guard and cause to be guarded the Political Constitution of the United Mexican States of 31 January 1917 and the Laws that emanate from it, and to fulfill the post loyally and patriotically."[173] Yet again, the fact that Assael was not Mexican was not seen as a deterrent to his ability to patriotically represent the Mexican government in his place of origin.

In February of 1918, inspired by his desire to be able to travel freely to Izmir, Assael again attempted to become naturalized as a Mexican, this time successfully. The naturalization process required him to relinquish other nationalities and several witnesses to attest to his identity and moral character. Assael declared that he had lived in Mexico for more than ten years, that he had a commercial business, and that he lived from the proceeds of that and from rent. He also renounced all submission, obedience, and fidelity to foreign governments, especially the Ottoman, of which he was a subject, and relinquished any protection other than those offered by the laws of Mexico and any rights that international treaties and laws conceded to foreigners.[174]

Assael's petition was witnessed by three witnesses whose nationalities point to Mauricio's extensive commercial ties. The first witness was a 41-year-old native of the northern Mexican state of Nayarít, who testified to having known Assael for "eight or ten years, and because of commercial relations that he has had with various members of the *colonia otomana*."[175] Mauricio's second witness was Beno Corkidhi, also from Izmir. He testified to having known Assael for more than twelve years through his commercial activities and other interests. The final witness was a 43-year-old French national, who also worked on Francisco I. Madero, who testified that he had known Assael for around twelve years as well, along with other members of the *colonia otomana* in Mexico.[176]

Assael's selection of witnesses also hints at several aspects of the life of the early Sephardi community in Mexico. First, one of his witnesses was another Sephardi Jew of shared geographical origins, who testified to having known Assael from roughly when he first arrived in Mexico. His commercial establishment, like Assael's, was on the street formerly known as Plateros, which was the site of many shops specializing in real and costume jewelry and ready-to-wear clothing in the latest styles. Assael's two other witnesses were not Sephardi, suggesting that Sephardi businessmen did not only trade with each other. The fact that one was Mexican and the other French is an indication of the international nature of commerce in Mexico and that business ties transcended nationality. However, the fact that both non-Sephardi witnesses mentioned knowing Assael as a member of a larger *colonia otomana* suggests that this community was prominent enough to be noticed, particularly in commercial interactions, and was perceived as being a coherent collective by those on the outside, in spite of internal fractures along lines of religion, language, and increasing conflicts over national movements.

On March 22, 1918, Mauricio Assael finally received his naturalization. The photograph his naturalization document bears offers a remarkably different portrait of Mauricio Assael. Unlike his earlier portraits, showing him in Ottoman garb or upon arrival in Veracruz, here he does not wear a hat, and his hair is carefully marcelled. He wears a dark suit, a vest, and a tie, with a white handkerchief tucked into his breast pocket. His mustache is carefully trimmed, but present enough to attest to his masculine virility (an Ottoman meaning of facial hair) and European roots (a Mexican meaning). In this portrait, he is neither an Ottoman nor a newly arrived adventurer braving the jungles of Veracruz. His origins are not obvious, but he is clearly portraying himself as a well-groomed man of wealth. While now Mexican by naturalization, there is nothing in his photo to suggest that he is not also Mexican by birth or by race.

Conclusion

In the face of Ottoman demands for active manifestations of patriotism and loyalty in the war effort, Ottoman Jews exhibited conflicting, layered, and transforming affiliations as Ottomans, as Sephardim, as Jews, and as members of humanity at large. Sephardi refugees fled the hostilities, some to larger cities like Constantinople or Izmir, while others looked abroad. Young men, desirous of avoiding conscription and in search of increased economic mobility, sought to leave the empire, whether by licit means or by falsifying documents and manufacturing intentions. These demographic transformations challenged Sephardi communities throughout the empire and its lost territory, as some communities found themselves without large swaths of the productive members of their populations, while other communities faced burgeoning costs to accommodate migrants and refugees.

The territorial losses of the Balkan Wars and the slaughter and expulsion of Armenians and Assyrian subjects made the empire increasingly Muslim and less secure for religious minorities who exhibited allegiances with non-Ottoman or Ottoman-allied powers. However, though Sephardim were each other's enemy combatants for the first time as they served in Ottoman, Bulgarian, and Greek armed forces, they continued to align themselves with coreligionists regardless of national affiliation. This perpetuated Sephardi and broader Jewish identifications that were not defined by Zionism and that at times ran in opposition to Ottoman political alliances. The borders that now divided the Sephardi *Kulturbereich*, and the oceans that separated emigrants from their natal lands, did not lessen manifestations of a shared Sephardiness that challenged Ottoman and other states' desires to determine allegiance.

While Sephardi Jews had started settling in Mexico from the turn of the century onward, drawn by the open Porfirian policies toward immigrants and by the allure of capitalizing on their foreignness to attain economic success, the political and social upheaval that accompanied the Balkan Wars and World War I propelled an increasing number of Sephardim to Mexico. Porfirio Díaz's accepting attitude toward immigration morphed into distrust of foreigners in Mexico following his overthrow, as revolutionary leaders blamed the *científicos* who had helped shape Porfirian policy, many of whom were of foreign descent, for the inequalities that the revolution aimed to address. In spite of the anti-Semitic form that the anti-*científico* sentiment of the revolutionary rhetoric assumed and the increasing use of executive power to expel foreigners deemed "pernicious" under Article 33 of the constitution of 1857, prior to and after the legislated inequality between Mexicans and foreigners in the Mexican constitution of 1917, Sephardi Jews continued to arrive in Mexico.[177]

As other foreigners fled the areas of conflict under the protection of their governments, Sephardim, under the leadership of Isaac Capon, united with other Ashkenazi and Syrian Jews to establish a Jewish community, Monte Sinaí, demonstrating their intentions to remain in Mexico permanently. The attachment of these new Jewish migrants to Mexico was exhibited by the purchase of land for a Jewish cemetery and the disinterment and reburial of Jews who had died and been buried elsewhere. Some Sephardim were able to take advantage of the upheaval of the revolution to create economic niches for themselves, capitalizing on their transnational Sephardi connections to acquire goods internationally even as the United States and its European allies attempted to control the flow of goods to enemy elements. Sephardim abroad relied on the office of the *Hahambaşı*, rather than on Ottoman diplomatic officials, to advocate for their interests. Although the Ottoman Empire sought to control manifestations of patriotism, it proved unable to do so. For some Sephardim in Mexico, particularly after the U.S. entry into the war complicated their acquisition of American goods to sell in Mexico, their sense of loyalty was shaped by a cosmopolitan utilitarianism as they altered their national identity or city of origin to covertly defy travel and trade restrictions on enemy nationals. Economic, familial, and religious ties bound migrants throughout the expanding Sephardi world, in spite of the borders and distances that divided them.

In the face of Ottoman demands for Jewish financial and military contributions to the war effort, the Ottoman Ladino press recognized and defended Jews' multiple affiliations and loyalties. While the 1917 article "Those without *Patria*" argues against the notion that Jews were not loyal citizens, it also defends the very "cosmopolitanism" that had marked Jews as outsiders and disloyal citizens. Citing Victor Hugo in an expression of utopian republicanism, the article asserts that

> humanity is wider than the fronts of the *patria*. . . . The citizen can and should love all the people, all the races, the universe outside the *patria*, and in loving the universe, are they not cosmopolitans? The *patria* is the soil that a natural feeling, birth, causes one to ardently love, and "humanity" is the superior terrain to which the spirit should incline its heart.[178]

While defending Jews from the calumny of being "rootless cosmopolitans" before Stalin had articulated the formulation, the article used French ideals, in spite of the war between France and the Ottoman Empire, to promote Jews as the best citizens. The highest goal of humanity should be the transcendence of borders in universal love. Jews, given their wide geographical distribution, had long ago learned not to be bound by space in their affection. What had been the source of aspersions on the Jewish character became a trait to which all people should aspire. Another article proclaimed that, by loving all humanity, "the Jewish nation is a sincere friend of peace," subtly castigating the existing wars that placed men in conflict with each other.[179] What ostensibly united all humanity was a philosophy common to Jews. *El Tiempo*, while espousing French republican values, transformed them into something inherently Jewish. In doing so, it recognized and defended the overlapping, conflicting, and multivalent loyalties and legacies to which Sephardim ascribed.

{ CHAPTER 3 }

UNCERTAIN FUTURES

GABRIEL YERMIA VALANCI'S PASSPORT told many tales, and hid many more. Unlike today's standardized booklets, this one was a large sheet of paper, folded many times over to fit within a wallet or breast pocket. Its front bore a large print of an eagle in profile, perched on a cactus and devouring a rattlesnake, in front of the looming Popocatepétl and Iztaccíhuatl mountains, reflective of the changes to Mexico's coat of arms that Venustiano Carranza had instituted in 1916. Below this, the *Secretaría de Relaciones Exteriores* (SRE) had noted that the passport was issued to Gabriel Yermia Valanci in July of 1920 for passage to the United States of America, France, and Turkey. A small photograph of a suited and bespectacled Yermia Valanci was affixed to the upper left corner. Lest someone be tempted to switch out the photograph for that of another—not an uncommon practice at the time but not one of the tales that this passport concealed—a series of identifiers was listed: Yermia Valanci was Mexican, 32 years old, single, a *comerciante*, brown-haired, brown-eyed, and beardless.

The reverse side of Yermia Valanci's passport was entirely covered by visas and stamps, so full that a smaller piece of paper had been taped to the side of the passport to allow for more. The stamps and visas attested to the complex trajectory, layers of bureaucracy, and overlapping authorities that Yermia Valanci traversed as he made his way from Mexico City to Constantinople and back over the course of a year: a visa from the consulate general of Greece in New York giving him permission to travel to Greece via France and Italy in August of 1920, a stamp from the Port of New York that he had passed through there later that August, a stamp attesting that he had arrived in Greece followed by an Ottoman-language stamp that he had made it to Constantinople, then a penciled note from Constantinople in October 1920 signed by the consul of Spain. Yermia Valanci then traveled back to France, passing through Marseille in June of 1921, received permission there from the Mexican consulate general to return to Constantinople in July, an entrance stamp from the French delegation of the Interallied Bureau of Passport Controls in the Orient, permission from the consul general of France in Constantinople to travel back to Mexico via France, and a visa from the consulate of Spain in Constantinople to travel to France by sea on August 9, 1921. The next day, he procured permission yet again from the French delegation of the Interallied Bureau of Passport Controls in the Orient, this time to travel to Mexico via France, and a stamp marked his departure from Constantinople on August 13, 1921. In Paris, the Prefecture of Police stamped his passport in December of 1921, the Mexican consulate general gave permission for return travel to Mexico City on December 21, and he departed the European continent from the Atlantic port of St. Nazaire in France.

The reason for Yermia Valanci's extended transatlantic voyage was also hinted at on the back of his passport. In May of 1921, the consul general of Spain in Constantinople made note that Yermia Valanci requested that his status be changed from "single" to "married." He had contracted marriage in Constantinople with a young woman by the name of Fanny Levy on February 2nd of that year.[1] On the surface of it, the folded, torn, taped, water-stained passport of Gabriel Yermia Valanci tells the tale of a young Mexican man who traveled across oceans and borders, stood in line at consulates and immigration checkpoints, and registered with police prefectures, all in pursuit of marriage with a woman who would return to Mexico with him, with whom he would soon have a son, and whose parents would soon join them. After all, what love story is complete without the hero overcoming obstacles to join his love? And the chaos at the end of World War I provided many obstacles.

This chapter explores how people made sense of what the Mexican historian Mauricio Tenorio-Trillo calls "the world adrift," cast into the deceptively calm seas of postwar chaos.² In a Mexico City reeling in the aftermath and reverberations of revolution, as in a Paris struggling to rebuild in the wake of war, a Salonica in the wake of fire, or an Istanbul or Izmir where war had merely shifted fronts and enemies, people held no clear consensus on what the future might hold. Over the course of the previous few years, millions of women, men, and children had died, whether on the battlefronts, in labor battalions, or of the famines and disease that wracked the home fronts. In 1919, representatives of the Great Powers and a plethora of national and religious contenders argued over fallen imperial territories and Woodrow Wilson's vision of national self-determination at the Paris Peace Conference—who might be deemed to have the right to their own sovereign state; who might instead come under the mandate of the Great Powers; where new state borders would be drawn—in the age of "national" self-determination, how nations were to be determined and what would become of people who did not fit neatly within the borders of states or nations; in effect, who would be declared the "winners" and "losers" of hostilities that had cost millions of lives?

Many individuals far removed from the halls of power understood that the world in 1919 was not what it had been a few years before. They perceived that they were living in a period of change, although it was unclear precisely what the future held. As the historian Dominique Reill argues in her work on the contested city of Fiume/Rijeka in the immediate postwar period, many imperial subjects in a newly post-imperializing world did not see nationalizing states as the obvious next progression.³ Postwar chaos upended clear conceptions of what the future was likely to hold and thereby what social, political, and economic order might look like. If longstanding empires had seemingly fallen, could not many options present themselves? And yet people need a sense of future to ground the present. In the immediate aftermath of war, when states, authorities, and global leaders were still in flux, multiple futures seemed open and possible. Individuals therefore had to try to make sense of what they envisioned their personal and communal trajectories to be within the existing state of flux, and to act accordingly. For individuals and communities, documentation proved ever more crucial for forging new futures and paths of belonging and for fitting into or moving between the new states and borders that were hardened in the aftermath of war.

Indeed, Yermia Valanci's passport concealed or gestured to other stories, at once less simple and romantic and more compelling for their complexity and authenticity. Yermia Valanci was not in fact the Mexican youth his passport said he was, though that was not discovered until several years later, after the birth of his son in Mexico. Nor was his father-in-law, Abraham Levy, who joined Gabriel and Fanny in Mexico in 1924, the retiree that he claimed to be on his migration paperwork, but rather the much-loved first rabbi of the growing Sephardi community in Mexico City, who traveled throughout the country to perform weddings and circumcisions and who sat without judgment among the Sephardi ambulant peddlers who, at the end of long days, gathered together at Café Bojor just south of the Zócalo while they drank *raki*, ate *mezes*, and sang familiar songs.[4]

In December of 1923, when Gabriel Yermia Valanci requested a new passport for travel abroad, Mexican authorities noticed that his birth in 1887 had been registered in 1919, attested to by a man who had been convicted of falsification of documents and fraud in 1914.[5] Although there was no direct evidence that Yermia Valanci had obtained his earlier passport based on a fraudulent birth certificate, the auxiliary attorney of the SRE noted:

> I believe that it would be prudent to make known to Sr. Yermia Valancí that the doubts around the legitimacy and veracity of the birth certificate that he provided are resulting in the denial of the passport he requests, and to hope that the interested party then makes the gestures that create opportunity to demonstrate that his civil status is as it appears on the birth certificate.[6]

Gabriel Yermia Valanci did not make the necessary gestures. However, in 1926, he successfully petitioned for Mexican naturalization, noting that he had arrived at the port of Veracruz in October of 1917 as a Turkish national.[7] The suspicions of fraud ignited by Yermia Valanci's 1920 Mexican passport might have resulted in its lack of renewal in 1923, but seem to have had little effect on his successful naturalization in 1926.

The date of Yermia Valanci's initial arrival in Mexico—October 1917—provides a hint as to why he might have needed a Mexican passport for travel to Constantinople in 1920. His naturalization petition did not note his port of embarkation for Veracruz in 1917 nor at what point he, a Turkish national according to the Mexican paperwork, had left the Ottoman Empire.

However, if he was born around 1887, Yermia Valanci would have been the prime age for mobilization into the Ottoman army during the Balkan Wars and World War I. Men of his age would have faced difficulty in leaving the Ottoman Empire legally in the years prior to his arrival in Veracruz. Although Yermia Valanci may have somehow finagled papers that authorized his exit from the Ottoman Empire, when he sought to return to Istanbul for a wife and a rabbi to lead the growing Sephardi community of Mexico, he was returning not to the capital of the Ottoman Empire but to a city under the control of a mélange of foreign occupiers. It was, perhaps, unclear whether his Ottoman-issued papers would be accepted, all the more so if they had not been entirely licit in the first place or if he had exited under false pretenses.

If the Mexican Revolution and World War I marked profound changes in the rule of law, political realities, borders, and even documentary regimes, the immediate postwar period was characterized by authorities, communities, and individuals seeking to make sense of those changes and what they entailed for the present and future. At any given moment, "hypothetical histories shadow actual ones."[8] Possible futures exert a powerful hold over individuals' decision-making processes, no less powerful in that moment for their failure to materialize later. The instability of the immediate postwar period renders particularly sharp the different ways individuals envisioned what they believed to be likely futures in light of present realities, and the choices they made to position themselves and those close to them most advantageously for that future. In doing so, their actions shaped the contours of what their lived future became.

Migrants and those who remained navigated transforming and unfamiliar layers of bureaucracy and authority, as borders and powers changed around them. This required imagining and implementing new social and communal realities in light of divergent futures; of fitting oneself, one's family, and one's community into what seemed the most plausible future at any given point in an era of many possible futures. In this period of chaos and possibility, borders were redrawn and new authorities imposed themselves; critically, too, meanings ascribed to nationality, class, race, and gender were in flux. Countless Sephardi individuals like Gabriel Yermia Valanci and Fanny and Abraham Levy made calculated choices based on their reading of the present in light of what they believed the future likely to hold, where they envisioned that they might belong, and how they shaped themselves to belong and shaped belonging to fit them.

Postwar Settlements

On October 30, 1918, the Ottoman minister of marine affairs, Rauf Bey, and the British admiral Somerset Arthur Gough-Calthorpe met onboard the British naval vessel *Agamemnon* in the Mudros harbor off the Greek island of Lemnos in the eastern Aegean. There, the two men signed the Armistice of Mudros, marking the end of Ottoman involvement in the hostilities of World War I. Several weeks later, Interallied troops composed of French, British, and Italian soldiers entered the Ottoman capital of Constantinople and set up a joint Allied military administration over the city. In a deliberate echo of Sultan Mehmet the Conqueror's entrance into Constantinople on a white horse when he captured the city from the Byzantines in 1453, but now reversing the power roles, the French general Franchet d'Espèrey rode from the quay below the Galata Bridge to the city's French embassy on a white horse given to him by a Greek Orthodox resident of the city.[9] The symbolism was not lost on the city's residents, who saw that the occupiers were upending the power dynamics between Muslim and non-Muslim populations. The Interallied forces saw themselves as the victors and the liberators of the city's Christian population, and they showed a marked preference for the latter in filling the jobs that emerged over the duration of their administration of the city.[10] These forces remained as occupiers of the erstwhile Ottoman capital until October of 1923 and the proclamation of the Republic of Turkey. At this point, the Turkish forces of Mustafa Kemal took over the city's administration, and Constantinople was consciously transformed, from the linchpin of an empire stretching across continents into Istanbul, a cosmopolitan backwater of a nationalizing state with its new capital in the Anatolian heartland. The Allied administration of Constantinople left multiple impressions on Yermia Valanci's passport—two visa stamps, signed and affixed with postage stamps, from the French delegation of the Interallied Bureau of Passport Controls in the Orient marked the Interallied authorities' permission for his sojourns in the city.

The Greek Orthodox and Armenian residents of Constantinople enthusiastically welcomed the Allied forces. Thousands of Ottomans crowded along terraces, high walls, and the Galata Bridge to watch the arrival of the British warships whose entrance marked the end of the Allied naval blockade of the city. Greek Orthodox Ottomans, in particular, cheered the arrival of the Greek warship *Averof*, whose sailors called to those assembled on land: "Awaken, poor subject, awaken and see liberty."[11] A Muslim student at the prestigious Galatasaray Lycée described with pain the British, French, Italian, and Greek flags that seemed to dangle from every window for the first days after the armistice. A neighboring Greek Orthodox tailor had even hung a blue-and-white bathrobe from his window in an approximation of the Greek colors and only removed it after three Ottoman mounted soldiers galloped down the thoroughfare tearing down foreign flags in a final gesture of Ottoman sovereignty.[12] Other residents of the city perceived a sense of doom permeating the air.[13]

With the signing of the Treaty of Mudros in 1918, the Ottoman Empire signaled its defeat. Over the course of the next five years, until the Lausanne Accords of 1923 marked the permanent end of the Ottoman Empire and the foundation of the new Republic of Turkey, the future of the Ottoman capital—and of all formerly Ottoman territory—remained uncertain. On an international political level, representatives of various groups argued for the partitioning of Ottoman territory at the Paris Peace Conference. The Treaty of Sèvres, ratified in August of 1920, divided Ottoman territory among the Entente powers and those deemed to have suffered under Ottoman domination.

The Treaty of Sèvres seemed to provide an internationally recognized template for the borders and the political control of the remnants of Ottoman Anatolia and Thrace. Armenia was recognized as an established state, and the treaty required that Ottoman authorities hand over to an Interallied tribunal those "responsible for the massacres committed during the continuance of the state on territory which formed the Ottoman Empire on August 1, 1914."[14] Izmir and its environs were placed under Greek administration, as was much of eastern Thrace; a referendum to take place five years hence would decide the ultimate status of the regions. Large parts of southern and western Anatolia were decreed to be under an Italian zone of influence, and some Italian colonial officials hoped to establish an Italian colony in the province of Antalya. Large portions of eastern Anatolia fell under French influence, with the provision that there should be a later referendum to decide the fate of a future Kurdistan. The Dardanelles, the Sea of Marmara, and the Bosphorus were to be internationalized, while certain ports, including Istanbul and Izmir, were to be free zones. Only a relatively small portion of the Anatolian plateau, centered around the city of Ankara, had been granted to a future Turkish state. However, even as the terms of the treaty were being hashed out, Mustafa Kemal set up a Turkish Grand National Assembly in Ankara in April of 1920, marking a definitive break with the Ottoman monarchy. In Constantinople, large public protests against the Allies decried government by the cross over the crescent and asserted that Greece's annexation of Izmir and its surroundings violated Wilson's principles.[15]

On January 11, 1920, Dr. Edgar J. Fisher, a professor of history at Constantinople's Robert College—an institution founded by American Protestant missionaries that educated the children of elite Christian families from throughout the empire and beyond—published an op-ed piece in the *New York Times*, "From Bad to Worse in Constantinople." In the immediate wake of the occupation, "in the minds of all, Christian, Jew, or Moslem, there was the universal conviction that, come what may, the future could bring nothing in its train more heartrending or more terrible than the years of the war." No one could have anticipated, though, that a year into the occupation, "the situation would be more difficult, more uncertain, and more unsettled."[16] Uncertainty engulfed Ottoman lands in and beyond the capital. Although the Balkan Wars and World War I had destroyed Jewish homes and businesses along the fronts and propelled Jewish refugees to Istanbul and Izmir, for Jewish residents in Izmir and its environs, the worst destruction came after World War I had finished. Greek forces, propelled by the irredentist *Megali Idea* (Big Idea) of expanding Greek borders to encompass the lands of the Byzantine Empire, clashed with tattered Turkish forces led by Mustafa Kemal. This propelled additional waves of Sephardi refugees to seek refuge in Izmir from cities in the Anatolian interior and along the Aegean coast. The Turkish forces ultimately succeeded in rebuffing the Greek army—the city of Izmir was burnt in the process—propelling the abrogation of the Treaty of Sèvres and the formation of the Turkish Republic under the leadership of Mustafa Kemal in 1923. This historical summary, though, glosses over the profound uncertainty that reigned supreme between the armistice of 1918 and the establishment of the Turkish Republic in 1923, uncertainty that was experienced and understood quite differently by Jewish residents throughout Ottoman lands and beyond.

The chaos at the international level mirrored chaos in the Ottoman capital and elsewhere as Interallied forces and those, like Greece, who benefited from the Treaty of Sèvres sought to realign economic and political norms within the areas they now governed. The strict press censorship of World War I, briefly relaxed after the armistice, had been reinstated with vigor by February of 1919; *El Tiempo*, the most widely read Ladino periodical of the capital, regularly bore blank spaces as a testament to articles that had been censored out.[17] Alexandre Ben Ghiat, author and editor of the Ladino periodical *El Meseret* in Izmir, meanwhile, complained that the high cost of paper itself made printing prohibitive.[18] The Allied blockade of the Dardanelles during the war years remained in effect for more than a year afterwards, preventing the delivery of commercial goods and foodstuffs into Constantinople, a situation that only augmented the war profiteering and inflation.[19] From December 1918 to March 1919, Constantinople's extensive tramway system was shut down; the firm that owned the plant powering the trams was a Belgian company with German roots.[20] Policing fell under the auspices of underfinanced Ottoman forces and a hodgepodge assortment of Interallied police, one-third of whom were English, one-third French, and one-third Italian. Interallied forces were only to interfere with Ottoman police in matters that concerned foreigners and speeding, and the seizure of illegal firearms.[21] The latter issue was of particular concern as frequent firefights broke out in Galata, Pera, and Stamboul, often along "national" lines.[22]

Meanwhile, the Great Powers lobbied for the reinstatement of the Capitulations, which the Ottoman state had abrogated in 1914, a measure that Ottoman authorities vehemently opposed. A key element of the Capitulatory regime was extraterritorial legal privileges. In the absence of the Capitulations, the legal regimes in occupied Constantinople were even messier than the policing systems. Ottoman legal codes dictated that matters of personal status should be adjudicated in accordance with the relevant *millet*'s religious laws, while all Ottoman subjects faced criminal charges within the Ottoman state court. At the same time, the Interallied police court had no jurisdiction over Ottoman subjects. In practice, this created loopholes that Ottoman subjects could exploit. U.S. military personnel were present in occupied Constantinople not as part of the occupying forces but to distribute aid in the form of foodstuffs and other goods to indigent residents of the city. When, in February 1921, several American soldiers were caught smuggling 70 sacks of sugar off a ship for resale by an Ottoman Jew named Joseph Meshullam, the American consular court brought a case against the soldiers. Meshullam, however, though he was involved in war profiteering, could not be tried. His illicit involvement with non-Ottoman subjects placed him outside the auspices of both the Ottoman and the American judiciary systems.[23]

Declarations of peace did bring immediate—if fleeting—changes throughout Ottoman lands. On October 6, 1918, Alexandre Ben Ghiat wrote in his diary in bold: "Peace! Peace! Peace!" All Izmir, he noted, was in celebration, and the high prices of sugar, petroleum, coffee, and soap declined almost immediately, although the price of bread did not decrease.[24] Within the next few weeks, Rahmi Bey, the governor of Izmir who was widely disliked by the city's Jewish denizens for having forcibly requisitioned the old Jewish cemetery in Karataş and used its stones to build schools and cinemas in Izmir and Ödemiş, was removed from his post and sent to Istanbul to face interrogation for his activities during the war. Izmir's police chief was imprisoned for having ordered prisoners caned. And day after day, attestations emerged of robbery, harassment, and killings of Armenian and Greek Orthodox subjects ordered by Enver, the Ottoman minister of war, and Talaat, the Ottoman minister of interior affairs and later grand vizier, and carried out by Ottoman governors and functionaries; Armenians and Greek authorities demanded the punishment of those responsible for the deaths of hundreds of thousands of Armenians and tens of thousands of Greek Orthodox Christians. Meanwhile, an order of the sultan dissolved the chamber of deputies, removing protections against arrest that deputies benefited from, and an arrest warrant was issued for all the Unionist ex-deputies who had been directly or indirectly implicated in "the dark deeds that were done in Turkey over the last four years."[25]

On October 29, an order was issued that hospitals, factories, shops, and homes that had been occupied by Ottoman and German soldiers be returned to their owners, and some Greeks who had been expelled from nearby villages and cities of the interior were permitted to return to their homes in and around Izmir.[26] With the signing of the armistice, German and Austro-Hungarian forces left Izmir in the middle of the night. According to Ben Ghiat, they feared that Izmir's angry population would stone them, but the cover of darkness did not protect them from catcalls and jeers.[27] When an English warship arrived in Izmir's port on November 6, "it was a joy for the non-Muslim population of Izmir, and particularly for the Armenians and the Greeks," who viewed the British flag as a bearer of hope and salvation. Greek households flew the Greek flag from balconies, but the Turkish police tore them down. The port was opened again for commercial ships, linking Izmir with Constantinople and the wider Mediterranean. In his final entry, dated March of 1919, Alexandre Ben Ghiat detailed that the prices of basic foodstuffs, merchandise, and manufactured goods continued to fall as ships came into Izmir's port, and he expressed hope that they would decrease still further. This would not come to pass.

In the first year of the Interallied occupation of Constantinople, Jewish individuals and communities viewed their future optimistically and sought to position themselves and their communities to align with what they believed the future to hold. Several satirical *haggadot* published in the immediate postwar period illuminate the divergent ways their authors envisioned the place of Ottoman Jews within this world while simultaneously emphasizing the profoundly transformative and unforgettable experience of the war for Ottoman Jewry.[28] Elia Karmona, the author of a wide array of Ladino novellas of varying quality and the editor of the long-running humoristic weekly *El Djugeton* (1908–1931), published the *Haggadah dela Gerra Djeneral* in 1920, and the otherwise unknown author Nissim Shem-Tov 'Eli published his *Haggadah dela Gerra por Dia de Pesah* in 1919, both in Constantinople. Alexandre Ben Ghiat, meanwhile, published *La Haggadah de Ben Ghiat* in Izmir, likely in 1919.[29] While they are similar in many ways—all three texts highlight the hardship of war, whether for men drafted into labor battalions or for those combating famine and disease on the home front—key differences among the three texts are illustrative of the diversity of opinions on possible futures for the Ottoman Jewish community.

The authors' divergent views on what the postwar future held becomes apparent in their treatment of the war and their views on who, beyond God, was ultimately responsible for salvation from the hardship of war. All excoriated Enver Pasha and Germany—Ben Ghiat's words for Enver were particularly harsh, calling him "el mamzer" (the bastard) and praying "may God kill him and dismember him."[30] Ben Ghiat likewise called for the punishment of Talaat Pasha and Rahmi Bey, the latter being the parallel to Pharaoh in his text.[31] The authors also all adopted some of the optimistic vision for the future that Erez Manela has characterized as "the Wilsonian Moment."[32] While Karmona explicitly mentioned U.S. president Wilson's words in favor of world peace, the other texts spoke positively of Wilsonian plans for national self-determination. For Ben Ghiat, English aid was crucial for a future time in which "we will be in Jerusalem seated in our house," and the Entente more broadly responsible for "removing us" from the oppression of Rahmi in Izmir. However, he specifies that it was "the people Israel from Poland" that were being taken out and would be given Palestine, not Ottoman Jews.[33] In 'Eli's text, the Allied forces served as the traditional Haggadic parallel to God leading the Israelites out of Egypt. For him, the four children of the *Haggadah* were the Jew, the Greek, the Armenian, and others "who suffer from the power of Turkey," who are rescued by Allied forces under the guise of divine will, who make for them homelands over which they will have dominion.[34] In 'Eli's text, the rewriting of the Passover song *Dayenu* ends with a reference to the establishment of a Jewish governing body in Palestine—"if the [victor] had made us patrons of *Eretz Israel* and not permitted us to form a chamber, it would have been enough for us."[35] His active advocating for the national self-determination of all Ottoman religious minorities, and of Jews in particular, casts a different light on narratives that paint Ottoman Jews as simply waiting to see what the outcome of the war would be.

But whereas in Ben Ghiat and 'Eli's texts, the Ottoman Empire was clearly defunct and the future for Ottoman Jews lay in Palestine as a result of the benevolent intervention of the Entente, Karmona's text offered a future in which the Ottoman Empire persisted. Though he cast Ottoman actions in World War I as the result of the Ottoman Triumvirate's desire to "destroy the people," his *Haggadah* ended with calling for praise of Sultan Mehmed VI Vahidettin, "who desired peace and brought it" together with the Allies. With no distinction between the various religious and ethnic components of Ottoman society, Karmona left open the possibility of an Ottoman future in which there would be "equality among the people."³⁶ The future he envisioned in his recounting of the war was one in which the Ottoman Empire persisted and in which Ottoman Jews, like all other Ottomans, had a place.

Within the Jewish communities of Constantinople and elsewhere, groups clashed over alignment with Zionism as a possible vision of a Jewish future. Ottoman Jewish leaders had spent years deliberately crafting an image of their community as the "model minority" within the Ottoman Empire, a minority that lacked the irredentist nationalist claims of Greek Orthodox and Armenian subjects. Even Ottoman Zionists, who became increasingly visible after 1909, presented a Zionism that would strengthen the empire as a whole, although anti-Zionists disbelieved this rhetoric.³⁷ After Allied forces occupied Constantinople, the New-York-based Ladino press recounted that a large number of Jews openly declared themselves in favor of Zionism and formed "a powerful national Jewish organization under the name *Agudat Bnai Israel* with the former deputy Nissim Russo and the director of the Or-Ahayim hospital Isaac Taranto at its head."³⁸ This organization aimed to take part "in the establishment of a Judeo-Ottoman national state in Palestine" and, among other goals and activities, organized English classes in Jewish schools and pleasure trips to Palestine, as well as helping to fund those who wanted to move there.³⁹ Nissim Benezra, a youth at the time, attested to the open support that Jews expressed of their own national projects. After the occupation of Constantinople, young Zionists came to "behave a bit like Constantinople was a conquered country," marching on parade through the city in full public view.⁴⁰ Chief Rabbi Nahum and his supporters clashed with the Zionists, insisting that "the Jews are nothing more than a religious sect and should not join in the Zionist idea."⁴¹

These tensions persisted but were increasingly refracted through a prism of continued attachment to the Ottoman sultan versus the Turkish nationalist movement of Mustafa Kemal; in an October 1922 Kemalist demonstration that passed through Balat, still a heavily Jewish area of Constantinople, one group of Jewish participants marched behind a portrait of Mustafa Kemal with a picture representing the Ottoman and Zionist flags. A group of counterprotesters, in contrast, shouted: "Long live Haim Nahum Efendi! Long live the Jewish nation," as they marched in favor of the sultan, with no overt Zionist symbol to be found.⁴² For the first group of protesters, it was possible simultaneously to support Mustafa Kemal and the Turkish nationalism he represented, the Ottoman Empire, and the Zionist project. After the establishment of the Turkish Republic the following year, however, the coexistence of such ideas became more and more untenable and public affirmation of support for Zionism increasingly disappeared.

In the absence of any clear political rule or reliable news sources, rumors became a powerful means of guessing at what the future might hold for Ottomans. Such rumors swirled around the Sephardi world, with Ladino papers in New York positing about the reports they had heard, unconstrained by the censorship that faced Ottoman periodicals. Sources like Ben Ghiat's wartime diary hint at how these rumors were experienced in daily life, when information was largely absent from newspaper reports. Several weeks before the Treaty of Mudros, the New-York-based *La Amerika* noted that Bulgaria's withdrawal from the war "made all of Turkey [sic] tremble." The Ottoman Empire should make peace with the Allies sooner rather than later, lest their delay result in being "entirely occupied and dismembered by the Allies."[43] In December of 1918, Ben Ghiat noted the rumors circulating in Izmir about the fate of Constantinople. It was, Ben Ghiat recounted, going to be the capital of a protectorate that would stretch from the Dardanelles to the outskirts of the city. This protectorate would be governed by the French, English, and Italians. Turks would not form part of the governing administration, and even the Turkish language would lose its status as an official language after nine years.[44] The loss of political power and the reduced status of Turkish was be a marked change from Ottoman rule for all the city's residents. In his last diary entry, from March 1919, however, Ben Ghiat recorded a different fate for formerly Ottoman lands from that of a scant four months before: the Great Powers would maintain control over Constantinople, Izmir and its environs would not be ceded to Greece but would remain under the control of the Entente, and a future Turkish state would be established with its capital in the Anatolian city of Konya.[45] Simultaneously, others were petitioning the United States to create an American mandate over Smyrna and Sivas.[46] Such rumors, and others that likely circulated unrecorded, might have provided listeners with some semblance of reassurance around which they could plan their lives, even as the frequency with which prognostications changed undermined any strong sense of security.

Ben Ghiat, who published his diary in March 1919, with its final entry predicting that Izmir would remain under Entente control, could not have known that two months later, Greek forces would disembark in Izmir and take control of the city in the name of addressing conflicts between Greeks and Turks, shortly to push into the Anatolian interior. Jewish sources soon began to attest to hostilities that local Greek populations perpetrated against them, noting that "in Aydın, in Manisa, and in Tire above all, we Israelites live in an atmosphere of suspicion on the part of the Greek residents."[47] From Izmir to Akhisar, Jewish administrators reported to AIU headquarters in Paris that the Greek administration's attitudes toward Jews changed markedly in the immediate aftermath of the Treaty of Sèvres. The treaty's terms that the ultimate fate of Izmir and its environs would be decided by a popular referendum transformed Jews into a useful voting block and highlighted their status as potential future subjects of the Greek state.[48] Relations between Jewish and Greek Orthodox residents of these towns briefly improved as well.

These attitudes soon cooled. In Tire, two young Jewish children were beaten by the local police for refusing to remove the fez, which was seen as a provocation, evoking Ottoman loyalty. When one of their mothers and a young Jewish man attempted to intervene, they too were beaten and the young man thrown in jail and beaten further.[49] In Salihli, a five-hour train ride from Izmir in an area that the Treaty of Sèvres had granted to Greece, Greek soldiers knocked over tombstones in the Jewish cemetery and transformed the Jewish school that was under construction into a stable for their cavalry. In Aydın, poor Jewish widows were prevented from working; in their place, olive harvesting jobs were given entirely to Greek women.[50] Albert Nabon, the principal of the AIU boys' school in Izmir, recorded a conversation with a visiting French admiral who asked his opinion about Greek dominion over the region. "I begged him to excuse me if I declared frankly that I was not at all reassured when it came to the future," he reported, "because I think of the situation of my coreligionists of Salonica upon the arrival of the Greeks in their city." This view was, he said, shared by the majority of Izmir's Jews.[51]

Izmir's Jews hoped that the Greek administration's conciliatory attitude toward Jews would enable the Jewish community to reacquire the cemetery in Karataş that Rahmi Bey had appropriated. However, this was not to be, and Jewish refugees from Aydın and elsewhere whom the Jewish community sought to house on the cemetery site were forcibly expelled by the Hellenic High Commissaire. These actions against the Jewish cemetery and Jewish refugees propelled Nabon to comment that "we see here a direct attack against these famous 'minority rights' which are so often spoken and of which we do not yet see any tangible evidence."[52] By 1920, the promise of minority rights was already, in the eyes of Nabon, so many empty words.

Hostilities between Turkish and Greek forces mounted, and Jews increasingly found themselves targets of violence and looting, whether from Greek Orthodox villagers or the Turkish bands of Ottoman deserters who still ravaged the countryside. In Aydın, a city with a Jewish population of roughly two thousand, eleven Jews died in the fighting between Greek and Turkish forces, many Jewish shops were looted by bands of Turkish irregular soldiers, and the fire that ravaged the city forced Jewish residents to take shelter in the Alliance schools, which still stood and were under French protection. Reports to the AIU headquarters in Paris noted that "Israelites are accused by the Turks of favoring the Hellenes and by the latter of favoring the Turkish revolt or Italian intrigues."[53] In spite of the intercession of Jewish leaders in Izmir with Hellenic authorities, they were unable to acquire the necessary permission for Aydın's Jews to take refuge in Izmir; fighting had destroyed telegraph lines and made rail travel dangerous.[54] Many Jews from Bergama, Manisa, and Akhisar, however, succeeded in fleeing to Izmir, where the Hellenic functionaries expressed a desire for cordial relations with the Jewish population. Those from Aydın arrived later, as did others from Nazilli, expelled from the town by Hellenic forces.[55]

Regional violence and the pouring of Jewish refugees into Izmir placed a heavy burden on the local Jewish community, not unlike the burden facing the Jewish community of Constantinople, with Ottoman Jewish refugees from Thrace and Jewish subjects of the former Russian Empire. While refugees could be housed temporarily in synagogues and schools, this meant that those spaces could not be used for their intended functions. Many new arrivals arrived with few resources and needed to be fed, clothed, and employed. By 1920, one frustrated AIU teacher noted that if the cost of living in Constantinople had increased to 1,125% of its prewar level, it had surged to between 1,500 and 2,000% in Izmir. "Living has become twenty times more expensive in 1920 than in 1914," he noted bitterly.[56] Ben Ghiat's assurances of a year earlier that the end of the Great War and the reopening of Izmir's port would result in lowered costs for basic goods no longer held true.

Philanthropy and Intra-Communal Tensions

The years of the war, and particularly the period of the postwar armistice, saw the arrival of a new philanthropic force in the Ottoman Jewish world to which Jewish communities and individuals turned for succor in Ottoman lands and in assistance in relocating elsewhere—the American-centered Joint Distribution Committee (JDC).[57] World War I threw Ottoman Jewish benevolent societies, whose resources were overstretched by large numbers of indigent women and children and burgeoning numbers of refugees, into a prolonged hiatus.[58] The central presence of the JDC's philanthropic efforts during and particularly after the war indicated a new prominence for American aid organizations on a global scale and paralleled large-scale American and League of Nations humanitarian endeavors in formerly Ottoman lands; the latter, manifesting in the actions of the Near East Relief Fund, particularly sought to provide humanitarian aid to thousands of women and children who had survived the Armenian genocide.[59] Once the Ottoman Empire and France were declared enemies, the power of the AIU waned in Ottoman lands, while the Interallied occupation of Constantinople led to the downgrading of the status of the German *Hilfsverein der deutschen Juden*. American Jewish relief organizations cast themselves to the forefront of Jewish humanitarianism in Constantinople and beyond. Tens of thousands of Ottoman Jews and thousands of Jewish refugees from pogroms in Russia were in dire need of assistance.

The distribution of American aid, however, at times exacerbated intra-Jewish tensions. In 1921, Jacques Rieur, a representative of the JDC, penned a report on the Near East and Balkan States. While his report was couched in terms of typical disdain for Jewish residents of the Orient, Rieur highlighted the diversity of Constantinople's Jewish population that numbered, he estimated, ninety thousand out of a total population of one million. Constantinople's Jews, he explained, were divided into four subgroups, which were further divided along class and subethnic lines within various distinct neighborhoods. The Sephardi community was the largest, numbering eighty thousand. The Ashkenazi community, into which he collapsed those from Austria and Poland, numbered five thousand people. The third group was the Italian Jewish colony, and the fourth group were Greek Jews, though he was unclear whether these individuals were of Sephardi origin bearing Greek papers, or Romaniote, whose residence predated the arrival of Sephardi refugees in 1492. Finally, there was a fifth and "unconsiderable" group of Jews from Persia, Georgia, Afghanistan, and other parts of the "Russian and Turkish Caucasus." Twenty-eight hundred of the Jewish population of the city consisted of orphaned children, and over two thousand were widows; since wealthy Ottomans—Jews and otherwise—often exploited loopholes to avoid conscription, most orphans were from the most indigent families.[60] Not included in this estimate of ninety thousand Jews were more than twenty-five hundred Russian Jewish refugees from Ukraine and Romanian-occupied Bessarabia.[61] These refugees, having fled villages and small towns to head to Black Sea ports, had left anti-Semitic violence only to find themselves in the most expensive city in Europe.[62] It was the presence of these Jewish refugees that had thrown Constantinople's various other Jewish communities into an uproar.

Although JDC officials claimed that neither the "Espanols" nor the Jews of German or Austrian origin "feel themselves very close to the Russian Jews," the Jews of Constantinople were not oblivious to the suffering of these Jewish refugees.[63] The new chief rabbi, Haim Bejarano, met with a number of orphaned children, drawing a parallel between the experiences of these Jews now forced to flee their homes and the experiences of Sephardi Jews four hundred years before.[64] The chief rabbi's secretary wrote to the AIU in France explaining that all the Jewish stores and establishments throughout the city were closed on November 13, 1919 in protest of the plight of these refugees. It was difficult for the Jewish community of Istanbul to aid them, though, for two reasons. First, "the political situation with the Entente in power makes it difficult for the Russian refugees to enter," and second, the housing crisis in Constantinople meant that refugees were often housed in bad areas.[65] Constantinople's Jews, grappling with an unfamiliar structure of authority in the occupied city, had difficulty in aiding coreligionists in the manner they would have preferred.

Ladino-speaking Jews were not inured to the suffering of Russian Jewish refugees, despite the claims of JDC officials. The Ladino press of Constantinople published emotional articles about Jewish children dying of hunger as a result of pogroms and civil war in Russia and Ukraine and organized subscriptions to aid "our brothers of Russia."[66] The Ladino press in New York regularly published on the plight of Russian Jewish refugees in Constantinople, noting in 1920 that thirty thousand refugees were reliant on American aid to alleviate their misery.[67] The following year, after clashes between Greek and Turkish nationalist forces sent thousands of Jewish, Turkish, Greek, and Armenian residents of Izmir, Bursa, and other cities to Constantinople, *La Amerika* proclaimed it "the sacred obligation of our Sephardim" to help alleviate their suffering, whether by donating money or old clothing.[68]

Russian Jewish refugees organized into a Federation of Russian Jews, specifically for "Russian Ashkenazim," a new communal group with its own synagogue that added to Constantinople's already diverse Jewish landscape. Many refugees were housed, at least temporarily, in the city's Jewish schools, synagogues, and orphanages. This displaced a number of orphaned children into private families.[69] A small number lived in the Messilah Chadashah Jewish agricultural colony founded by the Jewish Colonization Association, eighteen kilometers from Constantinople.[70] The close quarters in which refugees lived led to the proliferation of diseases in their residences. An outbreak of cholera in December 1919 resulted in a call for mass vaccinations to avoid an epidemic.[71] The following year, another outbreak was particularly acute in the camps holding Jewish refugees from the Crimea, resulting in widespread death within the camps and quarantine to ward off the disease spreading throughout the city.[72]

By 1922, there were a reported eighty thousand Jews relying on foreign aid, including two thousand recent arrivals fleeing pogroms in Russia and a number of war orphans.[73] The Rockefeller Foundation and other aid organizations called on the League of Nations to match their donations in aid of some hundred and fifty thousand refugees in Constantinople—Armenians, Greeks, Turks, Russians, and other nationalities—who were living in miserable conditions.[74] Within this morass of survivors of displacement and violence often living in close contact with those who had perpetrated violence against them, non-Jewish aid organizations were unlikely to devote specific attention to Jewish refugees. Jewish communities and individuals, whether local to Constantinople, Izmir, or elsewhere in Ottoman lands, or international organizations like B'nai B'rith or the JDC, were tasked with picking up the slack.

It was not only in Constantinople that local Jewish leaders sought aid and political intervention from the JDC. The president of Izmir's Jewish community requested that the JDC intervene with local authorities in the ongoing dispute over the status of the Jewish cemetery in Karataş. He asked for assistance for the large number of Jewish refugees from the interior sheltered in Izmir and housed haphazardly in synagogues and Jewish schools.[75] Later, once the city came under Turkish control, Izmir's Jewish leaders turned to American Jewish organizations to help provide for ten thousand Jewish refugees from the interior of Anatolia who fled to the city with nothing, their homes and shops destroyed.[76] Meanwhile, Jewish communities in the United States and even Rio de Janeiro sent donations to help the poor Jews of Izmir.[77]

The JDC's efforts in Constantinople oscillated between facilitating migration and providing refugees with the financial means to integrate into Constantinople. By August of 1920, they had secured more than a thousand visas for Ukrainian Jewish migrants to reunite with relatives in America; this number included the Mendeli Yiddish theater group, who faced difficulties in Constantinople because Sephardi Jews did not understand Yiddish, wealthy Ashkenazim "do not care for art," and the "immigrated Askenazim [sic]" could not afford the theater.[78]

Internal disputes among various factions of Constantinopolitan Jewry transformed this city into the JDC's Waterloo. In the words of a JDC report of 1921, "What I found was a beautiful fassade [sic] kept upright with great pains, awful confusion and unscrupulous, almost criminal circumstances inwardly."[79] On August 28, 1922, the preliminary organizing meeting for what would come to be known as the Central Reconstruction Committee of Constantinople was held at the chief rabbinate's office in Pera. Chief Rabbi Bejarano presided over a meeting that included representatives of the JDC, the Sephardi community, the *Commission Centrale de Secours*, the *Comité de Secours aux Réfugiés Juifs*, and the *Fédération de Secours Mutuel des Israélites de Russie*. The JDC expressed its commitment to reconstructing Jewish life in war-ravaged areas: "If the Jews of America have any right to be proud of," explained the JDC's representative, "it is the lesson of humanity and responsibility which the war has taught them." As the JDC's efforts shifted from relief to reconstruction, it saw its new burden not as giving alms, "humiliating for both the giver and receiver," but as contributing to stronger Jewish societies. "No distinction should be made between Russian Jews, Sephardim, Italian Jews and Ashkenasim [sic]. Funds are collected in America indiscriminately from all Jews. There should be no question of Sephardi Jews, Ashkenasim, etc., but only of Jews."[80]

In spite of calls for Constantinople's Jews to look beyond subethnic distinctions, members of the meeting expressed dissent. Representatives of the Sephardi community claimed that they were not sufficiently financially stable to contribute to reconstruction efforts. Russian Jews wanted autonomy from any central organization, since "the conditions of life of Russian Jews are quite different to those of other Jews who have already taken root in this country." Zionists, who refused to take part in the meetings, demanded that *chalutzim* (pioneers) be privileged over refugees; according to those opposed to this agenda, they were housed in luxurious conditions at the JDC's expense while other Jews languished.[81] All delegates complained of difficulties in communicating across numerous languages. While subsequent meetings led to the decision to establish a fund for small loans, Russian intransigence on the issue of participating in group efforts while simultaneously requesting that a substantial portion of aid be set aside for Russian refugees created continued friction among the delegates.[82] Delegates of the Italian community, meanwhile, objected to the initial denomination "Central Reconstruction Committee of Jews of Turkey," insisting that the organization's name be changed to the "Central Reconstruction Committee of Jews of Constantinople." The Jews of Constantinople, at least on the elite level, were more fractured along subethnic lines than ever before.

The actions of governmental authorities did nothing to ease tensions among the various Jewish communities. In 1922, Turkish authorities ordered the Sephardi chief rabbi to include only Turkish nationals on the Council of the Jewish Community. This excluded a number of Ashkenazi Jews and Sephardim who held foreign citizenship or protégé status. Not only did this create tension between the Sephardi and Ashkenazi communities of Constantinople, but the chief rabbi's unilateral exclusion of a number of prominent Jews who held Italian and other nationalities from positions of communal power exacerbated Sephardi antagonism toward the chief rabbi.[83] The dissatisfaction that Jews felt over governmental interference and the rabbinate's unilateral action to implement externally imposed changes highlights how Turkish Jewish elites sought to placate state authorities through acquiescing to their demands and emphasizing Jewish loyalty to the state. Not all members of the Jewish community of Turkey agreed with these actions, though dissent was not always voiced publicly.

The JDC also sought to assuage the suffering of refugees as they awaited the visas that would bear them abroad. It published calls for employment in English, Ladino, French, and Hebrew for "the unhappy Jewish emigrants now in Constantinople" addressed to "all Jewish employers in Constantinople."[84] One means that the JDC and representatives of the different Jewish communities of Istanbul saw of ameliorating the poor conditions in which Jews in Constantinople—refugees and others—lived was by establishing the *Caisse de Petits Prêts*. This organization gave small, low-interest loans to Constantinopolitan Jews in need of petty capital for business purposes. Loans were not to be disbursed to emigrants or *chalutzim*.[85] The *Caisse de Petits Prêts* offered loans to all groups of Constantinople's Jewish population, though its board was made up of Jews of Italian, Habsburg, and Sephardi origins with long roots in the Ottoman capital and the ability to process paperwork in Ottoman.[86] B'nai B'rith was the largest local contributor to the fund, followed by the Italian community and the chief rabbinate.[87] The Ashkenazi community, placed on equal footing with the Sephardi community in terms of representatives, contributed substantially less than the Sephardi community, leading to ire from the latter.[88]

Even though the Sephardi community objected to the low level of Ashkenazi contributions to the *Caisse*, it was Sephardi Jews who benefited from the vast majority of loans. In June of 1923, the *Caisse* received 232 applications, originating from 207 Sephardim, 10 Ashkenazim, and 15 Russian refugees. Of the applicants, 96 were small store keepers, 72 were peddlers, and the others artisans, employees, "professional people," laborers, or those without occupation.[89] Over the course of 1923, the *Caisse* gave loans totaling 142,030 Turkish lira to 1,852 applicants, 85% of them Sephardi, 4.32%

Ashkenazi, and 10.47% Russian.⁹⁰ The *Caisse*'s application forms, printed in French, Ladino, and Yiddish, asked questions ranging from family status and dependents, the location of a prospective business and whether the applicant already had capital and had paid off previous loans, whether he or she had a guarantor, the years of military service, and if he had been injured in the war or if she was a war widow.⁹¹ No questions were asked about communal affiliation or place of origin. For Jews intent on forging a future within what once was and what might still be the capital city of the Ottoman Empire, the *Caisse* provided a possible path to financial solvency.

Throughout formerly Ottoman territory, Jews sought to mobilize any connection they might have to a foreign power to protect their property, their movements, and their lives. At times, this required navigating layers of authority. AIU schools in the environs of Izmir flew the French flag to indicate to Greek and Turkish nationalist forces and antagonistic villagers or brigands that the properties and their contents were under French protection. Jewish refugees from Nazilli sought Italian intervention with Greek authorities to secure their passage from their place of origin through Antalya, which was in the Italian zone of influence, to Izmir, and to intercede with Greek authorities there to allow Nazilli's Jewish refugees to temporarily settle in the Karataş cemetery.⁹²

Jews' appeals to foreign powers also took the form of acquiring protégé status. The Italian consulate in Izmir was eager to expand its regional influence. It offered Italian protection to those who were able to prove even distant descent from an Italian subject or even who had simply been born in the Dodecanese Islands or Milas, now under Italian control. Affluent Jews of the region, in particular, jumped at the chance to garner Italian protégé status, though, as Sarah Abrevaya Stein has argued, understandings of the relationships among the statuses of protégé, national, and citizen were clear neither at the time nor later.⁹³ Still, in the moment, protégé status could provide those who were able to acquire it with a greater semblance of stability than did the uncertainty of their status as subjects of an empire that no longer existed, living in a territory under provisional Greek rule.⁹⁴ If nothing else, protégé status provided them options. Once it became clear that Turkish forces would regain control over Izmir, and as Turkish flags were raised throughout the city, some Jews who were protégés of foreign powers flocked to the consulates to ensure that they were registered as French or Italian to secure slots on boats leaving the city. One migrant who eventually ended up in Argentina recounted that his family in Izmir received two telegrams—one from a son studying in France, and another from an old family friend, Isaac Capon, now in Mexico—cautioning that "grave happenings are being prepared for Izmir." "My dear Bohor," wrote Capon, "If you have forgotten me, I have not forgotten you." Even though their family had relinquished French protégé status after the Ottomans entered World War I on the side of the Central Powers, they rushed to reinscribe themselves with the local French consulate, although in the eyes of the later Turkish state, they would remain Turkish citizens.[95]

For some Jewish individuals and communities in the Americas, the suffering of all Jews in areas that had once composed the empire provided an impetus to unite beyond national and linguistic divides. The *Alianza Monte Sinaí* in Mexico City raised 4,670 pesos destined for the "sufferers in Salonica, Damascus, Aleppo, Beirut, Izmir, Constantinople, etc.," some of which they sent directly to Rabbi Mair in Salonica and the rest, through the JDC, to Damascus, Aleppo, Izmir, and elsewhere. Donors' names, along with the amounts they gave, were published in the Ladino press of New York, revealing that they were of Sephardi, Syrian, and, to a lesser extent, Ashkenazi provenance. The largest amount given by individuals was 390 pesos from the Syrian Abadi family, followed by 150 pesos from Isaac Capon and 140 from his colleague Saul Carasso, both from Salonica. Women also featured among the donors, to a lesser extent—Mathilde Capon donated the largest sum of any woman, at 25 pesos, and Sara Palacci donated 10 pesos to her husband's 45. Mauricio Assael donated 40 pesos, his brother Ico 25. Less prominent individuals, male and female alike, donated smaller sums, the smallest donation recorded being 1 peso.[96]

Turkish nationalist and Greek forces clashed, and in early September of 1922, Turkish forces took control of Izmir. Thousands of Jews and others from the interior fled into Izmir as conflict raged around them. On September 13, a fire quickly spread from the Armenian quarter of the city. In a matter of hours, it engulfed the city's Greek and Armenian neighborhoods, the European quarter, and the city center. Thousands—mostly Greek Orthodox and Armenian Christians—were killed, and tens of thousands sought refuge along the quay, some throwing themselves into the sea in desperation to evade the flames. Although the Jewish area was spared, a number of Jewish commercial sites in the city center were now ash.

The city's destruction, coupled with political instability, propelled many of the city's prominent Jewish families to leave for Europe. The Jewish communal council, which before the fire had been composed of twelve members from rich, influential families, was diminished to three, the others having left.[97] This issue was even more acute in the Jewish communities of the interior, most of whose wealthiest families—upon which these communities depended to finance their schools and care for the indigent—had relocated to Izmir or abroad.[98] "Every boat carries hundreds of families to direct them either to America, Argentina, Cairo, or France, where they join a son, an uncle, or some relative," reported one AIU official. The regions of Aydın and Nazilli were totally devoid of Jewish families, while the Jewish communities of Tire, Bergama, and Kasaba were vastly diminished, their former inhabitants now in Izmir, Europe, Egypt, or South America.[99] In 1922, a British observer noted with alarm that even the Jews "are liquidating their property and leaving Smyrna."[100]

If some Ottoman Jews were invested in futures in which Ottoman Jews remained in what once was and might still be Ottoman territory, be it in Constantinople, Izmir, or Palestine, many others saw their future elsewhere. Although Jewish leaders hoped that Ottoman Jewish refugees could be repatriated once the situation stabilized, many individuals desired to stay in Izmir or Constantinople. Others, like many Jewish residents of Urla who had made their living in the raisin trade, moved to the Americas, leaving fewer than fifty Jewish inhabitants in their place of origin.[101] Armistice heralded the opening of Ottoman borders to prospective emigrants. The uncertain governance of the Ottoman capital meant that, rather than receiving a passport and an exit visa from Ottoman authorities as emigrants had done in the years before the armistice, those in Constantinople desirous of emigrating had to secure documentation from the British High Commission of the Allied Military Authorities in Constantinople.[102] What these individuals could not know at the time was that migrating on papers issued by Allied authorities would become a rationale for denaturalization under later Turkish law.[103]

"It is the beginning of one of these great events that you will encounter in history:... In all the ports of the world, hundreds or thousands of ships embark with immense quantities of men, women, and children to transport them from one hemisphere to another," proclaimed a 1920 article in *El Tiempo*. The European world was undergoing vast transformations that could potentially see storied cities like Vienna emptied of inhabitants.[104] Numerous articles reported that hundreds of Jewish migrants from Izmir and elsewhere in Anatolia had boarded ships for South America.[105] As it had done before the war, *El Tiempo* featured advertisements for companies that offered tickets and advice for travelers to the Americas.[106] Likewise, in 1923, the Bulletin for Constantinople's Or-Ahayim Jewish National Hospital featured three separate advertisements for Jewish firms lining the quay in Karaköy that sold tickets to destinations such as "North and South America, Cuba, Mexico, Buenos Aires, Canada," and "North America (New York, Canada, Mexico) and South America (Argentina, Buenos Aires, Brazil)."[107]

Geographic subtleties aside, Ottoman Jews who did not find themselves living under the French and British mandates confronted far fewer obstacles to emigration than they had in the years prior to armistice. For many, an uncertain future in foreign lands was preferable to an uncertain future in Ottoman territories, fast becoming foreign to its own inhabitants. The local Jewish communities in Constantinople and Izmir, who had to contend with skyrocketing costs of living and economic instability and whose resources were further strained by large numbers of internally displaced Ottoman Jews from border and interior regions and by destitute Russian Jewish refugees, encouraged and financially aided migration as a means of alleviating local burdens.

Prospective migrants looked to local and international Jewish philanthropic organizations for financial assistance. While Chief Rabbi Nahum was a key linchpin in a transnational network that linked Sephardi migrants throughout the world with family members in Ottoman lands, the philanthropic organizations assisting prospective emigrants sometimes operated along different subethnic or geographic axes. *HaMenora*, the French-language mouthpiece of the B'nai B'rith Lodge in Constantinople, announced that the city's Italian Committee of Assistance to Jewish Emigrants would financially assist Jews in transit for Italy or Italian colonies; it also helped other Jews. It aided 720 emigrants destined for North and South America in the first three months of 1922 and provided food for the entire journey to 230 migrants destined for South America.[108] Such benevolent activities underscored the place of Italian Jews at the top of Jewish hierarchies in the Ottoman world.[109] Many of Constantinople and Izmir's most prominent merchants, whose names filled the boards of philanthropic associations and the Or-Ahayim Jewish National Hospital and whose wives organized to distribute aid throughout the city, made claims to Italianness. Similarly, prominent Jews from Ottoman lands in Mexico, whose names were published in Ladino periodicals along with amounts donated to assist coreligionists in their natal lands, bore Italian surnames and, at times, Italian nationality. The JDC also sometimes aided Ottoman Jews—and Russian Jewish refugees—in migrating to new lands.[110]

The opening of Ottoman borders also allowed for the reestablishment of ties throughout a growing Sephardi diaspora, ties that were channeled through Haim Nahum, the former chief rabbi of the Ottoman Empire. In the immediate postwar period, the tenor of letters to Chief Rabbi Nahum shifted, even as Nahum went on an international tour to the United States, with rumored but unmaterialized stops in Cuba and Mexico, in an attempt to curry support for the AIU and Turkey's position in postwar negotiations.[111] A migrant in Cárdenas, Cuba sought his mother and two sisters, whom he had left nine years earlier in the heavily Jewish Balat district of Constantinople.[112] Another migrant, in New Brunswick, New Jersey, explained that he had not received any news of his parents since 1916 and that when he had last heard from them, they lived in Hasköy; like Balat, Hasköy was a predominantly Jewish and very poor district of Constantinople.[113] Others in Buenos Aires and New York contacted Nahum "as soon as the mail connections with Turkey were reestablished" in hopes that Nahum might use his influence to convince relatives, whose current addresses they no longer knew, to join them.[114] Similar letters searching for lost relatives came from Sephardi migrants in Tampico, Veracruz, New York City, San Francisco, Piraeus, and Bordeaux. While some wrote letters themselves, others, especially women, turned to rabbis in their new locales to pen missives on their behalf.[115] All attested to ruptures on a personal level that World War I had caused in an expanding Sephardi world, and to the fact that they still viewed the Ottoman chief rabbi in Constantinople as a linchpin.

The Ladino press also served as a means of connecting disparate parts of the Sephardi diaspora as individuals sought information about relatives. *La Amerika* boasted of agents in the United States in cities with substantial Sephardi populations like Seattle, Montgomery, Indianapolis, Chicago, and Los Angeles and throughout the western hemisphere, extending to Havana, Mexico City, Rio de Janeiro, Montevideo, and Buenos Aires.[116] One migrant from Constantinople now living in Havana wrote to *La Amerika* in New York in hopes of being put in touch with three of his brothers who, when he had last heard from them four years before, lived in Buenos Aires. *La Amerika* asked its readers in Argentina who knew the men to respond to the article with any information they might have on their well-being.[117]

The American Ladino press also provided information to prospective migrants on changes in immigration laws and suggested new destinations for migratory flows. After the 1921 implementation of American immigration quotas, *La Amerika* explained that Jewish migration to Cuba increased daily, those migrants hoping eventually to go from the island to the United States.[118] The following year, another American Ladino periodical, *La Luz*, reported that the Senate had extended the 1921 Emergency Quota Act until 1924 and had, at the same time, tightened restrictions that had allowed those who had resided in Canada, Cuba, or Mexico for one year to enter the United States regardless of quotas; the residency period was now extended to five years.[119] They reported on Senator Albert Johnson's proposition to limit migration altogether to the reunification of close relatives of American citizens; in 1924, Johnson was one of the two sponsors of the Johnson-Reed Act that drew on overtly racist and eugenicist principles of applying strict quotas against non-whites, southern and eastern Europeans, Middle Easterners, and Jews.[120] These articles alerted potential migrants to changes in legal codes and suggested alternative paths for arriving in the United States, should that be their intended endpoint, as well as other possible destinations.

The Ladino press frequently identified Spanish-speaking countries as locations where Sephardi migrants might thrive. The Sephardi community in Argentina had a flourishing social life, a Talmud Torah that taught "our true language," a society that aided ailing and needy Sephardi coreligionists, and a number of flourishing Sephardi commercial houses.[121] In Cuba, Sephardi migrants could acclimate easily because of the similarities between Ladino and Spanish. Should American laws restricting entrance not be reversed, "our new immigrants," especially those who could not be admitted in New York, could gather there instead of remaining in their natal countries in a situation of misery or being returned to Europe after their arrival in New York. Should the economic situation in Cuba continue in its bad state, "our Sephardim have the opportunity to emigrate from there to the nearby island of Puerto Rico or to Mexico where the Spanish language is also spoken."[122] Several Sephardi migrants who had migrated first to New York before heading to Mexico alerted *La Amerika* that commerce in Mexico was developing and that "our Sephardim in immigrating there would have a chance of a good future, especially because the official language of the state is Spanish."[123] Isaac Capon stopped by the editor's office in New York on his way to Paris to inform *La Amerika* that a new society had just been formed in Mexico to aid new migrants and that B'nai B'rith had pledged a large sum to purchase a locale with twenty-five beds where they could sleep. The newspaper once again noted that in Mexico, Sephardi Jews especially had a "great chance" due to the Spanish language.[124] At least one migrant in New York decided to relocate to Mexico, advertising his six-room apartment on Madison Avenue near 114th Street on the condition that the renter also purchase his furniture.[125]

The Ottoman Armistice and the Allied division of Ottoman lands reverberated throughout the Ottoman colony in Mexico. Shelomo Meyuhas, a regular correspondent on Mexico for *La Amerika*, reported in August 1919 that large numbers of "our brothers" had begun to gather and sell their goods in hopes of returning to their natal lands now under new administrations. The Abadi brothers, from Aintab [Gaziantep], now under French control, who had become quite wealthy in Mexico and whose names graced the board of Monte Sinaí and the Mexican society pages, were among the first to acquire French passports. They advised others to do the same. To obtain these passports, Meyuhas explained that one had to appeal to the French legation through the Syrio-Lebanese Union. This organization had been established in Veracruz in the later years of World War I by individuals with close ties to France originating in what would later become Syria and Lebanon. A letter of recommendation from this largely Christian union became unofficially mandatory for those seeking passports from the French legation.[126] But, as Meyuhas elaborated, the Monte Sinaí Society would write letters to the Syrio-Lebanese Union on behalf of Arabic-speaking Jews. French passports in particular would be of use even if one did not want to return to live in areas now under French control: they could ease the importation of clothing from the United States or obtaining permission to travel to Europe. However, Meyuhas explained, "only to the Syrians, speakers of the Arabic language, are they delivering the passports, and our brothers immigrated from Turkey and Europe cannot acquire them, being considered of Turkish nationality."[127] Other Ottoman émigrés, unsure of precisely what their nationality and passport documentation should be when the fate of Thrace, Constantinople, and Anatolia remained unclear, sought to reaffirm their status with Ottoman authorities.[128] And still others capitalized on the increasing fluidity in the boundaries of nationality, race, and origins in the wake of World War I. Ico Assael appeared on an American ship manifest in 1919 as an individual of the "Syrian race, French-protected nationality, from Smyrna, staying at a hotel in Paris, last lived in Mexico."[129] The acquisition of nationality and passports by Ottoman émigrés entrenched certain preexisting divisions along linguistic and regional lines while also creating new divisions among those of a shared Jewish faith who now found that some among them could access documentation that would ease their transnational travel and commerce, while others could not.

The Sephardi press did not always cast Mexico as a land of opportunity for new migrants. In October of 1919, a young Sephardi migrant from Rhodes was stabbed to death in Mexico after having migrated there from the United States to avoid the military call-up during World War I. A fellow *Rodesli* published a necrological poem in *La Amerika* in his honor, decrying Mexico City as "a deregulated and fatal city" and claiming that his relatives cried in sadness and the *Rodesli* colony sighed bitterly at the loss of the "youth full of courage and supreme ambition."[130] Such news from Mexico in the Ladino press potentially dissuaded new Sephardi migrants, highlighting as it did that the economic potential for Sephardi youths within Mexico did not come without risk, whether for new arrivals or established merchants.

Even as some Jewish migrants within Mexico made the decision to return to their natal lands following World War I and years of revolutionary violence, many others made their way to Mexico, diverted from the United States by the new quotas instituted in 1921 and 1924. Ashkenazi Jews, like their Sephardi coreligionists, headed to Mexico as American quotas made it increasingly difficult to obtain visas and enter the United States as immigrants. Some Jews—likely both Ashkenazi and Sephardi, though it has generally only been documented for Ashkenazi Jews—hoped to use a loophole in American quotas that enabled those who had been resident in Mexico and Cuba for a period of five years to bypass quotas, or simply hoped to cross the porous land or sea borders without documentation.[131] Others had heard rumors that the Mexican president, Álvaro Obregón, welcomed Jewish immigrants in hopes that they would help develop Mexico commercially and industrially in the wake of the revolution.[132] The American Jewish press published frequently on the potential desirability of Mexico as a destination for Jewish migrants, reporting that Obregón would not charge them the $250 tax on new immigrants and would help them financially until they were established and had become Mexican citizens.[133] Meanwhile, a Jewish lawyer in Chicago founded the Mexican Jewish Colonization Association in 1921, with hopes of convincing Obregón to allow Jews from Russia and elsewhere in eastern Europe to create a farming colony in Tamaulipas or Baja California.[134] British Jewish organizations dedicated to addressing the Jewish crisis in territories of the former Russian Empire, along with the American Jewish Congress, initially viewed such plans favorably and encouraged Ashkenazi immigration to Mexico; non-Ashkenazi Jews did not figure in their discussions.[135] Jewish farming colonies remained an unrealized and discarded path for Jews to fit within post-revolutionary Mexico, however. Those who arrived in Mexico or who were already settled there faced the challenge of adapting themselves to the new post-revolutionary reality in Mexico.

Mauricio Assael was likely thrilled when the photograph that he used for his 1918 Mexican naturalization appeared in *Excelsior* in April 1922, together with the image of the mansion at Córdoba 73 in Mexico City's fashionable Roma Norte neighborhood that he was donating for use as a maternity hospital.[136] The photograph accompanied a long article on Assael's endeavor in which he requested the newspaper's assistance in publicizing his call for others to donate materials for "so many unhappy women who do not have a manner of being conveniently assisted in the supreme hour in which they are going to become mothers, whether because they do not find a place in official institutions or because their homes, so poor and reduced, do not permit them to be attended to with the care that their state requires." *Excelsior* lauded Assael's efforts as an example of a type of "philanthropy that unfortunately is seen only rarely in our country" and later followed up this piece with another long article on Assael's maternity hospital and what role he envisioned for himself and his family within this institution.

Excelsior explained who Assael was in somewhat contradictory terms. It described him first as a "foreigner, very well known in our capital and in the Republic," before concluding the article with the note "we should state a fact that makes *señor* Mauricio Assael worthier of sympathy: foreign by origin, he is a Mexican citizen by naturalization." Assael, who had become a naturalized Mexican in 1918 to take up the post of Mexican honorary consul in his natal city of Izmir, was, in the eyes of the paper's editor, still a foreigner. Mexican citizenship could be obtained by naturalization, but citizenship did not necessarily remove the cast of foreignness. Assael's philanthropic endeavors made him the right kind of foreigner, however, a model of emulation for others who were attached, regardless of nationality, to Mexico's betterment.

The maternity hospital was not Mauricio Assael's first foray into philanthropy, nor the first time that his efforts had received press coverage. Several years earlier, when he was active as the consul in Smyrna, Assael had offered a large sum of gold for the formation of a central bank, as proposed by the Mexican constitution of 1917, that would control the issuance of money. *El Universal* opined that Assael's actions, in his capacity as a "prominent member of the Ottoman *colonia*," would inspire imitation "by many of his coreligionists." Even more satisfactory than the sum that Assael offered was that it demonstrated the growing confidence among Mexicans and foreigners alike that "the government emanating from the revolution inspired from the beginning."[137] In this instance, as in his later hospital project, Assael used his wealth to demonstrate his standing within the broader *colonia otomana*, which in turn helped to cement his belonging within the post-revolutionary order. His actions and his trust in the post-revolutionary government were worthy of emulation by those of his geographical origins and Mexican natives alike. The wealth that enabled these grand displays of patriotic fervor for his adopted country was, however, out of the realm of aspiration for most native-born Mexicans, naturalized Mexicans, and migrants.

Beyond the services that Assael hoped to provide through his maternity hospital or other endeavors and the Mexican press's bolstering of his honor and patriotism and identification of him as an example for Mexicans and foreigners alike, these activities gave Assael a pretext to form connections with higher echelons of state power. One week after the original piece on Assael's maternity hospital ran in *Excelsior*, Assael requested from President Álvaro Obregón that the concession of the lottery of the state of Sinaloa be used for ten years to help support his maternity hospital. Assael noted that he had already met with the president of the National Lottery, who had "found the project supreme," but requested that he receive approval from the Mexican president himself.[138] Several weeks later, Obregón's private secretary responded to Assael simply that he lacked the faculties to authorize the requested concession.[139]

Although Assael failed to receive presidentially approved funds for his endeavor, his letter to Obregón highlights how he sought to mark his belonging. Assael first identified himself as "a Mexican citizen by naturalization" and an owning partner of "La Exposición" jewelry store. No stranger to hyperbole, Assael explained that he had been living for eighteen years in "this land of God" and that from the beginning, he had been working to achieve his life's ambition of opening two hospitals, one a maternity hospital and the other a general hospital. Scattered throughout his missive were markers of Assael's reputation, established class status, and racialization as white. Assael enclosed the photograph that *Excelsior* had run of his face next to the impressive edifice in Roma Norte that was destined to become Assael's maternity hospital; within his letter, he noted that the mansion had previously been the residence and office of the former Spanish minister during his period of employment in Mexico. Assael cast himself as a naturalized Mexican citizen of long residence, a successful businessman of renowned image and reputation, and a dedicated philanthropist.

Middle class status, paternalism toward women and children, and the gentility conferred by perceived race were traits that constituted and marked honorable masculinity.[140] *Excelsior* further underscored the honorability of Assael's endeavor when it described his project as "an idea so noble that it honors him who conceived it and is putting it into practice no matter the obstacles." Mauricio Assael's donation of the former Spanish minister's residence for a desperately needed maternity hospital for Mexico City's impoverished mothers marked him as an honorable man. In laying the groundwork for an institution that he hoped would be "luxuriously outfitted conforming to modern hygiene," Assael used his wealth for the modern care of disadvantaged women at "the most critical moment of their lives." And this endeavor, he explained, was for the advantage of the nation: "those innocent *creaturas* [sic] who come to the light of the *Patria* will be received with all happiness." Through providing poor Mexican women with hygienic maternity care and bringing the children of the nation into a comfortable world, Assael showed himself to be an ideal masculine protector of the weak, not only within his own family but within the broader Mexican nation. In doing so, he implicitly advocated for the desirability of naturalized Mexicans like himself who worked for the betterment of the national family. He also countered the public discourse that would grow over the coming years that migrants like himself deliberately exploited the neediest of Mexican women and children while siphoning their profits to members of their own *colonias* in Mexico or to family abroad, to the detriment of the Mexican nation. His use of gendered discourse and practice contrasted markedly with practices in Argentina, where for Middle Eastern migrants, Christians and Jews alike, funding hospitals and health care, geared toward their own group, was the purview of women and a means for them to garner power in their communities.[141]

Two days after the initial article on Assael's planned maternity hospital, *Excelsior* printed a follow-up on the endeavor, this one featuring a large photograph of a young girl smiling at the camera in a white dress, a big bow on her head, bearing the simple caption of "the girl Saharita Assael."[142] This article reaffirmed Assael's honorability and standing, describing him as a "gentleman" whose altruistic project "once known by the public of Mexico has awakened the warmest elegies from everyone." The newspaper published the letter that Assael had sent to seek contributions for his endeavor from wealthy acquaintances—with the addition of several key words that emphasized the length of his stay in Mexico, his naturalized status, and his description of Mexico as a "land of God" and of the children that would be born in his hospital as belonging to the *patria*. Assael's appeals had made headway with "a group of honorable women of the best society of Mexico" and Assael assured *Excelsior*'s readers that all who helped with his project would receive a certificate and their donations would be made known publicly. Charitable giving would be a public mark of beneficence and status.

In this second article, Assael's four children became another way of connecting his future and theirs with that of Mexico. All his children were Mexican, he explained, although two were currently studying in Paris; Mauricio Assael's conception of his eldest daughter, Sara, as Mexican had changed drastically since her birth in Mexico City in 1909, when he had expressly requested that she keep Ottoman nationality.[143] Sara was now in her second year of secondary school in Paris, where she received top marks, and it was his greatest ambition that she "obtain her diploma to return to her *patria* and collaborate in the work that I have initiated."[144] In Mauricio Assael's estimation, Sara Assael, named after his mother according to Sephardi custom, was Mexican by birth, and Mexico was the homeland to which she owed fealty. A Parisian education did not negate her Mexicanness; if anything, even within the immediate post-revolutionary world, a French education continued to be a marker of the social and economic elite within Mexico. Sara Assael's future work as the director of a philanthropic institution designed to benefit indigent mothers was the completion of elite feminine duties par excellence. Wealth and the French language marked Sara as elite and as an integral member working for the betterment of Mexican society. Foreign residence did not negate her Mexican belonging, especially since her stint abroad was necessary to acquire skills that she would bring back to Mexico.

In the background of Mauricio Assael's endeavors to cast himself as a benevolent father figure deeply invested in the lives of Mexico's indigent mothers and the future of his adopted homeland was a broader project of stability and a new vision for Mexico in the wake of years of revolution, when yearned-for order had not yet fully materialized. The municipal government of Mexico City sought to create an image of public order. This took various forms: streets were renamed in honor of revolutionary figures; street vendors of food and clothing in the Plaza of the Constitution and other prominent locations in the city were outlawed, resulting, in one case, in a female vendor kicking an inspector in the testicles; and city markets assigned numbered and registered plaques to stands.[145] Wandering salespeople and vendors gave "a poor aspect to the city and gravely harm the hygiene and cleanliness of the public buildings near to which they station themselves."[146]

In November of 1920, 280 individuals signed a petition to the president of the municipality of Mexico City complaining of numerous individuals who were generally "Españoles y Turcos," popularly called *aboneros*, who sold goods on installment. These *aboneros* "exploited the misery of those people whose resources do not permit them to purchase with cash . . . being in their majority women."[147] Although installments allowed women to purchase clothing and other objects of primary necessity that they would be unable to buy otherwise, they did so at great cost—the *aboneros* charged "at least six times" the actual value of the items. These "Españoles y Turcos" also exploited Mexico by not paying taxes or getting required licenses. The petition alleged that they could cite "an infinity of houses who represent immense capital, in the streets of Capuchinas, Correo Mayor, and others whose proprietors not long ago were simply *aboneros*, individuals who arrived to our country without resources other than their will to make money in whatever form."[148] Capuchinas, Correo Mayor, and the other streets that encircled the Zócalo were the streets where new migrants crowded into colonial buildings transformed into tenements on the upper floors and where, as the petition noted, many former peddlers who had sufficient capital opened storefronts on ground floors and internal passages. There was little to separate the *aboneros* from those shopkeepers and, by extension, from wealthy merchants of foreign origin like Mauricio Assael whose storefronts were on streets leading from the other side of the Zócalo.

As city officials attempted to project an image of commercial order in the city center, the petition alleged that immigrants contributed only to disorder and their personal enrichment, to the detriment of Mexico as a country and particularly Mexico's most vulnerable populations. As the petition against *aboneros* clustered in the center of Mexico City suggests, however, even established businessmen like Assael were not far removed—metaphorically and geographically—from those "Españoles y Turcos" who deliberately exploited poor Mexican women and the largesse of the Mexican state to increase their personal wealth. The trope of going "from rags to riches" that was often a point of pride for Jewish migrants was undergirded, in the estimation of these petitioners, by the exploitation of Mexico City's most vulnerable residents, creating civic disorder and disrupting the ability of Mexican merchants to succeed.

Reports on *turcos* who sought to evade Mexican taxes by smuggling textiles from the United States or France caught the attention of French officials and the Mexican press alike. The French consul in Mexico noted in 1924 that Middle Eastern migrants traveled between France and Mexico smuggling silks and other luxury textiles in their personal luggage; this allowed them to undercut the prices of "honest merchants" of French origin and was the basis for their prosperity.[149] The Mexican press likewise published numerous pieces on *turco* smugglers, enforcing the sense that not all those of Assael's place of origin were benevolent and invested in the future of the new Mexico.[150] An article from Veracruz reported that a shop and restaurant called "La Colonia Otomana" sheltered textiles and other merchandise stolen by a band of thieves formed of *turcos*. When the police sought to search the establishment, they were fired on but ended up arresting six men, "part of a dangerous band of Turkish thieves who have chosen our port as a center of operations."[151] And when Mauricio Assael's jewelry store was robbed in 1922, he accused another individual of Ottoman origin, Kasem Salmen, of orchestrating the theft of 17,999 pesos worth of gold watches and other fine objects. Assael alleged that amid the empty boxes on the floor of his despoiled office, he had found a card with a black-and-white image of the Sacred Heart of Mary, upon which was written an advertisement for the cheap products of Kasem Salmen's notions store on Capuchinas.[152] Although no charges were filed against Salmen or anyone else in this case, Assael himself played upon popular conceptions of thieving *turcos* with shops on the street of Capuchinas or elsewhere on the southern and eastern edges of the Zócalo. Assael, though, was not one of these individuals, as was indicated not only by his physical presentation, wealth, political connections, and philanthropic activity. His store address on the fashionable Francisco I. Madero Street and his home address in the upscale neighborhood of Roma Norte likewise attested to his difference.

Even as Mauricio Assael sought to position himself, through his physical location and his philanthropic work, as an exemplary naturalized immigrant deeply attached to Mexico's betterment, other Sephardi migrants continued to play up their French connections to position themselves in Mexican society. In the immediate aftermath of the revolution, the possibility remained that strategies of belonging during the Porfiriato might still hold. At times, when foreign connections and wealth coincided and resulted in public visibility, this could still secure belonging within Mexico. In 1920, *El Universal* noted that Ico Assael, owner of "La Duquesa" jewelry shop, had just arrived in Mexico City from Europe, "where he had gone to purchase the latest novelties."[153] Similarly, Alberto Misrachi, who arrived in Mexico in 1918 from Monastir by way of Salonica, advertised subscriptions to the French fashion magazines of *Paris Elegant*, *Paris Mode*, and *Paris Chapeaux* at his foreign-language bookshop.[154] Foreign, and particularly French, connections, upended by years of war, still held salience for Sephardi migrants in their attempts to position themselves in post-revolutionary Mexico.

While some sought to use personal wealth, foreign connections, and status to forge a place for themselves and their progeny within the Mexican nation, however, wealth could not assure belonging, even within the Assael family. In April 1919, when Mauricio's older brother Isidoro (né Israel) was conned out of the astronomical sum of twenty thousand pesos, it made front-page news in Mexico City. Isidoro, like his four brothers, had migrated to Mexico in the first years of the 1900s; he had achieved prominence in the capital's jewelry trade, partnering with his younger brother Ico.[155] But as the capital's press described it, the *"joyero turco"* had been swindled out of the large sum by two "men of industry," taken in by their bespoke clothing and consumption of expensive alcohol. These men, one Russian and one German, defrauded Assael in a scheme to purchase American cattle and horses to sell in Mexico. Assael had been deceived, noted the major Mexican newspaper *Excelsior*, because he "lacked in all instruction," was illiterate, and could not read the documents the two men presented him with.[156] *El Democrata*, meanwhile, described Assael in their front-page story alternately as an "Arab" and a "Syrian," noting that Assael "was very well-known among us as an expert trafficker in jewelry."[157] In spite of his wealth, then, Isidoro, as a *turco*, *árabe*, or *sirio*, was described as an uneducated and illiterate foreigner. He was easily duped, a negative characterization that ran counter to the image of the cunning foreigner who exploited Mexico's most vulnerable in the marketplaces.

Isidoro Assael's name remained in the news. Several weeks after the robbery, his corpse was discovered in the Bosque de Chapultepec, the large city park in which Chapultepec Castle, the official residence of President Venustiano Carranza, was located. Assael had been shot, and the initial reports were that he had killed himself.[158] The articles on the death of the *"joyero turco*" in the April 13th edition of *Excelsior* ran over three pages, questioning whether Assael had killed himself given the position of the wounds. Given the details that Ico Assael, Isidoro's brother and business partner, had reported that Isidoro was "visibly sad" after the robbery, had not spoken to practically anyone, and had spent "long hours crying," it seemed possible that he had killed himself. However, Assael's brothers reported that the gun Isidoro usually carried was a .32-caliber, which was not the weapon that had left the wounds. Ico and "several compatriots of the deceased" recovered his body from the hospital the day after his death.[159] Newspapers in the capital and as far away as Texas debated for days whether Isidoro had killed himself or been murdered. *Excelsior* held out for homicide and *El Democrata* for suicide, noting that the Assael relatives believed that to have been the case.[160] However, a week after Isidoro's death, Ico Assael had revised his view that his brother had killed himself. He offered a reward of a thousand pesos to anyone who would aid in the capture of the two men who had robbed his brother and whom Ico and Mexican authorities now believed to be responsible for Isidoro's murder.[161]

Two weeks after Assael's death, the public prosecutor declared it a homicide and sought to link the murder with the charges of robbery already brought against the two foreigners who had defrauded Assael several days before his body was found.[162] Rumors were published that one of these men had asked after Assael "at the house of the *turco*" the day before his death and had looked disgruntled not to find Assael at home.[163] The two suspects, however, evaded capture by Mexican authorities, although their photographs were distributed throughout the country.[164] Isidoro's suicide-cum-homicide remained unsolved and unpunished.

Isidoro Assael's death reverberated beyond Mexico and Texas to the Ladino press of New York, where an article announced the "murder of a rich *turkino*." Assael was described as a *"djudio turkino"* from Izmir, a "rich businessman in jewelry" who was very well-known in the commercial world of Mexico. The Ladino newspaper went into greater detail than the Mexican press, explaining that the two suspects had for some time tried to convince Assael to go into business with them importing clothing from the United States, given that one had a brother in New York who could supply them with clothing.[165] Although the source was not given, the article sheds light on the greater role that the United States came to occupy as the supplier of ready-to-wear clothing, even as French fashion still held greater cachet.

Where the Mexican press had categorized Assael alternately as an *árabe*, a *sirio*, and a *turco*, wealthy but unlettered, willing to kill himself over the blow to his honor that the robbery caused, the Ladino press, in contrast, highlighted his wealth multiple times, his *Izmirli* origins, and the fact that he was a Jew and a *turkino*, a term that sought to emphasize the connections of Ottoman Jews to their place of origin and to the equalizing sentiment of the Ottoman Tanzimat reforms.[166] Isidoro's foreignness was emphasized in both accounts, but in very different ways. The Ladino articles mentioned Assael's Jewishness, but his religion never appeared in the Spanish press. While some readers may have guessed his religion from his surname or from the mention of his coreligionist José Benveniste, the casual reader would have only perceived him as a foreigner, someone from an unclear part of the eastern Mediterranean.

Isidoro Assael was interred in the Monte Sinaí Jewish cemetery, a fact that emphasizes, in and of itself, the centrality of Jewish burial practices to shaping this nascent community even through death. At the time he was buried, it was likely unclear whether he had killed himself or had been murdered, notable in Jewish law but not distinguished in where he was interred. His tombstone simply notes in Spanish that "he died in Chapultepec, Mexico, April 12, 1919," with the further indication on the back of the stone that he had been born in "the city of Smyrna, Turkey, in the year of 1878." The tombstone bears no Hebrew lettering, nor reliefs or blessings of any kind.

Conclusion

Many imperial subjects in a newly post-imperializing world did not see nationalizing states as the obvious next progression. Rather, some sought to align themselves with whatever they deemed the next great empire to be, while others sought to extricate themselves entirely by relocating to new lands.[167] Whether in stasis or flux, individuals of all stripes were forced to consider and reassess their own place and the place of their communities and to position themselves for whatever future they deemed most likely to come to pass.

The upheaval that accompanied the end of World War I marked the transformation of Jewish geographies. Longstanding land-based empires with large Jewish populations were defeated, while new, different types of imperial power exerted themselves over many of these lands. Many Jewish residents of now-defunct empires sought new lands where they could craft equally new futures, as uncharted as the potential futures they were leaving behind in lands themselves undergoing turmoil and transformation. This mobility—sometimes forced—propelled migrants and refugees around the globe, pushing them to engage with new, unfamiliar, and transforming documentary regimes. The chaos and uncertainty that reigned in the aftermath of global upheaval prompted individuals and communities to forge new trajectories and new paths of interaction even as they attempted to reconnect after years of upended communications. But increasing contact in a world suddenly more open to movement, but movement regulated by paperwork and oversight, did not entail the erasure of difference and lack of conflict.

When Gabriel Yermia Valanci made the decision to use falsified documentation to acquire a Mexican passport, he likely did so because he saw Mexican documentation as necessary for his complicated transatlantic voyage with transits through multiple countries, immigration and customs stations, and police prefectures. In the aftermath of World War I, when the Ottoman capital of Constantinople where Yermia had been born was under Interallied occupation, he may have considered it uncertain whether whatever Ottoman documentation he held would be valid or advantageous for such an endeavor. The archival record does not preserve Yermia's Ottoman travel documents nor any record of when and how he originally arrived in Mexico. When he returned to his natal city to marry Fanny Levy and to prepare later for the migration of her father Abraham, who would become Mexico's first Sephardi rabbi, he was likely very aware that the city to which he was returning was very different from the one he had left. For Gabriel and Fanny, navigating a world of still-possible and no-longer-possible futures required casting their lot elsewhere.

(CHAPTER 4)

"THEY ARE ENTIRELY EQUAL TO THE SPANISH"

SARA HALFON FISS DE LAHANA'S DEATH sent reverberations across the globe. The facts of her death were simple enough—the forty-seven-year-old woman died in April of 1925, of natural causes, and her body was immediately interred in the Monte Sinaí Jewish cemetery in Mexico City.[1] It was the lack of a will that complicated matters. This was compounded by the absence of acceptable documentation proving that she had been married to Simon Lahana, the man who came forward as her spouse, or that she was the mother of Salomon, Isaac, Fanny, and Zafira. "I can prove neither my marriage to Mrs. Halfon nor the birth of my children from the Civil Registry, as Mexican law requires," Simon Lahana attested in an appearance before the Third Civil Court in Mexico City. Civil marriage was not practiced in Turkey, where they had married, he explained, and their religious marriage was not recognized as legally binding in Mexico. Moreover, "as regards birth—the documents have been lost due to our many travels."[2] In spite of this, and in spite of testimony from three other Sephardi Jews in Mexico City—one from Bulgaria and one from Salonica who testified to having met the Lahanas after their recent arrival in Mexico and a third from Constantinople who claimed to have known the family from the Philippines—the Third Civil Court requested that an announcement be published in Istanbul soliciting that potential claimants to Sara de Lahana's estate come forward. On April

16, 1926, Scarlatt Tottu, Mexico's honorary consul in Istanbul, who would later lose his position as a result of widely publicized claims of fraud and bribery, published such an announcement in Spanish and Ladino in the city's Jewish newspaper *El Tiempo*.[3]

The Lahana family had traveled extensively, acquiring and likely losing an array of documentation in the process. Sara Halfon Fiss de Lahana had been born in Rodosto (Tekirdağ) and her husband in Constantinople, at the time part of the Ottoman Empire. Their two sons were born in the Ottoman capital around the turn of the century, although Salomon would claim on later documentation to have been born in either Manila or New York.[4] Fanny (Fania) was born in Athens, Greece in 1908 or 1909, and Zafira, the youngest, in the Philippines in 1912.[5] The Lahanas had lived in the Philippines for around a decade, where they had been in business with Sara's brother Joseph.[6] They arrived in Mexico and settled in Mexico City in 1924, the same year that two of Sara's other brothers moved to Mexico, one to Mexico City and the other to Chihuahua.[7] Sara and Simon had been born Ottoman subjects, though by the time of Sara's death, the Ottoman Empire had ceased to exist. Simon explained that all the members of the Lahana nuclear family were Americans by virtue of naturalization in the Philippines, which was under American control; the facsimile of his 1922 naturalization in Manila that Salomon Lahana included in his 1947 application for Mexican naturalization verified that he had been naturalized as a citizen of the Philippine Islands.[8] The American consulate in Mexico City did not wholly agree with the Lahanas' assessment of their belonging, however. Although it confirmed that Sara and the two daughters had traveled as dependents on Simon's passport, which had been issued in the Philippines for a period of six months for business travel in Hong Kong, Japan, and the United States, then extended in New York for travel in all countries, Simon and his sons were "citizens of the Philippine Islands, which owe obedience to the United States," rather than American citizens.

Even as Mexico sought to fix the identities of Sara de Lahana's husband and children through documentation that they lacked, and in spite of questions swirling around whether the Lahanas were American citizens, nationals, or neither, Simon Lahana and his children squeezed through a crack in Mexico's attempt to distribute Sara de Lahana's estate. Simon removed the intestate case from Mexico's jurisdiction by arguing that none of his deceased wife's assets were in Mexico, given that they had moved there only months before her death. On May 27, 1926, the *New York Times* announced that Sara de Lahana's estate of $6,000 was in probate, a process initiated by her son Salomon, a resident of 7 East 113th Street in Manhattan, on behalf of himself and the deceased's three other children.[9] Salomon and Simon had arrived together in New York City less than two weeks before from Veracruz, their entrance in the ship register noting that they had naturalized in the Philippines in 1922.[10] In moving the jurisdiction of the intestate case from Mexico to the United States, the Lahanas bypassed Mexico's stringent documentary requirements to prove family relations. They also confounded the efforts of Sara de Lahana's cousins in Turkey who sought to inherit from her estate. And by virtue of their naturalization in the Philippines, Simon and Salomon Lahana were able to enter the United States freely, a kind of movement that was heavily restricted for others of their geographical origin after the Immigration Act of 1924. By 1934, American legislation clarified that citizens of the Philippine Islands who were not also United States citizens would be considered aliens, subject to immigration quotas. In 1933, Simon Lahana, now living in Mazatenango, Guatemala, would declare himself stateless upon entrance to Mexico from its southern border; over the course of the 1920s, the Turkish government had progressively stripped citizenship from émigrés, eliminating that citizenship as an option for Simon.[11] In 1926, however, when the Lahanas traveled to New York, they benefited from the transnational legal forum shopping that was enabled by their relative freedom of movement.

The Lahanas' frequent movements, ambiguous nationality, lack of documentation, legal forum shopping, and transnational family connections posed a number of challenges for the various states with which they interacted and across whose borders they passed. World War I brought a preoccupation with monitoring and controlling the movement of individuals.[12] The end of hostilities did not entail the end of states' concerns with documenting, constraining, and containing people on the move in an effort to create legible, often homogenous, nations along specific parameters. American legislators sought to curtail migration through the implementation of quotas that strictly limited the immigrant visas available to those from southern and eastern Europe and the Middle East. Likewise, Mexico, in the immediate aftermath of its bloody revolution, and Turkey, legislated into existence by the Treaty of Lausanne, confronted the dilemma of the place of immigrants and emigrants in their nationalizing states. As the historian Tara Zahra notes, "in the aftermath of war and revolution, national classification represented one strategy through which governments sought to re-establish order, distinguishing citizens and foreigners, majorities and minorities."[13] National classification, the granting and recognition of citizenship, and the documentation of such prompted and constrained a number of deeper questions. Was national status determined by place of birth? Could someone born beyond the borders of the state assimilate into the nation? Did someone who had moved beyond state borders have any claim on the nation? Could someone who was born within the borders of the state and never left nonetheless be foreign, or inassimilable—and if so, by whose assessment? Did transnational connections mitigate against or aid the perceived assimilability of individuals? How were nativeness and foreignness determined in a nationalizing context? Hypermobile and transnationally connected individuals like the Lahanas provoked authorities to formulate responses to these questions even as such individuals sought to continue to travel along established networks in spite of constantly evolving circumstances.

"The Doors Are Open"

In 1922, Margot and Rafael Levi decided to return from Havana, Cuba—where they had been living for the previous twelve years, after a year in France—to their city of origin, Constantinople.[14] They had two main reasons for leaving Cuba. First, the country was in a steep recession in the wake of the collapse of sugar prices after World War I. Though Rafael had established a lucrative textile business in Havana, all the money that he had gradually accumulated had now been lost. Second, there was no significant Sephardi community in Havana, although the Levis lived in a house at Inquisidor 14 in Old Havana, across the street from the *Unión Israelita Chevet Ahim*. When the Levis arrived in Havana in 1910, fearing anti-Semitism, they adopted Margot's less-Jewish-sounding maiden name, Abouaf, as their surname and told people that they were French rather than Jewish. Given their past sojourn in France, performing Frenchness was not difficult. The

Levis' only child, Elvira, was enrolled in a Catholic school, but when, in 1922, at the age of 15, she began to attend Mass with her Catholic friends, that was the final straw for her mother, Margot. Margot insisted that the family return to Constantinople so that Elvira could be surrounded by Jewish relatives and learn to claim Judaism.

The Levis' plan was successful: after two years in Constantinople and socializing with other Jews, Elvira professed the Jewish faith. Her father, upon arrival, had purchased a large building that he named "Levihan." However, in 1924, one year after the creation of the Republic of Turkey, rumors began to circulate that Jewish-owned property in Turkey would be confiscated by the new government. Only two years earlier, Turkey had issued a ruling that in certain cases, the goods and property of "those who had deserted Turkey during the war" would be given to Muslim migrants from the Balkans or to the children of "martyrs" killed during the war.[15] Although the 1923 Treaty of Lausanne, which brought the Turkish Republic into existence, ostensibly guaranteed that non-Muslim property owners in Turkey would retain their property, the rumors that the government was acting against the treaty's minority protections proved to be a powerful motivator for migrating once again. The Levis, fearing appropriation of their property, quickly sold their building at a great loss and returned to Cuba in 1924. In 1926, Elvira and her mother traveled to Mexico, where they had a number of relatives, to find a husband for Elvira in Mexico's larger Sephardi community.[16]

For the nascent Turkish Republic, faced with massive rebuilding and nationalizing projects, religious minorities presented an obstacle to creating a homogenous Turkish nation. This was not a uniquely Turkish problem. The "minority problem" loomed large over the postwar deliberations and treaties dictating new borders and political structures. The Great Powers had been concerned with minority protection since 1878, when religious difference was the primary criterion for determining minority status, although the protection of minorities was sometimes less about safeguarding individuals and communities and more about having a pretext for gaining influence in other lands. By the Paris Peace Conference of 1919, "minority" peoples were defined by a descriptive formula of "race, language, and religion," which deliberately avoided the potentially explosive term "national," with its connotations of claims to self-determination.[17] The minority problem was deemed particularly salient within the 'war-breeding zone' of the dismembered Habsburg, Prussian, Ottoman, and Russian empires, and journalists, diplomats, and scholars fervently asserted that European peace and prosperity depended upon adequately settling this problem.[18] The guarantees of minority protection that emerged from these international treaties often had the opposite of the intended effect, however, with the stipulations viewed as unwanted infringements on national sovereignty that granted recognized minorities greater privileges than other citizens enjoyed. For Turkey and other post-Ottoman states and mandates, minority protection seemed strikingly similar to the pretense that the Great Powers had used to intervene in Ottoman economics and politics under the guise of the Capitulations.[19] Indeed, Turkish officials argued at Lausanne, if minorities were Turkish citizens, and all Turkish citizens had equal rights, what need was there for special minority protections?[20]

In contrast to other treaties that emerged from the Paris Peace Conference, with their definition of minority in terms of race, language, and religion, the Lausanne Treaty restricted the term to "non-Muslim nationals" living in Turkey.[21] As Tara Zahra notes in her comparison of national classification in French and Czechoslovak borderlands, French policies of national classification aimed to exclude those identified as Germans from the French nation, while officials in Czechoslovakia classified many self-declared Germans as Czechoslovaks against their will, to create the impression of a strong Czechoslovak minority.[22] The Treaty of Lausanne and the minority rights it ostensibly accorded offered protections for certain groups of Turkish citizens—Armenian and Greek Orthodox Christians, and Jews. Simultaneously, it negated the existence of other non-majority groups within the new Turkish Republic, most notably the substantial number of Kurds, thereby failing to extend protection over language and education to them. Other religious minority groups, including Assyrian and Chaldean Christians, were also omitted from the treaty's interpretation.[23]

The topics covered by the Lausanne Treaty ranged from international borders and control over waterways to the designations of nationality and minority protections. Articles 37 through 45 of the Lausanne Treaty addressed non-Muslim minorities. Article 38 noted that "the Turkish government undertakes to assure full and complete protection of life and liberty to all inhabitants of Turkey without distinction of birth, nationality, language, race or religion," and that "non-Moslem minorities will enjoy full freedom of movement and of emigration." Other articles promised equality before the law, freedom to communicate in any language, and adequate facilities "for the oral use of their own language before the courts"; the freedom to establish and manage charitable, religious, educational, and social institutions, with the right to exercise their own religion and use their own language therein; the right to settle questions of family and personal status law in accordance with their own customs; and protection of churches, synagogues, cemeteries, and other religious sites.[24] By the mid-1920s, first Jews and then Armenians and Greeks had relinquished the protections assured in the Treaty of Lausanne in the name of being equal citizens, but even prior to that, minority protection provisions were at times most observed in the breach.

In eastern Europe, Jews were often at the center of discussions over minority protection in newly created states.[25] In the Treaty of Lausanne, Jews as non-Muslim nationals figured into the discussion, but Armenians and Greek Orthodox communities were perceived and treated as particularly "suspect."[26] Jews were cited as a model minority for not having collaborated with outside forces, in contrast to Greek Orthodox and Armenian Ottomans.[27] Disloyal minorities were held partially responsible for Ottoman failure. İsmet [İnönü], the principal delegate representing Turkey at Lausanne and the future prime minister, viewed non-Muslim communities as potential fifth columns that might become weapons in the hands of foreigners and work against the interests of Turkish stability.[28] Greek Orthodox and Armenians in particular were seen as desirous of appropriating "Turkish" territory in their quests for national sovereignty, and memories of minority collaboration with Allied occupying forces remained fresh.[29]

The Lausanne Accords stipulated "unmixing" the peoples of the Aegean through a population exchange between Greece and Turkey based on ethnoreligious, rather than linguistic, categories; as the historian Laura Robson notes, "minority protection and minority expulsion had become two sides of the same coin."[30] An estimated 1.2 million Greek Orthodox residents of the Turkish Republic were relocated to Greece between 1923 and 1924, while approximately three hundred and fifty thousand Muslims were relocated to Turkey. The Dönme, a syncretic religious sect based in Salonica composed of the descendants of seventeenth-century Jewish converts to Islam, were included as Muslims in this exchange, while Jews were not.³¹ Greek Orthodox residents of Istanbul, called *établis*, were permitted to remain in Turkey, although this was a product of much debate. The Treaty of Lausanne legitimized the forced migrations of hundreds of thousands of people while juridifying the dispossession that had already occurred.³² While Lausanne guaranteed protection for recognized minorities within Turkey, the population exchange between Greece and Turkey underscored the fact that the absence of certain populations was not undesirable in the pursuit of national stability.

Key within the Lausanne Treaty's articles on minority protection was the provision stipulating free movement and emigration of minorities. Although the treaty presented this as protection for rights of movement, the Turkish officials responsible for drafting this language viewed minority emigration as a desired outcome to aid homogenization of the nationalizing state. In 1923, Rıza Nur Bey, the minister of health and one of the Turkish architects of the Lausanne Accords, explained to the Turkish parliament that the treaty had deliberately included clauses on migration. Immigration was to be left open to those deemed helpful for security and public order. But, as Rıza Nur explained, "We are particularly open to emigration. Let them go, their leaving is what we want." He went on to assert that "[m]inorities will not stay." When another parliamentarian mentioned Jews explicitly, Nur noted that "there are thirty thousand Jews in Istanbul. Up to this point, they are people who have not caused injury"—prompting an uproar from listeners, to which he responded, "concerning the Jews, they are people who will go wherever they are pulled. Of course, I would say it would be better if they weren't [here]."³³ Even though Rıza Nur Bey did not see Jews as having harmed Turkey in the past—in explicit contrast to the Armenians and Greek Orthodox—their continued presence in Turkey was not desirable.

Some Jewish families followed the Greeks when they left, although many others had fled from Thrace to Constantinople during World War I or during Greece's subsequent occupation.³⁴ Other Jews, from towns that had been at the center of hostilities, had chosen to emigrate entirely upon armistice; Mexican records attest to a spike in Sephardi migration from former Ottoman territories during the years after World War I and the early years of the Turkish Republic.³⁵ The Turkish government initially sought to prevent Jews who had fled to Istanbul while their towns were under Greek occupation from returning to their places of origin, perhaps as a means of reducing the presence of those deemed potentially disloyal in border regions.[36] While Lausanne protected minorities in Turkey, the state used the encouragement of voluntary emigration and controlling where minorities could live as a means to shape the Turkish nation.

The compulsory expulsion of Greeks in 1923–1924 and the earlier Armenian genocide aided the homogenization of the Turkish nation along lines that conflated religion and ethnicity. The Turkish government sought to fill positions of economic prominence vacated by departed minorities with Turkish Muslim merchants, a continuation of earlier CUP nationalist economic policies that had attempted to forge a Turkish Muslim commercial bourgeoisie at the expense of non-Muslims and foreigners.[37] At the same time, though Article 88 of the Turkish constitution articulated that "the people of Turkey, regardless of religion or race, are Turks as regards citizenship," Turkish parliamentary debates led to the assertion that not all Turkish citizens were members of the Turkish nation, thereby institutionalizing a gap between Turkish citizenship and Turkish nationality.[38] This peripheralized non-Muslims within the discourse and practice of the new state's developing national agenda, casting them as native foreigners.[39] By 1927, embracing "Turkish language and culture" became the main principle of the Republican People's Party and a key fulcrum around which Turkish national identity was articulated. This meant that minority languages should no longer be spoken in public and that the minority privileges that marked religious minorities as distinct from other Turkish citizens had to be relinquished.[40] The conceptualization of Turkish citizenship was intertwined with the fabrication of a new Turkish identity that hinged upon acceptance of a monolithic culture and rejection of ethnic or subcultural identities and foreign citizenship.[41] Such policies excluded religious and ethnic minorities, who became the target of increasingly fervent Turkification projects as the 1920s progressed.

Not all Jews in Turkey possessed Turkish citizenship, a legacy of historic tax advantages given to non-Ottoman subjects under the Capitulations and the recent division of Anatolia among Allied powers.[42] As the territory of Turkey was consolidated, the Turkish state regulated the movement of non-nationals and stripped Turkish citizenship from Jews who had acquired Italian nationality during the Italian occupation. Several Sephardim from

Rhodes who possessed Italian citizenship were forbidden to conduct trade in the Turkish port city of Finike or to continue in posts at AIU schools in Izmir unless they acquired Turkish citizenship.[43] Others, who had possessed Ottoman nationality but acquired Italian nationality while living under Italian occupation, had their Turkish nationality stripped from them following Turkish reacquisition of these territories. Still others voluntarily accepted Turkish nationality and relinquished their Italian papers.[44]

Lausanne Abroad

Turkey's efforts to fix the boundaries of Turkish citizenship after the Treaty of Lausanne extended beyond its borders. In November of 1926, the Mexican legation in Italy transmitted a request from the Turkish embassy in Rome to the Secretary of Foreign Relations in Mexico. Turkey wanted to ascertain the number of Turkish citizens currently in Mexico, including those from provinces of the former Ottoman Empire "separated from Turkey since 1914" who had not opted for new nationalities.[45] This request for information was conveyed to the governors of Mexico's states, who then transmitted it to local municipalities, some of which conducted investigations and reported their results back to Mexico City.

The rationale for this request can be gleaned from its timing and language. The Treaty of Lausanne, signed on July 24, 1923, contained a number of articles that dealt explicitly with the question of the current nationality of former Ottoman subjects. This forcible fixing of national classification was widespread in postwar European states, often articulated in postwar treaties or hashed out in immediate postwar practice.[46] Article 32 of the Treaty of Lausanne detailed that those who resided in "territory detached from Turkey ... and differing in race from the majority of the population of such territory" had two years to opt for the nationality of one of the states in which "the majority of the population is of the same race as the person exercising the right to opt, subject to the consent of that State."[47] Those who "are habitually resident abroad," Article 34 clarified, likewise had two years—later extended to three—to "opt for the nationality of the territory of which they are natives, if they belong to the race of the majority of the population of that territory." Article 36 stipulated that the status of married women was governed by that of their husbands, and children under eighteen by that of their parents.[48]

Nationality, as defined by the Treaty of Lausanne, was something that individuals of Ottoman provenance who resided abroad had to opt for within the set period of time. Unless they exercised the "nationality option," they defaulted to Turkish citizenship, an eventuality that the Turkish state did not want for the erstwhile empire's Arab subjects. The language of the treaty made it clear that individuals' nationalities should coincide with the implicitly understood racial character of the incipient nation-states. Migrants abroad could claim nationality either in the new states emerging in their homelands or in their countries of domicile, both options contingent upon acceptance by state authorities. In the event that the homeland was under a foreign mandate, as was the case for Syria, Lebanon, and Palestine, the mandate authority had to process claims and ensure the rights of migrants to exercise their nationality option. France capitalized on this moment to impose a French colonial citizenship in lieu of actual nationality.[49] Although the opportunity for individuals to opt for a nationality expired in 1926, by that point most Ottoman Arabs abroad still had not claimed their status as Syrians, Lebanese, or Palestinian. Émigrés from what had become the British Mandate of Palestine were required to repatriate within nine months in order to claim Palestinian passports, a process that was often made difficult by the lack of recognized documentation on which they could travel.[50] Individuals' decisions regarding opting for a certain nationality were connected to repatriation claims but also to their political views regarding various nationalist movements. By 1926, those who had not opted in were supposed to default to Turkish nationality, but instead they ended up in a liminal status, most of them ultimately taking citizenship in their country of domicile.[51] This conferral of citizenship was, however, dependent upon the agreement of the state in which they lived.

Turkey's 1926 request regarding the number of Turkish nationals resident in Mexico was likely in response to the impending deadline imposed by the Treaty of Lausanne for opting into nationality; earlier that year, French authorities, working together with local *Mahjari* notables, had instigated a scramble to register formerly Ottoman subjects within Mexico, relying on *Mahjari* commercial and patronage networks to disseminate information.[52] The request transmitted through Rome expressed no interest in former Ottoman residents who had already opted for other nationalities but only in those who maintained Turkish nationality, whether by design or accident. But the information on Turkish nationals that Mexican municipalities conveyed often did include details on former Ottomans who had registered with the French or British embassies in opting for Syrian, Lebanese, or Palestinian status. Most who maintained Turkish nationality were Jews, who, unlike Syrians or Lebanese, had no proto-state into which they fit in accordance with the stipulations of the Treaty of Lausanne. Such individuals were not explicitly discussed within the context of former Ottoman émigrés exerting the nationality option, but were defined elsewhere in the Treaty of Lausanne as "non-Moslem minorities" or "non-Moslem nationals" of Turkey.

Mexican municipalities did not all respond in equal detail. Tacuba de Morelos, in the Federal District, submitted a 33-page-long list of foreigners residing in the district and suggested that the requested information could be gleaned therefrom—the list was not appended to the archival file.[53] Many municipalities simply noted that there were no Turkish subjects there. Others, like Cárdenas in San Luís Potosí, clarified that "there do not exist subjects of Turkish nationality, but the Arab foreigners resident in this place are inscribed as Syrio-Lebanese, Syrians, and from Palestine, these nations being under the English and French protectorates."[54] Irapuato, Guanajuato received its information from a local Syrio-Lebanese man, who explained that "he did not know of anyone who had not yet inscribed himself with the French consulate" in Mexico City.[55] In a similar vein, the municipality of San Pedro, Coahuila explained that it had directed its query to several prominent members of the 250-person-large community of "persons of Turkish nationality." These individuals clarified that "we, members of the Syrio-Lebanese community of this city, upon the separation of the provinces from which we originate from the Ottoman Empire, opt to adopt the new nationality that our independence concedes us." This was also the view of the other members of their colony, "some from Mount Lebanon and others from Palestine."[56] Reliance on local Syrio-Lebanese communities for information may perhaps have yielded accurate numbers, but also potentially resulted in the undercount of those, particularly Ladino-speaking Jews, who were not networked into their communities and were the most likely to retain Turkish nationality.

The reported information did not always map onto state borders. San Luís Potosí provided the name, age, marital status, occupation, and date of arrival for some eighty individuals of "Sirio-Libanes" nationality, eight of whose nationality was "Sirio-Caldeo," four "Sirio-Trípoli," six "Siriaca," two "Mesopotamia," and just one "turca."[57] The basis for these divisions was unclear—was it how these individuals self-identified or how Mexican municipal officials categorized them?—nor was it clear what current nationality these individuals possessed. Meanwhile, the response from Xicohténcatl, Tlaxcala noted that there "exists no *raza* from Turkey," presenting their findings in racial rather than national terms.[58] The discursive imprecision of the term *turco* in the vernacular complicated responses, as with the results from Tenabo, Campeche, which noted that "there are five *turcos*, who recognized the French government, given that Syria Mount Lebanon is their country."[59]

Those most likely to claim Turkish nationality, as already noted, were Jews. In Iguala, Guerrero and Niltepec, Oaxaca, a small handful whose names suggest Arab origins retained Turkish nationality.[60] However, in Saltillo, Coahuila, an area with a large population of formerly Ottoman subjects, only six, all of whom bore clearly Jewish names, were listed as being Turkish in 1926: Moisés and Sarra Ycasday [Jasday], Roberto Machulan, Salomón Togel, Victor Calderón, and Salomón Bemarras.[61] In León, Guanajuato, there were two nuclear families of Jews whose names were provided and two women of Turkish nationality married to foreigners—one to a Syrio-Lebanese and one to a Greek.[62] Smaller municipalities might hold only one family claiming Turkish nationality, like the three Jewish individuals in Acámbaro, Guanajuato.[63] Veracruz provided a list of ninety Turkish nationals, all but three of whom had recognizably Sephardi names. Of these, all but eight had arrived in Mexico after 1921 and two-thirds after the establishment of the Turkish Republic.[64]

Even as Turkish officials expressed interest in identifying how many Turkish nationals lived abroad and who they were, Mexican officials expressed interest in attracting Turkish Jewish migrants, specifically. Scarlatt Tottu, mandated with establishing a Mexican consular post in Constantinople in 1923, found that as a result of regime change in both countries, the 1910 agreement between Mexico and the Ottoman Empire had been abrogated.[65] The new convention, written in 1924 and revised in 1926, delineated the rights of nationals in the other country. Each country had the right to authorize or prohibit immigration, but nationals of each state had the right to remain in the area of the other, to come and go freely, and to exercise all types of industry and commerce except those that were reserved for nationals only on the basis of laws, rules, or, in the case of Turkey, custom. The treaty stipulated that only the courts of the state from which nationals originated should deal with all matters of personal status, including inheritance. Lahana's intestate case had never belonged in the Mexican legal system, even though she died in Mexico.[66]

As honorary consul, Tottu sought to develop commerce between Mexico and Turkey. He invited prominent Turkish businessmen, particularly those in the tobacco trade, to his office on the fashionable Sıraselviler Caddesi in hopes of sparking trade between the two states. Tottu also sought to increase Mexico's standing in Turkey by supplying Turkey with medicine against typhoid and yellow fever.[67] He published numerous propaganda pieces in the Turkish, Armenian, Jewish, Russian, Greek, and French presses of Constantinople boasting of Mexico's riches and the constant progress of its industry. These articles were designed to entice immigration to Mexico. However, only 167 migrants left Turkey for Mexico in the entire year of 1924. By April of 1925, 40 migrants had relocated to Mexico. Although Tottu noted that of the handful who departed monthly for Mexico, most were Russian refugees, Armenians, or Jews, in reality almost all were Jewish. In 1924, he noted, only two of the migrants had been Turks—he most likely meant Muslim—and one Greek.[68]

The Mexican consul general in Vienna, who had demanded that Tottu's vacancy in Bucharest be filled by someone who was not Jewish "because the Jews are very much hated in Europe, they are immoral in their thirst for gold, and, not having the notion of *patria*, they care very little about the ruin of the world in light of their full coffers," saw Tottu's mission in Constantinople as a means of encouraging Turkish migration to Mexico. One of his reports explained that the Turkish lira exchanged quite favorably with the Mexican peso and that, consequently, "the Turk can emigrate more easily with his own funds and means to establish himself by his own account in another country." The consul general of Argentina in Constantinople informed him that Argentina issued dozens of visas every day for Turkish émigrés destined for the Southern Cone. Mexico should not miss out on attracting these migrants. A particular group of the population of Turkey would make attractive immigrants to Mexico:

> There are in Turkey a considerable number of Spanish Jews (*judíos españoles*), of those expelled from the Iberian Peninsula four hundred years ago, who conserve the Castilian language and who, in spite of being Jews, are not of the same abysmal moral condition as those of the north of Europe, given that these do assimilate and they are entirely equal to the Spanish. If some of these were to arrive in Mexico, they would not cause the damage that the others do to whatever state they tread on.[69]

In the wake of the Mexican Revolution, Mexico actively sought the arrival of new immigrants, particularly those who were economically solvent, who could propel the growth of Mexican commerce and industry, and who were perceived to be racially assimilable. An influential essay published in 1925, *La Raza Cósmica* by the Mexican intellectual Jose Vasconcelos, was ostensibly an attempt to counter conceptions of scientific racism and ethnic superiority propagated by Darwinists and others in the late nineteenth and early twentieth centuries. Nonetheless, embedded within the idea of creating a new "fifth race" in Latin America that was an amalgamation of the best qualities of European and indigenous was the necessity of selecting migrants who had desirable qualities to contribute to the formation of the mestizo race and the new Mexican nation. And in spite of the rhetoric of *mestizaje*, Mexico's economic and political elites often remained criollo, of Spanish or European descent, indexing class through race.[70] As the Mexican consul general from Vienna indicated, migrants should be able to fund their own migration and establish themselves financially in Mexico. They should have a strong sense of *patria*, which Jews did not, and should be racially beneficial and assimilable, which Jews were not. As Mexican immigration policies throughout the 1920s and 1930s would indicate, those of perceived Iberian descent, whether from the Iberian Peninsula itself or from Latin America, were seen as the most desirable because of their racial and cultural assimilability. In spite of the consul general's clear dislike of Jews, he drew on language that echoed the Spanish philo-sephardism of the early twentieth century, noting that Sephardi Jews were as Spanish as they were Jewish, assimilable, and not detrimental to Mexico's national future.[71]

At the same moment that Mexican authorities increasingly distinguished between the undesirability of Jewish immigrants in general and the desirability of Sephardi immigration on account of a perceived shared Iberian heritage and language, the Turkish government began to articulate policies that castigated Sephardi Jews in the newly constituted Turkish Republic precisely because their continued use of a Hispanic language and their perceived cultural and national affinities with Spain marked them as unassimilable and non-Turkish. In other words, while the Iberian heritage of Sephardi Jews complicated their efforts to Turkify in an era of increasing Turkish nation-building, it created a brief affinity between the Mexican government and Sephardi migrants. Small numbers of Sephardim had chosen to migrate to Mexico over the previous two decades due to the economic possibilities that Mexico offered. Turkey's increasingly stringent Turkification policies, targeting religious and ethnic minorities for either outright assimilation or the public appearance of such through the downplaying of religious and linguistic difference, while also removing those minorities from positions of economic prominence, propelled an increasing number of Sephardim to migrate. The closing of the American immigration gates through the Emergency Quota Act of 1921 and the Johnson-Reed Act of 1924, economic downturn in Cuba, and Mexico's relatively lax immigration policies until the end of the 1920s thrust a record number of Sephardi migrants towards the ports of Veracruz and Tampico. In Mexico, Sephardi Jews relied on transnational familial and commercial networks to acclimate to their new environment, translating the cultural affinity that they perceived with Mexico into economic upward mobility and the increasing acquisition of Mexican nationality.

Individual decisions to migrate were complex, informed by broad economic concerns and public discourse over how Jews could continue to belong in a nationalizing Turkish state. As individuals migrated, whether voluntarily or through compulsion, they left behind property and businesses, disrupting economic patterns as towns with large minority populations suddenly found themselves without pharmacists, physicians, and shopkeepers—occupations that had traditionally been filled by Greek Orthodox and Armenian subjects.

In a 1924 parliamentary discussion of the property rights of emigrating individuals who did not hold Turkish citizenship, it was explained that emigrating Armenians and Greek Orthodox should not benefit from these protocols. Armenians had wrought too much damage in eastern Anatolia, while Greek Orthodox subjects were blamed for wreaking havoc on western Anatolia during the War of Independence. The parliament could not simply make restrictions explicitly targeting the Greek Orthodox and Armenians, however, and so the measures were couched more obliquely. The speaker, Hasan Fehmi Bey, a representative of Gümüşhane, noted that prior to the National Struggle, trade had been in the hands of Greeks and Armenians. Non-Muslims still possessed large amounts of capital. Zeki Bey, another representative of Gümüşhane, challenged Fehmi about the Jews, asking if the Jews would be included in these protocols since "[t]he Jews are the ones sucking this state dry like leeches." Fehmi reiterated that the Armenians and Greeks were to be held accountable since "we saw it as our right" because of the disasters that Armenians and Greeks had wrought in prior hostilities. He left it open to the government to decide whether or not to include Jews in these restrictions, and the protocol remained in murky language.[72] While there were no state policies that actually stripped non-Muslims who remained in Turkey of their commercial or domestic property, there was likely to have been a great deal of confusion among residents of Turkey as to the seizure and redistribution of minority-owned property.

As Hasan Fehmi Bey and Zeki Bey's comments indicate, the Turkification of the economy, through shifting capital from the hands of religious minorities to those of Turkish Muslims, was central to the Turkish government's encouragement of minority emigration. It was expected that Muslim Turks would come to fill the positions that Greek Orthodox and Armenians left vacant. However, though some Muslims did become prominent businessmen in this period, so did a number of Jews, marking the latter as the next targets of hostility.[73] Claims that Jews were on their way to monopolizing Turkish commerce and industry were bandied about in the Turkish press. Such views were not universal. In 1923, the journal *Halk* from Adana responded to opinions of Jews as parasitic, assuring readers that "Jews are our compatriots and should enjoy the same rights as the Muslims." If Jews earned money, it was because they knew how to do so, having been habituated to it from childhood. In contrast to Armenians and Greeks, Jews proved themselves to be loyal citizens of whatever state in which they dwelt and had defended Turkish interests and individuals during the Balkan Wars. Jews could teach Turks how to engage in commerce effectively, and rather than worrying about Jews who kept money within Turkey, Turks ought to be worried about foreigners who drained Turkish capital.[74] Popular boycotts of Jewish merchants and employees sprouted up around Bursa in 1923. Jewish employees were fired, Jews forcibly expelled from some towns, and Muslims warned not to frequent Jewish-owned stores. In spite of reassurances from the authorities that those responsible would be held accountable, anti-Jewish activities in the region did not cease.[75]

The government sought to Turkify the economy by removing religious minorities from certain professions, further drawing the distinction that not all Turkish citizens were part of the Turkish nation. In 1923, the Commissioner of Public Works warned that if Greek Orthodox, Armenian, and Jewish employees in certain economic sectors were not let go, the government would stop the trams of Constantinople. They should be replaced by Turks—meaning Turkish Muslims—and not by those who held Turkish nationality alone.[76] By 1924, Jews and other religious minorities had been removed from positions in governmental administration, railways, and tramways, barred from admittance into commercial societies and forbidden to engage in occupations that Turks exercised, such as tanning and ironworking.[77] In a report to the AIU, David Fresco, the editor of *El Tiempo*, railed against these changes. Depriving individuals of their rights on account of their race and religion was incompatible with justice, honor, universal conscience, and Islam's principle of tolerance. "We, who have had an exemplary faithfulness; we, who have participated profoundly in the pains of the nation; we, who have bent for the triumph of its cause, deserve completely different treatment!" he fumed.[78] This enforced economic Turkification propelled a number of Jews who had lost employment to migrate to places like Mexico where they foresaw increased economic possibility or where they had friends or relatives who could help them gain a livelihood. In the words of the brother-in-law of a Jewish railway worker who lost his job due to Turkification policies and who saw little economic opportunity for himself in Turkey, Mexico "was more or less good," enough of an endorsement for the railway worker to relocate with his wife and child. Particularly for those who had dedicated their careers to aspects of public works, there remained few other options.[79]

The Turkish state and Turkish public opinion held that the minority rights established in the Lausanne Accords marked religious minorities as distinct from broader Turkish society. Separate educational and legal systems and, particularly, the continued use of languages other than Turkish, prevented these minorities from assimilating into the Turkish nation. As early as 1923, increased state intervention in minority schools mandated that certain subjects be taught only by Turkish Muslim instructors and that the Turkish language should become the language of instruction, to the detriment of French in the AIU schools.[80] In 1924, the Ministry of Public Education called for Jewish schools to relinquish all connection to the AIU. It decreed that although the minority rights had guaranteed that minorities could teach in their mother tongues, it was Hebrew that was the mother tongue of Jews, and these Jewish schools were teaching classes in French, rather than Hebrew. The Ministry of Public Education declared that French should be phased out of Jewish schools, to be replaced either by the Hebrew mother tongue [*lisan-i maderzad*] or by Turkish.[81] These demands that Jews only teach in their "mother tongue," Hebrew, which was not actively spoken, or in Turkish undermined the autonomy of Jewish institutions.

By late 1925, perhaps due to external pressure, the Turkish Jewish community had agreed to relinquish its rights to separate personal status laws and to follow the new Turkish civil code, which mandated the separation of religious and governmental affairs.[82] Soon after, the Armenian and Greek Orthodox communities followed suit.[83] For some, the nationalization of the court system created problems as the Turkish government sought to reconcile its civil code with the prescriptions of shari'ah law and the sometimes-conflicting minority legal codes. In 1927, Estrea Elnekave appealed a lower court's ruling that had allowed her husband, Salomon, to divorce her without her consent using the *talak-i selâse*, a Muslim form of a final, irrevocable divorce. Although the new legal system required that the Elnekaves conduct their divorce in a civil court before Turkish authorities, this civil court seemed to continue to employ shari'ah precepts and to be unaware that the *talak-i selâse* was not valid for Jews. Therefore, Estrea charged, her divorce was invalid.[84] Although the brief did not contain the final ruling, the fact that Estrea's appeal was published by a governmental press in Ottoman suggests that governmental legal authorities found this appeal to be noteworthy and its content worth spreading beyond the Turkish Jewish community.

Even after they relinquished some of their minority rights, the public pressure on Jews only intensified. On February 18, 1926, a mere day after the implementation of the new civil legal code, several organs of the Turkish press simultaneously published front-page articles attacking Turkish Jews for a letter of loyalty that had allegedly been sent to the Spanish government several months prior on the occasion of the anniversary of Columbus's discovery of America.[85] The following day, *El Tiempo* published a translation of an article from the Turkish periodical *Cumhuriyet* as an example of the form this "violent attack" had taken. *Cumhuriyet* alleged that three hundred Jewish notables from the intellectual class of Izmir and Istanbul had written a letter to the Spanish government attesting that "all of the Jews of the Orient consider themselves Spaniards and that they profit from these manifestations of the race." Jewish ingratitude for Turkish protection and their continued attachment to Spain, according to *Cumhuriyet*, had earlier manifested when a Spanish opera troop performed in Istanbul and Sephardim warmly applauded. At the time, this had been attributed to Jews' understanding of Spanish. However, following this Jewish profession of affiliation with Spain, "like those women who love that much more the husbands who beat them," it was clear that Turkish Jews continued to identify as Spanish, as part of the Spanish race, and were not loyal to Turkey. Their emigration, therefore, was encouraged: "The doors are open. Go ahead, *bâzergânlar*, to Spain and to the place that you want," wrote *Cumhuriyet*, employing a slur that referenced Jews' propensity to drive hard bargains.[86] The article simultaneously marked Jews as traitorous for an alleged attachment to Spain in spite of Turkish hospitality, as foreign through their celebration of Spanish cultural forms rather than Turkish equivalents, and as economically exploitative, unwelcome in Turkey on all accounts. Meanwhile, other Turkish-language press organs also asserted that the Jewish community of Turkey should be expelled. The periodical *Akşam* elaborated that "Turkish nationals who work for submission to a foreign state, who affix their signature to the bottom of such a document, are considered a species of traitor to the homeland. If we do not condemn them to death, the lightest punishment one can inflict on them is to lead them beyond our borders." The incident incriminated the totality of the Jewish community.[87] The collective responsibility of all Jews within Turkey's borders entailed that they collectively be expelled from Turkish territory.

The Jewish communities of Turkey reacted immediately to allegations of disloyalty and calls for the wholesale expulsion of Jews from Turkey. The chief rabbi went to the *vali* in Istanbul, who promised an investigation into the affair, though the infamous missive itself was never published nor the results of the investigation released.[88] Jewish notables including Abraham Galanté, Henri Soriano, Gad Franco, Simon Lévy, and Nissim Mazliah went to Ankara to assure Prime Minister İsmet [İnönü] that the Jews of Turkey had never sent such a letter and were entirely loyal to Turkey.[89] Meanwhile, representatives of the Jewish communities of Edirne,[90] Ortaköy-Beşiktaş,[91] Kadiköy,[92] and Galata-Pera-Şişli[93] reaffirmed Jewish loyalty to Turkey and gratitude for Turkey's hospitality by publishing declarations of loyalty in the French-language Turkish press.

Philon Fresco, a son of *El Tiempo*'s editor and the secretary of the Jewish community of Galata-Pera-Şişli, who had signed the communiqué of loyalty published in *La République*—the French-language version of *Cumhuriyet*—offered another reaction to this affair. In a letter written to the AIU, Fresco asserted that the affair was a calumny engineered to pressure the Jewish community to renounce further minority rights, an allegation he repeated in a letter to the director of the *Jewish Chronicles* of London. He noted that according to reliable information, the Turkish government had demanded from the Jewish delegation in Ankara that the Jews officially renounce the minority rights guaranteed in the Treaty of Lausanne while declaring to the national and international public that this renunciation had been spontaneous and not demanded by the government.[94] Supporting Fresco's contention that this affair had been fabricated as a means of encouraging the cultural, institutional, and linguistic Turkification of Jews in Turkey was the fact that concurrent to the Jewish delegation's foray to Ankara to affirm their loyalty to the Turkish Republic, the Ministry of Public Education demanded that the hours of Turkish education in Jewish schools increase and the hours of French education decrease.[95] Henri Soriano, one of the Jewish delegates to Ankara, assured the Turkish public that his delegation had promised that "the Jews will adopt Turkish culture and teaching in our scholastic institutions." This prompted the Turkish periodical *Milliyet* to note that Jewish compatriots understood better than "the other elements" that "the goal of the Republic is to found a Turkish state, united and pure," and that "as long as the non-Muslim elements live apart from their Turkish compatriots, enjoy rights and privileges superior to those that their Turkish compatriots possess legally, and speak a different language, with different ideas and cultures, one should anticipate similar misunderstandings."[96] Whether or not segments of the Turkish government had a direct hand in manufacturing or propagating press reports of continued Jewish affiliation with Spain,[97] Turkish Jews' relinquishment of institutional autonomy and conformity to Turkification programs that subsumed their distinct religious and cultural traditions played into governmental needs to forge a "united and pure" Turkish state.

In the face of intensifying pressure on Jews and other religious and ethnic minorities to conform to Turkification processes and to relinquish their occupations in favor of Turkish Muslims, a growing number of Jews, like Elvira Levi and her parents, sought new shores. The Turkish government, charged with the task of creating a new, modernizing state populated by a united and homogenous citizenry, did not attempt to dissuade religious minorities who sought to leave. Members of the Turkish governmental apparatus, like Rıza Nur Bey, viewed the emigration of religious minorities as desirable, a means of homogenizing the new Turkish state that augmented internal efforts to promulgate Turkish language and culture among religious and ethnic minorities. Mandating the exclusion of religious minorities from certain economic sectors while simultaneously pressuring religious minorities to relinquish the minority rights guaranteed them in the Lausanne Accords were means the state employed to undermine the autonomy of religious minorities. The emigration of Sephardim and other religious minorities only increased throughout the 1920s as Turkification efforts intensified, marginalizing them from the Turkish economic structure and from the Turkish nation itself. While some emigrants sought destinations in Europe or the United States, a growing number of Sephardim set their sights on Latin America, particularly Mexico.

Sephardi Migrants between the United States and Mexico

On February 2nd, 1922, the New-York-based Ladino periodical *La Luz* published a front-page article penned by "our friend" Albert Avigdor entitled

"Porke los Sefaradim Deven Pensar en Meksiko."[98] Avigdor, the editor explained, had arrived in New York five years earlier, dedicating himself to Spanish publications, export, and the progress of Sephardim in New York, and had been one of the most active Sephardi members of the B'nai B'rith lodge. However, Avigdor had decided to leave the United States. He chose Mexico as his destination, because "in all the countries in which I have traveled, there is no other that has left me with such a good impression as Mexico, in regard to the favorable conditions that this country offers to Sephardi Jews." Avigdor encouraged his Sephardi brethren to follow his example, elucidating numerous reasons why "Sephardi youth who have some confidence in themselves" would have "the best opportunity of making a better situation for themselves [in Mexico] than in any other country in the world."

Though Avigdor listed economic motivations, including Mexico's "incalculable" potential wealth in agriculture, the oil wells and mines "that have made many American millionaires rich," and favorably compared the Mexican economy to that of France and Italy in spite of the generally negative world economic situation, the reasons for migration that he emphasized had far more to do with perceived social and cultural similarities between Mexico and the familiar world that Sephardi migrants had left behind than fiduciary concerns. A shared Iberian heritage, resulting from the almost simultaneous creation of the Sephardi diaspora and the *puevlo meksikano* in 1492, would aid Sephardi migrants in Mexico and marked Mexico as a desired destination.[99]

The commonalities between Sephardim and Mexicans manifested both linguistically and behaviorally. First, Avigdor explained that Sephardim would not encounter difficulties in understanding the language. Mexican Spanish, he postulated, "although it contains some Indian words, possibly resembles our Ladino more than the modern Spanish that is spoken in Spain, because it should not be forgotten that the Mexican people of today began to be formed almost at the same time that the Jews were expelled from Spain." He surmised that a Sephardi, with three months of study, could speak Spanish "better than some of the Mexicans of the interior regions." Presumably, Avigdor was contrasting the ease with which Sephardim could acquire Mexican Spanish to the greater difficulty of English, and implying to his readers that Sephardi linguistic skills could enable Sephardim to distinguish themselves from the lower—indigenous—echelons of Mexican society. While Sephardi migrants in the United States occupied the lower rungs of society, those who went to Mexico, by virtue of their linguistic proficiency and their understanding of social and cultural norms, had greater opportunity for upward mobility.

Avigdor explained his characterization of Mexico as a favorable destination for migration in comparison to the United States with a description of behavioral characteristics that Mexicans and Sephardim shared. Mexican social life is "much more active than in the United States," the people "much more pleasant, more hospitable, and also with a courtesy that at times seems exaggerated." Attaining these qualities would not be difficult for a Sephardi because "they already form a part of his character." The customs in Mexico "remind one of the customs of the Levant (Turkey, Greece, etc.)." The pace of business is slower, people wander about, and though they are never content with the government, "they always endure no matter how bad it is." In short, "the country is not in the state of perfection of the great nations of Europe and America, and these nations suffer something more from the state of things than the Sephardi, who is already accustomed to all of this in the country of his birth."[100]

Avigdor presented it as a given that Sephardim, particularly the youth, were eager to migrate. Since the article was published in an American Ladino periodical, Avigdor's target audience seemed to be readers in the New York metropolitan area who were dissatisfied with their lives in the United States. Although scholars have suggested that the Johnson-Reed Act of 1924 marked the end of large-scale Sephardi migration to the United States and the increased diversion of migrants to Mexico and elsewhere in Latin America, the Emergency Quota Act of 1921 had already partially stanched the flow of Sephardi migrants by limiting immigration of any given nationality to three percent of their number in the 1910 U.S. census. Yet Avigdor made no mention of American legislation in his attempt to advocate Sephardi migration to Mexico, suggesting that his positive view of Mexico as a place where Sephardim could create a future for themselves was not solely based on the increasing difficulty of entering the United States. Avigdor himself had lived in the United States for five years before choosing to relocate. His personal decision to leave the United States had little to do with the recent immigration restrictions, which were not applicable to him.

Avigdor's message would also have been appealing to Sephardim across the Atlantic who faced unprecedented challenges in the territories of the now-defunct Ottoman Empire, as the cities in which they lived were divided among various powers. For many Sephardim, the necessity of rebuilding homes and livelihoods in lands marked by chaos, adopting new nationalities and languages, and acclimating to the demands that new national states placed on them, propelled them to look further afield for a place, like the Mexico that Avigdor described, where they could make a "better situation" for themselves.

In the years immediately after the Mexican Revolution, the Mexican government encouraged immigration, particularly for agricultural workers. It looked to immigrants to increase Mexico's economic growth, in spite of the socialist-progressive plan of development that the revolution heralded.[101] The demographer Sergio DellaPergola argues that Jewish migration follows socioeconomic development and political stability, but Avigdor's explanation that Mexico was a desirable destination for Sephardi youth precisely *because* it was less "perfect" counters DellaPergola's contention that, when given the opportunity to migrate either to a country at the core of the economic world system, like the United States or France, or to a semiperipheral country like Mexico, Jewish migrants would choose the former.[102] As discussed in chapter 1, it was precisely the ways in which Mexico was undeveloped that allowed Sephardim and other Middle Eastern migrants to create economic niches for themselves, facilitating their accrual of capital and their social ascent. In Avigdor's estimation, however, the importance of Sephardi economic interests was second to the ease with which Sephardim, particularly the youth, could adapt to life in Mexico. And while youth were not the only Sephardim migrating in the early 1920s, those under the age of thirty formed the vast majority of migrants.

Scholars have attributed the increase in Sephardi migration to Latin America in the wake of the American closing of the gates of immigration to the desire to gain eventual access to American soil, asserting that Sephardi migrants only remained in those countries due to the lack of opportunity to enter the United States.[103] American immigration restrictions did originally contain a loophole that allowed non-nationals resident in Mexico and Cuba for first one and then five years to bypass quota restrictions. A number of

Sephardim sought to capitalize on this loophole. Some, like David Tacher, who had arrived in Mexico from Constantinople in 1921 and in 1923 sought to migrate to New York where an uncle lived, were prohibited from entry due to the quota against Turkish nationals and sent back to Mexico.[104] Others, like Rafael Fais, who left Salonica in 1919 and sailed from Istanbul to Mexico, then crossed into the United States in 1925 at Laredo under the name Roberto Farias, Jr. and likely an assumed Mexican nationality, used subterfuge to bypass quota restrictions. By 1922, the U.S. State Department was sending complaints to Greece encouraging the implementation of stronger safeguards against the "undesirable emigration" of Sephardim from Salonica to Cuba, many of whom would then attempt to enter the United States illegally.[105] Meanwhile, in a 1925 report from Constantinople, Scarlatt Tottu noted that there were allegedly some migrants in Mexico "who leave from here or any other part of the world" with the aim of entering the United States, though Tottu expressed ignorance of any group in Constantinople that facilitated the entry of foreigners from Mexico into the United States.[106]

By 1924, U.S. State Department restrictions against those who sought to bypass quotas had gone into effect. The Sephardi *Unión Israelita Chevet Ahim* of Havana wrote a letter to the New-York-based Ladino periodical *La Vara* cautioning Sephardim in the United States to warn relatives in Turkey and Greece not to migrate to Cuba in hopes of eventually entering the United States. Due to the previous smuggling of many people, the American government had passed and now enforced more stringent laws. Life in Cuba was incredibly expensive, there was no work due to Cuba's recent economic collapse, and Sephardi youth in their period of florescence and families with small children wandered the streets of Havana in search of a livelihood or a piece of bread.[107]

In spite of the greater enforcement of immigration quotas in the United States, some Jews continued to seek illegal entry across its southern border.[108] It was particularly important for American Jews to stem this trend, because they feared that the arrests of Jewish migrants at the U.S.-Mexican border could be used to cast aspersions on American Jews. American Jewish organizations like B'nai B'rith sought to aid the integration of Jewish migrants in Mexico by creating Spanish language classes and small no-interest loans for recent migrants, in part to prevent illegal Jewish entry into the

United States.¹⁰⁹ However, Rabbi Martin Zielonka's report on arrested Jewish migrants from 1921 reveals that all of them were Ashkenazi.¹¹⁰ While U.S. immigration officials were cautioned to be on the lookout for Jews in general, because "the Jews and other oriental races can easily pass as Spaniards, i.e. Cubans, because of their oriental faces and dark skin," the Ladino language and Sephardi Jews' often ambiguous national origins likely aided their attempts to pass as Mexicans or Cubans.¹¹¹ This provided them with a critical tool for evading American quotas to which Ashkenazi Jews would not have had access, likely explaining the lack of Sephardi Jews among those arrested for illegal entrance.

However, as Avigdor's article indicates, not all Sephardim wanted to enter the United States, and a number of Sephardim who had previously gained access to U.S. territory and documentation chose to migrate to Mexico. In addition to the greater cultural affinities that Avigdor asserted Sephardim would feel with Mexicans due to their shared Iberian heritage, the common Iberian background also meant that Sephardim, given their knowledge of Ladino, did not have to learn a language that was entirely foreign. While most Sephardi migrants were multilingual, English was rarely in their linguistic repertoire, and the prospect of migrating to a country where they did not speak the language dissuaded some.¹¹² "My strongest impression was during my first nights [in Mexico] when I lay down and heard noise in the street of the people speaking Spanish, I would say 'But this city is full of Jews!'" recounted one Sephardi migrant, noting how Spanish made Mexico seem familiar to newly arrived Sephardi migrants for whom a Hispanic language indicated Jewish origins; as noted in the introduction, this was a common refrain among Sephardi migrants.¹¹³ In a similar vein, some who had intended to migrate from Mexico to the United States, upon arrival in Veracruz noted similarities between the Caribbean port city and their Aegean cities of origin and decided to remain in Mexico.¹¹⁴ In the United States, where Sephardim were a small minority of the Jews, the numerical, social, and cultural dominance of Ashkenazi Jews resulted in the marginalization of Sephardi migrants.¹¹⁵ In Mexico, on the other hand, while there was an Ashkenazi-Syrian-Sephardi divide, Sephardim outnumbered their Ashkenazi counterparts in the early 1920s and, as discussed in chapter 2, Sephardi individuals like Isaac Capon played a crucial intermediary role between Mexico's nascent Jewish institutions and the Mexican government.

For some Sephardim who had previously migrated to the United States and found themselves unemployed or working in menial positions, Mexico's less-developed economic structure provided more avenues for advancement. Ashkenazi dominance in American Jewish life and the difficulties of learning English relegated many in the first generation of Sephardi migrants in the United States to menial jobs as bootblacks, vendors, candy peddlers, and sweatshop laborers.[116] The New-York-based Spanish and Portuguese Sisterhood recognized that Sephardim in the United States could benefit from commerce with Latin America, and in 1924 offered free biweekly courses in Castilian Spanish at the Settlement House on the Lower East Side. It noted that these classes would be of special importance to those who wanted to conduct trade with Spanish-speaking countries or who sought positions as correspondents or secretaries in export houses.[117]

While some Sephardim based in the United States conducted trade with Mexico, others chose to relocate to Mexico for financial reasons. Marcos Reinah from the Dardanelles, who will be discussed in greater detail below and whose economic success as a merchant in Mexico six years later would propel jealous competitors to seek his expulsion, in 1917 lived in New York City, where he sold tickets in a movie theater.[118] Similarly, Daniel Montekio from Salonica described himself as a businessman in New York in 1916, but by 1921 he had relocated to Mexico City. There, he was one of the founders of *La Fraternidad*, the Sephardi benevolent association, and established a lucrative business selling imported stoves in a store just west of the Zócalo. This allowed him to accrue the capital necessary to build several apartment buildings in Colonia Roma by 1930.[119] Others, like Moreno Chicorel, who petitioned to be naturalized as a Mexican in 1927 after arriving in Mexico in 1922 and settling in Morelia, Michoacán, had previously lived in the United States for seventeen years. Though Chicorel's petition did not indicate why he sought Mexican nationality, he noted that he had an honest reputation as a businessman even in New York, indicating the transnational character of Sephardi financial networks between the United States and Mexico and implying that Chicorel must have been more successful in Mexico than in the United States.[120]

Some Sephardim who migrated from the United States to Mexico over the course of the 1920s had previously naturalized as Americans. As was the case for Sephardi migrants regardless of nationality, however, acquiring or retaining a particular nationality did not keep these individuals from continuing their travels or residing in a place that did not correspond to their nationality. For some, like Nissim Cadranel from Milas, Turkey, who had naturalized as an American in 1915, and his wife Mathilde from Rhodes, who acquired American nationality through her husband, it remained crucial to register their children, born in Guanajuato, Mexico, with the American consulate to ensure their American citizenship, even though by the time of the birth of their two daughters in 1923 and 1925, the Cadranels had not lived in the United States for several years.[121] For others, like Belina Cadranel de Eskenazi, a Greek national married to a fellow Sephardi who had become a naturalized American, relocating to Mexico provided access to a network of family support. Upon arrival in Mexico from the United States in 1922, she stayed with a sister and brother-in-law, who had previously migrated, and filed a successful claim for divorce and custody of her three children on the grounds that her husband was physically abusive. Though they had been married since 1913, Cadranel explained that a few months into her marriage, her husband had started to harm her, and although she had not wanted to separate from him, their life had become more impossible every day. She had gone to the authorities in Washington, who had sought to modify his behavior, but he continued to mistreat her, and a year after her arrival in Mexico she sought divorce on grounds of abuse.[122] While her husband Max, a tailor, returned to the United States to settle in Atlanta, Belina remained in Mexico, where she worked as a dressmaker, traveling once to New York to acquire merchandise, where she listed a brother there as her contact.[123] In Mexico's 1930 census, Belina was listed as a dressmaker in Puebla, maintaining custody of two of her children—the third having reached the age of majority—and calling herself a widow, likely as a means of deflecting the social stigma of being a divorcée.[124] For Cadranel, relocating from the United States to Mexico provided her with the family support and legal knowledge necessary to separate from her abusive husband and to begin to establish herself financially to care for herself and her children. As a divorced woman responsible for the well-being of her children, she, like many male Sephardi migrants, made use of transnational familial ties between the United States and Mexico to acquire merchandise. The presence of more established Sephardi migrants in Mexico allowed newcomers to draw on preexisting networks of family and patronage to propel their upward economic and social mobility. Others coming from the former Ottoman Empire likewise had their own, discrete patronage networks to ease the way for newer migrants,[125] but given that for Sephardi Jews, these networks hinged upon shared networks of knowledge undergirded by the Ladino language and family connections, the Ottoman Sephardim generally relied on their brethren and not on others of Ottoman origin.

While the networks that linked Sephardim in the United States and Mexico were primarily familial or financial in nature, and Sephardi migrants proved adept at navigating these networks to their advantage, these same webs also aided transnational Sephardi policing and internal coercive structures. In 1925, *La Vara* published a front-page article proclaiming "the horrible and tragic murder of a Sephardi brother." The piece, based on information sent from a correspondent living in Veracruz, explained that a 52-year-old Sephardi merchant named Moshe Alfassa who had lived in Veracruz for some years had been robbed of thirty years' worth of savings before being killed in a brutal manner. The author explained that the small Sephardi colony in Veracruz felt great consternation over this murder, only exacerbated upon the discovery that one of the alleged murderers was a fellow Sephardi migrant from Kırklareli, a young man named Alberto Ergas, a "damned youth who deserves to be stoned and burnt alive." Ergas had disappeared the day of the murder, and rumors circulated in Veracruz that he had fled to New York, where his brother lived. The correspondent in Veracruz informed *La Vara* of the address of Ergas's brother in New York, as well as the name and address of Alfassa's relatives in New York so that the latter could receive the remnants of Alfassa's estate. Though *La Vara* declined to publish the brother's name and address, it noted that it would do everything necessary to make sure that revenge be taken upon Ergas, because "the blood of the poor Alfassa is screaming from the earth."[126] The next week, however, *La Vara* published a correction. Having perused Mexican periodicals since Alfassa's murder, the editors had determined that the information supplied by the correspondent in Veracruz was incorrect. The murderer was, according to the Mexican press, someone by the name of "Marius." This person, *La Vara* noted, was not Sephardi.[127] Sephardim in the United States had recourse to Spanish-language Mexican press sources to verify news emanating from Mexico. More importantly, the reactions to the murder of Moshe Alfassa and the flight of Alberto Ergas, by the editors of *La Vara* and the anonymous correspondent in Veracruz, emphasize the extent of transnational Sephardi connections. Familial connections enabled the alleged flight of Ergas, while parallel networks allowed the editors of *La Vara* and the Mexican correspondent to ensure that a Sephardi migrant did not get away with murder. Sephardi Jews maintained lines of communication across borders, sharing news and cautionary reports as part of a common reading public. In doing so, they perpetuated the transnational connections that undergirded this Sephardi diaspora. These same networks of knowledge, communication, and travel also enabled the internal monitoring and control of Sephardi individuals who formed this diaspora.

Combating the Infamy of Success

In November of 1924, the government of the state of Puebla received a petition from "various residents of Tezuitlán," all of whom claimed to be Mexican by birth, requesting the expulsion of Marcos Reinah, a man of Turkish nationality. Article 33 of the Mexican Constitution granted Mexican authorities the power to expel foreigners from Mexican territory upon their being deemed "pernicious" for committing a crime, exploiting Mexican workers, or mixing in Mexican politics. In Reinah's case, petitioners cast him as pernicious for his alleged involvement in Mexican political machinations. Though a number of expulsion petitions had earlier been made throughout Mexico, and in this period they particularly targeted Chinese migrants in northern Mexico, this was the first such petition that sought to mark a Sephardi Jew as "pernicious."[128] The first of two such petitions against Reinah—the second would be filed in 1931—the complaint listed a number of allegations to demonstrate to the authorities that Reinah was a pernicious foreigner and therefore expellable.

The petition's authors had a clear sense of what would mark Reinah as detrimental to the Mexican state and attempted to tailor their petition in terms that authorities would find convincing. First, they noted that Reinah had been an open supporter of the rebel forces of Adolfo de la Huerta, the governor of Sonora who led the rebellion that killed then-president Venustiano Carranza in 1920 and the leader of a failed rebellion against Álvaro Obregón in 1923. The petition asserted that when constitutional forces had taken over the city plaza in Tezuitlán, Reinah had lent his services as a spy, aiding rebel forces in the procurement of arms. He had denounced out of "hatred and ill will" the individuals of the Syrio-Lebanese community in Tezuitlán. He was a discordant element in Tezuitlán due to his propensity for insult and was frequently detained and fined by local authorities, whom he publicly denigrated. Noting that most of the residents of the town were not natives but foreigners motivated by the desire to work, therefore "entirely foreign to political discords," the petitioners sought Reinah's expulsion. In casting Reinah as a foreigner who sought to disrupt political order by openly supporting revolutionary forces and who denigrated Mexican authorities and locals alike, the petitioners hoped that the *Secretaría de Gobernación* would look upon their petition favorably.[129] Unlike the 1931 petition for Reinah's expulsion, which stressed that Reinah was a "Jew" or a "Turkish Jew," the 1924 petition made no mention of Reinah's religion, which suggests that those who filed it were not aware of Reinah's religion or that this was not at the time deemed to be a factor that would provide weight to the case against Reinah.[130]

Marcos Reinah, from the Dardanelles, had arrived in Mexico on August 22, 1917, crossing through Nuevo Laredo. He had previously lived in New York City, where he worked in a movie theater.[131] He may have been encouraged to leave New York by the possibility of having to respond to the American draft; his name was published in the *New York Times* in a list of New Yorkers who had failed to respond to the draft and faced arrest.[132] Initially, he lived in Mexico City, where he performed the role of cantor for the Rosh Hashanah festivities shortly after his arrival.[133] In 1919 he married Julia Couriel, a fellow Sephardi Jew who had moved to Mexico City from Izmir with her parents and her two brothers, Albert(o) and Jacques (Jack).[134] Prior to migrating to Mexico, in 1914 (just before the outbreak of World War I), eighteen-year-old Alberto had headed to New York on a two-week voyage from Piraeus.[135] Jacques was based in New York and traveled frequently to Mexico for business and, according to Sálomon Levy, to visit his Mexican mistress in Mérida, while Alberto was based in Mexico and made yearly trips to New York for merchandise, alternately telling American officials that he was from Smyrna or Salonica, of Spanish, Turkish, or Greek nationality, and of the Hebrew, Spanish, Greek, or French race.[136] Marcos Reinah, in establishing a novelty store in Tezuitlán, likely tapped into the trade networks of his brothers-in-law to acquire wares.

In both the 1924 and 1931 petitions against Reinah, the *Secretaría de Gobernación* found that there were no grounds for expulsion. In 1924, the investigator noted that Reinah, though of Turkish origins, had been born to Spanish parents, a fact that required no exploration or explanation. Reinah's trade in novelties and clothing had earned him an honorable reputation in business, though he was a "joker" and excessively familiar in his social relations, which perhaps led to the souring of people's opinions toward him. The investigator linked antagonism toward Reinah to his financial success. Even though Reinah was of middling education, he had a natural business talent, overtaking other merchants who were also "*turcos*." These competitors and compatriots, "seduced by envy," used unfavorable terms against Reinah, "distancing him from their familiar relations of *paisanaje*."[137] The investigator attributed the case against Reinah to individuals whom the investigator perceived to be Reinah's fellow countrymen, though they were likely of a different linguistic and religious background, perhaps the same Syrio-Lebanese whom the petition accused Reinah of denigrating. The petitions for Reinah's expulsion, though signed by individuals claiming Mexican origin, were connected to Reinah's competitors, at least in the eyes of the Mexican investigators. These investigators were aware that expulsion could be used as a tool for eliminating economic competition. Particularly when the allegedly pernicious foreigner was damaging other foreigners and not Mexicans, Mexican authorities did not rush to assume such claims were true. The fact that Reinah was accused twice demonstrates the extent of the animosity of some members of Tezuitlán's society toward him, likely as a result of his economic success. The fact that he was twice exonerated indicates that the Mexican authorities gave no credence to these claims and did not view Reinah as pernicious.

During the early 1920s, a growing number of Jews sought residence in Mexico. Their migrations were facilitated by international aid networks that assisted Ashkenazi Jews as well as local networks formed by Sephardi Jews and Syrian Jews to support each other. Presidents Obregón and Plutarco Elías Calles expressed interest in Jewish colonization plans in northern Mexico, modeled after Jewish agricultural colonies in Argentina, but these unrealized colonies were meant to provide succor for Eastern European Jewish migrants, individuals who were the overwhelming concern of the B'nai B'rith Mexican Bureau and the Emergency Refugee Committee behind these colonization plans.[138] American Jewish benevolent associations spent little effort in aiding the migration of Ladino- and Arabic-speaking Jews, in contrast.

In settling in Mexico, Marcos Reinah, like the several thousand Sephardi migrants who arrived in Mexico during the 1920s, capitalized on transnational financial networks often solidified through family alliances. At the same time, these individuals tapped into existing patronage networks throughout Mexico, whereby Sephardi migrants who were already secure aided newcomers by providing them capital and goods or by serving as references for naturalization petitions for those who sought Mexican nationality; Aleppan and Damascene Jews established similar, though separate, networks.[139] In the early 1920s, Sephardi migrants established two charitable organizations in Mexico City to aid their Sephardi coreligionists: *La Fraternidad* was founded by Isaac Capón and others in 1923 and *Las Damas de Buena Voluntad*, led by married Sephardi women, was founded in 1925. Unlike conventional *landsmanshaftn* that aided those who shared a city of origin, and in contrast to Sephardi organizations in places like Paris and New York, these two organizations provided Sephardim, regardless of their city or country of origin, with money, medical assistance, and loans of cash or merchandise. *La Fraternidad* at times extended loans to male Sephardi migrants so that they could afford tickets to bring over family members still in Greece or Turkey, to be repaid in small installments.[140] *Las Damas de Buena Voluntad* explicitly aided new arrivals in attaining food, lodging, and other daily necessities.[141] By 1927, these two organizations taken together had at least two hundred and fifty members.[142]

Despite the Mexican government's favor toward Jewish migrants who would potentially cultivate the agricultural sector, in the early 1920s there was some popular antagonism toward Middle Eastern and other migrants. These sentiments grew as the 1920s progressed, eventually propelling the Mexican government to limit immigration. Although in the early 1920s

Mexican authorities had not established broad restrictions against immigration in spite of mounting popular xenophobia, there was budding concern about migrants evading even the existing limitations. In 1926, thirteen Syrio-Lebanese were forbidden entry in Veracruz because of trachoma in spite of the intervention of the French legation, mirroring earlier American restrictions against the entry of migrants with this disease.[143] Earlier, the secretariat of foreign relations had sought to prevent Chinese migrants in Mexico from sending visas that they had acquired, supposedly for their own use in returning to Mexico, to China for other Chinese to use in coming to Mexico with false papers. By requiring all Chinese subjects in Mexico to attend interviews in person, Mexican authorities sought to prevent the trade in falsified documentation.[144] The crackdown against Scarlatt Tottu for his alleged sale of falsified Mexican visas and passports in Istanbul reflected a similar attempt by the Mexican state to demonstrate its authority.

Travel and civil status documents could potentially be either lost or falsified. When they were lost, that complicated forays into the Mexican legal system, as exemplified by the challenges posed to Simon Lahana's children by the loss of their birth certificates in their attempt to be named beneficiaries in Sara Halfon de Lahana's intestate case.[145] It also complicated naturalization petitions, which required the petitioner to demonstrate legal entrance into Mexico and uninterrupted residence for at least five years. When Victor Cohen, born in Turkey but possessing French nationality, sought Mexican citizenship in 1926, he claimed that he had arrived in Mexico in 1914. He could not prove this, since his documentation had been stolen when the train he took to Mexico City was attacked. The outcome of his petition is unclear.[146]

During the early 1920s, the number of Sephardi migrants who sought to follow the legal path to Mexican naturalization grew. Though Mauricio Assael and several other Sephardim had attained Mexican nationality before and during the revolution, the number of naturalization petitions prior to the 1920s remained low. The growing wave of naturalization petitions by male Sephardi migrants in the early 1920s attests to several trends. First, these petitions highlight that the acquisition of Mexican nationality was increasing viewed as beneficial. Citizenship laws in the new Turkish Republic stipulated that those who acquired non-Turkish nationalities forfeited Turkish citizenship, but these individuals were willing to lose their earlier nationalities or to hope that Turkish officials would remain ignorant of their new nationalities. The relative ease with which these men acquired Mexican citizenship attests to the willingness of the Mexican government to envelop these men in the cloak of Mexican nationality.[147]

Additionally, these petitions, which required applicants to list their profession, assets, and references, cast light on the networks of patronage and alliance that existed within the Sephardi community and the nature of connections between Sephardi Jews and others in Mexico. In their petitions, migrants most often listed as their references large commercial houses—Lázaro Carillo's 1925 petition included the large department stores "El Puerto de Liverpool" and "El Puerto de Veracruz"—or prominent Sephardim in Mexico—Carillo's same petition also lists the firm of "Capon y Alazraki." Other petitions listed, among others, "Optica Mazal," belonging to Ruben Mazal;[148] the firm of "Cohen y Schoenfeld," in which one of the partners, Benjamin Cohen, was Sephardi;[149] and "La Ciudad de Lyon," owned by Isaac Lahana.[150] Petitioners also gave individuals as references, though often these individuals were linked explicitly to their commercial enterprises. When David Saul listed his references—Miguel Palacci, Roberto Chicurel, and Ico Assael—he noted that Palacci was the owner of a house of confections called "El Centro de Paris," Chicurel the proprietor of a clothing stand called "El Puente de Alvarado," and Assael the owner of the jewelry store "La Duquesa."[151] Elias Bemaras noted explicitly that his references—Isaac Capon, Nissim Eliakim, and Isaac Benuzillo—were his "paisanos," calling attention to the common origin and religion linking him and those who supported his petition, while Samuel Cuenca explained that he had known several of his references from Izmir prior to migrating.[152] Many petitioners listed their professions as "traveling salesman" or "salesman of clothing," implying that their lives were, in some way, itinerant. Sephardi migrants with established storefronts, such as the firm of "Capon y Alazraki" in Mexico City or Menahem Balli and Alberto Maya's "El Famoso 33" in Guadalajara, often contracted with or provided wares for Sephardi traveling salesmen and peddlers. For some petitioners, the individuals and companies listed as references may also have been their suppliers. By presenting as their references individuals who had known and determined physical locations and established commercial names in Mexico, migrants likely sought to strengthen their own cases. Their own personal and financial reputations were bolstered through links to those who had already solidified their social and economic presence in Mexico.

The petitions also shed light on personal ties between male Sephardi migrants and Mexican women. In 1923, the state of Sonora declared it a crime punishable by jail and a fine for Chinese men to marry Mexican women.[153] The Mexican press decried the degenerated racial characteristics that would be produced through the mixing of "the [male] smoker of opium and the [female] drinker of *pulque*."[154] However, there existed neither governmental nor social disapprobation of Jews marrying Mexicans. Among the Mexican consul general's rationale for the desirability of Sephardi Jewish immigrants, as opposed to Jewish immigrants in general, was his perception that as equally Spanish and Jewish, Sephardi Jews could and would assimilate. Naturalization petitions, petitions for the recognition of natural children, and oral histories attest to the existence of marital and extramarital relations between Sephardi men and Mexican women. Parallel relations between Mexican men and Sephardi women were rare, perhaps due to the smaller numbers of female Sephardim in the earlier waves of migration and to greater familial and communal regulation of female social and sexual relations. While some naturalization petitions stressed that the petitioners were married to women who shared their nationality,[155] others emphasized that they were married to Mexican women as a means of undergirding their petitions, at times going so far as to give their wives' names, a practice that does not appear in other naturalization petitions. The two Nyssen brothers who came from Constantinople in the early 1900s both married non-Jewish Mexican women, Alejandro Nyssen noting that his wife's name was María Luisa González.[156] Mauricio Benveniste, who arrived in Mexico in 1907 and was a traveling salesman, married a Mexican woman, Lucrecia Herrerías, with whom he had a child.[157] The continued ties of these men to other Sephardi Jews is apparent through the references they list, whether Mauricio Benveniste's brother and Mauricio Assael's former business partner Isaac Benveniste, Moises Camhi, or Samy Raphael. Likewise, oral histories suggest that marriages or sexual liaisons between Sephardi men and Mexican women were not uncommon, particularly among early migrants who arrived in Mexico as single men and who did not send home for wives. The non-Jewish wives of these men were often welcomed into the Sephardi community without any conversion process, and their offspring, who would not be considered Jewish according to Jewish law, were regarded as Jews and eligible marriage partners for later Jewish generations in Mexico.[158]

Not all relationships between Sephardi men and Mexican women occurred within the bonds of marriage. Rafael Jassan, a single shoe repairman from Izmir, filed a claim with the court to be recognized as the father of his two children, Rafael and María Elena, both born out of wedlock. In the case of his daughter, his relative Jack Jassan agreed to be the girl's custodian.[159] Sálomon Levy discussed the sexual relationships between several Sephardi migrants and Mexican women and hinted at several affairs himself, noting that even after his marriage he was a particularly popular dance partner with Mexican women "because I was foreign and the others were *medio prietitos* [kind of dark skinned]."[160] When the American Jack Mizrahi died in Mérida in 1932, the American consulate noted that though the deceased had a wife and brother in New York, his goods in Mexico remained in the custody of Angelina Arriola, whom the consulate called Mizrahi's "concubine."[161] As Levy suggested, the public perception of Sephardi Jews as racially white, in contrast to the Chinese, bolstered the conception expressed by the Mexican consul general to Vienna that Sephardi Jews were equally Spanish and Jewish. In some ways, these Sephardi migrants played into Mexican projects of "whitening" the racial composition of the Mexican nation.

However, the standing of Sephardi migrants in Mexico was solidified not through marriages or sexual relationships with Mexicans but instead through the acquisition and maintenance of economic status. Even though David Nyssen, who had arrived in Mexico in 1904 from Constantinople, was married to a Mexican woman, his petition for Mexican nationality was denied because he was a partner in a firm that was in liquidation.[162] However, as the example of Marcos Reinah indicates, too much financial success could mark Sephardi merchants as targets for falsified expulsion cases or increase public animosity toward them. In particular, the propensity of Sephardi merchants to take individuals to court for failing to keep up with payments for goods purchased on installment likely contributed to the perception that foreign *aboneros* preyed on the economically weak, particularly women. It was certainly not always the case that only the indigent purchased on installment. The woman that Mordo Babany sued for not having paid for a fur coat and the man whom Mauricio Assael took to court over not having fully paid for a gold watch purchased luxury items and were certainly not impoverished.[163] The historian Lore Diana Kuehnert has argued that the Mexican government and popular press favored the immigration of those who would be economically successful, but modestly so and not at the expense of Mexicans. The economic prominence of Chinese, Jewish, and Middle Eastern merchants in Mexico made them targets in debates over the desirability of foreigners who came to work in Mexico. Over time, the perceived financial prowess of Chinese, Middle Eastern, and Jewish businessmen led to increased popular resentment, the growth of nationalist groups targeting foreigners, and more stringent regulations against immigration.[164]

Although Presidents Obregón and Calles expressed favorable opinions toward Jewish immigration in the early 1920s, by the late 1920s Mexican popular opinion had propelled government officials to restrict immigration. Many of the early nationalist groups, such as the *Comité Anti-Chino* and *La Liga Nacional Pro-Raza*, targeted the Chinese, prompting the Chinese delegation in Chihuahua to seek protection for its nationals. At the same time, anti-Jewish sentiment also increased, in part as more Jews—whether Sephardi or their more visible Ashkenazi and Syrian counterparts—sought entry into Mexico.[165] In 1926, a magazine in Monterrey published an article entitled "The Jewish Plague and the Disastrous Consequences that Flow from It for the Country." Castigating Jews for their lack of scruples and morals, the article warned that Jews—explicitly those from Eastern Europe—would doom the Mexican economy. The article finished by questioning how the sudden opening of the doors of Mexico "to this element, the most pernicious of all the profiteers and usurers that exist in the world," could be justified.[166]

In 1926, at the intersection of the streets República de Peru and Allende, just to the north of the Zócalo in Mexico City, in an area where many Jewish migrants lived and worked, a local business owner hung large banners decrying Jewish merchants. "Mexican firms alert Mexicans that if you buy from or sell to the Jews," the banners cautioned, "you are not behaving patriotically. Boycott the Jews!"[167] This sign was hung above a store that sold men's suits. The ready-made clothing and textile trade were branches of business in which Jews—Sephardi and otherwise—and others from the Middle East were prominent. Here, it was economic competition, rather than "degenerated" racial characteristics, that propelled anti-Jewish agitation. The presence of such signs marks the beginning of a transition away from viewing Jewish migrants as welcome; by this point, the familiarity of Sephardi Jews' Iberian ancestry did not overcome their Jewish origins. Even as Sephardi Jews in Mexico sought to cement their status by drawing on Sephardi patronage networks and by becoming involved in relationships with Mexican women, the tides of popular opinion had begun to turn against foreigners in general and Jewish foreigners specifically. The Mexican government was forced to respond to concerns either that certain groups of migrants in Mexico would retard *mestizaje* through introducing deleterious racial characteristics or that they were economic parasites, leeching wealth from the Mexican economy by preying on vulnerable segments of the Mexican population.

Conclusion

Regardless of earlier perceptions that Sephardi Jews did not have the same negative characteristics as other Jews, anti-Jewish sentiment as one facet of the growing anti-foreigner resentment in Mexico could not but affect Sephardi Jews, individuals who were simultaneously becoming less welcome in their states of origin. Toward the end of the 1920s, Jews and other religious minorities in the Turkish Republic, though often bearing Turkish citizenship, were coming to be excluded from popular and official conceptions of who should constitute the Turkish nation. Turkish officials unofficially sought to encourage the emigration of religious minorities. The continued use of the Ladino language and allegations of Jewish loyalty to Spain became markers of Jewish difference and proof of Jewish disloyalty. These became tools that popular opinion used to force Turkey's Jewish community to relinquish the minority rights guaranteed to them by the Treaty of Lausanne. The steady erosion of Jewish communal and institutional autonomy, rumors of the seizure of minority-owned property, and the increasing marginalization of Jews and other religious minorities within certain economic sectors propelled many Sephardim to seek friendlier shores. These migrants sought out destinations in Europe and the Americas in which their cultivated transnational familial and economic networks offered them a means to flourish.

Simultaneously, it was precisely the continued use of a language of Iberian origin and the perception that Sephardi Jews shared cultural and social norms with Mexicans because of their distant Spanish provenance that propelled certain Mexican officials to regard Sephardi Jews as desirable immigrants. These perceived commonalities prompted the establishment of a Mexican diplomatic presence in Constantinople to lure Sephardi Jews to Mexico and compelled some Sephardi migrants to choose Mexico as a destination over the United States. While Mexican officials sought immigrants who would aid the Mexican economy and contribute beneficial racial characteristics to the Mexican nation, Sephardi migrants saw Mexico as one key link in transnational Sephardi networks, a place where Sephardi patronage and commercial ties would aid the migration and acclimation processes and the gradual accrual of capital. Because of the shared imprint that Spain had left on the Mexican and Sephardi peoples, Sephardim could more easily adapt to life in Mexico than elsewhere. Some Sephardi men married Mexican women, an increasing number acquired Mexican nationality, aided in part by references provided by other Sephardim, and some Sephardi merchants succeeded economically. Economic success, however, sometimes made them targets of the public animosity of business competitors and opened them and other foreigners in Mexico up to charges of being economically parasitic, feeding off of the poor, women, and children.

Growing public animosity and governmental concern led the Mexican government in 1927 to issue its first large-scale restriction of immigration into Mexico. This legislation prohibited the entry of workers and laborers who possessed under ten thousand pesos in capital from Syria, Lebanon, Armenia, Palestine, Turkey, and Arab countries and restricted the entrance of Indians, Chinese, and blacks. Although initially a two-year temporary measure, it was made permanent in 1929. These restriction were motivated by economic concerns, the *Diario Oficial* noting that the immigrants did "not constitute a useful economic factor in the development of the public wealth" and "occasioned a notable unstableness in the large trade and had deprived our own countrymen of the small trade."[168] Mexico also sought to avoid the mixing of races that were "scientifically" deemed to degenerate its descendants.[169] The Turkish government issued a statement deploring this restriction, which went against the spirit of the treaty of friendship between the two states, and decreed the suspension of Turkish visas to those bearing Mexican passports.

In 1927, an internal memo by the subsecretary of the secretariat of foreign relations (SRE) condemned the inclusion of Turkish citizens in the restriction against "oriental immigration."[170] By 1930, the disagreement within the Mexican government over whether to include Turkish citizens in restrictions became more apparent. The subsecretary of the SRE and future Mexican ambassador to Spain, Portugal, and Turkey, Genaro Estrada, explained that he was not opposed to the restrictions against workers of Lebanese, Armenian, Palestinian, Chinese, Arab, or Russian origin. However, "[f]or that which concerns the Turks, it appears that there exists a certain general propensity to confuse them with the Arabs and the Syrio-Lebanese, which in reality are populations with very distinct customs and mentalities." Therefore, he opposed restricting the entrance of Turkish citizens.[171] Estrada's distinction between Arabs and Syrio-Lebanese on the one hand, and Turkish citizens on the other, suggests that he viewed the former as posing a greater economic and social threat to Mexico than the latter. While this could be attributed to the far greater numbers of Syrio-Lebanese in Mexico and their wider geographic dispersal, there could also be an alternative rationale behind Estrada's contention that Turkish citizens' customs and mentalities were distinct from those of the Syrio-Lebanese and not detrimental to Mexico. Of those bearing Turkish nationality who had arrived in Mexico prior to 1930, all but a handful were Sephardi Jews. For Estrada and others in the Mexican government who were unopposed to continued and unrestricted Turkish migration into Mexico, the referent for "Turk" was the Sephardi Jew.

(CHAPTER 5)

THE SEPHARDI CONNECTION

ON JUNE 1ST, 1928, "Mexico's greatest scandal" since 1915 made international waves.[1] General José Álvarez, the chief of staff to the Mexican president, Plutarco Elías Calles, was dismissed for "smuggling merchandise into Mexico in connivance with certain foreigners."[2] In the course of their investigations, Mexican police raided the luxurious Mexico City house of María Conesa, a retired Spanish actress, dancer, and "intimate friend" of General Álvarez. There, they discovered seven hundred and fifty thousand dollars' worth of silks to be sold by "Spanish-Syrian" merchants.[3] Further cases of contraband silks were captured en route to Matamoros and Monterrey, having been smuggled into Mexico across the northern border.[4] Álvarez testified that he had issued orders, in Calles's name, for the free entry of the contraband silk "in the belief that his associates were bringing in from the United States documents which would incriminate clerical elements behind the Catholic rebellion."[5] Calles's anticlericalism, manifested in his implementation of the anti-Church provisions of the 1917 constitution; his attempts to end what he deemed the intrusion of the Catholic Church into secular affairs; his mandating the registration of all clergy and demanding the deportation of foreign-born priests; and his suppression of popular religious celebrations in local communities had instigated a large-scale rebellion in 1926. *La Cristiada*, or the Cristero Rebellion, was in full swing in 1928 and claimed the lives of sixty-five to eighty thousand Mexicans before it ended in 1929.[6] General Álvarez cast himself as a loyal supporter of Calles who had turned to all means at his disposal, including those skirting the edge of legality, in an overly zealous attempt to aid his president. However, Álvarez was sent to prison and Conesa exiled to the United States.[7] Likewise, the implicated merchants—who numbered over a dozen and included two naturalized Mexican citizens—were expelled from Mexico as "pernicious foreigners" under Article 33 of the 1917 constitution.[8]

As the description "Spanish-Syrian" may or may not suggest at first glance, the merchants purportedly involved in reselling this contraband silk were all from lands that had been part of the Ottoman Empire. They were native speakers of Arabic and Ladino, Christians and Jews. Their citizenships ran the gamut from Syrian and Turkish to Mexican, American, and Portuguese, and they had been born in places as distinct as Monastir and Salonica in the Ottoman Balkans and Aleppo and Damascus in the Arab provinces. Though the implicated merchants were expelled to the United States, Guatemala, and Cuba, all were eventually permitted to return to Mexico, a process this chapter explores. This was a direct result of their mobilization of connections within and outside of Mexico in their defense and their deep knowledge of overlaps in masculinity and femininity, criminality, nationality, and class. Meanwhile, General Álvarez remained imprisoned and María Conesa exiled.

From the late 1920s into the 1930s, Sephardi Jews faced growing obstacles from expanding regulation on migration and internal monitoring of their movements and actions as they tried to continue their patterns of hypermobility facilitated by recourse to transnational networks and overlapping nationalities. As the world economy convulsed, migrants in Mexico came to be lambasted for causing or exacerbating Mexico's economic woes, which had been made worse by the repatriation of Mexican nationals from the United States.[9] Jews, regardless of origin, and Chinese and Syrio-Lebanese migrants became frequent targets of nativist fervor, while the protectionist economic policies that the Mexican state favored led to progressive limitations against migrants regardless of origin. Meanwhile, in Turkey, policies toward the public erasure of minority difference became more overt. Though the emigration of minorities was not advocated as a means of propelling the ethnic and religious homogenization of the Turkish state as it had been in the earlier 1920s, the Turkish government adopted strategies to minimize discrepancies between those whom it deemed to form the "Turkish nation" and those who bore Turkish citizenship. The Turkish government enacted laws that stripped Turkish citizenship from emigrants. This removal of citizenship complicated the return to Turkey of those whose citizenship had been revoked, excising minority émigrés from the Turkish state and the Turkish nation. The Turkish state sought to end the practice of maintaining non-Turkish nationalities in spite of Turkish geographical origins. At the same time, to be able to identify those whose Turkish citizenship should be continued or revoked, Turkish authorities sought to monitor and control Turkish citizens abroad. Their actions toward minority émigrés revealed discrepancies between being a citizen of the Turkish state and an accepted member of the Turkish nation.

This chapter explores how Sephardi migrants contended with closing borders that restricted the movements of goods and their own movements. While states enacted laws limiting the movements of certain goods and peoples deemed undesirable, individuals could and did subvert border controls, penetrate territories, seek markets, find customers, and make spaces of belonging for themselves and their communities.[10] Such mobility demanded financial capital, transnational connections, and deep knowledge of laws and norms at many points of one's trajectory. Illicit activities, whether the smuggling of textiles or the falsification of family relations or documents to enable entry, often ran parallel to, or within the same networks as, the legal movements of goods and people.[11] Focusing on the activities and connections that undergirded the illicit and licit traffic of people and goods casts light on how transnational individuals contended with, adapted to, and helped to shape legal and social regimes at international, national, and local levels that outlawed their movements and merchandise. So, too, does it expose the political and geographical limits of sovereignty, particularly when mobile individuals with connections and know-how employed strategic mobility to play states' divergent definitions of legality and desirability against each other.[12]

Transitions to Invisibility

In December 1933, the Mexican secretariat of foreign relations (SRE) named Albert Cazés, a Sephardi Jew from Istanbul holding Spanish citizenship, as

Mexico's honorary consul to Istanbul with jurisdiction over the Turkish Republic. Although they did not provide a justification for their choice of Cazés, their previous recourse to Mauricio Assael and their search for consular officials with knowledge of Spanish and French suggests why Cazés, proficient in both, would have been an attractive candidate. In his acceptance letter of February 8th, 1934, Cazés wrote: "I will do all that is in my power for the protection of Mexican interests in Turkey, to execute my mission and the development of commercial relations between Mexico and Turkey," and that he would look to the Mexican ambassador to Madrid and the consul general in Milan to help him obtain the Turkish government's approval of his nomination.[13]

Seven months after his nomination, Cazés had still not received his exequatur from the Turkish government granting him authorization to fill his post. Fernando Pesqueira, the Mexican consul general to Milan, requested that Cazés begin his duties anyway, even without official approval. By November 1934, Pesqueira was clearly losing his patience. His office in Milan had already sent Mexico's seal and flag to Istanbul, and all that was lacking was Cazés's ability to take on his duties. Pesqueira asserted that this lack of Turkish approval was abnormal and suggested that the SRE undertake inquiries to ascertain the reasons for this delay. In August of 1935, the Turkish government had still not approved Cazés's nomination. Cazés noted that the honorary consul of Portugal, who was also a Spanish citizen (and likely also Sephardi), had also been waiting for his exequatur for two years. The Turkish government desired that the honorary consuls of foreign powers in Turkey be either nationals of the country that they represented or Turkish citizens. However, rather than explicitly prohibit the use of foreign nationals as honorary consuls in Turkey, the Turkish government preferred to simply "indefinitely retard the concession of the exequatur" in hopes that such delays would propel foreign governments to nominate Turkish citizens. After intervening with Turkish representatives in Mexico, the SRE was finally able to attain Cazés's exequatur in November 1936, just under three years after his initial nomination.[14]

The Turkish government's deliberate hesitation to approve Albert Cazés's nomination was a manifestation of the occasionally fractious negotiations of power between the Mexican and Turkish states. Although Mexico had nominated a candidate that it deemed best able to serve its interests, Turkey delayed its approval as a means of displaying its dissatisfaction with the nominee. The Turkish government's dawdling speaks to broader Turkish attempts to encourage the Turkification of minorities. Cazés's retention of Spanish citizenship despite his Turkish origins, and his proficiency in the Spanish language, flew in the face of the Turkish authorities' desire for minority assimilation. Increasing government intervention in the affairs of religious minorities in the wake of their relinquishment of minority rights entailed individual and communal transformation. However, this dissolution of difference, both imposed from without and emanating from forces within the Jewish community, did not always proceed smoothly as Jews and other minorities were compelled to assume public invisibility.

Language was critical to Turkey's efforts to create a unified nation, and the Turkish language—subject to a series of reforms in 1928—became a matter of national pride and a locus for binding the Turkish nation.[15] Gripes over Jews' lack of Turkish language abilities and their use of Ladino or French grew. In 1928, the "Vatandaş, Türkçe Konuş!" [Citizen, Speak Turkish] campaign began among the Law Faculty Students' Association of Istanbul University, appealing to Turkish citizens to speak Turkish in public and to take an active stance against those who did not. This campaign, which mobilized university students, teachers, intellectuals, and journalists in favor of a homogenous Turkish nation manifesting through a common language and culture, argued that those who spoke languages other than Turkish did not recognize Turkish law and were therefore not good citizens.[16] The campaign targeted non-Muslims, whom a columnist for the *Hizmet* periodical called "Passport Turks" ready to exchange their Turkish passports for those of an enemy nation when expedient. Jews, this columnist asserted, were the primary offenders.[17] By not speaking Turkish, Jews displayed a lack of respect toward Turkishness, a number of Turkish periodicals alleged. Some went so far as to suggest that Turkish Jews should either take up Turkish or leave.[18] Posters and placards were placed in Istanbul's trams and ferries, encouraging individuals to speak Turkish in public and to castigate those who spoke other languages. Speaking non-Turkish languages in public could have comic results—one Sephardi memoirist recounted an Ashkenazi orphan living in the Jewish orphanage in Ortaköy proclaiming in French, the only language he shared with his Sephardi counterparts, that the ground was "beaucoup mouillée" [very damp], which a passing Turkish youth understood as "bokumu ye" [eat my excrement].[19] However, a youthful act of public defiance could also result in detention by police, and Jewish and Armenian children alike were embarrassed by their parents' noticeable accents when speaking Turkish.[20] Even assisting foreign visitors to Turkey in the visitors' language could occasion public disapprobation.[21] By 1936, municipal governments in Edirne and Tekirdağ—towns with not-insignificant Jewish communities even in the wake of a 1934 pogrom that rent apart Jewish life in Turkish Thrace—as well as in Bursa and Lüleburgaz, passed decrees fining those who spoke languages other than Turkish in public.[22]

Pressure on Jews to relinquish Ladino and French in favor of Turkish did not arise only from outside the Jewish community. A Jewish committee for the diffusion of the Turkish language was founded. "Never had an initiation been more opportune or more patriotic," noted a former AIU instructor, who explained that "the community of language will render closer the relations between the different elements and will eliminate antagonism" and that "the principal means of truly becoming Turks is to learn Turkish."[23] Munis Tekinalp published a pamphlet in 1928 called "Türkleştirme" [Turkification], in which he advocated for Jewish Turkification through language, names, and culture. Tekinalp, who was born Moiz Cohen in Serres, educated in AIU schools, and active in the Committee of Union and Progress in Salonica before relocating to Istanbul after Salonica's fall to Greek forces in 1912, published widely in Turkish-language periodicals and was a strong supporter of pan-Turkism and an ardent proponent of Jewish Turkification.[24] In "Türkleştirme," Tekinalp asserted that Jews, "like Frenchmen in France, Englishmen in England, Italians in Italy, have no reason to not become a Turk at once in Turkey," arguing that for Jews not to accept the Turkish language as a mother tongue confounded mind and logic, material and spiritual interests.[25] According to Tekinalp, the French historian Anatole Leroy Beaulieu had proven that Sephardi Jews had the greatest aptitude among Jews for adaption and integration. Turkifying should cause little difficulty for Turkey's Sephardi population. He believed that Jews, in contrast to Christians, were capable of assimilating into the Turkish language, culture, and ideals. They would thereby cease to be "an ethnic minority among the Turks."[26] This possibility was predicated upon Jews speaking Turkish.

Within this environment of public advocacy for the linguistic and cultural Turkification of minorities, the Turkish government sought to limit the public denigration of Turkishness. In 1926, the Turkish state passed Article 159 of the penal code, which made the "public insult or ridicule" of Turkishness, the parliament, government, state officials, military, security forces, and judiciary a crime punished by "no less than three years in prison." The justice ministry required approval from the Turkish parliament to file charges.[27] The vitriol and public support behind the "Citizen, Speak Turkish" campaign provided the necessary slogans and atmosphere for the laws against insulting Turkishness.[28]

Non-Muslims were the primary target of this article, which was often applied in an arbitrary manner. In practice, if someone made a statement to a friend during a private conversation that was overheard by someone who thought that the statement was critical of Turkey, the speaker could be accused and prosecuted under Article 159. In other instances, individuals made allegations propelled by personal vendettas.[29] Numerous cases were brought against Jews and other minorities under this new article, while only a few were brought against Muslims, most of whom bore names that marked them as non-Turkish.[30] Jews throughout the Republic were tried, in areas with large Jewish populations, such as Istanbul, Izmir, and Edirne as well as in smaller Jewish centers such as Manisa, Çanakkale, Bursa, and Uzunköprü.[31] Although the Turkish parliament dismissed a few cases before prosecution, it deemed the vast majority worthy of prosecution.[32] Protecting "Turkishness" from those in some way external to it was at the heart of the majority of prosecutions, although several cases were brought against Jews for insulting the government. The latter included cases against Isak Effendi, a former employee of the rabbinate in Edirne,[33] and Josef Revah, the director of the French-language section of the Turkish Trade periodical,[34] while a Jew from Vienna was charged with "insulting the government and its employees."[35] In cases of denigrating Turkishness, the prosecution targeted both women and men. Occasionally, more than one individual was brought to prosecution under the same case, suggesting that they had denigrated Turkishness together.[36]

Prosecutions for insulting Turkishness served as a deterrent for expressing opposition to, or even disapproval of, Turkification or governmental policies. Within the press, *La Boz de Oriente*, the only remaining Ladino newspaper in Istanbul after the death of David Fresco shuttered *El Tiempo*, vociferously defended Turkey from charges of anti-Semitism. "There is no anti-Semitism," proclaimed one article in bold font, as it argued against an article published on the topic in the *Daily Express* of London. Even as it refuted the *Daily Express*'s claims, it alerted its readership to the fact that foreign Jewish press organs believed that there was anti-Semitism in Turkey and were openly discussing it.[37] While predominantly a Ladino publication, *La Boz de Oriente* also included articles in Turkish by Tekinalp advocating for Turkification and adopting the Turkish language. It noted with pride that *La République*, the French-language version of the Turkish periodical *Cumhuriyet*, had detailed that in a gathering in honor of Atatürk at a Galata synagogue, no language other than Turkish was heard throughout the entire ceremony.[38] Numerous articles lauded Turkish leaders and distanced those leaders from the violence that accompanied the 1934 *Trakya Olayları*, violent pogroms targeting Thrace's Jewish populations that resulted in most of the region's Jews relocating to Istanbul.[39] "In the Republic of Turkey, there are not Muslims, nor Christians, nor Israelites, there are none other than Turks and all who bear this name earn the same rights and bear the same responsibilities, above all, to love the country and to contribute to its grandeur," a 1935 article on Turkey and the Jews proclaimed.[40] Given the intense scrutiny of Jewish individuals within Turkey, which likely spread to the country's remaining Ladino newspaper, such articles should not be taken at face value. They should also be read as attempts by certain elite members of the Jewish community to accommodate public discourse and policies regarding Turkey's minorities and to model for Turkey's Jews the types of speech and actions that would most effectively skirt negative attention. But, as Leo Strauss notes, persecution leads to a particular type of writing in which the truth is presented exclusively between the lines. Authors and readers alike would have been alert to the various layers of meaning these articles contained.[41]

Despite the public proclamations by Turkish leaders, members of the Jewish community, and the sole remaining Ladino press organ that the designation "Turk" encompassed all members of Turkish society willing to embrace the Turkish language and culture, fissures became increasingly apparent, particularly in regard to nationhood and citizenship. During the late 1920s and into the 1930s, Turkish authorities passed a series of decrees to denaturalize Turkish citizens. Law 1041 declared that those who had not participated in the National Struggle and who had not returned since could be denaturalized, while Law 1312 denaturalized those who had acquired other citizenship without special permission or who had served a foreign state in any capacity. Several years later, the 1933 Statute on Traveling prohibited the return of those who had left Turkey on foreign passports; exit papers extended by Interallied authorities during their occupation of Istanbul were counted as foreign passports. Individuals like Menahem Balli, born in Silivri, who departed from Constantinople in 1920 on travel documents from the British High Commissioner, would find themselves unable to return to Turkey under these new regulations.[42] Although these laws stated that those who left with an Ottoman passport or without any passport, or who had been abroad for more than five years without registering with a Turkish consulate, could return upon successful petition to Turkish authorities, most petitions were denied.[43] Many Ottomans migrated on travel documents rather than the passports required by law, many never acquired an Ottoman passport, and others had exited on falsified papers that might not bear up to scrutiny.[44] Regardless of émigrés' intentions on leaving or desire to return, once the Turkish government became aware that citizens might qualify for denaturalization, this process could begin. Such actions distinguished between Ottomans and Turks on the level of what certain documentation meant; just because one had been an Ottoman subject did not mean that one had the right to make claims to Turkish citizenship.

In theory, denaturalization laws were applicable to all who violated their terms, regardless of ethnic or religious background. In practice, given who it was who left the Ottoman Empire in its final years or before the establishment of Turkey, most of the several thousand denaturalized individuals were religious minorities. While records do not give the names of individuals in cases where more than a hundred people were denaturalized with one decree, when they *are* given the names emphasize that it was predominantly religious minorities whose Turkish citizenship was revoked.[45] In September of 1932, fourteen people were stripped of their Turkish citizenship in accordance with Law 1041. Of these, one was clearly of Greek Orthodox provenance, ten were Armenian, and three—Viktor Hayon, Daniyel Levi, and Harun Levi— were Jewish.[46] In a February 1934 denaturalization of twenty-six individuals, eleven were Jewish, including four women.⁴⁷ Given that Armenians migrated at greater numbers than Jews and Greek Orthodox, it is unsurprising that Armenians are most prominent among those denaturalized. Jewish names also appear frequently in the large lists of those denaturalized in accordance with Law 1041 and the smaller number denaturalized in accordance with Law 1312. Sources occasionally note former Turkish citizens' new nationalities, as when Merkado Kohen and his wife Nelli lost Turkish citizenship after they had acquired Austrian citizenship in 1930, although they still lived in Istanbul, or when Victoria Arditi acquired American nationality after passing through France.⁴⁸ Most cases involving denaturalization due to Law 1312 provided neither the names nor the new nationalities of those stripped of Turkish citizenship, however.

Having one's citizenship stripped and being unable to reenter Turkish territory could have very personal consequences. In 1928, Lina Behmoiras, an AIU teacher who had once taught in Essaouira, Morocco and who was the daughter of the former chief rabbi of Edirne, sought a week's leave from her current post in Edirne.⁴⁹ She informed the AIU central office that she and her parents planned to travel together to Phillipoli [Plovdiv] in Bulgaria. Her brother was there, recently arrived from America after an absence of more than fifteen years. However, he could not enter Turkey, requiring the family to travel to Bulgaria to visit him. Her director had given her three days off, but Lina begged the AIU for more time, since with only three days' leave she would have only one day with her brother, and if she did not travel to Bulgaria, she ran the risk of never seeing him again.⁵⁰

The enforceability of denaturalization laws depended on the Turkish government monitoring nationals abroad. Turkish nationality could be retained through regularly registering with Turkish embassies. Turkish authorities tried to track those who had acquired new nationalities without special permission. Often this required the cooperation of authorities in other countries, who did not, however, consistently do as Turkish officials requested, as well as the cooperation of migrants, whose interests often ran counter to those of the Turkish state. In 1935, the Turkish legation in Mexico submitted a request to the SRE regarding the "many Israelite families originating from Istanbul, Andrinople (Edirne), Kirklar-Eli, Izmir, Los Dardanelos (Chanakkale), Silivri etc., [who] have immigrated to Mexico with a Turkish passport or without one" since 1900.⁵¹ Upon arriving in Mexico, many of these people registered as Turkish citizens, whether on the basis of the documents they carried or verbal declarations, while others acquired Mexican nationality without permission from the Turkish government. The legation requested a list of the latter. Many of these Jews had preserved their Turkish citizenship but without having registered with the Turkish consul general in New York, and traveled to Europe or throughout the American continent on Turkish papers, an "abnormal state that should not continue." The legation asked that Mexico not extend passports to Jews registered as Turkish citizens but, rather, to direct them to the first consul of Turkey in New York.⁵² The SRE, though, did not cooperate with the request to compile this list for the Turkish legation, and it was not until 1946 that Mexico created a list of Turkish nationals who had naturalized as Mexicans. This list of 430 individuals, almost all of whom were male, included many who had originated from Syria, Lebanon, and other areas that were once Ottoman but never Turkish.⁵³

Mexican and Turkish officials had divergent senses of who was and was not a Turk and who could or could not make claims to Turkishness or Turkish citizenship. In November of 1934, Mehmet Munir Bey, the Turkish ambassador to the United States, traveled to Mexico City to meet with President Abelardo Rodríguez. Although the purpose of the visit was to secure trade—particularly of coffee and tobacco—between Mexico and Turkey, easy relations were marred by Mexico's limitations on the entrance of Turkish citizens, in effect since 1927. Ambassador Munir penned an official complaint to the Mexican minister of foreign affairs, asserting that he

> could not discover the trace of any Turk who had gone to Mexico with the intention of exercising commerce or industry there, or with the view of establishing himself there definitively. The restrictive measure in question had been taken, it appears, against certain peoples and certain minorities [who were] subjects of the old Ottoman Empire and do not have any connection now with the government of the Turkish Republic.⁵⁴

Although the immediate Turkish response in 1927 had been to deplore restrictions against "Turkish citizens" in general, Munir's problem was not the restriction per se. Rather, it was that it erroneously targeted Turks by lumping them together with "certain peoples and certain minorities" who, as subjects of the now-defunct Ottoman Empire, no longer had relations with the Turkish government, at least in Munir's eyes.

Munir's distinction between "Turks" and others was more explicit in the internal report that he wrote about his trip to Mexico:

> I have never come across a Turk here in Mexico even until now, but rather, some Syrians, Arabs, Armenians, and Jews are found here under the name "Turk" from portions of the old Ottoman Empire. And these [peoples] have no connections with Turkishness [*bunların Türklükle hiç bir alâkaları olmadığını*], while the Turks, who have a very old civilization and history, are welcomed with much respect in every place.[55]

The problem was not that the Mexican government had legislated against the immigration of Turkish *citizens*. Rather, the Mexican government had falsely equated those who pertained to "portions" of the now-defunct Ottoman Empire with Turks. These other peoples—Syrians, Arabs, Armenians, and Jews—were former Ottoman subjects but did not share in the historic Turkish past or in Turkish civilization. They were not "Turks," but they were responsible for causing the Mexican government to view Turks negatively. Munir's disavowal of these individuals did not, however, mean that the Turkish government bore no interest in the actions of Turkish citizens in Mexico. Munir's assertion that such minorities "had no connection with Turkishness" reflected the widespread view in Turkey that religious minorities, though bearing Turkish citizenship, were not part of the Turkish nation. Distance only increased this separation.[56] Although minorities might not be "Turks," this did not inherently mean that they were not Turkish citizens. However, Turkish denaturalizations particularly targeted minority émigrés, suggesting that the Turkish state wished to remove Turkish citizenship from those who were, by virtue of religion or ethnicity, deemed distinct from the Turkish nation.

The Turkish state was clearly aware of Jews in Mexico bearing Turkish citizenship, going so far as to note the towns and cities whence they originated in requesting that Mexico monitor them. It was also clearly interested in controlling the travels and the nationalities of such individuals. Stripping Turkish citizenship from those who had acquired other nationalities without permission served as a means of preventing the existence of "passport Turks." Individuals like Albert Cazés, who, though born in Turkey, bore a non-Turkish nationality and worked in the employ of a foreign government, were quickly becoming anathema. The thousands of denaturalizations in the late 1920s and through the 1930s demonstrated the determination of the Turkish state to restrict citizenship as well as its success in ascertaining who, according to new legislation, no longer qualified as Turkish citizens. However, the fact that individuals—such as the many Jews in Mexico noted in the request of the Turkish legation—continued to hold both Turkish and another nationality revealed the limits of the ability of the Turkish state to control the movements and actions of those intent on perpetuating conceptions of citizenship that had markedly more in common with an imperial system than with that of a modernizing nation-state.

Undesirable Foreigners?

As much as Ambassador Munir wanted to disavow them, there were in Mexico thousands of individuals who had belonged to the erstwhile Ottoman Empire, some of whom, like the twelve merchants implicated in the textile smuggling case with which this chapter opened, drew negative attention to those grouped together under the designation *turco* or "Spanish-Syrian." Cases like this brought a negative focus upon migrants to Mexico. Widespread campaigns against foreigners in general, and specifically those who were from the Middle East or China or were Jewish, resulted in increased focus on the movements into and within Mexico and the activities of those categorized as such, and in the association of migrants in the public imagination with smuggling and other illegal activities. Pro-fascist brown-shirt groups proliferated, focused on Jews in particular. At times, this resulted in investigations and expulsions, even of those who had naturalized as Mexican, for being economically or politically pernicious. In turn, Jewish migrants and others made extensive recourse to patronage networks within Mexico and abroad to continue their geographical mobility and make space for themselves within Mexico. The networks these individuals drew upon highlight the distinct spheres in which these merchants operated and their deep understandings of how Mexican ideals of masculine honor and obligation to family and country could be mobilized to counter claims of their perniciousness.

In many ways, the apprehension and expulsion of the "Spanish-Syrian" merchants for their involvement in textile smuggling was not surprising.

Jewish and non-Jewish Ottomans had occasionally been caught smuggling textile goods from the United States into Mexico ever since the Mexican Revolution.[57] Sephardi migrants to Mexico were asked by coreligionists in Mexico to carry suitcases packed with outdated Parisian styles when crossing the Atlantic. These would be sold later in apparel venues that Sephardi migrants owned throughout the country.[58] From when Sephardi Jews first began to arrive in Mexico, in the early 1900s, most Sephardi migrants settled into various aspects of the textile trade. These ranged from the small-scale peddling of ties, socks, and towels, or the temporary erecting of street booths, to larger-scale stores targeting a wealthy clientele and small manufacturing plants. While Sephardi Jews did not monopolize the clothing niche, they, like their coreligionists of Ashkenazi and Syrian provenance, or like fellow former Ottomans from the Levant, formed a substantial contingent within that market.[59] But in 1928, Mexican merchants in Coahuila, a cotton-producing state in northern Mexico, announced their intent to report suspicious transactions and potential smugglers to federal officials. In opening their campaign, merchants across Mexico declared that "smuggling has become not only a disgrace to Mexico but that the practice is undermining the business existence of honest merchandisers," because it meant those who worked with the smugglers could offer high-quality cloth, fine silks, and apparel at prices that "legitimate merchants could not possibly quote and remain in business."[60] There was growing interest in the illicit activities of textile smuggling, increasingly coming to be associated with those of Ottoman provenance.

The twelve merchants expelled for their participation in this smuggling ring had extensive recourse to their own particular networks in order to advocate for their return. As in other expulsion cases targeting members of their community, the Lebanese Chamber of Commerce mobilized a letter-writing campaign in defense of one of those expelled. Ten letters from prominent Lebanese-owned firms throughout Mexico stressed the expellee's honor and enthusiasm for work, the extent of his time in Mexico, and his perfect history in the country. Communal institutions like the Lebanese Chamber of Commerce, as well as prominent Lebanese merchants within Mexico, were critical in advocating for those included in their community.[61] Rarely did this include Jews from that regional provenance, who instead made recourse to different networks of coreligionists, generally from their respective geographical and linguistic community.

There was no Jewish institution parallel to the Lebanese Chamber of Commerce until 1931, but this did not mean that the Jews who were expelled in this case did not employ patronage networks to argue for their return to Mexico. Sara Cohen, a Jewish migrant from Monastir, turned to the National Chamber of Commerce to investigate the cases of her husband and brother-in-law, both of whom had been expelled. She bemoaned the fact that her husband and brother-in-law had been forced to abandon their families and their business interests, highlighting her own feminine fragility in the absence of male family members. In response, the Chamber of Commerce attested that a detailed investigation had determined that the two men were renowned for their honorability in Mexico City's business world and emphasized the fact that both had become naturalized Mexican citizens, indicating their attachment to Mexico. Cohen then used this attestation to make a successful claim against the *Secretaría de Gobernación* for the repatriation of her husband and brother-in-law. Likewise, two expelled Syrian Jewish brothers requested letters from firms in the United States, a strategy that proved successful for their repatriation. Several other expelled merchants relied on family members to advocate for them. Bribes were likely also paid, though these do not appear in the historical record. In practice, those of upper-class status had roughly a fifty-percent chance of having expulsion orders revoked, a number that dwindled to under fifteen percent for those of middle-class status or lower.[62] All those expelled in this case successfully returned to Mexico, some in as little as a year. The actions of these individuals in having recourse to commercial and family networks, highlighting their class status, and playing into gendered tropes of vulnerability and honor, along with the successful results that these interventions bore, emphasize the proficiency with which these merchants and their female family members understood and navigated Mexico's legal, social, and commercial waters.

Abraham Salem, a Portuguese citizen from Salonica expelled to Guatemala, did not mobilize a similar network of merchants or family members. Yet he also employed the terms of honor, dedication to work, and a clean history to be allowed to return to Mexico. Writing from Guatemala that he had been working in Mexico for many years, Salem asserted that he always imported his materials from Europe, never the United States. His receipts and the import taxes he paid could prove as much. He was absolutely innocent of trading in contraband. "The unjust measure that has been taken against me greatly harms me morally and materially," he concluded, "not only because of my credit as a merchant, but also because my family has remained alone and helpless in Mexico." In a letter several months later addressed to President Calles, Salem wrote that Calles's "love for justice" and "kind heart" were welcome

> in these moments in which I find myself separated from my family and my little businesses and from the soil that I love like my *patria*, because although I am Portuguese by birth, I am Mexican of heart, because it was in Mexico that I made myself a man, where I formed for myself a future, where I have my home and my dearest aspirations of being an honorable man, and where I want my bones and those of my children, who are Mexicans, to rest.[63]

In highlighting his Portuguese birth, Salem downplayed his Ottoman origins, distancing himself from the negative associations with *turcos* and the immigration restrictions on Turks. A confidential telegram permitted Salem to return, although Mexican officials decided to keep an eye on him. When he went on a later business trip to France, they refused to give him a visa identifying him as a resident foreigner. This required him to reenter Mexico under the status of "traveling agent," which involved a five-hundred-dollar deposit and leaving the country again within six months. The lack of a presidential order revoking his expulsion caused difficulties when Salem sought to naturalize as a Mexican several years later.[64] This was in spite of letters from prominent Sephardi-owned commercial houses in Mexico City that attested to his good reputation.

All those expelled merchants who sought to return to Mexico employed gendered notions of honor and responsibility for female family members and children left behind. In Mexico, where notions of who precisely could possess honor were imbricated with class and racial status, the employment of such terms, and their corroboration by others, was likely a deliberate strategy aimed to counter notions of perniciousness and undesirability.[65] This was particularly important given that popular discourse connected the undesirability of foreigners to their exploitation of the weak and poor within Mexico, particularly women. Salem's expression of his desire that he and his Mexican children die in Mexico countered Mexican fears that certain foreigners—particularly Jews—had no desire to contribute to Mexican society. In this framework, Jews accrued wealth in Mexico to distribute among family members abroad, without returning any money into the Mexican economy. Their familiarity with Mexican social and cultural norms enabled the expelled merchants to employ rhetoric that might persuade authorities to decide in their favor. Due to their ability to mobilize widespread networks of commercial patronage and their use of the gendered rhetoric of masculine responsibility, then, all those who were expelled in this, the greatest scandal in Mexico for over a decade, were allowed to return within several years.

In response to the worsening economy and the growth of anti-immigrant sentiment, the Mexican state restricted the entrance of foreigners. Many of these restrictions depended on economic status rather than nationality. The "temporary" 1927 decree, made permanent in 1929, had already limited entrance based on nationality. In spite of disagreements between the SRE and the *Secretaría de Gobernación* as to whether or not Turkish nationals should be excluded, the *Secretaría de Gobernación* decided that Syrian, Lebanese, Armenian, Palestinian, Arab, Chinese, Turkish, Russian, and Polish immigrants should be barred. A number of factors contributed to their overall undesirability. These included their overwhelming presence in urban centers and the allegation that many had acquired permission to immigrate as farmers and yet, upon arrival in Mexico, never dedicated themselves to the fields. Most damning was the contention that their occupations "do not constitute a useful economic factor of the development of public wealth, nor can they be considered as a contingent of production." Many of these migrants devoted themselves to "petty commerce and usury" based on meager capital and precarious credit, and "have produced a notorious disequilibrium in high-volume trade, displacing our conationals from small trade."[66] The 1929 law guaranteed that immigrants possessing at least ten thousand pesos could attain exemption from nationality-based exclusions. Additionally, the spouses, parents, descendants, and minor siblings of foreign individuals whose residency was fixed in Mexico and who had obtained Mexican naturalization could bypass nationality-based restrictions. Mexican consular posts abroad were charged with enforcing these controls, marking the shift toward what the historian Aristide Zolberg has described as "remote control" in migratory practices.[67] The concern that migrants from Russia and Poland could cause political instability by promoting communist or socialist ideology was not mentioned as a rationale for restriction, even though some were expelled from Mexico on those grounds.[68] Instead, economic concerns were the primary reasons stated for immigrant exclusion. Most salient was the fear that the occupations of these immigrants damaged the Mexican economy by displacing Mexican nationals.

It was not only the Mexican government that viewed certain immigrants as economically detrimental. During the *Maximato*, the six-year period from 1928 to 1934 after Calles had relinquished the presidency but continued to exert influence, an increasing number of organizations were founded that voiced their views on foreigners and immigration to the Mexican government. Some groups, like Mexico City's *Unión Revolucionaria de Mexicanos Naturalizados*, encouraged foreigners to naturalize as a sign of their "profound sense of gratitude."[69] Other organizations, like the *Comité Permanente Pro-México de Afuera*, emphasized that "it should be understood by all merchants who come from abroad to establish themselves here that they are not coming to a conquered country," but that they should contribute through "their honest labor" to the society that has extended them hospitality.[70] In 1933, the *Cámara Nacional de Comercio, Industría y Minería* in Guadalajara requested that "only honorable people who come to work in a field of equality and honorable competition, thus cooperating for the betterment of the state, be allowed to nationalize." It requested that the state surveil the legal status of all foreigners who wanted to engage in commerce.[71] These groups were not against all immigration. But they only supported the naturalization of foreigners who demonstrated their gratitude for the hospitality of the Mexican state and society by engaging in honorable work and not exploiting fellow Mexicans.

Other organizations, however, called for restrictions on the immigration and naturalization of foreigners along lines that conflated economic and racial concerns, often highlighting foreigners' propensity to engage in contraband trade as a rationale for exclusion. These groups, many of whose members had lower-middle-class origins, sought to convince the Mexican government to limit migration. The historian Alicia Gojman notes that although the national government did not draw directly on the support of these organizations, the organizations' programs found indirect support in local and regional governments, which in turn pressured the national government to restrict immigration.[72] In 1930, the *Campaña Nacionalista de Labor*, based in Irapuato, Guanajuato, expressed that they were in favor of the nationalization of foreigners who had lived in Mexico for many years, possessed good customs, and were "of blood and customs perfectly assimilable into our own, not races that are going to degenerate the species."[73] While this group did not articulate precisely who was assimilable, other groups, like the *Unión Nacionalista Mexicana Pro-Raza y Salud Pública*, made their targets more explicit. According to this group, individuals of Chinese and Jewish origins were undesirable because they displaced Mexican workers and undermined established businesses by importing contraband and not paying taxes.[74] Chinese and Jewish immigrants were a racial and public health threat. A pamphlet that the *Unión de Comerciantes Mexicanos de Fresnillo* distributed in Zacatecas reiterated these claims. It proclaimed, "Jew means War, Hunger, and Prostitution; Chinese means Syphilis, Trachoma, Degeneration, and Tuberculosis," warning Mexicans that they should teach their children to have affection for their *patría* by extricating it from the tentacles of the "foreign octopus." Although this group singled out Jews and Chinese, it also cautioned Mexicans not to purchase from "*aboneros*, Arabs, Russians, Poles, Lebanese, and any other undesirable race."[75] Similarly, the *Liga de Defensa Nacional* founded a periodical that featured articles on "The Merchants Facing the Jewish Invasion of the Country" and "The Pro-Mexico Committee in the Markets."[76] These groups marked certain nationalities, races, and religions as unassimilable, parasitic to the Mexican economy and the Mexican nation. Although the Mexican government phrased its opposition to certain immigrants on national or economic grounds, these nationalist organizations had no qualms about conflating such categories with racial undesirability.

Complaints emerged from throughout Mexico. The *Comerciantes en Pequeño del Mercado la Lagunilla* in Mexico City denounced "Russians and other foreigners" who were killing the commerce of Mexicans,[77] while the formation of the *Comité Nacionalista* in Aguascalientes elicited complaints from the French legation in Mexico for its targeting of Syrians, Lebanese, and others.[78] The *Cámara Nacional de Comercio* in Iguala, Guerrero decried the "plague" of foreigners who had entered the country under false pretenses, claims reiterated by the *Asociación Regional de Comerciantes e Industriales Mexicanos* in Tampico, Tamaulipas.[79] The *Campaña Nacionalista del Estado de Puebla* reserved much of its vitriol for foreigners. "Don't make yourself an accomplice to national scarcity by buying from Jewish *aboneros*" warned one slogan, while another cautioned "Citizen: close the doors of your house to the *aboneros*, who almost always sell contraband merchandise."[80] Some anti-immigrant groups allied beyond state borders, such as the *Liga Defensa de Propietarios de Zapaterías, Peleterías, y Similares* in Mexico City, uniting with the *Centro Mercantil de Pieles y Calzados* in Monterrey, Nuevo Leon and the *Unión de Industriales y Comerciantes de la Ciudad de León* and the *Cámara Nacional de Comercio e Industría* in León, Guanajuato. These groups urged "the uniting of all good Mexicans" for the "well-being of our regions and the *patria*" against those foreigners who ruined the Mexican economy by making false claims, smuggling contraband, and declaring false bankruptcy to avoid paying debts.[81] The organizations involved, uniting shoemakers, furriers, leatherworkers, businessmen, and industrialists, highlight the array of the branches of commerce that viewed themselves as victims of foreigners. Their distribution throughout the country emphasizes the extent to which migrants and the perceived threats they posed became a national issue. For these groups, migrants were a plague that needed to be quarantined and neutralized for the good of the Mexican body politic. It was the duty of the Mexican state and Mexican workers to assure the prosperity of the Mexican economy by frequenting Mexican-owned businesses that sold Mexican-made goods.

The agitations of these groups had greater repercussions for Chinese migrants, who faced a massive pogrom in northern Mexico in 1931 and left Mexico en masse in its wake, and for Ashkenazi peddlers, who found themselves legislated against in Mexico City in the early 1930s, than it did for Sephardi Jews.[82] Mexican anti-foreigner sentiments reverberated in the Ladino press in Istanbul, where they were linked to the rise of Hitler.[83] In 1931, Alberto Farji, a Sephardi Jew from Izmir living in Culiacán, Sinaloa, wrote several letters of complaint to various branches of the Mexican national government. Farji, whose business partner in a clothing store was a Mexican national, alleged that the local government taxed him disproportionally because he was a foreigner. According to Farji, the local treasurer had been unduly influenced by the *Comité Pro-Raza*. The *Comité Pro-Raza*, which sent translations of Henry Ford's *The International Jew* and *The Protocols of the Elders of Zion* to Presidents Abelardo Rodríguez and Lázaro Cárdenas, voiced particular antagonism toward Chinese, Jews, and Lebanese, whose presence it regarded as detrimental to Mexico's welfare.[84] Farji alleged that the treasurer of Culiacán wanted all foreigners to leave Mexico and that, although he was constitutionally prohibited from expelling those who were not deemed pernicious, the treasurer was trying to drive Farji out through overtaxation. These actions were harmful to Farji and also infringed on the rights of his Mexican business partner. Farji threatened to contact the Turkish ambassador to Washington, DC, in charge of the affairs of Turkish nationals in Mexico, to intervene on his behalf should the Mexican national government not take appropriate actions to protect his interests.[85]

Anti-foreigner and specifically anti-Jewish agitation propelled Jews to organize for purposes other than social or religious gatherings. B'nai B'rith's YMHA organization at Tacuba 15 in Mexico City had existed since the early 1920s, providing frequenters with a Jewish library containing books in Russian and Hebrew and lounge areas where young Jews could mingle with each other. Many Sephardi men, particularly those not of the economic elite, preferred to spend their evenings, after a day of peddling, seated in the Café Bojor on Capuchinas Street (renamed 'Venustiano Carranza' in 1928) to the south of the Zócalo, drinking *raki*, eating *mezes*, and playing dominoes or dice while singing in Ladino or Turkish.[86] But now, facing rising anti-foreigner sentiment, Jews in Mexico began to organize to advocate for their economic rights. Some organizations, like the *Asociación Israelita de Aboneros*, founded in 1930, which defined itself as "a cultural group for young people" that offered loans, financing, protection, intervention, and legal help, had a membership that was solely Ashkenazi. Others, like the *Asociación de Comerciantes Israelitas en Pequeños*, founded in 1930 in response to the "medieval attitude" of the Mexican press toward Jews, included Sephardi and Ashkenazi members.[87] Most notable was the founding of the *Cámara Israelita de Industría y Comercio de México* (CIICM) in 1931, whose leadership and membership crossed subethnic divides and which thrust itself to the fore in protecting Jews throughout Mexico.

The actions the CIICM undertook fell into two categories. First, it sought to unite all Jews, regardless of national origin or linguistic background, so that it could serve as the spokesperson for Jewish ethical, moral, and commercial interests in Mexico.[88] To that end, its board featured Ashkenazi and Syrian Jews, while the president of the organization, Jack Penhas, was Sephardi. To unite its diverse membership, in 1932 the CIICM published the "Directorio Comercial, Industrial, y Profesional," which featured informative articles in Spanish and Yiddish on how to issue letters of change, how to fill out checks, and Mexican labor laws. It provided members with contact information for Mexican consular officials abroad and foreign consular representatives in Mexico, a list of all members, their contact and business information sorted alphabetically and by occupation, and advertisements for Jewish-owned businesses in Mexico.[89] The articles demonstrate the effort that the CIICM put into educating its Jewish membership about Mexican business regulations in order to ensure that Jews in Mexico did not accidentally violate laws, a sign of Jewish willingness to integrate into the Mexican economy and abide by Mexican legal codes. On the other hand, the registry of Jewish businessmen provided members of the CIICM with knowledge of precisely which Jews were engaged in which distinct economic activities, potentially facilitating intra-Jewish interactions rather than encouraging Jews to conduct commerce with Mexicans and others.

Further belying the integrationist intentions of the CIICM was the arbitration that it established to allow members to mediate financial disputes without involving the Mexican courts. In 1934, a financial conflict between Jack Penhas and Max King, a prominent Ashkenazi jeweler, reached the Mexican courts. The CIICM, aware of "the very unfavorable consequences that this matter could have for our colony," sought to mediate their conflict within the confines of the CIICM; as a result of this arbitration, King withdrew his complaint against Penhas from Mexican civil court.[90] While bringing a case before the Mexican court could serve as a means of forcing the hand of one's opponent within CIICM arbitration, the efforts that the CIICM went through to ensure that intra-Jewish cases be settled without recourse to the Mexican legal system were a means of combating views of Jews as pernicious. If Jews, regardless of subethnic identification, could mediate their disputes within the confines of a Jewish organization, this would keep Jews out of the limelight and potentially ameliorate negative public opinion.

The CIICM also intervened with the Mexican government as the representative of a unified Jewish community. Jews, unlike the Lebanese, Poles, or Chinese, had no government to represent their interests, the leaders of the CIICM explained, and the CIICM sought to fill that void to combat the rising anti-immigrant and anti-Jewish sentiment of nationalist groups. In a manner similar to how the French legation protested anti-Lebanese activity, the CIICM asked the federal government to intervene to guarantee the safety and livelihood of Jewish residents in locales ranging from Hermosillo and Mazatlán to Morelia and Veracruz.[91] Jack Penhas and the CIICM secretary, Jacob Landau, sent numerous telegrams to President Rodríguez, meeting with him to advocate for the protection of the livelihoods and persons of their coreligionists and to try to stem the rising tide of anti-Jewish publications.[92]

Embedded within growing concerns that foreigners were racially and economically detrimental to Mexico were worries that these foreigners exploited Mexican workers. Although legislation sought to protect Mexicans' access to work by mandating that Mexicans make up ninety percent of workers in all companies, in 1932 the *Departamento Confidencial*, Mexico's central intelligence agency, began an investigation into "Armenian, Jewish, Polish, and Russian foreigners who own businesses" to ascertain the number of Mexican employees they had, whether or not they had entered Mexico legally, and any related material. The *Departamento Confidencial* sought to ensure that the Mexican employees had contracts stipulating eight-hour days. These investigations included Sephardi Jews of Turkish origin who had become nationalized as Mexicans, though their focus was on Polish and Russian Jews and on Syrian and Lebanese Jews and Christians.[93] Although all Mexican employees surveyed conveyed satisfaction with their working conditions, a 1934 report on the expulsion of foreigners from Mexico expressed surprise that only one foreigner had been expelled for violating the *Ley de Trabajo*, which the report's author attributed to bribery.[94]

Allegations that foreigners exploited Mexican workers constituted a frequent trope in petitions for expulsion, though the targets of these cases were more often Syrio-Lebanese than Sephardi. In 1928, the *Liga Nacional Campesina* in Veracruz petitioned for the expulsion of the Grayeb brothers, of Syrio-Lebanese provenance, for collusion and for having assassinated several Mexican workers who protested conditions on their coffee plantation. The Grayebs were expelled, though they were eventually allowed to return on the condition they not reside in Veracruz.[95] Similarly, Manuel Mina, a Syrio-Lebanese youth whose father owned a clothing stand, was targeted for expulsion after having allegedly beaten a Mexican worker who had not wanted to purchase his merchandise. Although *El Universal* clarified that Mina had gotten into an altercation with a Mexican merchant who had tried to set up a stall next to Mina's in La Lagunilla market, a letter in *El Gráfico* in response to the Mina case castigated "the inhumane and immoral form of exploitation of Mexican female workers [*obreras*] by the Syrio-Lebanese, Arabs, Poles, Russians, and Jews." It alleged that the only way foreigners were able to sell at such low prices was by forcing Mexican workers to sew clothing in poor conditions for long hours at low pay, causing them to lose their health for the rest of their lives. Workers were afraid to complain, lest they lose their jobs.[96] The protection of the well-being and working conditions of Mexican laborers became another argument against foreigners in the Mexican workplace and in Mexico in general. Jews were by no means the sole, or even primary, target of anti-immigrant agitation in Mexico. Rather, anti-Jewish tropes were a facet of broader xenophobic utterances and actions.

During the *Maximato*, fears of the moral threats that migrants could pose also emerged. Although Mexico did not participate in international conferences on sex trafficking during the Porfiriato,[97] by the late 1920s, the Mexican state was increasingly concerned about the sexual propriety of foreign women and the possibility that they were entering Mexico in order to engage in prostitution. By 1930, married women were no longer allowed to travel alone or with their children without the written permission of their spouses.[98] In 1930, the French legation in Mexico warned the SRE that a ship heading to Veracruz from France bore ten girls of Greek nationality destined for "white slavery."[99] Mexican investigators discovered that the only woman of Greek nationality on board was a Sephardi woman, Lili Naar, who was traveling to Mexico to join her husband, Mario. Although Naar was briefly detained upon arrival in Mexico, she was permitted to enter.[100]

The lack of morality of foreign men served as justification for expulsion petitions and court cases. In 1928, the twenty-year-old Constantinopolitan Victor Pessah, who had been naturalized as a Mexican in 1926 and was an importer of novelties from the United States and Europe, was sentenced to prison for "insults to morality." Pessah was convicted of having publicly pulled down his pants and underwear, grabbed his genitalia, and shouted at several passing women "Look! Know me well, *hijas de la chingada*."[101] The Mexican public could understand such cases as illustrative of the disregard in which foreign men of Middle Eastern provenance held Mexican women, their lack of respect for Mexican gender and social norms, and their overall undesirability.

The growing number of expulsion cases against Sephardi and other migrants in Mexico during the *Maximato* is an indication of the Mexican government's crackdown on those it deemed pernicious. Mexico, wary of the costs of repatriating expelled foreigners, frequently placed expellees on ships from Veracruz to Havana, eliciting complaints from the Cuban government.[102] In 1934, the *Dirección General del Gobierno* issued a report breaking down those who had been expelled from Mexico by reason and nationality. Of the eight hundred and fifty expulsions, almost one-third were Guatemalans expelled for violating of the *Ley de Migración*; overall, half of the expulsion cases, regardless of nationality, involved violations of that law. Included among the expellees were twenty-seven Greeks and twenty-one Syrians; Greeks only began being expelled in 1931, more than one-third of them on the grounds of having defrauded customers. Although popular groups blamed foreign merchants for dealing in contraband, only twenty-seven out of all of the expulsion cases hinged on smuggling goods; more than half of those involved Chinese or Americans. The report noted that Mexico had a small population and that immigrants could contribute fruitfully, but only those who were selected for health, economics, culture, social life, and were "good elements who could be put to work in favorable conditions, in light of their customs, capacities, and racial characteristics." The report concluded with calls for the Mexicanization of foreigners, particularly those who resided in urban areas.[103]

In 1933, the Department of Migration issued the "strictly confidential" Circular 250, which defined which races and individuals should be excluded from Mexico. Individuals were to be excluded along racial and ethnic lines, for political reasons, for bad customs, and for being "adventuring people"—a euphemism for the Romani. While no mention was made of Jews in this circular, when it was revised in April of 1934 as Confidential Circular 157, Jews were presented as the "most undesirable of all."[104] According to Circular 157, Jews would nearly always declare their religion when asked. Although Mexico was forced to accept American Jews because of reciprocity agreements, Jews of all other origins, regardless of nationality, should be prohibited. If it was determined that a visa had been granted to a Jew, the authorities should revoke it immediately and telegram the central government.[105] This Mexican restriction against immigrants along lines that explicitly linked race and religion marked a shift from earlier legislation, which had not obviously targeted particular races as undesirable. This circular made it clear that the economic rationale employed to justify immigration restrictions was intimately intertwined with racial and religious concerns. Just as foreigners posed a moral and economic threat to Mexican society, certain races and religions—particularly Jews—could undermine the Mexican state and the Mexican nation. There remained a firm belief that Jews would never conceal their religion and would therefore be easily identifiable and excludable if asked directly.

Within the context of growing popular and governmental sentiment against migrants, Jews with Turkish nationality intent on entering Mexico despite the restrictions developed multiple strategies for circumventing the new measures aimed at excluding them. On August 24th, 1927, ten migrants with Sephardi names arrived in Veracruz from Havana. Of these ten, six were male—only one of them unmarried—and four were female—of the women, likewise, one was unmarried. Two bore Cuban nationality, two were Turkish citizens, and the rest had Greek papers.[106] Many of these migrants were related, traveling with spouses, parents, or more distant relatives. Unsurprisingly, since many Sephardi Jews from Thrace migrated to Cuba, two were from Silivri and three from Kirkkilise (Kırklareli). However, none of those from Kırklareli claimed Turkish nationality. Only four of the ten listed their religion as "Jewish" on their migration cards; the rest declared themselves "Orthodox."

One migrant's identification card for travel to Mexico was particularly revealing. Rebecca Mitrani, a married forty-six-year-old, listed her place of birth as "Kir-Klissé," but rather than locating her city of birth in Turkey as was geographically accurate, she gave her country of origin as "Greece." At this time, the ban against the entrance of Turkish citizens into Mexico, discussed in chapter 4, had gone into effect. In claiming that she was born in Greece, Mitrani and her family could evade the new Mexican restrictions barring Turkish nationals. Mitrani's subterfuge went unnoticed by Mexican officials, who likely had no detailed knowledge of precisely where borders lay in Thrace.

Striking, too, was Mitrani's claim of the Orthodox religion. Several Sephardi migrants had declared non-Jewish religions on earlier naturalization petitions, though this practice was not widespread—some, like Elias Sevy and Peppo Saltiel, claimed their religion as "Catholic" on failed naturalization petitions in the early 1920s before reverting to claiming the Jewish religion on successful naturalizations in the later 1920s or early 1930s.[107] Sevy, mirroring the strategy that Rebecca Mitrani used in her 1927 entrance into Mexico, altered his place of birth from "Smyrna, Turkey" on his 1924 naturalization petition to "Salonica, Greece" in his successful 1929 naturalization. Mitrani's 1927 identification card bears several clues as to her Jewish origins, hints to which those who processed her papers were not attuned. First, Mitrani was a particularly prominent surname among Thracian Jews.[108] Mexican officials, like their American counterparts, associated Jewishness with stereotypically Ashkenazi names, making it easier for Sephardi migrants to avoid being labeled "Jewish" when it was not expedient. Second, Mitrani signed her name in *soletreo*, the Sephardi Hebrew cursive script, which might have been mistaken for Greek by Mexican officials unfamiliar with non-Latin alphabets. And even the name she used for her city of birth—"Kir-Klissé"—hints at Jewish origins; known in Turkey as Kırklareli since 1924, the city was called "Saranda Ekklisies" by Greek Orthodox residents.[109] Only Jews would have persisted in referring to it as Kirkkilise. By the time she registered as a foreigner in Mexico in 1930, as a result of Mexico's monitoring of foreign nationals in Mexican territory, Mitrani was signing her name in a halting Latin hand. But her earlier use of *soletreo* characters belied her claims to the Orthodox religion. Mexican officials either did not notice or did not care.

Numerous migrants entered with a nationality that belied their origins in cities in Turkey. Many, like Mitrani, identified their natal city as being located in Greece rather than Turkey. This practice was the most common for Sephardi migrants who entered Mexico after living in Cuba for some years. The Becherano family, who entered Mexico in July 1928, noted their place of birth as "Kirklisse, Greece" and bore Greek nationality. Several people with the surname "Behar" who entered Mexico from Cuba at various points in the late 1920s and 1930s declared their origin as "Edirne, Greece" or "Silivri, Greece." A migrant who arrived in Mexico on a tourist visa from Cuba in 1929 (only to stay until at least 1937, when he had a child with a Sephardi Jew of Turkish origin whom he had met in Mexico) declared his place of origin to be "Rodosto, Greece."[110] This strategy of evading the 1927 ban against the entrance of Turkish nationals relied on Mexican consular and immigration officials' ignorance of where, precisely, borders lay. These migrants likely also had false documentation to support their claims of Greek origins—false papers were notoriously easy to come by in Cuba, though scholars have focused on how such individuals sought to enter the United States rather than Mexico.[111] The methods developed for evading American restrictions were equally effective for bypassing Mexican ones.

Although some Sephardi migrants used illicit documentation to circumvent Mexican regulations, many others used transnational family ties and networks to enter Mexico. While Sephardim of Serbian, Bulgarian, or Greek origins and nationalities were not explicitly restricted until 1934, when Jews of all origins were prohibited, an increased focus on immigration and exclusion catalyzed a greater interest in requiring visas for all would-be migrants. Family reunification remained a loophole that migrants could exploit, although greater enforcement of legal codes complicated even legal attempts at migration. To attain permission for family reunification visas, Mexican residents needed to write to the *Secretaría de Gobernación* and then, once permission was granted, send a card with the visa to their family members who intended to migrate.[112] Moises Cohen, from Monastir and living in Guadalajara, petitioned for three of his younger brothers to come to Mexico in 1929. His brothers, all in their early twenties, lived in Havana. Cohen asserted that "they have the means to live honestly and to bring their capital to our country," attempting to assuage concerns that migrants were economically detrimental.[113] The brothers were initially turned away in Veracruz for not having the requisite visa. The Mexican consulate in Belgrade promised to send the appropriate documentation, allowing the brothers to disembark in the Mexican port.[114] Nonetheless, Mexico's growing concern with keeping out those who could burden the economy or take the place of Mexican workers meant that although provisions were made to allow some family reunification, petitions were not guaranteed to succeed. Because claiming family relations was one means of circumventing restrictions against certain types of migrants, the Mexican government became invested in ensuring that such family relations were genuine. They increasingly required those petitioning to provide documentation of purported ties. Such documentation could be falsified, often as prospective migrants gathered in Paris while attempting to secure authorization to travel to any number of destinations throughout the Americas. France, as always, was a crucial fulcrum in transnational Sephardi connections.

The French Connection and Transnational Travel

Even for Sephardim who maintained residency in Mexico or refrained from frequent international travels, the ability to perform alternative national identities was a means of facilitating upward social, cultural, and economic mobility. While Julia Phillips Cohen has aptly demonstrated that Sephardi migrants in the United States identified themselves as Ottoman and "Oriental" through their engagement with Ottoman products and symbols upon emigration,[115] Sephardi Jews in Mexico most adamantly did not. A few played up their Middle Eastern connections while passing off French-produced cotton carpets, with oriental motifs stamped on them, as wool carpets of Turkish origin, actions that mirrored earlier French accusations against Armenians and Jews of selling counterfeit oriental rugs in Paris.[116] In contrast to the large number of Syrio-Lebanese who capitalized on their origins to sell trinkets from the Holy Land,[117] or the Armenian Odabachian family that established a business selling Oriental carpets in Mexico City that survives to this day,[118] Sephardi migrants by and large sought to distinguish themselves as "Europeans" in Mexico. They did this in part by selling wares that they had imported from the United States or France. Even in the CIICM directory, the advertisements of Sephardi-owned businesses were far more likely to emphasize that their goods were imported from Europe or the United States than were the advertisements for Ashkenazi or Syrian Jewish establishments.[119] For Sálomon Levy, who never saw a reason to become naturalized as a Mexican, performing French identity was a means of selling his wares to Mexicans who were desirous of the social capital that French fashions conveyed. He dutifully invented tales of Parisian life for his clients, although he had never set foot in Paris. Given the rising anti-Jewish, anti-Turkish, and anti-Lebanese agitation in Mexico, publicly identifying oneself as French proved far more lucrative than conveying Jewish or Turkish origins to Mexican clientele. As French migrants selling goods, Sephardi Jews were more likely to be received as "educated foreigners."[120] Maintaining transnational ties and performing French origins allowed Sephardi migrants to reinvent themselves as bearers of social and cultural capital while simultaneously deflecting anti-Jewish sentiments that otherwise would have targeted them.

Other migrants looked to temporary or permanent relocations to France as a means of undergirding their connections to Mexico. In 1928, Mauricio Assael filed for bankruptcy, seeking protection from a naturalized Costa Rican named Max Weinberg who alleged that Assael had not repaid a mortgage on a property that Assael had purchased in the Colonia Roma. During his bankruptcy proceedings and several related court cases, Assael was not in Mexico. As was accepted practice, when Assael left Mexico for France and the United States, he first left his jewelry business, "La Exposición," in the hands of his wife, Rachel Corri. When she, too, left Mexico, control of the business passed into the hands of a fellow Sephardi, Salvador Azicri.[121] Mauricio was seeking the latest technology, invented in France and now found in "all the developed countries," that would allow him to make glass and plastic jewels appear to be of the same quality as real stones. To this end, Assael traveled to New York in August of 1927,[122] writing to Azicri that though he had found factories that could potentially produce the goods he wanted, they did not have the proper machinery. "You need the patience of the devil to succeed in this," he told Azicri, expressing the hope that there would be no need to return to Mexico but that "God will make everything good." Only on August 17, 1928 was Mauricio able to tell "my very dear Salvador" that he had received the necessary patent from Washington, DC: "You can only imagine my happiness." He also requested that Azicri send one thousand francs to a B. Assael in Izmir.[123]

At the time of his bankruptcy, then, Assael, though a Mexican citizen since 1918, was not in Mexico. Nor would he or his wife and children return to live in Mexico. Even in the face of greater surveillance of and restrictions on mobility in and between Mexico, Turkey, France, the United States, and other countries, vestiges of Sephardi reliance on transnational networks and geographical mobility persisted. Transnational ties and transnational lifestyles were still noticeable. Sephardi Jews retained active connections between multiple states, as the example of Assael demonstrates. Assael's nationality and business were Mexican, he imported goods from the United States and France, lived in France, and sent remittances back to relatives in Turkey.

Acquiring Mexican citizenship did not entail continuous or permanent residency in Mexico. Throughout the early 1930s, when Assael and his wife, Rachel Corri, and their children relocated to the Fontenay-sur-Bois suburb of Paris, other Sephardi Jews who had acquired Mexican nationality also continued to be mobile, drawing on French connections or perpetuating ties with other countries in Latin America or the United States. Though Assael never returned to live in Mexico, he maintained his business interests in Mexico City while living in Paris, with Salvador Azicri canceling Assael's bankruptcy proceedings in 1931. Likewise, other Sephardi migrants who acquired Mexican citizenship continued to renew their permission from the Mexican government to live and travel abroad, all the while retaining Mexican nationality.[124]

In spite of restrictions on mobility, many Sephardi Jews in Mexico relied on retaining a French connection. Manuel Modiano, from a prominent Salonican Sephardi family and a relative of Mauricio Assael, and who was naturalized as a Mexican in 1931, repeatedly traveled to Paris with his wife, Rebecca, in the late 1920s and early 1930s. He listed his contacts there as a Sephardi firm, Misrachi, Carasso, and Company, on Rue de Trevise in the neighborhood of Montmartre.[125] Some migrants retained Parisian familial connections, listing them as references in their travels from Mexico to Paris.[126] Others retained French commercial connections through the maintenance of a family presence in Paris; although two of the Alazraki brothers had acquired Mexican nationality in 1928, a third brother, Moïse, lived in Paris and was listed as a contact when his brothers traveled to Paris. Moïse acquired a Mexican visa in 1932, though he drew on commercial connections with a Sephardi coreligionist, Santiago Cohen, rather than having his brothers petition for him.[127] Moïse continued to travel back and forth between Paris, Mexico City, and New York with his wife and son, alternating residency in these three cities.[128] Drawing on familial connections for economic reasons continued to be a potent option for some Sephardi migrants, even in the face of growing restrictions on international mobility.

Some Sephardim, like the Alazrakis, Assaels, Capons, Carassos, and others, drew on their economic success in Mexico to further their upward mobility in Paris. While the majority of Sephardi Jews of Ottoman and post-Ottoman origins in Paris lived in the working-class neighborhood of the Roquette, in the eleventh *arrondissement*, when Sephardi Jews who had sojourned in Mexico resided in Paris, they lived in middle- or upper-class regions of the city, often, and perhaps not coincidentally, near the headquarters of the Alliance Israélite Universelle in the ninth *arrondissement*. When the Carassos and the Capons relocated to Paris in the 1930s, they listed residences in the ninth *arrondissement* and in the seventh, right off of the plaza facing the Eiffel Tower, though they continued to travel back to Mexico frequently.[129] Acquiring Mexican nationality and establishing a successful business endeavor in Mexico provided Sephardi migrants a means of increasing their social and economic capital to the extent that they could relocate to Paris as Mexicans and live in neighborhoods that were not readily available to most Sephardi migrants in Paris. Mexican nationality and financial success in Mexico aided upward mobility in locales such as France that Sephardim, given their propensity to view France as the paragon of culture par excellence, saw as bearing greater social capital than Mexico. As a Sephardi Jew, one could make it in Paris, but it was easier to do so as a Mexican national.

While some Sephardim in Mexico retained active commercial and familial relations with coreligionists in France, others perpetuated transnational connections with the United States or elsewhere in Latin America. For some, like Isaac Behar, a Sephardi Jew born in Mexico in 1910 to parents who later relocated to Colombia, obtaining the Mexican nationality to which he had gained access by birth in Mexico became an issue worth contesting with Mexican authorities. Obtaining Mexican nationality on the grounds of jus soli was the only means by which Behar could acquire a nationality, since he was not eligible for Colombian citizenship and did not possess the citizenship of his parents.[130] For others, retaining active commercial or familial relations with Sephardim living in Cuba, Argentina, or Guatemala provided a means of facilitating cross-border economic connections. When Jacobo Yaffe applied for Mexican naturalization, Mexican authorities discovered that Yaffe had left the country, traveling first to Cuba, then Colombia, and was unsure of his return to Mexico. Other Sephardi migrants traveled between Mexico and Guatemala, and the Sephardi migrant Jacobo Elnecave, who lived in Tapachula, Chiapas, served as a contact for some Sephardi residents of Guatemala who entered Mexico. Others ended up returning to Mexico, like Simon Lahana, who had relocated to Guatemala while his four children remained in Mexico but returned to Mexico in 1933, though he only officially gained immigrant status in 1939. By his 1933 reentry into Mexico, Lahana possessed no citizenship, having lost the United States nationality he had acquired through his earlier stay in the Philippines, after the United States changed its laws regarding extending American nationality to Filipinos.[131] Still others traveled between Mexico and Colombia, Argentina, and Cuba.[132] Thus, despite greater restrictions on mobility in the postwar period, some Sephardim were able to maintain their transnational connections, traveling back and forth between Mexico and cities in the United States or elsewhere in the Americas.

Conclusion

In August of 1934, a circular was distributed to Mexico's foreign service officers bearing the heading "CONFIDENTIAL," in capital letters. This circular explained that "the ethnic, economic, political, and demographic conditions that prevail in the Republic require the replacement of the prohibitions and restrictions established in the confidential Circular 250 [regarding immigration] with the following additions." In what followed, the granting of visas to those of the black race, whether of African or Australian origins, was banned. So, too, was the granting of visas to those of the "yellow or Mongolic race" (exceptions were made for Japanese and Koreans, while Filipinos and Hawaiians were viewed as American); anyone of the "Oriental Indo-European race" (encompassing those from India, Ceylon, Central Asia, Iran, and elsewhere); and those of the "olive or Malayan Race" (including all those from Oceania). In addition to the racial categories, this new circular also prohibited the entrance of Poles, Lithuanians, Czechoslovaks, Syrians, Lebanese, Palestinians, Armenians, Arabs, Turks, Bulgarians, Romanians, Persians, Yugoslavs, and Greeks. Individuals from the USSR were prohibited on political grounds. Albanians, Afghans, Ethiopians, Algerians, Egyptians, and Moroccans were banned because their "mix of blood and indices of culture, habits, and customs make them exotic for our psychology." In regard to "the problem created by Jewish immigration," Jews, more than any other group, "due to their psychological and moral characteristics, for the class of activities to which they dedicate themselves and the procedures that they follow in the commercial branch in which they inevitably wind up, are undesirable." This new circular thereby stipulated that they should be banned.[133]

This circular, which drew from Circulars 250 and 157, marked a transition in Mexican attitudes toward immigration and toward citizenship itself. While earlier restrictions were couched in economic terms, this new circular subsumed those economic concerns under racial concerns. Noticeably absent from the long list of nationals and races banned from entry into Mexico were those of Western European, Latin American, and American origins, those whose race, customs, and psychology would supposedly allow them easily to mix into Mexico's population. In this new immigration policy, economic concerns gave way to ethnic and racial worries about the assimilability of immigrants. Restricting immigration to those deemed socially, culturally, racially, and economically assimilable served as a means of protecting the Mexican body politic, economic, and ethnic. Sephardi migrants and other former Ottomans adapted to this by performing Europeanness and by entering into public debates to construe themselves racially as European.[134]

As Mexico's policy shifted from restricting immigration on economic grounds to viewing immigrants in racialized terms, Turkey used emigration as a means of homogenizing the religious composition of its population. Turkey's acceptance of thousands of Muslim refugees from the Balkans and simultaneous stripping of citizenship from several thousand members of religious minority groups emphasized the extent to which religion still played a role in the conceptualizations of who should constitute the Turkish nation, in spite of the ostensibly secular nature of the Turkish Republic. Policies that urged citizens to speak Turkish exclusively and trials against those who had insulted Turkishness propelled ethnic and religious minorities to play down their public performance of a distinct, non-Turkish identity.

Sephardi Jews were increasingly, yet not completely, caught up in global redefinitions of citizenship in Mexico, Turkey, and elsewhere. While progressively restrictive measures on migration and citizenship marked an end to patterns of geographic mobility and flexible uses of nationality for some, this was not the case for all Sephardi migrants in Mexico and beyond. Some, like Rebecca Mitrani and her family, bypassed Mexican restrictions by altering their place of origin, nationality, or religion on paperwork. Others drew on family and commercial ties in Mexico to migrate. And still others, like Isaac and Mathilde Capon, or Mauricio Assael and his family, acquired Mexican nationality before temporarily or permanently relocating to Paris. In spite of global obstacles to the freedom of movement, Sephardi migrants continued the patterns of hypermobility that maintained their diasporic connections.

(CHAPTER 6)

FORGE YOUR OWN PASSPORT

IN APRIL OF 1946, Mauricio Fresco, a former first secretary of the Mexican foreign service—whose diplomatic career had begun with an honorary position in Shanghai in 1932 and encompassed positions as first secretary in Bordeaux, Lisbon, Nazi-occupied Paris, and Marseille under Vichy—requested that the Mexican General Archive send him the original of his birth certificate, which he would replace with a facsimile.[1] The general director of the secretariat of foreign relations (SRE) saw no reason not to accede to Fresco's request.[2] On October 16, 1946, Fresco signed that he had received the original and the chief of archives attested that the facsimile was accurate.[3] The copy preserved in Fresco's diplomatic personnel file matched the original, recorded by the director of the civil registry in Mérida, Yucatán, in 1926; a fine of five pesos had been assessed for Fresco's delayed registration at the age of 26, an unremarkable occurrence. Fresco's registration in the Mérida civil registry attested that he had been born in Mérida on May 13, 1900, to David Fresco, a married businessman from Mexico City, and his wife, Rebeca Fresco, also from Mexico City. Two businessmen from Mérida, Manuel J. Acevedo and Edilberto Barrera, attested to the veracity of Fresco's late registration.[4]

On the face of it, Fresco's birth certificate was unremarkable, the delayed registration of his birth a frequent occurrence in the Mexico of his day. It was granted because it was an unexceptional request; but even if the request had been unusual, it might have been granted to Fresco, given the heights that he had achieved in his diplomatic career and in the numerous publications he had authored in his travels, affirming key controversial political tenets of Mexican foreign and domestic policy.

Fresco's birth certificate proving his Mexican origins, which were, in part, what undergirded the career and persona that he fashioned, casting himself as a staunch defender of Mexican interests, contained several crucial inaccuracies. Fresco had indeed been born in May of 1900 to parents named David and Rebeca Fresco. But his parents had never been residents of Mexico City. In fact, they had never set foot in Mexico. Rather than being a native of the Yucatán, Fresco was born in the Ottoman capital of Constantinople, one of nine children and the youngest son of the region's most prominent Ladino newspaper editor, the irascible David Fresco. Mauricio himself had first arrived in Mexico only in 1924, already a young man.[5] He had left his place of birth at the age of 17, a difficult feat in the midst of World War I as the Ottoman Empire clamped down on the emigration of men of conscriptable age. He spent several years wandering before setting sail for Veracruz from Boulogne-sur-Mer in September of 1924, on a Turkish passport, issued in Paris, bearing a Mexican visa issued in the French capital on June 23, 1924.[6] In 1929, three years after Fresco had falsified the registration of his birth in the Mexican Civil Registry, he applied for Mexican naturalization through official means, his petition attesting to his Turkish and Jewish origins.[7] This petition languished, seemingly supplanted by Fresco's relocation to Shanghai in 1930 and by his apparent trust—not misplaced—in his falsified Mexican origins.

This chapter uses the life of Mauricio Fresco as a foil for exploring the multiple tensions, at times coexisting and at times conflicting, that undergirded global Sephardi life in the tempestuous years of the late interwar and World War II eras. It draws the narrative of transnational Sephardi networks into a period in which they began to break down, just as they became most crucial. While in many ways an exceptional character, Fresco embedded himself within, contributed to, and drew on Sephardi ties within and outside of Mexico. Simultaneously, he rocketed to prominence as a Mexican diplomat, traveling the world and bearing written witness to some of the era's greatest calamities—the Japanese invasion and occupation of Manchuria, the Nazi occupation of Paris and its subsequent liberation, Spanish Civil War refugees languishing in French concentration camps. In a love for journalism inherited, albeit not without ambivalence, from his father, Fresco published numerous books in several languages on what he witnessed in the Mexican diplomatic corps, and served as a correspondent for newspapers throughout Europe, vociferously defending Mexican positions. His work as a photographer in Manchuria prior to his appointment as Mexican honorary consul in Shanghai led to his detainment by Japanese soldiers in 1931,[8] but by the time of World War II, Fresco was secure enough in his diplomatic credentials to take photographs of a bejowled Eugénie Pétain leaving the Notre Dame Cathedral in Paris, the Vichy premier Pierre Laval leaving the Spanish embassy, and a crowd of young children excitedly saluting Benito Mussolini. The Mexican press reported his early endeavors with pride, noting that this man who spoke seven languages was "more Mexican than a *nopal*," the prickly pear cactus that adorns the Mexican flag.[9]

This chapter explores how Mauricio Fresco, who left Constantinople at age seventeen, drew on and contributed to transnational Sephardi networks even as he traveled the world as a member of the Mexican diplomatic corps, crafting an image of an idealized Mexico and himself as its staunch proponent. Fresco's position depended on the social capital he could access as a member of transnational Sephardi networks, networks that he used in the service of the Mexican state and, later, to critique the purposes of states more broadly. Fresco's naturalization petition and his initial post as honorary consul in Shanghai were predicated on Sephardi patronage networks within Mexico to which Fresco, in Shanghai, had recourse. The linguistic skills that enabled him to successfully pass as Mexican and to navigate later Mexican diplomatic positions in Vichy-governed Marseille and in Paris were grounded in his Sephardi origins. And the ways in which Fresco drew on these patronage networks and his linguistic heritage to perform a new nationality was an equally common ploy, adopted by numerous other Sephardi migrants. Fresco's story serves as a framework through which to explore how Sephardi migrants drew on all networks at their disposal to remain mobile in a period where mobility increasingly meant the difference between life and death.

On April 6, 1931, Manuel Tello, the Mexican consul in Yokohama, passed along to the SRE a report written by Mauricio Fresco, whom Tello described as a Mexican in Shanghai as the commercial agent of a French company.[10] Fresco—Tello reported—had recently become aware of a number of Mexican women married to Chinese men who, after waves of anti-Chinese violence intensified in Mexico in the 1920s, had been deported—along with their husbands—to China. Some of these women, Fresco reported, had been abandoned by their Chinese husbands or had discovered that their husbands were in bigamous marriages with Chinese women. These women of Mexican birth found themselves in legal limbo; Mexican law stipulated that upon marriage, a woman take her husband's nationality. Fresco fashioned himself as an advocate for these women and was able to successfully petition for their repatriation, along with that of their Chinese-Mexican children, an effort that has earned him footnotes in every study of Chinese in Mexico.[11]

Fresco capitalized on the notoriety of his interventions to launch a meteoric and drama-filled career in the Mexican diplomatic corps. By his own and other accounts, Fresco was a perfect Mexican patriot who made a name for himself advocating for those who were vulnerable, casting Mexico by extension as a country that protected the helpless. In 1932, Fresco was named the Mexican honorary consul to Shanghai, a post he held for several years.[12] During this time, he hosted prominent Mexican officials, including the former president, Rodríguez.[13] Almost immediately after his appointment, Fresco faced the challenge of defending Mexico's actions in regard to the Chinese, averring that there was no anti-Chinese boycott in Mexico and that he had no information regarding recently deported Chinese residents of Mexico. A World Overseas Chinese official anonymously responded that Fresco had "falsely accused the overseas Chinese with having transacted unlawful business, etc., for which reasons they were being deported."[14] In June of 1933, Fresco wrote a letter to the consul in Yokohama complaining that with the arrival of two hundred and fifty Chinese from Mexico, the Chinese press had again begun to write articles denigrating Mexico and Fresco himself. In the two interviews requested of him, Fresco asserted that "the government of Mexico has not initiated any movement against the Chinese and that he has received no news that atrocities were committed against them," but that this was the only thing he could say to defend the Mexican government.[15]

Fresco advocated for Mexican economic interests while in China. In his official capacity as consul, he published articles in English on trade between Mexico and China, decrying the low volume of trade between the two countries. He lauded Mexico as an "agricultural and mining country" with universally recognized potential wealth in both fields and "the programme of National reconstruction started and carried out by our revolutionary governments" that enabled Mexico to attain "national economic independence."[16] The geographical proximity of the Mexican cities of Ensenada and Tijuana to the United States, and Mexico's favorable import policies, were advantages for Chinese exporters wanting their wares to reach into the Americas. However, he cautioned that Chinese businessmen should not "limit their radius of action to whatever territory their own Chinese agents can cover, but [should] spread such a radius by direct contact with Mexican dealers all over the country."[17] Fresco did not mention anti-Chinese violence in the same regions where he advocated conducting business in Mexico. Rather, he drew on his knowledge of English to seek to benefit Mexico, whether by burnishing the image of the success of post-revolutionary economic policies, stimulating trade in a period of global economic downturn, or encouraging Chinese exporters to rely on Mexican dealers rather than remaining within an economic network made up of Chinese agents.

According to Fresco's later reports, he was forced to flee Shanghai under the threat of death after the 1937 publication of his English-language book *Shanghai, The Paradise of Adventurers* under the pseudonym "G. E. Miller, Diplomat."[18] Local periodicals shared the most controversial allegations made in *Shanghai, The Paradise of Adventurers*, including reports on the easy sale of passports, the Lytton Commission's reliance on Japanese military sources for information on the Manchurian situation, and tax evasion and gambling activities by missionary orders. The book was particularly critical of extraterritoriality and how it permitted the exploitation of Chinese: "The flag of extraterritoriality is the largest banner ever devised. It reaches up to the heavens and ... smells that high, too," noted Fresco under his pseudonym.[19] Advance copies of the book, reports noted, had been sent to Chiang Kai-shek by airmail on the first westward flight of the China Clipper at the end of April.[20] While Fresco disavowed authorship of the controversial exposé in the Shanghai press, claiming to know nothing about the book, "he was grinning widely and appeared to have his tongue in his cheek."[21]

In a 1937 letter to President Lázaro Cárdenas, Fresco described his book as exposing "the machinations and abuses of the Imperialist powers," and "of the war in Manchuria and Shanghai and the indifferent attitude towards it of certain League of Nations members." According to Fresco, the international press had been "excessively favorable and all of them say that my book is the best defense of the abolition of the Rights of Extraterritoriality in China." Because of its sympathetic portrayal of the Chinese, it remained in print long after the Communist Revolution.[22] Fresco quoted Chinese reviews of the book to Cárdenas, reviews that described Fresco as "the first white man who has had the courage to defend the Chinese people in this way, and he had to be a Mexican citizen, whose country, whether in the case of Manchuria, Ethiopia, or Spain has always been the one to raise its voice." Being Mexican, Fresco explained, he felt it was his duty to share the book with Cárdenas. Cárdenas responded that he looked forward to reading it with great interest.[23]

Yet Mauricio Fresco's story as an ardent Mexican patriot conceals and is undergirded by another trajectory and network of connections. During multiple stages of his life, his reliance on and contribution to Sephardi networks proved critical. Mauricio Fresco's 1929 naturalization petition attests to his reliance on these intra-Mexican Sephardi patronage networks. Listing his profession as a "traveling salesman," Fresco noted that he had two thousand pesos of commercial credit with two commercial houses—Alazraki and Atri, and Fua Hermanos. Both commercial clothing establishments were run by Sephardi migrants: the Alazraki brothers from Izmir, having arrived in Mexico on Italian passports; the Fuas from Constantinople, with French papers. The Fua brothers, who earlier in the decade had owned "El Centro de Paris" with Miguel Palacci, arrived in Mexico before World War I. Though from Constantinople, they had somehow acquired French papers, whether through the remnants of protégé status, the acquisition of French nationality itself, or by exploiting the amorphous boundaries of these categories.[24] The Fuas imported women's clothing from Paris and London.[25] In his naturalization petition, Fresco also noted that members of "his *colonia*" could supply character references, the lack of definition of "his colony" implying understood parameters.[26] Fresco himself was a character witness for the naturalization of another Sephardi migrant from Constantinople, a man named Roberto

Sovrado.[27] Sovrado and Fresco would later encounter each other across the Atlantic, where Fresco, as a Mexican consular official in Nazi-occupied Paris, succeeded in securing Sovrado's release from the Drancy internment camp.

It becomes even more interesting to look at Fresco's recourse to Sephardi patronage networks once he was in Shanghai. A few scholars have mentioned Fresco because of his role in advocating for the repatriation of Mexican women abandoned by Chinese spouses or for his later involvement in the migration of thousands of Spanish refugees fleeing Franco to Mexico. Few note anything about Fresco personally, and nothing beyond that Fresco was able to transform his success in Shanghai into a diplomatic career. Mauricio Tello, the Mexican consul in Yokohama, recommended Fresco for the initial post in Shanghai, preferring him over his competitor who had held the post previously because of the favorable pieces on Mexico that Fresco had published in the Shanghai press and because of "his good connections"—particularly useful in light of the diplomatic quagmire between Mexico and China as a result of the deportation of thousands of Chinese from Mexico. Tello's opinion, formed through private correspondence between himself and Fresco, was that Fresco was a young man "full of enthusiasm and activity," whose degree of dynamism had propelled him to investigate the conflict over Japan's occupation of Manchuria.[28] Fresco was well-connected, particularly in Shanghai's journalistic spheres, which could be used for information and propaganda, and Mexicans who had passed through Shanghai had attested to Fresco's amicability. Fresco, unlike his competitor, was Mexican, and had good letters of recommendation from Mexico supporting him.

These letters of recommendation reveal how Fresco mobilized Sephardi patronage networks to achieve his diplomatic career. In February 1931, several months before Tello contacted the SRE, Fresco, then representing a French commercial house in Montmartre, wrote a letter in French to "Mon cher Jacques" in Mexico City. The "Jacques" to whom he wrote was Jacques Benuzillo, one of the founders of the Sephardi benevolent association *La Fraternidad*. Benuzillo had arrived in Mexico in 1915, where he opened a clothing establishment named "La Ciudad de Paris." Like the Fua brothers with their "El Centro de Paris" clothing boutique and numerous other Sephardi merchants in Mexico, Benuzillo recognized the commercial appeal of French fashion to his Mexican clientele.

In this letter, Fresco explained that since arriving in Shanghai, he had had the opportunity to meet several influential Mexicans, including the Mexican consul to Japan, who, Fresco noted, "was also from the Yucatan." This suggests that Benuzillo was also aware of Fresco's deception regarding his place of birth. Benuzillo had, Fresco reminded him, promised to offer support should Fresco need it. "I believe there is something you can do, my dear Jacques, that I would recognize for my entire life," Fresco elaborated, before requesting that Benuzillo intervene with his father-in-law Alberto Misrachi, who had a "certain influence over" Genaro Estrada, at that time the director of the SRE. Benuzillo was married to Amelia Misrachi, a Portuguese citizen, whose father, Alberto Misrachi from Monastir, had been a Serbian citizen until acquiring Mexican nationality in 1920. Alberto Misrachi was the crucial intermediary to whom Mauricio Fresco sought access. Misrachi owned the prominent "Agencia Misrachi," a large bookstore and later art gallery in central Mexico City, one of the only places in the city that sold printed materials in English and French. Genaro Estrada would visit Misrachi's bookstore every day and speak Ladino with him.[29] By 1933, the bookstore and art gallery had moved to Juárez 4, facing the Palacio de Bellas Artes, and had become a gathering place for connoisseurs of English and French, Mexico's literati and politicians, and the prominent artists David Alfaro Siquiros, José Clemente Orozco, Doctor Alt, and Diego Rivera and Frida Kahlo; the latter two painted portraits of members of the Misrachi family.[30] Misrachi indeed wrote a letter on Fresco's behalf, to which a response was given that the position in Shanghai was already filled satisfactorily. Yet, several months later, the consul in Yokohama indicated that it was Fresco's letters of reference that had propelled him to recommend Fresco for the position that was already filled. Although there is no direct evidence of such, we can therefore surmise that Fresco's Sephardi patrons in Mexico continued to pull strings on his behalf.

Fresco's multilingualism and journalistic skills helped him to propagate his vision of Mexico—one that aligned with revolutionary ideology, proud of its Spanish and indigenous roots, populist, independent of foreign economic intervention and control, and a staunch defender of the oppressed, regardless of location. In a questionnaire required of Mexican consular employees, Fresco noted that he was a journalist who had studied in France, worked as a correspondent for various newspapers around the world, and been a commercial representative and traveling salesman for European factories. Not only was he a native speaker of Spanish, but he could speak, write, and translate English, French, and Italian, and he spoke German.[31] When, in 1942, Fresco threatened to withdraw from his post as chancellor in Lisbon because he felt he had not been granted a deserved promotion, the minister of the Mexican legation in Lisbon reiterated that in addition to Fresco's work ethic, knowledge, honesty, and "definite" revolutionary ideology, his devotion to journalism made him useful for collaboration.[32] Fresco used publishing as a means of propagating views that aligned with those in vogue with Cárdenas and other Mexican leaders, thereby underscoring his own utility as a Mexican representative. Critically, Fresco's publications also helped to shape the legacy of an independent Mexico dedicated to the defense of the world's downtrodden, a legacy that has overshadowed the practices of exclusion of those—such as Jews—that occurred simultaneously with the practices of inclusion that Fresco was personally involved in, lauded, and published about.

In Fresco's writings, he used appeals to Mexico's colonial and indigenous heritage to provide subtle—as well as at times unsubtle—rebukes of narratives of exclusion. In contrast to definitions of "America" that centered on the United States, Fresco emphasized the literary contributions of Mexico to the American Library of Congress, noting that the first Library of the Americas was founded in Mexico. He highlighted a statement from the director of the Library of Congress describing the shared heritage of those republics encompassed by the term "America."[33]

Beyond reinscribing Mexico's importance within broader conceptions of "America," Fresco used Mexico's indigenous heritage as a means of directly rebuking Nazi policies in Europe. In his self-published 1944 book *Yo He Estado en Paris con los Alemanes* [I was in Paris with the Germans], Fresco describes his experiences as one of the last Mexican consular officials in the French capital as the city came under Nazi occupation. Protected in encounters with Nazi officials by his status as a consular representative of a neutral state, Fresco repeatedly expressed distaste for the Nazi occupiers of Paris and for Nazi endeavors in Greece and elsewhere.[34] He decried the occupiers as people who "seemed to have bathed themselves in a sea of bleach; all are identical, without color and without flavor."[35] In response to the "Heil

Hitler" of a German superior officer who had sojourned in Mexico and wanted to chat with Mexicans, Fresco described himself as replying "Heil Mexico!"[36] He recounted that a Cuban friend of his, the proprietor of the popular La Cabaña Cubana cabaret in Montmartre, shouted a similar "Heil Bautista!" in response to a Gestapo officer who had informed him that La Cabaña Cubana would be shuttered because Cubans were non-Aryans, "impure elements" with whom German soldiers should not come into contact.[37] Not long after, a building owned by a Mexican citizen was commandeered and made into a German mess hall; when Fresco complained to the military commandant, he was told that Mexicans and "the other peoples of the Americas" were classified as "non-Aryans" and therefore merited neither attention nor privileges. "Very well," Fresco recounted himself as having answered, "if tomorrow morning at nine the locale is not evacuated, I will cable my government so that the properties of the German 'Aryans' can be occupied by 'non-Aryan' Mexican Indians [los indios mexicanos "no arios"]." This threat proved effective, Fresco noted, because there were more German interests in Mexico than Mexicans in Paris.[38] Fresco's rhetoric underscored that the indigenous component of *mestizaje* was central to Mexican identity—and to the broader continental American heritage. This idea was shared by other urban Mexicans who otherwise might have viewed far-right political stances sympathetically. In 1938, a German migrant to Mexico from Silesia married a Mexican woman of Spanish ancestry and sought to have her declared an Aryan woman by the NSDAP race department in Berlin. He was so offended by their demand for proof that she was free of indigenous heritage as far back as 1800 that he went to the anti-Nazi *Liga Pro Cultura Alemana*. The organization then copied the German response, using the heading "Mexicans, do you know that you are a second-class race?" and distributing it throughout Mexico City, forcing the German minister to publish rebuttals in leading Mexican papers.[39] The non-Aryan nature of the Mexican populace served as a means by which Fresco, in Paris, could resist Nazi practices in occupied Paris and rebuke Nazi configurations of racial hierarchies while simultaneously reaffirming Mexico as a proudly mestizo nation.

But if Mexico's indigenous heritage gave Fresco the fodder with which to make a stand against Nazi policies, his accounts reveal a more ambiguous attitude toward intersections between Jewishness and Mexicanness.

He described anti-Jewish measures implemented by Nazis, included signs forbidding Jewish entry into hotels, restaurants, and cafés—sufficient, he remarked, to encourage French Catholics not to visit these places in solidarity; the appropriation of Jewish shops, businesses, bookstores, and movie theaters; the suspicious death of the Jewish proprietor of the Luna Park amusement park; and the establishment of the Drancy internment camp on the outskirts of Paris, where, he noted, some fifteen thousand Jews were confined and where, daily, small groups were shot as hostages or as communists.[40] Fresco never mentions his own Jewish origins. Nor does he mention the Jewish antecedents of his friend, the prominent editor, bookstore owner, and former Mexican chargé d'affaires to Argentina, Enrique Freymann; in discussing Freymann's initial encounters with several German officers who sought to discover whether this accomplished man were German or at least Aryan, Fresco describes Freymann as having countered that he was "Mexican and had Indian blood."[41] Freymann's father was a German Jewish migrant and his mother Mexican. For him, as perhaps for Fresco, highlighting the indigenous component of *mestizaje* served as a means of critiquing the Nazi racial taxonomies of "Aryan" and "non-Aryan" but in a way that elided the more problematic issue—for Nazi formulations—of Jewish blood.

Fresco downplayed Jewishness even in the case of a Mexican citizen interned in the Drancy camp on the northern outskirts of Paris, focusing instead on his Mexican citizenship. Drancy, initially used by German forces for prisoners of war, was transformed into an internment camp for Jewish men in August of 1941 after a raid on Paris's eleventh *arrondissement*, with its substantial population of Sephardi Jews, resulted in the arrest of 4,230 Jews, the majority of whom were Sephardi or Polish. By the following summer, Jewish women and children were also being sent to Drancy, through which passed ninety percent of the Jewish deportees from France to extermination camps.[42] An agreement between German occupiers and the Vichy government entailed that in exchange for a promise from the German authorities to deport only foreign and stateless Jews, the French police would arrest and turn over Jews in the "free" zone; this resulted, in 1942, in the deportation of forty thousand Jews to extermination camps.[43] The Vichy authorities denaturalized foreign-born French Jews, facilitating their deportation, along with many Ottoman-born Jews who were formally stateless as a result of Turkey's policies of stripping citizenship, discussed in chapter 5.[44] Jewish citizens of states at war with Germany, including "almost the totality of Salonican Jews of Greek nationality," who were caught up in a November 1942 raid in Paris, had little recourse once arrested.[45] Meanwhile, citizens of neutral or friendly countries could appeal to their local consulates to intervene with Nazi authorities for release from internment camps. Turkish authorities intervened on behalf of some Jews interned in Drancy—often those of financial means—while stripping Turkish citizenship from numerous others for failing to register with Turkish consulates or renew their Turkish passports.[46]

Diplomatic representatives of countries neutral or friendly to the Nazis played a pivotal role in the potential survival of Jewish nationals. José Papo, the cantor of the Sephardi community of Paris, recounted that upon his release from Drancy, he immediately alerted the consulates of neutral and friendly countries to agitate for the release and repatriation of their citizens. The consul of Italy and the vice-consul of Portugal, he noted, were the most proactive.[47] The lack of diplomatic representation for neutral countries could occasionally prove useful; the Swiss consulate, which represented Uruguayan interests in France, extended relief to several Sephardi Jews who had formerly naturalized as Uruguayan before relocating to France and losing their Uruguayan citizenship.[48]

Fresco, too, noted his intervention on behalf of Mexican citizens caught by Nazi forces. While Fresco cast himself as assiduously defending the rights of Mexicans in his capacity as consular representative, once the consulate was forced to close, the Germans detained many Mexicans. Fresco continued to advocate for the detainees: "after many negotiations, upon obtaining the liberation of Mexican Roberto Sobrado [Sovrado], who had been interned in the Camp of Drancy, we had to take him to his house in an ambulance, because the poor youth was half dead."[49] Sobrado was one of the few individuals Fresco mentioned by name, but his Jewishness was not noted, solely the fact that he was Mexican. Nor does Fresco mention his personal connection with Sobrado; when Sobrado was naturalized as Mexican in 1927, having entered Mexico in 1921 with a birth certificate rather than a passport, Mauricio Fresco was one of three references given in support of his petition.[50] Fresco's mentioning of his role in releasing Sobrado alludes to what was at stake for Fresco personally. On the one hand, affective ties bound the two men, who had known each other for at least fifteen years by the time of Sobrado's internment, and who had likely, in the past at least, had a close relationship, given that Sobrado had listed Fresco as a character reference. On the other hand, the familiarity of the two men highlighted the precarity of Fresco's position; Sobrado had known Fresco when Fresco was still a Turkish Jew, before he adopted the mantle of Mexican parentage, birth, and citizenship, and could potentially expose his secret.

Fresco's endeavors in Paris to advocate for Sobrado were one example of how Jews in Mexico sought to mobilize national and transnational networks in the face of the Nazi presence in France and elsewhere in Europe. In 1933 and again in 1935, the broader Jewish community of Mexico had organized boycotts of German businesses and goods in protest of Nazi persecutions of Jews.[51] Various Mexican Jewish organizations sought to advocate with the governments of Cárdenas and Manuel Ávila-Camacho to extend visas to Jews fleeing the Nazis. These organizations included already established groups such as the *Cámara Israelita de Industria y Comercio de México* as well as organizations like the *Comité Pro Refugiados*, founded in 1938 in direct response to Mexico's participation in the Evian Conference; the *Comité Pro Refugiados* was later absorbed into the *Comité Central Israelita*, also founded in 1938, which endeavored to serve as the unified representative of Mexico's Jews to the Mexican government.[52] These organizations' efforts, however, were mostly unsuccessful. A 1937 report prepared for Cárdenas assessing Jewish immigration to Mexico came to three conclusions: that Jews were "not useful to the racial integration of our nationality," but rather the opposite, always constituting "an ethnic, linguistic, and religious minority, irreducible and unassimilable BY US"; that there was a sentimental reaction of "our people that is, in general, anti-foreigner, and in particular toward the Jews, anti-Semitic"; and finally, that "the Israelite, in himself, is unassimilable and irreducible."[53] Even as Jews within Mexico tried to advocate for their coreligionists fleeing Nazi persecution, the overtly anti-Jewish attitudes at popular and governmental levels proved almost impossible to surmount.

The Mexican government largely classed Jews as economic migrants who were migrating voluntarily, and therefore undesirable, or, after 1940, as racial refugees, which were distinct from political refugees. In 1938, the *Secretaría de Gobernación* declared that Mexico would only receive migrants when they were "dedicated fighters for social progress, valiant defenders of Republican institutions, or exponents of the science and arts."[54] These refugees would not displace the Mexican working classes.[55] Those who were deemed "political refugees," a classification from which Jews were largely excluded, had a better chance of receiving visas to Mexico. The 1934 restriction against Jewish entry was still in effect, though the many Jews who requested asylum in Mexico were unaware of this.[56] Even some Jews who successfully argued that they were political refugees were denied visas for inconsistencies in documentation.[57] Only between eighteen hundred and two thousand Jews were accepted as asylum seekers into Mexico during the twelve years of Nazi rule.[58]

Individual Jews within Mexico struggled to maintain contact with and act on behalf of friends and relatives in France and elsewhere. At times, their activities involved Mexican consular officials abroad, including Mauricio Fresco. Guy Benveniste recounted how his father, from Salonica but in France since the 1920s, reached out to Saul Carasso, a fellow *Selanikli* who had been naturalized as a Mexican and who spent a good deal of time in Paris. Carasso paid a bribe in Mexico City that aided the procurement of visas for Benveniste, his wife, and son, stamped, according to Benveniste, by the consul in Marseille. The family arrived in Mexico after passage through Spain and a long stay in Lisbon while waiting for a ship to Veracruz via Casablanca and Havana, and were met at the pier in Veracruz by Carasso, his wife, and the chauffeur of their large Buick.[59] Perhaps as a result of the illegal means by which the Benvenistes acquired visas, their names do not appear in the *Registro de Extranjeros*, hinting at the documentary absence of Sephardi migrants and others who escaped Europe on paperwork acquired through back channels.

Some Sephardi Jews who had been naturalized or been born as Mexican, or who had acquired visas to Mexico, but who had family members in France, frantically tried to track those family members down through Mexican consular officials. In 1944, Guedalia [Eduardo] Assael, Ico Assael's son, sought information about his cousins, Mauricio Assael's children, who had all been born in Mexico and possessed Mexican nationality, but now lived in France. Saying that he would pay transportation costs and support his cousins in Mexico, he noted that one cousin, Esther Assael, was currently in the Vittel internment camp, in which Nazis housed citizens of neutral or enemy countries whom they hoped to exchange for German citizens interned abroad; a second cousin, with whom he shared the name "Guedalia," was a German prisoner of war; a third cousin, Sara, "is or was in France." Mexican officials responded that Esther lacked documents proving her Mexican nationality, but should Eduardo verbally attest that she was Mexican, a provisional Mexican passport could be extended. On August 29, 1945, Esther Assael received a provisional passport; the archival record is silent on the fates of Guedalia and Sara Assael.[60]

It was not only Mexican citizens who turned to Mexican consular officials for intervention. The brothers Gaston and Michel Gerassy, movie distributors born in Salonica who lived in France, acquired visas through the Mexican legation in Lisbon to enter Mexico in October 1941 as "political refugees."[61] In 1944, Michel Gerassy solicited Mexican consular officials in France for information about his relatives—all Greek citizens.[62] Mauricio Fresco, investigating from Paris where he had reopened the Mexican legation in August, telegraphed a week later that several relatives were in their homes and "perfectly healthy."[63] Two weeks later, a second telegram informed Gerassy that Alberto and Mercada, likely his parents, had been deported to Germany on October 5, 1942, destination unknown. Several other relatives were safe; his sister, Laure, received a visa in 1946 to join him in Mexico.[64]

Even as Jews in Mexico clamored for, and were often denied, entrance visas for coreligionists in Europe, Fresco and his superiors in the Mexican consular corps in France and Portugal focused on granting succor to another group of refugees, thereby helping to propagate the image of Mexico as welcoming of refugees and defending the downtrodden. The Spanish Civil War had displaced tens of thousands of Republican supporters to southern France, where many languished in concentration camps; though Fresco did not mention it, his elder brother Isaac had fought alongside the Republicans before relocating to a small house in Vence, outside of Nice, where he would pass the remainder of his life.[65] An agreement between Mexico and Maréchal Pétain in August of 1940 put thousands of Spanish refugees under Mexican protection.[66] Upon Fresco's relocation from Paris to Marseille, Consul General Gilberto Bosques—part of Cárdenas's inner circle—placed him in charge of the Office of Migration for Spanish Refugees. Fresco detailed his interactions with these refugees, "crying women and dying children" waiting in Toulouse for documentation and those interned in concentration camps, noting that within five weeks, he prepared close to eleven thousand files for immigrants.[67] His efforts, together with those of Bosques, earned him the recognition of Spanish exiles in Mexico.[68]

In a book published in 1950, Fresco emphasized the importance of the work he and his colleagues had done in providing refuge for the Spanish Civil War refugees, part of his attempt to highlight how these individuals benefited Mexico.[69] He contradicted several periodicals and magazines in Mexico that were critical of the selection process for refugees. Fresco asserted that there had been no discrimination on racial or political grounds for the granting of visas, though he explained that he was particularly drawn by the Basques and Catalans, for reasons he did not specify, and by the university-educated; in spite of this, he asserted, he completed his duty even with regard to those who did not belong to these groups.[70] Although Mexico harbored past resentment for the treatment suffered during the Spanish conquest and colonial period, "time has made those old wounds healthy; so old that their scars have already been erased."[71] Mexicans of the current generation "hold the idea that our blood is half Indian and half Spanish."[72] Once again, Fresco sought to underscore the essential mestizo character of the Mexican people. Mexico performed a humanitarian duty in accepting refugees from the Spanish Civil War, which in turn enriched the Mexican population through an influx of people who provided a crucial component of Mexican identity.

Implicitly, the indigenous-Spanish amalgam of *mestizaje* in Fresco's formulations excluded other admixtures, including Jews. On May 24, 1939, the Ministry of the Interior acknowledged in a press bulletin that in exchange for welcoming Spanish Civil War refugees, Mexico had closed its borders to Jewish applicants.[73] The willingness to aid Spanish political refugees did not extend to Jewish refugees from the Nazis and their collaborators.[74] While performing his consular duties and, later, lauding the work of Bosques and others including himself in accepting thousands of Spaniards, Fresco made no reference to the other group of individuals that had sought Mexican visas and had been largely rebuffed. In formulating "our blood" as being half indigenous and half Spanish, Fresco elided his own heritage and his contribution to *mestizaje*. At no point did he reveal what, if any, personal cost this entailed.

However, Fresco simultaneously maintained Sephardi ties that stretched to family members in Los Angeles as well as back to Turkey. In April of 1949, Fresco wrote to Abraham Galanté, a prominent Sephardi historian living in Istanbul who had been friends with his father and whom Fresco had met twenty-nine years earlier. Fresco sketched his life for Galanté, noting that "I have worked in America as a journalist; I have published many books, and I have contributed to dozens of newspapers and journals in various languages." His pursuits paralleled the occupation to which his father "sacrificed his life, and that of our family." He mirrored his father's obsession with the Ladino language as a corrupted jargon, too, declaring that *La Boz de Türkiye*, a Ladino-language political, scientific, and literary magazine published from 1939–1949 in Istanbul, "should be written *La Voz*, as in Spanish."[75] He recommended that the editor of *La Boz de Türkiye*, Albert Kohen, follow Fresco's father's approach in trying to reconcile Ladino with Spanish, which would remove "the impression that it is filled with errors" and would have the added benefit of teaching the readers Spanish.

Fresco recounted his diplomatic exploits, though he did not mention that he had served Mexico nor that he had long passed himself off as a Mexican born in the Yucatán. His diplomatic career, he noted, had led him to prepare a book called *Forge Your Own Passport*, which was never published. Though Fresco remarked that it would likely cause him a great deal of trouble, he noted that in the book, "I seek to prove the stupidity of passports, visas, nationalities, races, etc." "With eighteen years of service in consular and diplomatic positions," he went on, "I will bring to light many examples that prove how humanity is exploited. Certainly everyone engages in exploitation, but this does not mean that one should abstain from denouncing it."[76] Several years earlier, Fresco had denounced another type of exploitation, publishing an explosive charge in *El Excelsior* that the Argentine embassy in Madrid sold passports to Nazis leaving for the Americas through Portuguese and Spanish ports.[77]

Although Fresco did not mention to Galanté that he himself had acquired false papers, the title of his book could have been drawn from his own actions, those of Sephardi compatriots, and the many practices he had witnessed in the diplomatic service. Fresco, born a Sephardi Jew seemingly excluded on all sides from the nationalizing states that emerged in the wake of World War I, had seen firsthand the horrors that restrictions on mobility and ideas of scientific racism posed. Perhaps his own itinerary and use of false papers made him particularly attuned to questions of documentation and citizenship. In Shanghai, Fresco sought to expose the facility with which one could acquire passports that were either falsified or "imported," the latter being an authentic passport purchased from its original owner, from almost any country.[78] There were "millions of people without the documents necessary to prove the nationality to which they belong," Fresco noted in 1937, a situation that had been exacerbated by how World War I "modified the map of most of the world. Countries and cities changed hands; men and women entered or left before or after the reappointment; many evaded military service or deserted . . . so that today thousands upon thousands are refused the right to a passport or even recognition of their nationality." Endless immigration restrictions "in force everywhere" prohibited the entry of people "from such and such a country either for economic or racial reasons."[79] Though Fresco's 1937 tome did not mention this in particular, Ottoman-born Jews like himself continually contended with the lack of documentation to prove their nationality and with obstacles to their movement based on economic and racial rationales. This hints at why Fresco might have acquired false papers in Mexico: to leave the Ottoman Empire in 1917 in the midst of World War I, Fresco likely needed forged papers, which would later have complicated his retention of Turkish citizenship. Fresco's false papers facilitated his diplomatic career and mobility, just as countless other Sephardi migrants adopted false identities to aid geographical and economic mobility.

Fresco's success depended, in part, on his personal charm; in the words of his niece, Fresco was "bright, articulate, opinionated, traveled, and debonair," inspiring "intimacy and trust in men and thinly veiled lust in women."[80] His endeavors, though, were predicated on his false papers and his success in convincing those he encountered that he was more Mexican than the cactus. As scholars of racial passing in the United States have argued, passing often entails an "anxious decision" to turn one's back on a racial identity, losing what you pass away from as you claim to belong to a group to which you are not legally assigned.[81] If racial passing within the American context required negotiating a permeable border between black and white and, in doing so, highlighted the specious and utterly real concept of race,[82] passing across borders required a deep knowledge of racial systems within two national contexts but also enabled the exploitation of porosities in the color lines and borderlines through capitalizing on hidden vulnerabilities and inconsistencies.[83] For African American former slaves or for Sephardi Jews, cultivating a specific type of foreignness in a given national context allowed one to accrue advantages not available to certain natives or to foreigners of a different nationality or ethno-religious background.[84]

Fresco faced different challenges. Unlike many of his coreligionists in Mexico who capitalized on their knowledge of the French language and French connections to cultivate French identities, or who acquired false papers from countries in the eastern Mediterranean that neighbored their countries of origin, Fresco sought to cultivate nativeness. He did so in part, counterintuitively, by publishing in multiple languages for a variety of audiences. Several of his books defended controversial Mexican policies, including a French-language book for an international audience on Cárdenas's nationalization of petroleum and a later Spanish-language text vociferously arguing for the benefits accrued from Mexico's decision to welcome Spanish Civil War refugees, a policy for whose implementation Fresco, as first secretary in Marseille, was responsible.[85] Even in his books that were not explicitly about Mexican policies—his controversial exposé of extraterritorial life in Shanghai, his account of the early days of the Nazi occupation of Paris—Fresco crafted a narrative of Mexico as the consummate defender of the rights of the downtrodden and himself as one charged with upholding Mexico's reputation in this regard. This carefully constructed narrative of Mexico and of himself, and the facility with which Fresco was able to propagate these views through publishing in multiple languages, helped to solidify his importance in the Mexican diplomatic sphere.

Fresco's success in cultivating Mexicanness also depended on deliberate ignorance, at least on paper, on the part of prominent Mexican diplomatic figures—Fresco's immediate superiors and colleagues—who almost certainly were aware that Fresco was not exactly who he claimed to be. In October 1939, Gilberto Bosques, then Mexico's consul general in Paris, processed the diplomatic examination of Mauricio Fresco, first secretary of the consulate in Paris. Fresco's highest score, four points, was in French, while he received threes in English, the SRE's archival system, diplomatic and consular laws and rules, and fiscal and mercantile accounting. In contrast, he received a single point in stenography in Spanish and two points each in speaking and writing Spanish correctly and in Mexican history and geography. Given this distribution of points, it seems unlikely that Bosques and others could have been unaware that Fresco was not of Mexican birth, but this does not seem to have affected his diplomatic career. The primary flaws on Fresco's Spanish test consisted of leaving off the initial unvocalized "h" on several words, a letter not represented in Ladino spellings of words like *habrían* or *hechas*.[86] As with his coreligionists who dissimulated in various ways to ease their entry into countries where their presence was undesired or to aid their social and economic mobility, Fresco's position was fraught with the precarity of potential discovery.

Fresco's final book, published in 1962, contains clues that others outside of a closed Sephardi sphere were familiar with Fresco's origins. Entitled *Un Mundo Curioso* [A curious world] after Fresco's decade-long column in *Excelsior*, the book contained short and often humorous anecdotes about events, habits, and practices throughout the world, a far cry from the politically motivated volumes of his earlier days. The cover of the book displays a caricature of Fresco, his hair thinning, smiling as he gazes down at a typewriter he is tapping away at in his lap. He is seated on top of the world, an uncomfortable parallel to Nazi propaganda posters for a reader aware of Fresco's Jewish heritage. The volume's introduction was written by Carlos Freymann, the son of Enrique Freymann, whom Fresco had lauded in his earlier publication on Paris, gesturing toward the tight and often invisible ties that bound together his world. Freymann the younger made numerous references to Fresco's life that implied, but never stated, Fresco's unique origins—he had lived a "random and wandering life" and his surname "had the distinction of not being common," but Fresco addressed "with grace" the frequent questions as to its roots. Over the course of his life, Fresco had been a sailor, diplomat, author, reporter, businessman, pater familias, and friend; as a sailor, Freymann elaborated, Fresco "is one of the Mexicans who best knows the ports of the basins of the Mediterranean Sea and the Black Sea."[87] Freymann's allusion to Fresco's deep knowledge of the seas so close to Fresco's real birthplace of Ottoman Constantinople suggest that he was aware that while Fresco, with his life of wandering and his somewhat odd family name, was indeed Mexican, he had a trajectory that did not match his Mexican birth certificate.

However, even though Fresco successfully cultivated his Mexican public persona, likely with the knowledge and tacit permission of certain associates and superiors, this did not mean that he disavowed his extensive ties with Sephardi family members and contacts around the world. Scholars of passing in the African American context have argued that successful passing often necessitated a deliberate disconnection from those who could reveal one's "true" nature. For Fresco, this was not the case. Although he claimed Yucatecan origins, he was also embedded within familial and commercial Sephardi networks that extended across the seas. He drew on Sephardi patronage networks to secure his initial diplomatic appointment and in turn contributed to such networks when asked to serve as a character witness on Mexican naturalization petitions. He visited his sisters and their families in Los Angeles, sent them gifts from his global travels, and hosted their friends on visits to Mexico City. He also sent his friends and former lovers to be hosted by his Californian relatives.[88] The reciprocal flow of contacts between Fresco in Mexico and his family in California suggests that Fresco's Yucatecan origins were a known fiction, an act of dissimulation that did not hold any substantial weight. If some in the Mexican government sought to prevent the entry of Jews into Mexico and believed that Jewish migrants would always declare their religion, others even within the Mexican diplomatic corps seemingly did not care.

Passing, when successful, has often been seen as a clandestine act, intended to leave behind no trace.[89] Yet this chapter attempts to piece together the many clues that Fresco left behind to paint a portrait of a man who simultaneously lived seemingly disparate lives—in which one mode of being constantly threatened the existence of the other—which were nevertheless, at times, mutually constitutive. As his diplomatic career and frequent publications in many languages attest, Fresco thrived in the public spotlight, promoting his image of an idealized Mexico and of himself as its ardent advocate. Simultaneously, though, like many other Sephardi Jews, he maintained strong ties with his family members, who themselves had migrated to Los Angeles, Paris, or Lyon or had remained in the erstwhile Ottoman capital. His life was profoundly shaped by his Sephardi cultural background, and he was embedded within transnational Sephardi commercial and patronage networks, as were many of his coreligionists. Fresco's life encourages the critical exploration of what, precisely, "Jewishness" comes to signify to a man seemingly without a strong Jewish religious identity—neither of Fresco's wives was Jewish; his daughter Anne-Marie Fresco Lynette was baptized in the Nuestra Señora de Lourdes church in the center of Mexico City[90]; and Fresco asked to be and was cremated upon his death[91]—who nonetheless cultivated and maintained strong ties with fellow Sephardim.

Mauricio Fresco appears at first glance to be an anomalous individual. Upon closer inspection, however, his exceptionality lies only in the fact that his life manifested extreme versions of what countless others experienced and did during the tumultuous first decades of the twentieth century. Fresco, like millions of others of his era, contended with the transition from empire to nationalizing state, uniquely challenging for those on the uncomfortable peripheries of ethno-religiously defined national imaginings. Geographical mobility was the means by which many sought to improve their future, particularly when, as Devin Naar astutely points out, the almost-constant upheaval of the early twentieth century meant that the decision was not truly between an old world and a new but rather in which new world they would choose to cast their lot.[92] Individuals of Sephardi Jewish origins, this book argues, relied on mobility more than most; hypermobility within and across shifting national borders enabled them to cultivate the transnational commercial, familial, religious, and patronage networks that cohered an expanding Sephardi world. Fresco was hypermobile, and his trajectory encompassed regions far beyond the Mediterranean and Atlantic peregrinations of many of his coreligionists. In migrating, individuals were forced to contend with increasingly restrictive visa and citizenship policies as regulating migration, territorial ingress, and citizenship became a key strategy for nationalizing projects. Sephardi migrants drew on their transnational connections, multilingual backgrounds, a legacy of varied citizenship and protégé statuses, and complex geographical origins to perform or acquire the national identities that would enable their geographical and socioeconomic mobility. Fresco, likewise, acquired Mexican citizenship by falsifying his birth in Mérida, which enabled his future travels across the globe, his career in the Mexican diplomatic corps, and his self-fashioning as an ardent shaper and defender of Mexico's global reputation. All the while, he drew on ties to well-connected Sephardim within Mexico to attain his initial diplomatic post and used his cultivated multilingualism to advocate for Mexico and reinscribe his own utility. Fresco, like countless other coreligionists from Ottoman lands, achieved success, but only through his willingness to live on a knife's edge, calling in favors and expecting officials to turn a blind eye.

CONCLUSION

OVADIA NATHAN CONSTANTLY FLED from failure, but failure was never far behind. He left his home in Constantinople as a young man sometime before 1909, when his travel from France via Havana, Cuba to Tampa, Florida, left its trace in the archival record. He was twenty-two at the time, literate, single, and a laborer. American authorities noted that he was of Turkish nationality and initially categorized him as being of the Turkish race, but that was then crossed out and replaced by "Hebrew."[1] In 1912, he attempted to enter Canada to try his hand at farming. Turned away at the Canadian border because Canadian law stipulated that only migrants arriving directly from their place of origin would be admitted—a measure implemented largely to prevent the entry of Asians and other "undesirables"—he returned to the United States. Several months later, a Duluth, Minnesota woman had him arrested, alleging that Nathan had insulted her when he came to her house as a peddler, violating the social contract that existed between male peddlers and their largely female clientele.[2]

Like many young men, migrants and Americans alike, Ovadia Nathan went west. He worked for several years on the railroad, a laborer for the Southern Pacific Company, and continued to peddle. Having filed his declaration of intent to become a citizen, the first step in the process of American naturalization, he enlisted with the U.S. Army during World War I at the rank of private, serving from May through September of 1918, when he was honorably discharged.³ In a 1919 advertisement that Nathan put in the *San Francisco Chronicle* seeking employment, he emphasized that he was a "commercial traveler" who spoke six languages: English, French, Spanish, Italian, German, and Turkish.⁴ Nathan, like other Sephardi migrants, sought to use his multilingualism to his economic advantage. The 1920 Federal census noted that he lived alone in Petaluma, that he was a retail merchant in dry goods, and that he had submitted his papers for naturalization. By 1921, Nathan was listing himself in the San Francisco Buyers' Guide as an importer and exporter on Market Street.⁵

Nathan's efforts to establish himself in the United States were not successful. In 1918, he penned a despondent missive in Ladino and smatterings of Hebrew in the Latin alphabet to Haim Nahum, the Ottoman chief rabbi, in which he explained his tragic circumstances. He had studied in the Jewish seminary in the Hasköy neighborhood of Istanbul but had been unable to complete his studies. At age fourteen, he had left school and the country "to go after nothing," and he wrote that "I have already traveled the four parts of the world but I have still not found the end" [*ya a viaji 4 partes de el mundo yine no topi el cavo*]. Nathan had sent every penny that he earned in Europe to his parents while they were still alive. But after they died, his brothers-in-law had "opened their mouths to consume" everything—jewelry, money, houses, fields [*joyas paras qazas qanpos*]—that his father, who had lived off rental income, had left as an inheritance. He asked the chief rabbi for assistance in contacting his brother-in-law Moises Belleli, who was a life insurance agent in Galata but whose exact address Nathan did not know.⁶

Nathan's traces in the archival record disappear for several years at this point, but he reappears in Mexico in the later 1920s. On June 29, 1929, a few weeks after his forty-first birthday, his marriage to a French citizen, Mary Menier Clark, was witnessed by the American vice consul in the Mexican port city of Tampico, who noted that both lived there.⁷ A week earlier, on June 20th, the two had married in Mexican civil court, their matrimony witnessed by four Mexican men.⁸ These were civil marriages, legally binding and recognized in Mexico and the United States; it is unclear whether Clark was Jewish and whether the couple also married in a Jewish ceremony, which would not have been legally binding or recognized in Mexico. But Clark left him on the day of their American wedding and he never saw her again, or so he claimed several years later in a Texas court in his successful petition for divorce.[9] Immediately after his marriage, he moved to Monterrey, Mexico, where he described himself as a widower.[10] He listed as his contacts his sister Esther and her husband Moises Belleli, who had both left Turkey in 1926 to work as merchants in Mexico City.[11]

Soon, Ovadia Nathan left Mexico and his failed marriage behind, trying his luck once again in the United States. He first roomed with a family in the border city of Laredo, Texas. The 1930 U.S. census also listed Nathan as a widower, born in the United States to American-born parents, his occupation and a number of other slots left blank. Though Nathan may have given inaccurate information himself, it is also plausible that one of the family members in the house conveyed what they believed to be Nathan's history, that he had described himself to them as a widower to conceal his wife's abandonment, and that he had created an alternative narrative about his parents' nationality.[12]

Whereas in San Francisco, Nathan had attempted to capitalize on his extensive knowledge of foreign languages to secure employment, when he returned to the United States, he embraced the role of purveyor of Oriental carpets, an economic niche that Sephardi Jews in Mexico eschewed but that Sephardi Jews in the United States did not.[13] He first opened an Oriental rug store in Ballinger, Texas in 1930, before relocating to El Paso, where he advertised himself as an importer of Oriental rugs and a buyer and seller of antique carpets.[14] A 1933 article on Nathan's "little antique shop" noted that he was "recently from Turkey and a great lover of Orientals," which were the perfect gift to oneself and one's home "to dress it up for Christmas."[15] Nathan had not, in reality, returned to Turkey in years. He marshaled his origins to bolster his purported expertise in this new commercial sphere.

After a prolonged battle with stomach cancer, during which time he moved from Austin, Texas to the Veterans Administration Center in Temple, he died in 1957 at the age of sixty-nine and was buried in the Agudath Jacob Cemetery in Waco. His death certificate, which categorized his "color or race" as "Hebrew," noted that Nathan had been a merchant. It also noted that he had remained unmarried his whole life, not factually correct, although perhaps his one-day marriage in Tampico decades earlier was not something that Nathan had made known.[16] Waco's rabbi applied for a military headstone in flat granite with a Star of David to mark Nathan's grave.[17]

By many benchmarks of success established by his peers—whether economic or familial—Ovadia Nathan failed. He earned no accolades from governmental authorities, no consular posts, honorary or official. He had occasional contacts and conflicts with state and religious authorities, but nothing sustained. His name appeared in print, but often in the form of advertisements, as opposed to laudatory articles or opinion pieces. He left behind no children or grandchildren and had a contentious relationship with his siblings even as they remained in contact. It is unclear who mourned his passing. Ovadia Nathan was not an individual whom history often remembers.

But it is precisely his insignificance that makes him noteworthy. Ovadia Nathan, over the course of his life, drew on the same strategies of hypermobility—emphasizing his wide knowledge of languages, moving from peddler to shopkeeper, drawing on ties to family and coreligionists—as did the many others whose personal and communal histories this volume weaves together. He negotiated an array of civil and criminal legal codes, navigated how he was perceived and classified in different contexts, and contended with layers of documentation, bureaucracy, and behavioral and economic expectations linked to gender, religion, and nationality. In this, he was like so many others of his generation, among the last of those born into an empire that ceased to exist in their formative years, who sought opportunity in new locations and sometimes achieved success. The fact that Ovadia Nathan would have been deemed unsuccessful in his attempts to forge a secure life for himself even as he employed the same strategies that worked for many others emphasizes the narrow tightrope that all these individuals had to walk to gain any measure of security, be it financial, social, or personal. All of the individuals explored in this volume contended with constant precarity.

Although states "emerged as powerful organizers of human life during an important era of transnationalism," we should not assume the perspective through which nationalizing states viewed people on the move.[18] As the historian Elliott Young argues in his work on Chinese migration in the Americas, through the lens of the state the alien is viewed as marginal, anxious, and deviant. The various states that sought to stem what they deemed to be undesirable flows of Sephardi people across the Mediterranean and Atlantic marked such individuals as pernicious. If we move our gaze from the level of the nation or state to the level of individuals who occasionally left traces as they moved between many states, we can explore how such individuals became fluent—literally and figuratively—in multiple languages and legal systems. This fluency provided them with the tools necessary to subvert such systems. The histories of state control over the mobility of certain goods and people highlights how state attempts to solidify national borders and national identities provided the impetus for the solidifying of transnational diasporic networks of Sephardi Jews and others.[19] As Mexican officials struggled to unite the Mexican people in the years after the Mexican Revolution, foreign men and women became markers against which to construct deviancy and the boundaries of the nation.[20] Sephardi migrants, in turn, responded by mobilizing commercial and familial networks that spanned the Mediterranean, Atlantic, and Caribbean to subvert state restrictions against their entry into Mexico.

As Young suggests, if we adopt the views of the migrants themselves, "we begin to see a transnational community that fits poorly into the national boxes to which historians too often consign their subjects."[21] For many individuals, migration was not a linear trajectory from one country to another but entailed internal displacement before international travel and, often, prolonged passage through multiple transit points prior to arriving at a destination. But, as this book argues, for this generation of Sephardi migrants, even the destinations themselves were often transitory, whether by coincidence or design. Many individuals who left the Ottoman Empire or its successor states intended to settle in the United States, and even went so far as to petition for first papers or to naturalize entirely, before realizing that they might have greater possibility for upward economic and social mobility in Mexico. Others lived in France, Cuba, Mexico, sometimes for upwards of a decade, and then relocated, sometimes bearing new nationalities. Even among those who remained primarily in one country for the remainder of their lives, many took frequent extended international trips to acquire merchandise or spouses, to visit aging relatives, or to reconnect with friends and family. And mobility continued for those who did not travel abroad; as with so many other migrant Jews of this and earlier epochs throughout the world, peddling provided a well-trodden path to economic advancement with relatively little investment of capital.[22] Mobility, rather than stasis, was a defining characteristic of the lives of the women and men explored in this book. States' perspectives on these mobile people as "emigrants" or "immigrants" captures only one crucial aspect of their experience, a framework with which these individuals contended but against whose dominance they struggled. These individuals' hypermobility and the diaspora that they created and maintained through their dense networks of communication demonstrates that not all people participate in linear or finite migration, and that some groups, like Sephardi Jews, have relied on an intensive process of nonlinear movement among multiple regions and through multiple states. This provokes broader questions on the nature of migration, whether it should ever be categorized as linear, and when and how some groups deploy tactics of hypermobility that may be either not available or not advantageous in the same way to all groups.

The migrants' presence and movements, and governmental responses to such, provoke larger questions about the meaning of citizenship: What is the obligation of a state to its citizens, both those within and beyond its borders, and what happens to those individuals if the state disavows them, officially or unofficially? When a state officially strips citizenship from or grants citizenship to a person, when does that matter for the person in question? Is citizenship only relevant when crossing borders or in specific types of encounters with state authorities? How much does the citizenship of a migrant matter in daily life, and in what ways does this enable an individual to subvert state power? What are means and measures other than citizenship that a migrant can employ to create space for him- or herself and to belong? How is this contingent upon how they are perceived and classified by society and bureaucracies around them? And how do transnational networks of patronage, family, and friends facilitate movement and settlement, mitigating against exclusion even as they perpetuate connections beyond state borders? This examination of the networks of Sephardi migrants indicates the extent and durability of transnational Sephardi networks that could be mobilized to facilitate trade or mobility. Such mobility often relied on the falsification or use of multiple passports and identity documents. In this, the early years of the "passport regime," when states throughout the world sought to solidify the borders of state and nation, Sephardi Jews excelled at subverting passport requirements almost as soon as they were implemented.

This book also provokes questions on the importance and meaning of Jewishness. On an empirical level, during the final decades of the Ottoman Empire, religious difference was perhaps the central category through which the Ottoman state saw its subjects. It was Jews as Jews that Mexico's regulatory migration practices sought to exclude after 1934. Those who remained in their places of origin were at the center of debates over precisely who could make claims on new nation-states, and in what ways. Jewish law and custom governed whom Ottoman Jews could marry, how people divorced, and who would inherit. Jewishness in a broad sense informed the types of organizations migrants formed, including cemeteries, aid organizations, synagogues, and schools, while rabbis constituted key intermediaries in local, national, and transnational networks, both for religious guidance and for personal matters.

But Jewishness, this book suggests, should be understood more capaciously. Jewishness and religion writ large are not defined only by certain halakhic or institutional practices governing life cycle events, foods, or conventional sacred spaces such as synagogues or churches. Religion, culture, and social relationships operate in concert, inseparable from the networks of individuals they link. Jewishness can be "domesticated," home and family forming the core of a modern Jewish identity; or consuming luxury items or vacations can become a sacred act.[23] Religion—like diaspora—is active, processual, and relational, imbricated within the webs of meaning that humans use to create themselves and relate to others.[24] Any set of networks that carries organizing principles and practices for how a group lives constitutes a form of religion. Maintenance of Sephardi trade networks, circulation of knowledge, marriages contracted or dissolved transnationally, and the other networks of communication, relation, and interaction explored herein enabled the perpetuation of a modern Sephardi diaspora. These activities are also a form of ritual. Regardless of the personal beliefs of those, like Mauricio Fresco and others, who may have distanced themselves from Judaism in a traditional sense, their participation in dense networks of communication and interaction with other Sephardi migrants created shared ritual spaces.

They created and bound together a dispersed community through common practices, knowledge, norms, and even transgressions.

Migrants make states even as states create migrants. The figure of the migrant looms large in today's popular and political discourse, but the migrant has occupied a primary position in the public imagination for far longer. I use the term "imagination" deliberately, since as this volume has shown, migrants—cast as a beneficial contributor of labor, capital, or genetic material, or as a nefarious, diseased and criminal influence undermining general welfare—exist as a foil for projecting broader social, political, and economic concerns. In such discourse, the humanity of migrants is overlooked and their stories, in all their complexities, disregarded. As Mauricio Fresco, fresh out of his Mexican diplomatic career, wrote to his father's old colleague in Istanbul in 1949 regarding his manuscript that sought to prove "the stupidity of passports, visas, nationalities, races, etc.," "certainly everyone [engages in exploitation], but this does not mean that one should abstain from denouncing it."[25]

NOTES

Introduction

1. Galanté contributed to the Ladino-language periodicals *El Telegrafo* and *El Tiempo*, both run by David Fresco. See Abraham Elmaleh, *Le Professeur Abraham Galante: Sa vie et ses oeuvres* (Istanbul, 1947), 20.

2. I quote from the letter published as "'Forge Your Own Passport': The Unlikely Rise of an International Author and Diplomat," translated by Julia Phillips Cohen, in *Sephardi Lives: A Documentary History, 1700–1950*, ed. Julia Phillips Cohen and Sarah Abrevaya Stein (Stanford, 2014), 379–380.

3. "Lista de Nuestros Adjentes," *La Amerika*, 4/16/1920, 3; "A Todos los Abonados," *La Amerika*, 2/4/1921, 4.

4. Ben Yitzhak Saserdote, *Refael i Miriam: Novela de la Vida de los Djudios del Oriente* (Constantinople, 1910); Elia Karmona, *El Mayoral Djudio* (Constantinople, 1910); Elia Karmona, *La Novia Aguna: Romanso Nasional Djudia* (Constantinople, 5682).

5. Carlos Monsiváis, "Notas sobre cultura popular en México," *Latin American Perspectives* 5, no. 1 (1978), 108; Rivka Havassy, "Con el Tiempo y Progreso (With Time and Progress): The Sephardi Cantigas at the Dawn of the Twentieth Century," *European Judaism* 44, no. 1 (Spring 2011), 129.

6. Elías Arditti, *Izmir, París, Buenos Aires: Odisea de un inmigrante* (Buenos Aires, 1993), 15.

7. José M. Estrugo, *Los Sefardíes* (Havana, 1958), 64. Daniela Gleizer cites an interview with Isaías Nizri, who related that "everyone spoke Spanish, my mother thought they were Jews." See Daniela Gleizer, "Judíos Sefardíes: De España a México a través del Imperio Otomano," in *La Ciudad Cosmopolita de los Inmigrantes*, ed. Carlos Martínez Assad (Mexico, 2010).

8. John Torpey, *The Invention of the Passport: Surveillance, Citizenship, and the State* (Cambridge, 2000), 1–2.

9. Will Hanley, *Identifying with Nationality: Europeans, Ottomans, and Egyptians in Alexandria* (New York, 2017), 8, 285.

10. Exceptions include Rebecca Kobrin, Sarah Abrevaya Stein, and Tobias Brinkmann.

11. Thomas Nail, *The Figure of the Migrant* (Stanford, 2015), 3.

12. Extensive transnational diasporic connections and travels were also a salient aspect of the histories of Syrio-Lebanese migrants in the same time period. See Andrew Arsan, *Interlopers of Empire: The Lebanese Diaspora in Colonial French West Africa* (London, 2014), 8–10.

13. Donna Gabaccia, "Is Everywhere Nowhere? Nomads, Nations, and the Immigrant Paradigm of United States History," *Journal of American History* 86, no. 3 (Dec. 1999), 1117.

14. Matthias B. Lehmann, "Rethinking Sephardi Identity: Jews and Other Jews in Ottoman Palestine," *Jewish Social Studies* 15, no. 1 (Fall, 2008), 83.

15. Ibid., quoting James Clifford, *Routes: Travels and Translation in the Late Twentieth Century* (Cambridge, 1997), 246.

16. Rogers Brubaker, "Migration, Membership, and the Modern Nation-State: Internal and External Dimensions of the Politics of Belonging," *Journal of Interdisciplinary History* XLI, no. I (Summer, 2010), 63.

17. Sandra McGee Deutsch, *Crossing Borders, Claiming a Nation: A History of Argentine Jewish Women, 1880–1955* (Durham, 2010), 6; Liz Hamui de Halabe, *Identidad Colectiva: Rasgos Culturales de los Inmigrantes Judeo-Alepinos en México* (Mexico City, 1997), 104.

18. Devi Mays, "'I Killed Her Because I Loved Her Too Much': Gender and Violence in the 20th Century Sephardi Diaspora," *Mashriq and Mahjar* 2, no. 1 (2014), 9.

19. Nail, *The Figure of the Migrant*, 235.

20. Interview with Vitali Meshoulam by Monika Unikel, 1/16/1989, AAUHJ.

21. Tobias Brinkmann, "From Immigrants to Supranational Transmigrants and Refugees: Jewish Migrants in New York and Berlin before and after the Great War," *Comparative Studies of South Asia, Africa, and the Middle East* 30, no. 1 (2010), 52.

22. Manuel Delgado, "Marca y Territorio: Sobre la Hipervisibilidad de los Inmigrantes en los Espacios Públicos Urbanos" in *La inmigración en la Sociedad Española*, ed. Joaquín García Roca and Joan Lacomba Vázquez (Barcelona, 2008).

23. Aihwa Ong, *Flexible Citizenship: The Cultural Logics of Transnationality* (Durham, 1999), 88–92.

24. Ignacio Klich and Jeffrey Lesser, "'Turco' Immigrants in Latin America," *The Americas* 53, no. 1 (July 1996), 2–4, 8.

25. Sarah Gualtieri, *Between Arab and White: Race and Ethnicity in the Early Syrian American Diaspora* (Berkeley, 2009), 131.

26. Eric L. Goldstein, *The Price of Whiteness: Jews, Race, and American Identity* (Princeton, 2006), 2, 5.

27. Arsan, *Interlopers of Empire*, 152; Isa Blumi, *Ottoman Refugees, 1878–1939* (London, 2013), 93; José Najar, "The Privileges of Positivist Whiteness: The Syrian-Lebanese of São Paulo, Brazil (1888–1939)" (PhD diss., 2012); Ruth Fredman Cernea, *Almost Englishmen: Baghdadi Jews in British Burma* (Lanham, 2007); Jeffrey Lesser, "(Re)Creating Ethnicity: Middle Eastern Immigration to Brazil," *The Americas* 53, no. 1 (July 1996): 45–65.

28. Camila Pastor, *The Mexican Mahjar: Transnational Maronites, Jews, and Arabs under the French Mandate* (Austin, 2017), 19.

29. Interview with Nathan Sissa by Monika Unikel, 4/17/1989, AAUHJ.

30. Interviews with Fortuna Camacho and Jaime Mitrani, AAUHJ; Pastor, *The Mexican Mahjar*, 36. Gualtieri notes that as many as 80% of Syrian female migrants in the United States peddled in the early years of their migration. See Sarah Gualtieri, "Gendering the Chain Migration Thesis: Women and Syrian Transatlantic Migration, 1878–1924," *Comparative Studies of South Asia, Africa, and the Middle East* 24, no. 1 (2004), 71.

31. Devin Naar, "From the 'Jerusalem of the Balkans' to the 'Goldene Medina'": Jewish Immigration from Salonika to the United States," *American Jewish History* 93, no. 2 (Dec. 2007); Devin Naar, "Between 'New Greece' and the 'New World': Salonikan Jewish Immigration to America," *Journal of the Hellenic Diaspora* 35, no. 2 (Fall 2009), 47; Adriana Brodsky, *Sephardi, Jewish, Argentine: Community and National Identity* (Bloomington, 2016), 67–73; Marquesa Macadar, "Sephardic Diaspora: A Case Study in Latin America" (PhD diss., 2009), 186–189; Albert Adatto, "Sephardim and the Seattle Sephardic Community," (MA thesis, 1939).

32. For an overview of *francos*, see Dina Danon, "Francos," in *Encyclopedia of Jews in the Islamic World*, ed. Norman Stillman. Consulted online on August 29, 2019.

33. Esther Benbassa and Aron Rodrigue, *Sephardi Jewry: A History of the Judeo-Spanish Community, 14th-20th Centuries* (Berkeley, 2000), xix.

34. Brodsky, *Sephardi, Jewish, Argentine*, ch. 3.

35. Liz Hamui de Halabe, *Identidad Colectiva: Rasgos Culturales de los Inmigrantes Judeo-Alepinos en México* (Mexico City, 1997), 21, 80–117.

36. Michel de Certeau, *The Practice of Everyday Life* (Berkeley, 1984), esp. ch. 7.

37. Matthias B. Lehmann, *Emissaries from the Holy Land* (Stanford, 2014), esp. ch. 5.

38. Here, I build on Lehmann's work on eighteenth-century Jewish philanthropic networks. See Lehmann, "Rethinking Sephardi Identity," 83.

39. I am grateful to the second reviewer of my book manuscript for this list. There is a growing body of scholarship on Middle Eastern diasporic populations in Mexico and elsewhere; for the ways in which Syrio-Lebanese non-Jewish migrants used these tactics, see the works of Alfaro-Velcamp, Arsan, Ballofet, Fahrenthold, and Pastor, among others; for Aleppan Jews, see Hamui; for Armenians, see Carlos Antaramián, *Del Ararat al Popocatépetl: Los Armenios en México* (Mexico City, 2011) and Antaramián, "La Merced, Mercado y Refugio, El Caso Armenio," ISTOR IX, no. 36 (Spring, 2009).

40. Pastor, *The Mexican Mahjar*, 47.

41. Theresa Alfaro-Velcamp, *So Far from Allah, So Close to Mexico* (Austin, 2007); Jacob Norris, "Exporting the Holy Land: Artisans and Merchant Migrants in Ottoman-Era Bethlehem," *Mashriq & Mahjar* 2 (2013).

42. Pastor, *The Mexican Mahjar*, 57, 59, 189.

43. Hanley, *Identifying with Nationality*, 98.

44. Adam M. McKeown, *Melancholy Order: Asian Migration and the Globalization of Borders* (New York, 2008), 1–2.

Chapter 1: Fabricating the Foreign

1. Klaus Kreiser, "Turban and Türban: 'Divider between Belief and Unbelief'—A Political History of Modern Turkish Costume," *European Review* 13, no. 3 (2005), 451.

2. Julia Phillips Cohen, "Oriental by Design: Ottoman Jews, Imperial Style, and the Performance of Heritage," *American Historical Review* 119, no. 2 (April, 2014), 368.

3. Kreiser, "Turban and Türban," 451; Cohen, "Oriental by Design," 389.

4. Kirsten Fermaglich has convincingly shown that American officials at Ellis Island rarely changed the names of Jewish immigrants, but that what happened instead was that a disproportionate number of Jewish immigrants and their descendants formally changed their surnames to avoid antisemitism and to assert their whiteness. See Kirsten Fermaglich, *A Rosenberg by Any Other Name: A History of Jewish Name Changing in America* (New York, 2018), 5, 10.

5. Cohen, "Oriental by Design"; Theresa Alfaro-Velcamp, *So Far from Allah, So Close to Mexico: Middle Eastern Immigrants in Modern Mexico* (Austin, 2007), 29–30.

6. John-Paul A. Ghobrial, "The Secret Life of Elias of Babylon and the Uses of Global Microhistory," *Past & Present* 222, no. 1 (Feb. 2014), 58.

7. Emphasis in text. Joseph Schemonti, *États des Ottomans au Méxique: Devoirs de l'Empire à leur Égard, Remèdes* (Constantinople, 1909), 19, located in gömlek: 11, dosya: 77, HR.SYS, BOA.

8. Ibid., 7.

9. Andrew Arsan, "Failing to Stem the Tide: Lebanese Migration to French West Africa and the Competing Prerogatives of the Imperial State," *Comparative Studies in Society and History* 53 (2011), 464–465.

10. "Les livres," *Correspondance d'Orient*, 9/15/1909, 32; "Une visite de S.E. José

Castellot: Les Ottomans au Mexique," *La Jeune Turquie*, 3/29/1911, 2; "Un Interesante Folleto del Doctor A. Shemonti: Pide que Haya Representantes de Su País," *El Imparcial*, 4/15/1911, 8.

11. "Djovenes Djudios Otomanos Profetad," *El Tiempo*, 6/11/1908, 3–4; "El Enseniamiento de la Lingua Turka en los Talmudei Torah," *El Tiempo*, 13/11/1908, 7–8.

12. N. Sason, *Silabario en Turko-Espanyol* (Istanbul, 1905), 1; Jacques Gueron to AIU headquarters, 6/8/1909, TU-09/Turquie I E 21, AIU; Albert Benaroya, 8/7/1910, TU-15/Turquie V E 84, AIU. On the rhetoric of giving thanks to the Ottoman Empire, see Julia Phillips Cohen, *Becoming Ottomans: Sephardi Jews and Imperial Citizenship in the Modern Era* (Oxford, 2014).

13. Letter from Isaac Fernandez, 5/20/1909, TU-02/Turquie I B 6.15, AIU.

14. Albert Benaroya, 8/7/1910, TU-15/Turquie V E 84, AIU.

15. Eric Lohr, *Russian Citizenship: From Empire to Soviet Union* (Cambridge, 2012), esp. ch. 4; Tara Zahra, *The Great Departure: Mass Migration from Eastern Europe and the Making of the Free World* (New York, 2016), 29–31.

16. Clifford Rosenberg, *Policing Paris: The Origins of Immigration Control between the Wars* (Ithaca, 2006), 2.

17. David Gutman, "Armenian Migration to North America, State Power, and Local Politics in the Late Ottoman Empire," *Comparative Studies of South Asia, Africa, and the Middle East* 34, no. 1 (2014), 177–178.

18. Donald Quataert, *The Ottoman Empire, 1700–1922* (Cambridge, 2005), 65–68.

19. Gutman, "Armenian Migration," 178.

20. David Gutman, "Agents of Mobility: Migrant Smuggling Networks, Transhemispheric Migration, and Time-Space Compression in Ottoman Anatolia, 1888–1908," *InterDisciplines* 1 (2012), 78–79.

21. Cohen, *Becoming Ottomans*, 10; Kemal Karpat, *The Politicization of Islam: Reconstructing Identity, State, Faith, and Community in the Late Ottoman State* (New York, 2001), 314; İsmail Aydıngün and Esra Dardağan, "Rethinking the Jewish Communal Apartment in the Ottoman Communal Building," *Middle Eastern Studies* 42, no. 2 (March, 2006), 324–325.

22. See Engin Deniz Akarlı, "Ottoman Attitudes Towards Lebanese Emigration, 1885–1910," in *The Lebanese in the World: A Century of Emigration*, ed. A. Hourani and Nadim Shehadi (London, 1992), 110, 116; Kemal Karpat, "The Ottoman Emigration to America, 1860–1914," *International Journal of Middle East Studies* 17 (May 1985), 187.

23. Gutman, "Agents of Mobility," 50–51.

24. David Gutman, "Migrants, Revolutionaries, and Spies: Surveillance, Politics, and Ottoman Identity in the United States," in *Living in the Ottoman Realm: Empire and Identity, 13th–20th Centuries*, ed. Christine Isom-Verhaaren and Kent E. Schull (Bloomington, 2016), 287–288, 292.

25. Akarlı, "Ottoman Attitudes," 110, 116; Karpat, "Ottoman Emigration,"; Mutaz M. Qafisheh, "The International Law Foundations of Palestinian Nationality: A Legal Examination of Palestinian Nationality under the British Rule" (PhD diss., 2007), 40.

26. Gutman, "Migrants, Revolutionaries, and Spies," 288.

27. Alfred Northrup to Bie Ravndal, Trebizond, 5/4/1914, Vol. 277, RG: 84, NARA.

28. Akram Fouad Khater, *Inventing Home: Emigration, Gender, and the Middle Class in Lebanon, 1870–1920* (Berkeley, 2001), 118–127; Arsan, *Interlopers of Empire: The Lebanese Diaspora in Colonial French West Africa* (London, 2014), 38–39.

29. Elia Karmona, *La Novia Aguna* (Constantinople, 5682), 44–45, 75.

30. Nedim İpek and K. Tuncer Çağlayan, "The Emigration from the Ottoman Empire to America," in *Turkish Migration to the United States: From Ottoman Times to the Present*, ed. A. Deniz Balgamış and Kemal H. Karpa (Madison, 2008); Karpat, "Ottoman Emigration," 186–188; Arsan, *Interlopers of Empire*, 29.

31. Gömlek: 30, dosya: 2031, DH.MKT, BOA.

32. Gömlek: 23, dosya: 104, DH.MKT, BOA.

33. Steven Hyland, Jr., *More Argentine than You: Arabic-Speaking Immigrants in Argentina* (Albuquerque, 2017), 33. For similar practices among Moroccan Jews, see Jessica Marglin, "The Two Lives of Mas'ud Amoyal: Pseudo-Algerians in Morocco, 1830–1912," *International Journal of Middle East Studies* 44, no. 4 (Nov. 2012).

34. Elia Karmona. *Komo Nasio Elia Karmona: Komo Se Ingrandisio i Komo Se Izo Direktor del "Djugeton"* (Istanbul, 1926).

35. Julia Phillips Cohen and Sarah Abrevaya Stein, "Sephardic Scholarly Worlds: Toward a Novel Geography of Modern Jewish History," *Jewish Quarterly Review* 100, no. 3 (Summer 2010), esp. 351; Albert E. Kalderon, *Abraham Galanté: A Biography* (New York: 1983).

36. Aron Rodrigue, "Jewish Society and Schooling in a Thracian Town: The Alliance Israélite Universelle in Demotica, 1897–1924," *Jewish Social Studies* 45, no. 3/4 (Summer–Autumn 1983), 268.

37. Alberto Confino, "Report of the Jews of Silivri," 7/8/1907, TU-04/Turquie I C 1.5s, AIU; Haim Nahum, "Report on the Jews of Silivri," 7/8/1910, TU-04/Turquie I C 1.5u, AIU; David Nabon, "Report on the Israelites of Silivri," September, 1901, TU-04/Turquie I C 1.5u, AIU.

38. Sálomon Levy, interview by Monika Unikel, 1/4/1989, AAUHJ; Jaime Mitrani, interview by Anita Viskin, 12/14/1988, AAUHJ; Mary C. Neuberger, *Balkan Smoke: Tobacco and the Making of Modern Bulgaria* (Ithaca, 2013), 68–69.

39. Yitzchak Kerem, "The Migration of Rhodean Jews to Africa, 1900–1914," *Jewish Affairs* 61, no. 3 (Sept. 2006).

40. On Salonica's wealthiest Jewish families, see Orly C. Meron, *Jewish*

Entrepreneurship in Salonica, 1912–1940: An Ethnic Economy in Transition (Brighton, 2011), 24. See also Sara Assael, Acta de Nacimiento, México, Distrito Federal, Registro Civil, Nacimientos, 1861–1934. Archivo Estatal de Distrito Federal. Courtesy of the Academia Mexicana de Genealogia y Heraldica, 27.

41. Ico Assael, "Liquidación judicial," July 1935, folio: 237135, caja: 2783, serie: archivo histórico, sección: siglo XX, TSJDF, AGN.

42. Sarah Abrevaya Stein, *Making Jews Modern: The Yiddish and Ladino Press in the Russian and Ottoman Empires* (Bloomington, 2004), 55; Olga Borovaya, *Modern Ladino Culture: Press, Belles Lettres, and Theater in the Late Ottoman Empire* (Bloomington, 2012).

43. "Korrespondensia de Buenos Aires," *El Tiempo*, 10/16/1908, 9–10; "La Inkisision en el Meksiko," *El Tiempo*, 11/2/1908, 7–8; "La Kolonizasion Djudia en el Kanada," *El Tiempo*, 11/13/1908, 5; "La Independensia de la Isla Kuba," *El Tiempo*, 1/13/1909, 8; "Mumias de Djudios en Meksiko," *El Tiempo*, 1/17/1917, 5.

44. Moses Ben Ghiat, "Tipos de Imigrasion," *El Meseret*, 1/5/1908, 5.

45. Marc David Baer, "Turk and Jew in Berlin: The First Turkish Migration to Germany," *Comparative Studies in Society and History* 55, no. 2 (2013); Aviva Ben-Ur, *Sephardic Jews in America: A Diasporic History* (New York, 2009); Devin Naar, "Between 'New Greece' and the 'New World': Salonikan Jewish Immigration to America," *Journal of the Hellenic Diaspora* 35, no. 2 (Fall 2009); Naar, "From the 'Jerusalem of the Balkans' to the 'Goldene Medina': Jewish Immigration from Salonika to the United States," *American Jewish History* 93, no. 2 (Dec. 2007); Margalit Bejarano, "From All Their Habitations: Sephardic Jews in Cuba," *Judaism* 51, no. 1 (Winter 2002); Adriana Brodsky, *Sephardi, Jewish, Argentine: Community and National Identity* (Bloomington, 2016). For a detailed analysis of Sephardi commercial and financial relationships connecting Salonica with the Macedonian hinterland, see Meron, *Jewish Entrepreneurship*.

46. Moshe Emanuel Matalon, "La Imigrasion," *La Epoka*, 1/8/1904, 4.

47. Ben Ghiat, "Tipos de Imigrasion."

48. "Buenos Aires en Izmir," *El Meseret*, 1/23/1908, 7; Şule Toktaş and Fatih Resul Kılınç, "Jewish Immigration to the American Continent," *The Journal of Migration Studies* 4, no. 1 (Jan.–June 2018), 54.

49. "Karta de Buenos Aires," *El Meseret*, 4/7/1910, 1–2.

50. "Letra de Inglatiera, La Imigrasion," *La Epoka*, 1/29/1904, 9.

51. "De *La Epoka*," *El Meseret*, 1/16/1908, 3.

52. "Los Imigrantes," *El Meseret*, 5/17/1907, 9.

53. "Karta de Buenos Aires," *El Meseret*, 4/7/1910, 1–2.

54. Ibid.

55. Ben Ghiat, "Tipos de Imigrasion."

56. "Avizo—Buro de Imigrasion," *El Meseret*, 7/20/1911, 1.

57. "La Imigrasion," *La Amerika*, 8/4/1911, 1.

58. "Las Sufriensas de Nuestros Djudios de Turkia en Elis Island por No Konoser las Leyes de la Imigrasion," *La Amerika*, 6/9/1911, 1. *La Amerika* published a booklet with the translation of American immigration laws into Ladino in 1916. See Devin Naar, "A Guidebook for Sephardi Immigrants," https://jewishstudies.washington.edu/sephardic-studies/a-guide-for-sephardic-immigrants/ (accessed 9/10/2019).

59. "A la Atansion de los Djudios de Turkia ke Imigran en Amerika," *El Meseret*, 7/6/1911, 4.

60. Aviva Ben-Ur, "In Search of the American Ladino Press: A Bibliographical Survey, 1910–1948," *Studies in Bibliography and Booklore* 21 (2001), 13.

61. "La Amerika," *El Meseret*, 7/13/1911, 2.

62. Aron Rodrigue, "Jewish Society and Schooling," 264; Rodrigue, *French Jews, Turkish Jews: The Alliance Israélite Universelle and the Politics of Jewish Schooling in Turkey, 1860–1925* (Bloomington, 1990).

63. Edgar Morin, *Vidal et les siens* (Paris, 1989), 28. See also Karmona, *La Novia Aguna*; A.H. Navon, *Joseph Pérez: Juifs de Ghetto* (Paris, 1925).

64. Eliezer Caraco, 6/12/1906, TU-04/Turquie I C 4.2b, AIU.

65. Letters from M. Fresco, 1907, TU-06/Turquie II C 8.04 b, AIU.

66. Letters from Marcel Aranias, 1908, TU-14/Turquie IV E 57, AIU.

67. Letters from Jacques Taranto, 1913, TU-200/Turquie LXXXIX E 1046, AIU.

68. Meron, *Jewish Entrepreneurship*, 55. See also "Turkey Plans to Boycott Italy," *The Wall Street Journal*, 10/14/1911, 4; "To Close Italian Banks in Turkey," *The New York Times*, 12/25/1911, 3; "Death to Italians," *The Washington Post*, 10/11/1911, 1. It is unclear whether any Jews were expelled.

69. A member of the prominent *franco* Picciotto family served as the Austrian consul in Aleppo during the 1840 Damascus Affair. See Yaron Harel, "The Rise and Fall of the Jewish Consuls in Aleppo," *Turcica* 38 (2006); Jonathan Frankel, *The Damascus Affair: Ritual Murder, Politics, and the Jews in 1840* (Cambridge, 1997).

70. Morin, *Vidal*, 45. For additional discussions of the benefits and complications of extraterritoriality, see Sarah Abrevaya Stein, "Protected Persons? The Baghdadi Jewish Diaspora, the British State, and the Persistence of Empire," *American Historical Review* 116, no. 1 (Feb. 2011); Ziad Fahmy, "Jurisdictional Borderlands: Extraterritoriality and 'Legal Chameleons' in Precolonial Alexandria, 1840–1870," *Comparative Studies in Society and History* 55, no. 2 (2013); Frank Castiglione, "'Levantine' Dragomans in Nineteenth Century Istanbul: The Pisanis, the British, and Issues of Subjecthood," *Osmanlı Araştırmaları / The Journal of Ottoman Studies* 44 (2014): 169-195.

71. Morin, *Vidal*, 44.

72. André Aciman, *Out of Egypt: A Memoir* (New York, 1994), 4–5, 7, 43–44.

73. Morin, *Vidal*, 60–61; Meron, *Jewish Entrepreneurship*, 22.

74. Letter to the Ottoman chief rabbi from Verona, 7/2/1912, HM2 9070.1, CAHJP.

75. Meron, *Jewish Entrepreneurship*, 45, 55.
76. Corry Guttstadt, *Turkey, the Jews, and the Holocaust* (Cambridge, 2013), 180.
77. Annie Benveniste, *Le Bosphore à la Roquette: la communauté judéo-espagnole à Paris (1914–1940)* (Paris, 1989), 16, 45–48.
78. Cohen, "Oriental by Design," 394.
79. Guttstadt, *Turkey, the Jews, and the Holocaust*, 182.
80. Annie Benveniste, "The Judeo-Spanish Community in Paris," in *From Iberia to Diaspora: Studies in Sephardi History and Culture*, ed. Norman A. Stillman and Yedida K. Stillman (Leiden, 1999), 172; Guttstadt, *Turkey, the Jews, and the Holocaust*, 182.
81. Guttstadt, *Turkey, the Jews, and the Holocaust*, 181.
82. "Echos," *La Jeune Turquie*, 6/11/1910, 1.
83. Quoted in Liz Hamui de Halabe, *Transformaciones en la Religiosidad de los Judíos en México* (Mexico City, 2005), 116.
84. Daniela Gleizer notes that no Sephardi migrant referenced Rivas, nor have I come across any allusion to him in historical sources. See Gleizer, "Judíos Sefardíes: De España a México a través del Imperio Otomano," in *La Ciudad Cosmopolita de los Inmigrantes*, ed. Carlos Martínez Assad (Mexico, 2010).
85. Albert Assael, NYPL, 1820–1957, Year 1901, line: 10, Page: 42, microfilm role T715_169, Serial 15, NARA.
86. The United States immigration officials at the time noted Ottoman nationality as "Turkish."
87. Johanan Assael, NYPL, 1820–1957, Year 1901, line:4, Page: 176, microfilm role T715_169, Serial 15, NARA.
88. Isaco Assael, NYPL, 1820–1957, Year: 1903, Line: 30, Page: 15, Roll: T715_328, Serial: T715, NARA.
89. Martin Zielonka, "Letters from Mexico," *The American Israelite*, vol. 55, no. 2, 7/9/1908.
90. Daniela Gleizer, "De la Apertura al Cierre de Puertas: La Inmigración Judía en México durante las Primeras Décadas del Siglo XX," *Historia Mexicana* 60, no. 2 (Oct.–Dec. 2010), 1182–1183. For more on Mexican Francophilia in the Porfiriato, see Mauricio Tenorio-Trillo, *Mexico at the World's Fairs: Crafting a Modern Nation* (Berkeley, 1996). Buchenau asserts that Mexican elites modeled their modernization after the French Third Republic: Jürgen Buchenau, "Small Numbers, Great Impact: Mexico and Its Immigrants, 1821–1973," *Journal of American Ethnic History* 20, no. 3 (Spring 2001), 32. For financial interactions between France and Mexico involving Jews of French and German origin, see Steven C. Topik, "When Mexico Had the Blues: A Transatlantic Tale of Bonds, Bankers, and Nationalists, 1862–1910," *American Historical Review* 105, no. 3 (Jun. 2000), 721–736.
91. Benjamin Orlove and Arnold J. Bauer, "Giving Importance to Imports," in *The Allure of the Foreign: Imported Goods in Postcolonial Latin America*, ed. Benjamin Orlove

(Ann Arbor, 1997), 12–13, 16; William H. Beezley and Linda A. Curcio-Nagy, "Introduction," in *Latin American Popular Culture: An Introduction* (New York, 2000), xvii; Jeffrey D. Needell, *A Tropical Belle Epoque: Elite Culture and Society in Turn-of-the-Century Rio de Janeiro* (Cambridge, 1987), 28, 156.

92. William H. Beezley, *Judas at the Jockey Club and Other Episodes of Porfirian Mexico* (Lincoln, 1987), 13–66; Jeffrey M. Pilcher, "Many Chefs in the National Kitchen: Cookbooks and Identity in Nineteenth-Century Mexico," in *Latin American Popular Culture*, ed. William H. Beezley and Linda A. Curcio-Nagy (New York, 2000), 128–131.

93. Camila Pastor, *The Mexican Mahjar: Transnational Maronites, Jews, and Arabs under the French Mandate* (Austin, 2017), 46.

94. Gleizer, "Apertura," 1185; Pastor, *The Mexican Mahjar*, 19.

95. Ana María Alonso, "Conforming Disconformity: 'Mestizaje,' Hybridity, and the Aesthetics of Mexican Nationalism," *Cultural Anthropology* 19, no. 4 (Nov. 2004), 461–462. Díaz, who was ashamed of his partially indigenous background, notoriously whitened his skin in photographs and public appearances. For an analysis of the relationship between Porfirian economic policy, his view of Mexicans as racially inferior, and the perceived need to infuse Mexico with foreign blood, money, and technology in hopes of economic betterment balanced against the threat of foreign domination, see Richard Weiner, "Battle for Survival: Porfirian Views of the International Marketplace," *Journal of Latin American Studies* 32, no. 3 (Oct. 2000), 660–662; on how American paternalistic attitudes toward Mexican employees fomented anti-foreign sentiment under the slogan "Mexico for the Mexicans," see Jonathan C. Brown, "Foreign and Native-Born Workers in Porfirian Mexico," *The American Historical Review* 98, no. 3 (Jun. 1993). On "whitening" the population and attitudes toward race, see Buchenau, "Small Numbers, Great Impact," 31–32; Martin S. Stabb, "Indigenism and Racism in Mexican Thought: 1857–1911," *Journal of Inter-American Studies* 1, no. 4 (Oct. 1959); T. G. Powell, "Mexican Intellectuals and the Indian Question, 1876–1911," *The Hispanic American Historical Review* 48, no. 1 (Feb. 1968). Miguel Angel Aviles-Galán examines the links among *mestizaje*, national identity, race, and nation in the work of Vicente Riva Palacio to argue that for him, the mestizo was the "modern race": Miguel Angel Aviles-Galán, "Measuring Skulls: Race and Science in Vicente Riva Palacio's *México a través de los siglos*," *Bulletin of Latin American Research* 29, no. 1 (2010), 94, 98, 99. José Angel Hernández, however, argues that Mexican colonization policies were aimed not at "whitening" the Mexican population but at incorporating indigenous groups into the "Mexican family" while excluding others, particularly Spaniards, and that allegations of Porfirian attempts to "whiten" Mexico were historiographical inventions to solidify the critique of Díaz as despotic and anti-Mexican. He notes that "[t]he official Mexican ideal of *mestizaje*, which articulates a painful, if invented, community of miscegenation, has conveniently overlooked the nation's violent practices of expulsion and exclusion

that ultimately contributed to a hostile environment for European settlement." José Angel Hernández, "From Conquest to Colonization: Indios and Colonization Policies after Mexican Independence," *Mexican Studies/Estudios Mexicanos* 26, no. 2 (Summer 2010), 292.

96. Gleizer, "Apertura," 1180–1181; Corinne Krause, *Los Judíos en México: Una Historia con Énfasis Especial en el Periodo de 1857 a 1930* (Mexico, 1987); Liz Hamui de Halabe and Fredy Charabati, eds., *Los Judíos de Alepo en México* (Mexico City, 1989), 98.

97. Hamui de Halabe and Charabati, *Los Judíos de Alepo*, 122; Paulette Kershenovich Schuster, *The Syrian Jewish Community in Mexico City in a Comparative Perspective* (Saarbrücken, 2012), 113–114; Alfaro-Velcamp, *So Far from Allah*, 31–39, 52–53. This preoccupation with the United States as a final destination for migrants to Mexico is not confined to the study of Middle Eastern migrants. Erika Lee offers a nuanced analysis of Chinese migrants entering the United States from Canada and Mexico but does not examine Mexico as a viable destination: Erika Lee, "Enforcing the Borders: Chinese Exclusion along the U.S. Borders with Canada and Mexico, 1882–1924," *Journal of American History* 89, no. 1 (Jun. 2002).

98. Rana Razek, "Trails and Fences: Syrian Migration Networks and Immigration Restriction, 1885–1911," *Amerasia Journal* 44, no. 1 (2018), 111–116.

99. "Noticias Maritimas," *El Mundo*, 3/29/1916, 5; Saul Carasso, 6/24/1906, NYPL, 1820–1957, Year: 1906, Page: 118, Line: 1, Roll: T715_731, Serial: T715, NARA; Saul Carasso, 7/19/1906, NYPL, 1820–1957, Year: 1906, Line: 3, Page: 127, Roll: T715_742, Serial: T715, NARA; Saul Carasso, NYPL, 1820–1957, Year: 1906; Page: 127, Line: 3, Roll: T715_742, Serial: T715, NARA; Saul Carasso, 4/5/1907, Nonstatistical Manifests and Statistical Index Cards of Aliens Arriving at Laredo, Texas, May 1903–November 1929, Roll: 10, Serial: A3379, RG: 85, NARA.

100. Isaac Capon, 12/10/1906, NYPL, 1820–1957, Year: 1906, Line: 5, Page: 133, Roll: T715_808, Serial: T715, NARA.

101. Clement Gabai, Manifests of Statistical and Some Nonstatistical Alien Arrivals at Laredo, Texas, May 1903–April 1955, Roll: 20, Serial: A3437, RG: 85, NARA; Albert Salem, 7/29/1911, NYPL, 1820–1957, Year: 1911, Line: 5, Page: 199, Roll: T715_1714, Serial: T715, NARA.

102. Juan Assael, NYPL, 1820–1957, Year 1907, Line: 1, Page: 80, Microfilm Role T715_1066, Serial T715, NARA.

103. Exp. 590, vol. 512, sec.: certificaciones, fondo: Ayuntamiento, AHDF.

104. Correspondence with Dina Danon; Joseph Nalpas, *Annuaire des commerçants de Smyrne et de l'Anatolie* (Smyrne, 1894). Leon Alazraki was one of the witnesses to Saul Carasso's 1912 marriage to Mexican national Concepción Gómez. Mauricio Assael and Isaac Benveniste became partners in the longstanding "La Exposición" jewelry store in central Mexico City in 1912, and Benveniste and one of Alazraki's brothers got arrested together in Havana for smuggling merchandise in 1914. "Presentaciones," *El*

Diario, 9/12/1912, 3; "Cruz Blanca Neutral Mexicana," *Diario del Hogar*, 7/14/1911, 3; "Por Defraudación a la Aduana," *El Mundo*, 4/2/1914, 8.

105. Naturalization petition of Mauricio Assael, Alberto Assael, Isidoro Assael, Leon Alazraki, Salomon Castro, Isaac Benveniste, exp. 590, vol. 512, sec.: certificaciones, fondo: Ayuntamiento, AHDF.

106. Avigdor Levy, "Introduction," in *The Jews of the Ottoman Empire*, ed. Avigdor Levy (Princeton, 1994); Cohen, *Becoming Ottomans*.

107. Robert Weis, "Immigrant Entrepreneurs, Bread, and Class Negotiation in Postrevolutionary Mexico City," *Mexican Studies/Estudios Mexicanos* 25, no. 1 (Winter 2009), 75.

108. Buchenau, "Small Numbers, Great Impact," 28–29.

109. Pastor, *The Mexican Mahjar*, 87–88.

110. For a comparison of the economic activities and success of Syrio-Lebanese in Brazil and the United States, see Oswaldo M. S. Truzzi, "At the Right Place at the Right Time: Syrians and Lebanese in Brazil and the United States, a Comparative Approach," *Journal of American Ethnic History* 16, no. 2 (Winter 1997). See also Alfaro-Velcamp, *So Far from Allah*, esp. ch. 6.

111. Zielonka, "Letters from Mexico," 7/23/1908, *The American Israelite*, vol. 55, no. 4; Zielonka, "Letters from Mexico," 8/15/1908, *The American Israelite*, vol. 55, no. 7.

112. Alfaro-Velcamp, *So Far from Allah*, 56.

113. Judit Bokser de Liwerant, *Imágenes de un Encuentro: La Presencia Judía en México durante la Primera Mitad del Siglo XX* (Mexico City, 1992), 75.

114. "Ecos del Incendio del Teatro Guerrero en Puebla," *El Imparcial*, 2/13/1909, 5; "Fué casi Completo el Saqueo á la Joyería Assael," *El Imparcial*, 4/22/1909, 5.

115. "Sociales y Personales," *El Imparcial*, 10/11/1911, 7; "Hotel Arrivals," *The Mexican Herald*, 11/9/1912, 8; "Hotel Arrivals," *The Mexican Herald*, 1/14/1913, 8; "Presentaciones," *El Diario*, 9/12/1912, 3; "De Sociedad," *El Universal*, 9/28/1918, 6.

116. Alejandro Portes, Luis Eduardo Guarnizo, and William J. Haller, "Transnational Entrepreneurs: An Alternative Form of Immigrant Economic Adaptation," *American Sociological Review* 67, no. 2 (Apr. 2002), 279.

117. Martin Zielonka, "Letters from Mexico," *The American Israelite*, vol. 55, no. 5, 7/30/1908; Hamui de Halabe and Charabati, *Los Judíos de Alepo*, 97.

118. Alberto Assael, 5/12/1908, NYPL, 1820–1957, Year: 1908, Line: 3, Page: 134, Roll: T715_1101, Serial: T715, NARA; Ico Assael, 6/1/1909, NYPL, 1820–1957, Year: 1909, Line: 16, Page: 100, Roll: T715_1278, Serial: T715, NARA.

119. Paul Dubois y Cia. vs. Alberto Assael, folio: 141050, caja: 851, serie: archive histórico, sec.: siglo XX, TSJDF, AGN; Alberto Assael, Quiebra, folio: 149630, caja: 845, serie: archive histórico, sec.: siglo XX, TSJDF, AGN.

120. "La Turquesa," *El País*, 12/15/1912, 5.

121. Annie Benveniste, *Le Bosphore à la Roquette*, 67, 80–82.

122. Isaac Capon, NYPL, 1820–1957, Year: 1927, Line: 14, Page: 61, Roll: T715_4030, Serial: T715, NARA; Isaac Capon, NYPL, 1820–1957, Year: 1927, Line: 30, Page: 133, Roll: T715_4165, Serial: T715, NARA; Manuel Modiano, NYPL, 1820–1957, Year: 1929, Page: 39, Line: 30, Roll: T715_4561, Serial: T715, NARA; José Saltiel, NYPL, 1820–1957, Year: 1930, Line: 30, Page: 31, Roll: T715_4856, Serial: T715, NARA; Rafael and Ida Eskenazi, NYPL, 1820–1957, Year: 1934, Line: 23, Page: 21, Roll: T715_5564, Serial: T715, NARA.

123. Isaac Capon et al., 4/30/1909, NYPL, 1820–1957, Year: 1909, Line: 2, Page: 110, Roll: T715_1255, Serial: T715, NARA; Msi Cohen et al., 4/9/1910, NYPL, 1820–1957, Year: 1910, Line: 5, Page: 18, Roll: T715_1448, Serial: T715, NARA.

124. Isaac Capon, 4/15/1910, NYPL, 1820–1957, Year: 1910, Line: 12, Page: 120, Roll: T715_1454, Serial: T715, NARA; Leon Alazraki, 7/8/1910, NYPL, 1820–1957, Year: 1910, Line: 1, Page: 96, Roll: T715_1514, Serial: T715, NARA; Isaac Capon and Leon Alazraki, 10/3/1910, NYPL, 1820–1957, Year: 1910, Line: 2, Page: 6, Roll: T715_1568, Serial: T715, NARA.

125. Naar, "Jerusalem of the Balkans"; Naar, "New Greece," 47.

126. Abuof vs. Habif, Injurias. 11/2/1907, folio: 96907, sección: siglo XX, serie: archivo histórico, TSJDF, AGN.

127. For a discussion of male same-sex sexual encounters and views of such prior to the mid-nineteenth century, see Yaron Ben-Naeh, "Moshko the Jew and His Gay Friends: Same-Sex Sexual Relations in Ottoman Jewish Society," *Journal of Early Modern History* 9, no. 1–2 (2005). In the broader pre-twentieth-century Ottoman context, Khaled El-Rouayheb and Dror Ze'evi have argued that while being the active male partner in a male same-sex sexual encounter was not frowned upon, being the penetrated "passive" partner was considered "shameful" and "unmasculine" once a man had left his youth. Joseph Massad argues that the conception of "homosexuality" and a "homosexual identity" as such were twentieth-century byproducts of the hegemonic cultural and sexual norms of Western imperialism. See Khaled El-Rouayheb, *Before Homosexuality in the Arab-Islamic World, 1500–1800* (Chicago, 2005); Dror Ze'evi, *Producing Desire: Changing Sexual Discourse in the Ottoman Middle East, 1500–1900* (Berkeley, 2006); Joseph A. Massad, *Desiring Arabs* (Chicago, 2007).

128. Joseph A. Schemonti to Rifaat Pasha, 9/20/1909, gömlek: 11, dosya: 77, HR.SYS, BOA.

129. Report of Gonzalo Esteva to the Secretaría de Relaciones Exteriores, 7/14/1904 and M. Rechid, letter to Gonzalo Esteva, 7/14/1904, 7-19-12, SRE.

130. Letter from the legation, 1/22/1905, 7-19-12, SRE.

131. Letter from the legation, 6/18/1909, 7-19-12, SRE.

132. Ottoman-Argentine relations were also propelled by the large number of Syrio-Lebanese Ottoman subjects in Argentina and intended to facilitate trade relations, and were also conducted through Rome. See Ignacio Klich, "Argentine-Ottoman

Relations and Their Impact on Immigrants from the Middle East: A History of Unfulfilled Expectations, 1910–1915," *The Americas* 50, no. 2 (Oct. 1993), 181–182. Copies of the Ottoman consular protocols with Argentina, Brazil, and Mexico are located at gömlek: 341, dosya: 10/-ç., Fon: A.MTZ.(05), BOA, while negotiations for the protocol with Argentina are at gömlek: 283405, dosya: 3779, BEO, BOA.

133. Letter from the SRE, 11/30/1909, 7-19-12, SRE.
134. Letter from the legation, 2/10/1910, ibid.
135. Letter from the SRE, 3/11/1910, ibid.
136. Gömlek 11, dosya: 78, HR.HMŞ.İŞO, BOA.
137. Michael J. Gonzalez, "Imagining Mexico in 1910: Visions of the *Patria* in the Centennial Celebration in Mexico City," *Journal of Latin American Studies* 39, no. 3 (Aug. 2007), 498.
138. Letter from Francisco León de la Barra, 6/15/1910, L-E-117, SRE.
139. "Recuerdo del Centenario," *El Imparcial*, 8/8/1910, 4.
140. Mauricio Tenorio-Trillo, "1910 Mexico City: Space and Nation in the City of the Centenario," *Journal of Latin American Studies* 28, no. 1 (Feb. 1996), 76–78. Comité Patriotico Otomano to the Director General de Obras Publicas, 7/1/1910, exp. 4, vol. 603, subsection: Festividades, sec.: Consejo Superior de Gobierno, Fondo: Ayuntamiento, AHDF.
141. Aslı Odman, "Meksika'daki Osmanlı Saat Kulesi," *Toplumsal Tarih* 167 (Nov. 2007), 44, 48.
142. Selim Deringil, "'They Live in a State of Nomadism and Savagery': The Late Ottoman Empire and the Post-Colonial Debate," *Comparative Studies in Society and History* 45, no. 2 (Apr. 2003); Deringil, *The Well-Protected Domains: Ideology and the Legitimation of Power in the Ottoman Empire, 1876–1909* (London, 2011), 31, 135–149; Mehmet Bengü Uluengin, "Secularizing Anatolia Tick by Tick: Clock Towers in the Ottoman Empire and the Turkish Republic," *International Journal of Middle East Studies* 42 (2010).
143. Letter from the *colonia otomana* in Mexico to the Mexican ambassador in Washington, 10/3/1910, 7-19-12, SRE; letter from Anthony Houry, Mexico City, to Hilmi Pasha, 8/14/1909, gömlek: 11, dosya: 77, HR.SYS, BOA; "El Monumento de la Colonia Otomana, Inaugurado Ayer," *El País*, 9/23/1910, 1.
144. Casino Otomano, exp. 1389, vol. 1638, sec: Juegos Permitidos, Fondo Ayuntamiento, Gobierno del Distrito Federal, AHDF; Casino Turco, 1911, exp. 1426, bis, vol. 809, sec: diversiones publicas, Fondo: Ayuntamiento, Gobierno del Distrito Federal, AHDF.

Chapter 2: Patriot Games

1. Annie Benveniste argues that it was common for individuals to change their ages, names, and nationalities to avoid military service. Benveniste, "The Judeo-Spanish

Community in Paris," in *From Iberia to Diaspora: Studies in Sephardic History and Culture*, ed. Norman A. Stillman and Yedida K. Stillman (Leiden, 1999), 170.

2. Lying to officials about the purpose and extent of travel, particularly claiming to be going to France temporarily to continue education, is also attested to in other accounts. See Benveniste, "The Judeo-Spanish Community," 46. Dr. Markus, one of the leaders of the B'nai B'rith Lycée in Istanbul, reported that nearly eighty students left for Switzerland between 1916 and 1917 to avoid conscription. See Markus to Abram Elkus, 4/3/1917, ID: 10721, folder: Turkey, General, 1917–1918, 1914–1918 NY Collection, JDC.

3. Margalit Bejarano, "From All Their Habitations: Sephardic Jews in Cuba," *Judaism* 51, no. 1 (Winter 2002), 100, 101, 104.

4. Sálomon Levy, interviewed by Monika Unikel, 1/4/1989, Mexico City, AAUHJ.

5. See Avner Levi, "The Jewish Press in Turkey," in *Jewish Journalism and Printing Houses in the Ottoman Empire and Modern Turkey*, ed. Gad Nassi (Istanbul, 2001), 19; and Sarah Abrevaya Stein, *Making Jews Modern: The Yiddish and Ladino Press in the Russian and Ottoman Empires* (Bloomington, 2004), 57.

6. Esther Benbassa, *Haim Nahum: A Sephardic Chief Rabbi in Politics, 1892–1923* (Tuscaloosa, 1995), 9–14.

7. "Las Suskripsiones," "Reunion de Damas," "El Movimiento Patriotiko," "Yamada a Nuestros Ermanos," *El Tiempo*, 2/3/1913, 3–4. Throughout *El Tiempo*, the word *patria* is used to denote "homeland," in contrast to *nasion*, "nation," or *pais*, "state."

8. Gendering of nation as a female mother whose honor was in danger to rally the (male) nation in her defense was a common trope. See Afsaneh Najmabadi, *Women with Mustaches and Men without Beards: Gender and Sexual Anxieties of Iranian Modernity* (Berkeley, 2005), esp. 97–132; and Lisa Pollard, *Nurturing the Nation: The Family Politics of Modernizing, Colonizing, and Liberating Egypt, 1905–1923* (Berkeley: 2005).

9. Ottomanist ideology, reaching back to the reign of Abdülmecid I (1839–1861), aimed to guarantee equality between Muslims and non-Muslim citizens, offering a panacea to ward off separatist nationalisms among the residents of the empire. Escalating Ottoman military losses, increasing social polarization between ethnic and religious groups, the secession of the Balkan provinces during the Balkan Wars, and emerging Armenian, Greek, and Arab nationalisms finally enabled Turkish nationalism to triumph over Ottomanism, however, particularly in the wake of the Balkan Wars and throughout World War I. The various nationalist movements—whether Turkish, Armenian, Greek, or Arab—were predicated on the political mobilization of new visions of history, literature, and education by new organizational forms of philanthropic associations, secret societies, and political parties. See Fatma Müge Göçek, "Decline of the Ottoman Empire and the Emergence of Greek, Armenian, Turkish, and Arab Nationalisms," in *Social Constructions of Nationalism in the Middle East*, ed. Fatma Müge Göçek (Albany, 2002). See also Erol Köroğlu, *Ottoman Propaganda and Turkish Identity:*

Literature in Turkey during World War I (London, 2007), 24–25; Hasan Kayalı, *Arabs and Young Turks: Ottomanism, Arabism, and Islamism in the Ottoman Empire, 1908–1918* (Berkeley, 1997); Reşat Kasaba, "Dreams of Empire, Dreams of Nation," in *Empire to Nation: Historical Perspectives on the Making of the Modern World*, ed. Joseph W. Esherick, Hasan Kayalı, and Eric Van Young (Lanham, 2006), 200.

10. "Prizonieros Djudios en Bulgaria," *El Tiempo*, 2/3/1913, 4, emphasis mine.

11. Yiğit Akın, *When the War Came Home: The Ottomans' Great War and the Devastation of an Empire* (Stanford, 2018), 18, 26–27.

12. Bora Isyar, "The Origins of Turkish Republican Citizenship: The Birth of Race," *Nations and Nationalism* 11, no. 3 (2005), 343, 346–347; Göçek, "The Decline of the Ottoman Empire," 43, 46–47; Eyal Ginio, "Mobilizing the Ottoman Nation during the Balkan Wars (1912–1913): Awakening the Ottoman Dream," *War in History* 12, no. 2 (2005), 170–171.

13. Letter from Tchourlou, 1/15/1914, microfilm at CAHJP, HM3/694, AIU Turquie XCVI E 1125.01, CAHJP. According to Alexis Alexandris, the CUP's economic policies during the war benefited Turkish and Jewish merchants, who exhibited a "frantic pace of economic activities." While individual Ottoman Jewish subjects may have benefited economically during the war from the displacement of Greek and Armenian subjects, the trope of overall Jewish economic success is not borne out by the sources, which overwhelming display unprecedented displacement and economic challenges. See Alexis Alexandris, *The Greek Minority of Istanbul and Greek-Turkish Relations, 1918–1974* (Athens, 1992), 44.

14. Zafer Toprak, "Nationalism and Economics in the Young Turk Era (1908–1918)," in *Industrialisation, Communication, et Rapports Sociaux en Turquie et en Mediterranée Orientale*, ed. Jacques Thobie and Salgur Kançal (Paris, 1991), 260–261.

15. Feroz Ahmad, "War and Society under the Young Turks, 1908–1918," *Review (Fernand Braudel Center)* 11, no. 2 (Spring, 1988), 267, 269, 277; Elizabeth B. Frierson, "Gender, Consumption, and Patriotism: The Emergence of an Ottoman Public Sphere," in *Public Islam and the Common Good*, ed. Armando Salvatore and Dale F. Eickelman (Leiden, 2006), 115. According to Alexis Alexandris, in 1914, fifty percent of the actual capital investment in the Ottoman Empire was controlled by Ottoman Greeks, twenty percent by Armenians, and five percent by Jews; ten percent was controlled by foreign nationals, many of whom were religious minorities who had acquired foreign nationality to benefit from the Capitulations. Fifteen percent of capital investment before World War I was held by Turkish Muslims. Alexandris, *The Greek Minority*, 32.

16. Kemal Karpat, "The Ottoman Emigration to America, 1860–1914," *International Journal of Middle East Studies* 17 (May 1985), 180.

17. Edward J. Erickson, "From Kirkilisse to the Great Offensive Turkish Operational Encirclement Planning, 1912–22," *Middle Eastern Studies* 40, no. 1 (Jan. 2004).

18. Rena Molho, "Popular Antisemitism and State Policy in Salonica during the

City's Annexation to Greece," *Jewish Social Studies* 50, no. 3/4 (Summer 1988–Autumn 1993), 254, 256.

19. Jacques Rieur, "Report on the Near East and Balkan States," 12/1/1921, ID: 352180, Folder: Turkey: Subject Matter, Child Care, 1921–1928, 1921–1932 NY Collection, JDC.

20. Sarah Abrevaya Stein, *Extraterritorial Dreams: European Citizenship, Sephardi Jews, and the Ottoman Twentieth Century* (Chicago, 2016), 25–26, 38; Rena Molho, "The Jewish Community of Salonica and Its Incorporation into the Greek State, 1912–1919," *Middle Eastern Studies* 24, no. 4 (Oct. 1988), 391, 395.

21. For the relocation of *Selanikli* Jews to Constantinople, see Yomtov Baruch to the Hahambaşı, 8/25/1914, HM2/9072, CAHJP.

22. For a first-hand account of the 1917 fire and the devastation it wrought, see T. Yaliz, *El Insendio del 17–18 Agosto 1917* (Salonica, 1919). Sephardi Jews in the United States raised funds to send to Salonica to alleviate the misery of their compatriots; see The Sephardic Relief Committee of America, 8.20/1918, JDC; and Sephardic Relief Committee, 9/2/1917, JDC. For more on the reconstruction of Salonica and the erasure of Muslim, Bulgarian, and Jewish elements from the cityscape, see Mark Mazower, *Salonica: City of Ghosts* (New York, 2004) 333–346.

23. "La Emigrasion de Salonik," *La Amerika*, 10/1/1915, 2.

24. K. E. Fleming argues that Salonican Jews were not identified, nor identified themselves, as "Greek" until they were in Auschwitz and labeled as such by Nazi forces and fellow Jewish prisoners, or later in Israel. See K. E. Fleming, *Greece: A Jewish History* (Princeton, 2008), 145–165, 190–204.

25. Devin Naar, "Between 'New Greece' and the 'New World': Salonikan Jews en route to New York," *Journal of the Hellenic Diaspora* 35, no. 2 (Fall 2009), 76.

26. A. Guéron, *Journal du Siège d'Andrinople, 30 octobre 1912–26 mars 1913* (Istanbul, 2002), 29, 37, 69; Avigdor Levy, "The Siege of Edirne (1912–1913) as Seen by a Jewish Eyewitness: Social, Political, and Cultural Perspectives," in *Jews, Turks, Ottomans: A Shared History, Fifteenth Through the Twentieth Century*, ed. Avigdor Levy (Syracuse, 2002).

27. Haim Bejarano Papo, 9/26/1913, TU-17/Turquie VI 100 A, AIU.

28. Letter from Kirkkilise, 9/18/1913, microfilm at CAHJP- HM3/693 Turquie XCIV E 1110.01a, CAHJP; Saul Cohen, "Tchourlou," 11/23/1912, 12/1/1912, TU-07/Turquie II C 13, AIU; David Levy, "Rodosto," 1913, TU-07/Turquie II C 11.2, AIU; Haim Rodrigue, "Kirkilisse," 9/21/1913, microfilm at CAHJP HM3/693, AIU Turquie XCIV E 1110.08, CAHJP.

29. Gömlek: 290, dosya: 57, DH.ŞFR, BOA. In this period, the Ottoman government also relocated several Jewish individuals engaged in prostitution, most of whom were Russian or Romanian, to the Anatolian interior. See Gömlek: 47, dosya: 22, DH.EUM.5.Şb, BOA.

30. Bejarano, "Habitations," 100, 104.

31. "List of Emigres in Or-Ahayim Hospital," June 1913, Correspondence to Hahambaşı, HM2/9070.3, CAHJP; Nissim Nathan Catalan, 1/14/1914, HM3/694, AIU Turquie XCVI E 1124.2, CAHJP.

32. *Commission Centrale de Secours aux Israélites Ottomans éprouvés de la guerre* (Constantinople, 1917).

33. "Relief Work for the Benefit of Families, Widows, and Orphans of Jewish Soldiers," Altaber, 7/2/1916, JDC; *Reports Received by the Joint Distribution Committee of Funds for Jewish War Sufferers* (New York, 1916), 110–130. On soup kitchens, see Abram Elkus, 3/2/1917, ID: 10734, folder: Turkey, General, 1917–1918, 1914–1918 NY Collection, JDC.

34. See Nissim B. Benezra, *Une Enfance juive à Istanbul (1911–1929)* (Istanbul, 1996), 9–11, 31, 44–45, 60–61.

35. Felix Warburg to Albert Lucas, 2/1/1917, ID: 10709, Folder: Turkey, General, 1917–1918, 1914–1918 NY Collection, JDC; Letter to Albert Lucas, 1/26/1917, ID: 10705, Folder: Turkey, General, 1917–1918, 1914–1918 NY Collection, JDC.

36. Judith Russo, "Los Djudios Otomanos," *El Tiempo*, 12/9/1912, 7.

37. Julia Phillips Cohen, "Between Civic and Islamic Ottomanism: Jewish Imperial Citizenship in the Hamidian Era," *International Journal of Middle East Studies* 44 (2012), 248.

38. "Askier de Toda Nasion i Djudios Tambien," *El Meseret*, 8/8/1908, 3.

39. Albert Benaroya, 7 August 1910, TU-15/Turquie V E 84, AIU.

40. Gad Franco to Hahambaşı, 1/29/1912, HM2/9070.1; AIU, TU-14/Turquie IV E 56.

41. Akın, *When the War Came Home*, 32.

42. Akın, *When the War Came Home*, 104; Alexandre Ben Ghiat, *Livro-Jurnal de la Gerra Djeneral* (Izmir, 1919), 18.

43. Yomtov Baruch to the Hahambaşı, 8/14/1914, HM2/9072, CAHJP.

44. Jewish Community of Bourgas to Hahambaşı, 8/12/1918, HM2/9073.3, CAHJP.

45. Leyla Neyzi, "Trauma, Narrative and Silence: The Military Journal of a Jewish 'Soldier' in Turkey during the Greco-Turkish War," *Turcica* 35 (April, 2003), 297; Erik J. Zürcher, "Little Mehmet in the Desert: The Ottoman Soldier's Experience," in *Facing Armageddon: The First World War Experienced*, ed. Hugh Cecil and Peter H. Liddle (London, 1996); Erik J. Zürcher, "The Ottoman Conscription System in Theory and Practice," in *Arming the State: Military Conscription in the Middle East and Central Asia, 1775–1925*, ed. Erik J. Zürcher (London, 1999).

46. Elia Karmona, *Haggadah dela Gerra Djeneral* (Constantinople, 1920); Nissim Shem-Tov Eli, *Haggadah dela Gerra por Dia de Pesah* (Constantinople, 1919).

47. "Una Trajika," 11 October 1910, *El Tiempo*, 4.

48. "Los Djudios en la Armada Otomana," 11 July 1913, *El Tiempo*, 6; "Petisiones de los Djudios de Salonica i de Ismirna por Modifikar la Ley Militara," 24 April 1912, *El Tiempo*, 6.

49. Karmona, *Haggadah*.

50. Ben Ghiat, *Livro-Jurnal*, 73.

51. Edward J. Erickson, *Defeat in Detail: The Ottoman Army in the Balkans, 1912–1913* (Westport, CT, 2003), 329.

52. Benezra, *Une Enfance juive*, 79.

53. Commission Interclub Israelite of Salonica to Hahambaşı, 4/3/1913, HM2/9070.3, CAHJP.

54. "Prizyoneros Djudios Bulgaros en Turkia," *El Tiempo*, 3/3/1913, 5; "Los Prizyoneros Djudios Bulgaros," *El Tiempo*, 8/25/1913, 3.

55. Grand Rabbinate of Bulgaria to the Hahambaşı, 4/21/1913, HM2/9070.3, CAHJP; Grand Rabbinate of Bulgaria to the Hahambaşı, 6/11/1913, HM2/9070.3, CAHJP; Grand Rabbinate of Bulgaria to the Hahambaşı, 8/27/1913, HM2/9070.3, CAHJP.

56. "Soldados Djudios Otomanos Prizyoneros en Filipoli," *El Tiempo*, 5/25/1912, 7; "Ringrasiamientos de prizyoneros Djudios Otomanos en Filipoli," *El Tiempo*, 1/20/1913, 8.

57. This contrasts with the Jews of France and Germany during World War I, who stopped seeing themselves as brothers in favor of a fully French or German identity. See Vicky Caron, *Between France and Germany: The Jews of Alsace-Lorraine, 1871–1918* (Stanford, 1988); Nadia Malinovich, *French and Jewish: Culture and the Politics of Identity in Early Twentieth-Century France* (Oxford, 2008).

58. "Askerlik," *El Meseret*, 10/2/1909, 2.

59. Naar, "'New Greece,'" 52–53.

60. Alexandre Ben Ghiat, "Askeres Djudios Fuidos en Egypto," *El Meseret*, 5/4/1911, 1.

61. Politi Argi, 4/5/1913, TU-03/ Turquie II B 10.7, AIU; Zürcher, "Little Mehmet," 234.

62. Zürcher, "Little Mehmet," 234.

63. Letter, 10/30/1913, HM3/694, AIU Turquie XCVI E 1125.01, CAHJP.

64. *Société de Bienfaisance Israélite de Marseille* to the Hahambaşı, 10/13/1913, HM2/9072, CAHJP.

65. Naar, "'New Greece,'" 60–61.

66. Sublime Porte to Habsburg Ambassador, 7/3/1916, Konstantinopel GesA 105, HHSA; Sublime Porte to Habsburg Ambassador, 12/20/1916, Konstantinopel GesA 105, HHSA; Stacy D. Fahrenthold, *Between the Ottomans and the Entente: The First World War in the Syrian and Lebanese Diaspora, 1908–1925* (New York, 2019), 48.

67. Leon Graciani, Letter, 10/18/1912, TU-21/ Turquie VII E 144, AIU.

68. Zürcher, "Little Mehmet," 234; Karpat, "Ottoman Emigration," 182.

69. Conorte Canneti to AIU headquarters, 7/22/1919, HM3/693, AIU Turquie XCIV E 1110.04a, capitals his.

70. Gömlek: 26, dosya: 9, DH.EUM.SSM, BOA.

71. For more on Ottoman Syrians in the French and U.S. armies, see Fahrenthold, *Between the Ottomans and the Entente*.

72. Gömlek: 52, dosya:1, DH.EUM.5.Şb, BOA; Akarlı 131–133.

73. Benveniste, "The Judeo-Spanish Community," 170; Benveniste, *Le Bosphore à la Roquette*, 77; Sarah Abrevaya Stein, "Citizens of a Fictional Nation: Ottoman-Born Jews in France during the First World War," *Past & Present* 226 (2015), 235.

74. José M. Estrugo to Robert Lansing, Los Angeles, 11/5/1918; document: 763.72115/3308, microfilm 0353; Series M367; Civil prisoners: Enemy Noncombatants; Records of the Department of State Relating to World War I and its Termination, 1914–1929; General Records of the Department of State, 1763–2002, NARA. For more on soldiers of Ottoman origins serving in the American army and elsewhere, see Stacy D. Fahrenthold, "Former Ottomans in the Ranks: Pro-Entente Military Recruitment among Syrians in the Americas, 1916–1918," *Journal of Global History* 11, no. 1 (March 2016).

75. Aviva Ben-Ur, "Identity Imperative: Ottoman Jews in Wartime and Interwar Britain," *Immigrants and Minorities: Historical Studies in Ethnicity, Migration, and Diaspora* (2014), 9–10; Stein, "Citizens of a Fictional Nation," 239.

76. Benveniste, *Le Bosphore à la Roquette*, 57.

77. John Foran, "Race, Class, and Gender in the Making of the Mexican Revolution," *International Review of Sociology* 6, no. 1 (March, 1996), 140.

78. Letters from the American Embassy, Constantinople, to the Imperial Ministry for Foreign Affairs, Sublime Porte. gömlek: 69, dosya: 50, HR.SYS, BOA; "Meksiko i los Estados Unidos," *El Tiempo*, 4/20/1914, 7.

79. Pablo Yankelevich, *¿Deseables o Inconvenientes?: Las Fronteras de la Extranjería en el México Posrevolucionario* (Mexico, 2011), 88–89.

80. "Extranjería y Naturalización," 1917, 17-10-40, SRE.

81. Bella Cherem, "La Integración de los Judíos Alepinos en la Historia de México," in *Los Judíos de Alepo en México* (Mexico City, 1989), 134. In 1915, the U.S. State Department, acting as the representative of Ottoman interests in Mexico, filed an informal protest against the execution of three Syrians by Obregón's forces. Obregón explained that "If I had known that these three were foreigners, I would have ordered that a more formal investigation be done." "Representación de los súbditos otomanos," 16-15-116, SRE; George Addison Hughes, "Outrage and Slaughter in Mexico City," *Los Angeles Times*, 3/29/1915, 1.

82. "Extranjeros que desean salir de la Ciudad de México," 16-14-174, SRE. Robert McCaa puts the total human cost at 2.1 million, making it the greatest demographic catastrophe of the twentieth century in the Americas. Robert McCaa, "Missing

Millions: The Demographic Costs of the Mexican Revolution," *Mexican Studies/Estudios Mexicanos* 19, no. 2 (Summer 2003), 397.

83. Yankelevich, *¿Deseables o Inconvenientes?* 128.

84. Pablo Yankelevich, "Extranjeros Indeseables en México (1911–1940): Una Aproximación Cuantitativa a la Aplicación del Artículo 33 Constitucional," *Historia Mexicana* 53, no. 3 (Jan.–Mar. 2004), 693–696; Yankelevich, *¿Deseables o Inconvenientes?* 129; Beatriz A. Almanza Huesca, "La Entrada de los Ejércitos Revolucionarios a la Ciudad de México (1913–1915)," *Revista Mexicana de Sociología* 56, no. 3 (Jul.–Sep. 1994), 163. For deportations and restrictions on Americans in Mexico during the Revolution, see Yankelevich, "Explotadores, Truhanes, Agitadores y Negros: Deportaciones y Restricciones a Estadounidenses en el México Revolucionario," *Historia Mexicana* 57, no. 4 (Apr.–Jun. 2008).

85. Foran, "Race, Class, and Gender," 150.

86. Theresa Alfaro-Velcamp, *So Far from Allah, So Close to Mexico: Middle Eastern Immigrants in Modern Mexico* (Austin, 2007), 73–89.

87. Camila Pastor, *The Mexican Mahjar: Transnational Maronites, Jews, and Arabs under the French Mandate* (Austin, 2017), 252; "In re: Marcus Natan, Mexico, Alleged Viol. Selective Service Act," 6/4/1918, M1085, Investigative Reports of the Bureau of Investigation, 1908–1922, series: Old German Files, 1909–21, case number: 207715, NARA; "Ruben Beraha, visa application." 7/17/1918. M1085, Investigative Reports of the Bureau of Investigation, 1908–1922, series: Old German Files, 1909–21, case number: 234151, NARA.

88. Sandorf, "El Conflicto Turco-Xalapeño en el Mercado Jáuregui," *La Opinión*, 3/7/1914, 4.

89. "Se Multa a un Comerciante Turco," *El Democrata*, 5/21/1916, 4.

90. Denise Benbassat interview by Linda Behar, 7/10/1987, AAUHJ.

91. Almanza Huesca, "La Entrada de los Ejércitos Revolucionarios," 161–162, 165.

92. "Nuestros Korelidjionarios Sefaradim del Meksiko Se Empesan a Organizar," *La Amerika*, 8/30/1913, 2.

93. Liz Hamui de Halabe, *Identidad Colectiva: Rasgos Culturales de los Inmigrantes Judeo-Alepinos en México* (Mexico City, 1997), 266–267.

94. See entries for 10/8/1906, 1/1/1916, 7/1/1916, 4/9/1917, United Hebrew Congregation of Cuba, Minute Book 1906–1923, INV/7667, CAHJP. See also Bejarano, "Constitutional Documents"; for Argentina, see Adriana Brodsky, *Sephardi, Jewish, Argentine: Community and National Identity* (Bloomington, 2016), especially chapter 1.

95. Exp. 50, Vol. 3563, sec. panteones en general, fondo Ayuntamiento, AHDF; Exp. 1142, Vol. 3462, sec. panteones en general, fondo Ayuntamiento, AHDF.

96. Daniela Gleizer, "De la Apertura al Cierre de Puertas: La Inmigración Judía

en México durante las Primeras Décadas del Siglo XX," *Historia Mexicana* 60, no. 2 (Oct.–Dec. 2010), 1188–1189.

97. "La Aliansa 'Monte Sinai' en Meksiko," *La Amerika*, 2/18/1916, 3.

98. "Se Demanda," *La Amerika*, 6/8/1917, 1.

99. Shelomo Y. Meyuhas, "Nuestros Djudios de Meksiko," *La Amerika*, 9/28/1917, 4.

100. "La Aliansa 'Monte Sinai' en Meksiko." The few Jews who were buried in the year of 1918, the only year for which I have records, were Syrian and Sephardi. See exp. 486, sec. panteones en general, vol. 3547, fondo: Ayuntamiento, AHDF.

101. Exp. 9, Vol. 3553, subsec.: inhumaciones, sec. panteones en general, fondo Ayuntamiento, AHDF; Exp. 1142, Vol. 3462, sec. panteones en general, fondo: Ayuntamiento, AHDF; exp. 97, vol. 3473, subsec: de Dolores, sec: panteones, fondo: Ayuntamiento, AHDF. Burial in accordance with Jewish precepts was a matter of concern for Sephardi migrants. In the 1918 case of a Sephardi peddler who died in Lima, Peru, the local Jewish community sent the little money he had to the Ottoman chief rabbi in hopes that Nahum would forward it to his family but also informed Nahum that "it will console his family to know that he was buried according to Mosaic prescriptions in the Jewish cemetery of Bellavista, 8 km from Lima." Letter from David Hasson to the Hahambaşı, 12/24/1918, HM2/9073.4, CAHJP.

102. Gömlek 58, dosya: 221, HR.HMŞ.İŞO, BOA.

103. "Atansion a Nuestros Ermanos Suditos Otomanos del Meksiko," *La Amerika*, 11/26/1915, 1.

104. Gömlek: 9, dosya: 77, HR.SYS, BOA.

105. Margalit Bejarano, "Constitutional Documents of Two Sephardic Communities in Latin America (Argentina and Cuba)," *Jewish Political Studies Review* 8, no. 3/4 (Fall 1996), 131.

106. Fahrenthold, *Between the Ottomans and the Entente*, 48.

107. David Pisante to the Hahambaşı, 6/16/1914, HM2/9072, CAHJP.

108. David Hasson to the Hahambaşı, Lima, Peru, 12/24/1918, HM2/9073.4, CAHJP.

109. *La Amerika* to the Hahambaşı, New York, 7 Av, 5673, HM2/9072, CAHJP. Jewish women abandoned by their husbands were known as *agunot*, prohibited by Jewish law from being able to divorce their absent husbands or to remarry. For more on *agunot* in Imperial Russia as a result of emigration for the Americas, see ChaeRan Y. Freeze, *Jewish Marriage and Divorce in Imperial Russia* (Hanover, NH, 2002).

110. Marco Bonomo to the Hahambaşı, 12/6/1913, HM2/9070.1, CAHJP.

111. O. Camhi to the Hahambaşı, Paris, 9/6/1919, HM2/9073.4, CAHJP; Chief Rabbi of Buenos Aires to Hahambaşı, 11/16/1913, HM2/9070.3, CAHJP; Jewish Association for the Protection of Girls and Women, 1/22/1912, HM2/9070.1, CAHJP; President of the Jewish Community of Athens to the Hahambaşı, 7/31/1913, HM2/9070.1, CAHJP; Sephardic Community of Rouschouk to the Hahambaşı, 4/9/1912, HM2/9070.3,

CAHJP. A particularly heart-wrenching example is a letter from Nissim Farache, whose daughter Lisa married a trafficker and was taken to Bulgaria. After his daughter's disappearance, Farache searched for her fruitlessly until she wrote him a letter in Turkish giving her whereabouts. His query to the chief rabbinate of Bulgaria was then forwarded to the chief of police and to the Hahambaşı. The records do not reveal whether father and daughter were reunited. See Nissim Farache, 9/16/1914, HM2/9072, CAHJP.

112. Simon Lahana to the Hahambaşı via the American Consulate, 11/30/1914, HM2/9073.2, CAHJP.

113. For a more detailed analysis of the relationships between migration and transforming family and gender structures, see Devi Mays, "'I Killed Her Because I Loved Her Too Much': Gender and Violence in the 20th Century Sephardi Diaspora," *Mashriq and Mahjar* 2, no. 1 (2014).

114. Maurice Assael, 10/15/1913, Year: 1913, Line: 9, Page: 151, Roll: T715_2199, Serial: T715, NYPL, 1820–1957, NARA.

115. M.A. Gaillard de Assael vs. Raul Bermudez, caja: 1288, folio: 244908, serie: archivo historico, sección: siglo XX, TSJDF, AGN.

116. Gömlek 40, dosya: 18, HR.HMŞ.İŞO, BOA.

117. In discussing similar inheritance cases among Baghdadi Jews in Shanghai, Stein notes the complication inherent in cases where multiple nationalities claimed adherence to multiple legal systems in the same case, revealing how individuals could appeal to the legal protection of different countries as a tool for achieving what they hoped would be a ruling favorable to their cause. See Sarah Abrevaya Stein, "Protected Persons? The Baghdadi Jewish Diaspora, the British State, and the Persistence of Empire." *American Historical Review* 116, no. 1 (Feb. 2011).

118. Throughout this period, Turkish and Mexican law held that a woman, upon marriage, acquired the nationality of her husband, requiring her to formally petition to regain her original citizenship following the divorce or death of her husband.

119. M.A. vda. de Assael vs. Mauricio Assael, injurias, folio: 226298, caja: 1297, sección: siglo XX, serie: archivo historico, TSJDF, AGN.

120. Fahrenthold, *Between the Ottomans and the Entente*, 48–55; Steven Hyland, Jr., *More Argentine than You: Arabic-Speaking Immigrants in Argentina* (Albuquerque, 2017), 91.

121. 11/30/1917, *Al-Jawater*, Vol. IV, no. 304.

122. Randa Tawil, "Racial Borderlines: Ameen Rihani, Mexico, and World War I," *Amerasia* 44, no. 1 (2018), 84.

123. Pastor, *The Mexican Mahjar*, 60.

124. "En un Garito Árabe, Estuvo a Punto de Ser Muerto un Periodista Turca," *El Democrata*, 3/25/1918, 7.

125. Gömlek: 67, dosya: 35/-1, DH.H., BOA; 13-3-5, SRE. A 1911 newspaper article notes that by September 11, 1911, five Ottoman subjects had been killed, and over thirty grievously injured. See Protección de la Colonia Otomana, 1911, 16-4-4, SRE.

126. Casino Turco, 1915, 16–15–220, SRE.

127. Tawil, "Racial Borderlines," 93–94.

128. Erby E. Swift, "In re: Turkish Jews Vio. Conscription Act," 9/12/1917, in Visa Matter; role: 8000–72405, case number: 362282, series: Old German Files, 1909–21, M1085, Investigative Reports of the Bureau of Investigation, 1908–1922, NARA.

129. Chief to William M. Offley, 10/1/1917, Ibid.

130. Fahrenthold, *Between the Ottomans and the Entente*, 65–66.

131. Letter from American consul in Veracruz to U.S. Secretary of State, 9/17/1918, Number: 763.72/7183, Roll 0055, M367, Neutral Commerce, Records of the Department of State Relating to World War I and its Termination, 1914–1929, NARA.

132. Enemy trading list, June 1918, 763.72112A/1868, Roll 0248, M367, Neutral Commerce, 1918, June, Records of the Department of State Relating to World War I and its Termination, 1914–1929, NARA.

133. Alfaro-Velcamp, *So Far from Allah*, 73–89.

134. Jacobo Elnecabe, *El Mundo*, 12/10/1914, 13; Jacobo Elnecave to the Chief Rabbi, 5/24/1919, Incoming Correspondence of the Hahambaşı, HM2/9073.4; Asociación Unión Israelita Chevet Ahim to the Chief Rabbi, 4/9/1915, Incoming Correspondence to the Hahambaşı, HM2/9073.2.

135. Olga Borovaya, *Modern Ladino Culture: Press, Belles Lettres, and Theater in the Late Ottoman Empire* (Bloomington, 2012), 209; Yaron Ben-Naeh, "The Zionist Struggle as Reflected in the Jewish Press in Istanbul in the Aftermath of the Young Turk Revolution, 1908–1918," in *Late Ottoman Palestine: The Period of Young Turk Rule; Studies in Honor of Prof. Haim Gerber*, ed. Yuval Ben-Bassat and Eyal Ginio (London, 2011), 248.

136. "Address to American Ambassador," 4/3/1917, ID: 10725, folder: Turkey, General, 1914–1918 NY Collection, JDC. Following the American entrance into the war, American Jewish organizations continued to supply aid to their coreligionists in the Ottoman Empire by means of the Swedish ambassador. They justified their support of indigent Ottoman Jews by guaranteeing that "to the best of our knowledge and belief none of these funds will be delivered by us or by our agents or representatives to any individuals who are subjects of, or agents, or representatives of, an enemy country or of an ally of an enemy country (except subject races of the Turkish government)." See Albert Lucas to the State of New York, 11/30/1917, ID: 10750, Folder: Turkey, General, 1917–1918, 1914–1918 NY Collection, JDC; Secretary of JDC to Abram Elkus, 11/25/1917, ID: 10751, Folder: Turkey, General, 1917–1918, 1914–1918 NY Collection, JDC.

137. Jacobo Elnecave, 9/4/1916, Line: 10, Page: 113, Year: 1916, Roll: T715_2486, Serial: T715, NYPL, 1820–1957, NARA.; Victor Elnecabe, 9/11/1916," Year: 1916, Line: 27, Page: 157, Roll: T715_2488, Serial: T715, NYPL, 1820–1957, NARA; Jacobo

Elnecabe, 2/6/1917, Year: 1917, Line: 2, Page: 27, Roll: T715_2513, Serial: T715, NYPL, 1820–1957, NARA; Victor Elnecave, 2/6/1917, Year: 1917; Line: 2, Page: 18, Roll: T715_2513, Serial: T715, NYPL, 1820–1957, NARA. The categorization of Jewish immigrants to the United States as "Hebrew" began with the United States Immigration Service developing its own conception of race and racial categorization in the late 1890s in an effort to improve statistics at Ellis Island. This list was problematic, in that racial and national definitions at times coincided or conflicted. This "List of Races or Peoples" was eventually distributed to other ports of entry in the United States. While the racial designation of "Hebrew" was initially embraced by many Jews in the United States as a manifestation of pride and in the absence of an articulated conception of "ethnicity," in the early twentieth century, American Jews unsuccessfully challenged this classification, fearing that being marked as such could be the first step in Jewish exclusion from the United States. In the period under discussion here, Jews as such were not targets of exclusion by American immigration officials; rather, for Sephardim, it was their nationality as enemy subjects that made them objects of inquiry. See Marian L. Smith, "Race, Nationality, and Reality: I.N.S. Administration of Racial Provisions in U.S. Immigration and Nationality Law since 1898," *Prologue: Quarterly of the National Archives and Records Administration* 34, no. 2 (Summer 2002); Eric L. Goldstein, "Contesting the Categories: Jews and Government Racial Classification in the United States," *Jewish History* 19, no. 1 (2005): 79–107. For a brief discussion of Ellis Island officials' difficulties in identifying and categorizing Sephardic Jews, see Naar, "New Greece," 64–65.

138. *Djidio* is a regional pronunciation of *djudio*. It is unclear whether this spelling in *La Boz del Pueblo* reflects the speech patterns of the authors, editors, or intended audience.

139. "Djidios Turkinos en el Meksiko," *La Boz del Pueblo*, 5/5/1916, 4.

140. Ibid.

141. "Un Contrabandista Pidió Amparo," *Excelsior*, 3/9/1920, 9.

142. "Jacobo Elnecave, enemy trading list, 8/2/1918, number: 763.72112A/2955, Roll 0248, Neutral Commerce, 1918, August M367, Records of the Department of State Relating to World War I and Its Termination, 1914–1929, NARA.

143. "Jacobo Elnecabe," 1925, 2/361.254, exp. 72, caja: 3, DGG., Grecia AGN; "Jacobo Elnecabe," 1928, 2/361.2671, exp. 66, caja: 29, DGG., Grecia, AGN; "Jacobo Elnecave," 1931, 2/361.5215, exp. 15, caja: 56, DGG, Grecia, AGN. Elnecave is listed as the reference on the cards of Isaac Mizrahi, tarjetas 189 and 193, Caja 2, serie: Turquía; and Maria N. Harabon de Mizrahi, 42, Caja 2, Turquía, Registro de Extranjeros [RE], DM, AGN.

144. Denise Benbassat, Interview.

145. Liquidación judicial de Julio Fuentes y Hermanos. Credito de Corkidhi, Palacci, y Cía, folio: 223653, caja: 1281, serie: archivo historico, sección: siglo XX, TSJDF, AGN.

146. "Dona Dionisia Pallaci y Levy de Benbasat, Naturalization." 31–9–28, SRE.

147. Benjamin Corkidhi, 12/24/1912, Year: 1912, Line: 7, Page: 129, Roll: T715_1995, Serial: T715, NYPL, 1820–1957, NARA.

148. "Paris-Bijou," *Excelsior*, 5/15/1917, 5.

149. Corkidhi and Palacci, enemy traders, 5/29/1918, number: 763.72112/8938, Roll 0228, Neutral Commerce, 1918, August, M367, Records of the Department of State Relating to World War I and Its Termination, 1914–1929, NARA.

150. "Michel Palacci, Visa Matter," 5/27/1919, case number: 362282, role: 797, series: Old German Files, 1909–21, M1085, Investigative Reports of the Bureau of Investigation, 1908–1922, NARA.

151. Miguel Palacci, 7/8/1920, Roll: 68, Serial: A3437, Manifests of Statistical and Some Nonstatistical Alien Arrivals at Laredo, Texas, May 1903–April 1955; RG: 85, NARA.

152. Nissim Roffe, 3/21/1916, NYPL, 1820–1957, Year: 1916, Line: 1, Page: 35, Roll: T715_2458, Serial: T715, NARA; Nissim Roffe, 10/16/1915, Nonstatistical Manifests and Statistical Index Cards of Aliens Arriving at El Paso, Texas, 1905–1927, Roll: 104, Serial: A3406, RG: 85, NARA.

153. Nissim Roffe, 5/17/1917, NYPL, 1820–1957, Year: 1917, Line: 18, Page: 53, Roll: T715_2526, Serial: T715, NARA; Nissim Roffe, 1/27/1927, Nonstatistical Manifests and Statistical Index Cards of Aliens Arriving at Laredo, Texas, May 1903–November 1929, Roll: 87, Serial: A3379, RG: 85, NARA; Nissim Roffe, 1/26/1928, Nonstatistical Manifests and Statistical Index Cards of Aliens Arriving at Laredo, Texas, May 1903–November 1929, Roll: 87, Serial: A3379, RG: 85, NARA. For citizenship, see Nisim Roffe, 1921, exp. 72, vol. 1171, sec. gob., nacionalización de extranjeros, Fondo: Ayuntamiento, AHDF; Nissim Roffe, exp. 44, vol. 1171, sec. gob., nacionalización de extranjeros, Fondo: Ayuntamiento, AHDF; Nissim Roffe, 1927, 2/361.2058, exp. 11, caja: 23, DGG, AGN.

154. Maurice Asher, 10/8/1918, NYPL, 1820–1957, Year: 1918, Line: 17, Page: 40, Roll: T715_2603, Serial: T715, NARA. Asher was not alone among Sephardic merchants in Mexico who declared themselves Syrian to bypass restrictions. When Isaac Capon, from Salonica, was detained by American authorities while traveling to New York City in 1917, though he traveled at the time under a Spanish passport, he declared that he was born in Syria, rather than Salonica. Elias Atri, an Aleppan Jew who was a partner of the Alazraki brothers, travelled with him; Atri bore a French passport. Both were permitted to enter. Investigation of Isaac Capon, Case Number: 85416, Series: Old German Files, 1909–1921, M1085, Collection: Investigative Reports of the Bureau of Investigation 1908–1922, NARA. When David Arditti, from Smyrna and a resident of Veracruz, sought a U.S. visa to come to New York for business purposes in 1918, he possessed a passport issued by the French government, "as I was born in Smyrna, French Protectorate." The naturalized Syrians in New York that he listed as contacts

affirmed that "he was born in Syria to French parents." David Arditti, visa application, 4/1/1918, case number: 171320, series: Old German Files, 1909–21, M1085, Investigative Reports of the Bureau of Investigation, 1908–1922, NARA.

155. Stacy Fahrenthold, *Between the Ottomans and the Entente*, 115–118.

156. Jacques Couriel, 8/21/1916, NYPL, 1820–1957, Year: 1916, Line: 5, Page: 68, Roll: T715_2485, Serial: T715, NARA; Jacques Couriel, 12/26/1916, NYPL, 1820–1957, Year: 1916, Line: 6, Page: 7, Roll: T715_2508, Serial: T715, NARA; Jacques Couriel, 12/2/1917, NYPL, 1820–1957, Year: 1917, Line: 1, Page: 68, Roll: T715_2554, Serial: T71, NARA; Jacques Couriel, World War I Draft Registration Cards, 1917–1918, New York County, New York, Draft Board: 157, Roll: 1786818, NARA; Jacques Couriel, 10/8/1918, NYPL, 1820–1957, Year: 1918, Line: 17, Page: 40, Roll: T715_2603, Serial: T715, NARA.

157. Jacques Couriel, 3/3/1923, NYPL, 1820–1957, Year: 1923, Line: 7, Page: 236, Roll: T715_3260, Serial: T715, NARA; Jacques Couriel, 5/6/1934, NYPL, 1820–1957, Year: 1934, Line: 4, Page: 186, Roll: T715_5496, Serial: T715, NARA.

158. Elías Arditti, *Izmir, París, Buenos Aires: Odisea de un Inmigrante* (Buenos Aires, 1993), 13–14.

159. David Barsimonton [sic], 9/11/1917, Manifests of Statistical Alien Arrivals at El Paso, Texas, May 1909–October 1924; NAI: 2843448; RG Number: 85; Roll: 2, NARA.

160. 1/9/1923, Manifests of Statistical and Some Nonstatistical Alien Arrivals at Laredo, Texas, May 1903–April 1955; RG: 85; Serial: A3437; Roll: 78; NARA; Nonstatistical Manifests and Statistical Index Cards of Aliens Arriving at Laredo, Texas, May 1903–November 1929; NAI: 2843448; 1787–2004; RG Number: 85; Roll: 006, NARA.

161. Sálomon Levy, interview. Cards for the Levy family can be found in the Registro de Extranjeros under tarjetas 4,5,10,11, 12, Caja: 3, serie: Griegos, DM, AGN.

162. Mauricio Assael, personnel file, 1–7–6, SRE.

163. "Consules de Mex. en Petrograd y en P. de Esmirna," 5/11/1916, *El Democrata*, 1.

164. Alicia Gojman de Backal, *Jacobo Granat: Una vida de contradicciones entre la comunidad y el cine* (Mexico City, 2012), 70.

165. Mauricio Assael, personnel file, 1–7–6, SRE. While the Ottoman Archives also contain records relating to Assael's appointment, they are unavailable to researchers, despite repeated requests.

166. Jews living in the Ottoman Empire had a long history of serving as consular representatives for various European powers. For more on Jewish consuls in Aleppo, see Yaron Harel, "The Rise and Fall of the Jewish Consuls in Aleppo" *Turcica* 38 (2006).

167. Mauricio Assael, personnel file, 1–7–6, SRE.

168. Ibid.

169. Letter of Y. Alcarate, Leon Simarro, Rafael Altamira, Angel Pulido, and N. Nordau, 3/28/1917, ID: 6753, folder: Refugees in Spain, 1916–1919, 1914–1918 NY Collection, JDC.

170. Maurice Assael, 7/13/1916, NYPL, 1820–1957, Year: 1916, Line: 3, Page: 74, Roll: T715_2478, Serial: T715, NARA.

171. Mauricio Assael, renuncia su nacionalidad sobre casa, 9/2/1916, 7–24–199, SRE.

172. John Lear, "Mexico City: Space and Class in the Porfirian Capital, 1884–1910," *Journal of Urban History* 22 (1996), 469–470.

173. Mauricio Assael, personnel file, 1–7–6, SRE.

174. Mauricio Assael, Naturalization, 1918, 43–9–246, SRE.

175. Ibid. Mexican legal documents tend to be transcribed, and first-person testimony is generally written in the third person.

176. Ibid.

177. Claudio Lomnitz, "Anti-Semitism and the Ideology of the Mexican Revolution," *Representations* 110, no. 1 (Spring 2010); Yankelevich, "Extranjeros Indeseables," 693–696.

178. "Los sin Patria,", *El Tiempo*, 8/13/1917, 7–8.

179. "El Pueblo Djudio Ama Sinsiramente la Pas," *El Tiempo*, 9/28/1914.

Chapter 3: Uncertain Futures

1. Gabriel Yermia Valanci passport, 10–21–69, SRE.

2. Mauricio Tenorio-Trillo, *I Speak of the City: Mexico at the Turn of the Twentieth Century* (Chicago, 2012), 93.

3. Dominique Reill, *The Fiume Crisis: Surviving in the Wake of the Habsburg Empire* (Cambridge, forthcoming).

4. Rosalynda Pérez de Cohen, Simonette Levy de Behar, Sophie Bejarano de Goldberg, *Sefarad de Ayer, Oy i Manyana: Presencia Sefardí en México* (Mexico City, 2010), 48, 63; Interview with Jaime Mitrani, AAUHJ.

5. Caja 1276, Archivo Historico, Siglo XX, TSJDF, AGN.

6. Auxiliary Attorney to the Subsecretary of the SRE, Mexico City, 12/5/1923, 10–21–69, SRE.

7. Gabriel Yermia, Naturalization. DDG., SRE, Turquia, 2/361.729, caja 10, exp. 8, AGN.

8. Gary Saul Morson, *Narrative and Freedom: The Shadows of Time* (New Haven, 2007), 118–119.

9. Charles King, *Midnight at the Pera Palace: The Birth of Modern Istanbul* (New York, 2014), 42.

10. Ibid., 41, 64.

11. Catherine Laskaridhis, *Quinze mille jours à Constantinople ma patrie* (Athens,

1987), 93–96, quoted in Hélène and Stéphane Yerasimos, "Rêves et cauchemars d'une ville perdue," in *Istanbul, 1914–1923: Capitale d'un monde illusoire ou l'agonie des vieux empires*, ed. Stéphane Yerasimos (Paris, 1992).

12. Suat Aray, *Bir Galatasaraylının Hatıraları* (Izmir, 1959), 116–117, quoted in Stéphane Yerasimos, "Jeunes et Vieux Turcs dans la tourmente," in *Istanbul, 1914–1923: Capitale d'un monde illusoire ou l'agonie des vieux empires*, ed. Stéphane Yerasimos (Paris, 1992).

13. Üstün Bilgen-Reinart, *Porcelain Moon and Pomegranates: A Woman's Trek through Turkey* (Toronto, 2007), 112.

14. *The Treaties of Peace 1919–1923, Vol. II* (New York, 1924), 863.

15. "Grandiozo Miting en Konstantinopla kontra los Aliados," 5/28/1920, *La Amerika*, 1.

16. Edgar J. Fisher, "From Bad to Worse in Constantinople," 1/11/1920, *New York Times*, 45.

17. Alexandre Ben Ghiat, *Livro-Jurnal de la Gerra Djeneral* (Izmir, 1919), 68.

18. Ben Ghiat, *Livro-Jurnal*, 4.

19. Fisher, "From Bad to Worse," 45; Yiğit Akın, *When the War Came Home: The Ottomans' Great War and the Devastation of an Empire* (Stanford, 2018), 121.

20. Erol Ülker, "Foreign Capital, Allied Occupation, and Class Politics in Istanbul: Constantinople Tramways and Electric Company," Paper presented at Middle East Studies Association, Washington, DC, November 2014.

21. Clarence Richard Johnson, ed., *Constantinople To-Day, or The Pathfinder Survey of Constantinople, a Study in Oriental Social Life* (New York, 1922).

22. Fisher, "From Bad to Worse"; Johnson, *Constantinople To-Day*, 112–113. In some ways, this violence paralleled earlier violence between refugees in Istanbul in the Hamidian period. See Roger A. Deal, "War Refugees and Violence in Hamidian Istanbul," *Middle Eastern Studies* 49, no. 2 (2013).

23. United States of America vs. George Gaugh et al., Consular Posts, Istanbul, Turkey, Vol.: 332, RG 84, NARA.

24. Ben Ghiat, *Livro-Jurnal*, 43.

25. Ibid., 45–46.

26. Ibid., 44.

27. Ibid.

28. For more on these *haggadot*, and on Ladino literary interpretations of World War I, see Devi Mays, "Recounting the Past, Shaping the Future: Ladino Literary Responses to World War I," in *World War I and the Jews*, ed. Marsha Rozenblit and Jonathan Karp (New York, 2017), 201–221.

29. As Eliezer Papo notes, although the Ben-Zvi Institute has catalogued Ben Ghiat's text as being written in 1914 or 1915 on the basis of a handwritten note on the front page, the text's overt references to the Russian Revolution in fact preclude it

having been written prior to 1917. Papo posits the likely publication date as 1919. See Eliezer Papo, *Ve-hitalta le-vinkha ba-yom ha-hu: Paradyot Sefaradiyot-Yehudiyot 'al ha-Hagadah shel Pesah*, Vol. I (Jerusalem, 2012), 147–148, 151, 153.

30. Alexandre Ben Ghiat, *La Haggadah de Ben Ghiat* (Izmir, 1919) quoted in Papo, *Ve-hitalta le-vinkha ba-yom ha-hu*, Vol. II (Jerusalem, 2012), 53, 61.

31. Ben Ghiat, *La Haggadah de Ben Ghiat*, Quoted in Papo, *Ve-hitalta le-vinkha ba-yom ha-hu*, Vol. I, 149, 150.

32. Erez Manela, *The Wilsonian Moment: Self-Determination and the International Origins of Anticolonial Nationalism* (Oxford, 2007).

33. Ben Ghiat, *La Haggadah de Ben Ghiat*, quoted in Papo, *Ve-hitalta le-vinkha ba-yom ha-hu*, Vol. 1, 149–150; Papo, *Ve-hitalta le-vinkha ba-yom ha-hu*, Vol. II, 52–53.

34. Nissim Shem-Tov Eli, *Haggadah dela Gerra por Dia de Pesah* (Constantinople, 1919), 6–7.

35. Ibid., 17–18.

36. Elia Karmona, *Haggadah dela Gerra Djeneral* (Constantinople, 1920), 3, 7.

37. Michelle Campos, *Ottoman Brothers: Muslims, Christians, and Jews in Early Twentieth-Century Palestine* (Stanford, 2011), ch. 6.

38. "La Revolusion Nasionala Djudia en Konstantinopla," *La Amerika*, 9/19/1919, 2.

39. "Organizasion Tzionista en Konstantinopli," *La Amerika*, 7/11/1919, 5.

40. Nissim M. Benezra, *Une Enfance juive à Istanbul (1911–1929)* (Istanbul, 1996), 83–84.

41. "La Revolusion Nasionala Djudia en Konstantinopla," *La Amerika*, 9/19/1919, 2.

42. "Manifestasion Kemalista en Balat," *La Amerika*, 10/27/1922, 3.

43. "La Turkia Tembla," *La Amerika*, 10/4/1918, 5.

44. Ben Ghiat, *Livro-Jurnal*, 45.

45. Ibid., 77.

46. Fahrenthold, *Between the Ottomans and the Entente*, 109–110.

47. AAIU, Turquie, II C 9, Smyrna, politique, Nabon, 7/17/1919, in *La grande guerre et la guerre gréco-turque vues par les instituteurs de l'Alliance Israélite Universelle d'Izmir*, ed. Henri Nahum (Istanbul, 2003), 17.

48. Ibid., 43.

49. Ibid., 45–46.

50. Ibid., 47–48.

51. Ibid., 48.

52. Ibid., 54.

53. Ibid., 27.

54. Ibid., 18, 24–25.

55. Ibid., 38–39.

56. Ibid., 29.

57. Charles W. Fowle to Alfred Abrevaya, New York, 12/31/1919, ID: 238679, folder: Turkey, Transmission of Funds, 1919–1921, 1919–1921 NY Collection, JDC.

58. Extracts from Letter from Ambassador Elkus, Constantinople, 3/3/1917, ID: 10734, Turkey, General, 1917–1918, 1914–1918 NY Collection, JDC.

59. Keith Watenpaugh, "Between Communal Survival and National Aspiration: Armenian Genocide Refugees, the League of Nations, and the Practices of Interwar Humanitarianism," *Humanity* 5, no. 2 (Summer 2014); Keith Watenpaugh, "The League of Nations' Rescue of Armenian Genocide Survivors and the Making of Modern Humanitarianism, 1920–1927," *American Historical Review* (Dec. 2010).

60. Statistiques des veuves, orphelins et orphelines de la capitale, 11/4/1920, Constantinople, ID: 238699, Folder: Turkey, Child Care, 1920–1921, 1919–1921 NY Collection, JDC.

61. Jacques Rieur, "Report on the Near East and the Balkan States," 12/1/1921, ID: 352180, folder: Turkey, Child Care, 1921–1928, 1921–1932 NY Collection, JDC, pp. 1–2; Report on the Activity of the Emigrant Office of the JDC, Constantinople, 12/31/1920, JDC.

62. Jacques Maguite to the JDC, New York, 7/7/1920, JDC.

63. Ibid.

64. *Journal d'Orient*, 1/18/1921.

65. Isaac Eskenazi Hazan to Jacques Bigart, Constantinople, 12/31/1919, TU-02/Turquie I B 6.03, AIU.

66. "20,000 Kriaturas Djudias Mueren de Ambre," *El Tiempo*, 1/23/1920, 1; "Una Subskripsion en Favor de Nuestros Ermanos de Rusia," *El Tiempo*, 3/5/1920, 3; "Una Yamada ala Umanidad," *El Tiempo*, 9/23/1919, 2–3.

67. "30 Mil Djudios Resfuidos en Konstantinopla," *La Amerika*, 6/4/1920, 4.

68. "Konstantinopla Yeno de Resfujiados de Anadol," *La Amerika*, 9/2/1921, 1.

69. Bejarano and Marcus, Report on the Committee of 33, 2/10/1921, Constantinople, ID: 238820, Folder: Turkey, Refugees and Emigrants, 1919–1921, 1919–1921 NY Collection, JDC.

70. Rieur, "Report on the Near East and the Balkan States."

71. "Kolera en Konstantinopla," *La Amerika*, 12/5/1919, 5.

72. "Kolera en Konstantinopla," *La Amerika*, 12/24/1920, 4.

73. "80 Mil Sufrientes Djudios en Konstantinopla," *La Amerika*, 1/13/1922, 1.

74. "Ayudo a los Refuidos en Konstantinopla," *La Amerika*, 5/5/1922, 1.

75. Boaz Menasche to Rabbi Dr. Teitelbaum, Izmir, Dec. 3, 1919, 1919–1921 NY Collection, Folder: Turkey, Adrianople, Angora, Constantinople, Gallipoli, Smyrna, ID: 238890, JDC.

76. Nahum, *La grande guerre et la guerre gréco-turque*, 74–75.

77. Ibid., 88.

78. Letter, Constantinople, 8/3/1920, JDC; Abstract of a Yiddish letter from Constantinople, 8/28/1920, ID: 238707, Folder: Turkey, Cultural and Religious, 1919–1921, 1919–1921 NY Collection, JDC.

79. Kahn, Report on Constantinople, 23–31 August, 1921, ID: 351994, Folder: Turkey, Administration, General, 1921–1922, 1921–1932 NY Collection, JDC.

80. Minutes of the Meetings of the Central Reconstruction Committee, 8/28/1922, ID: 352336, Folder: Turkey, Reconstruction, 1922–1924, 1921–1932 NY Collection, JDC; Letter from Constantinople to Jacques Bigart, Constantinople, 8/28/1922, HM3/696, AIU Turquie, I.H/ 1.A 04, CAHJP.

81. Kahn, Report on Constantinople.

82. See the meetings 8/29/1922, ID: 352336, Folder: Turkey, Reconstruction, 1922–1924, 1921–1932 NY Collection, JDC.

83. Rosenblatt, Report on Constantinople. 9/1/1922, ID: 352340, folder: Subject Matter, Reconstruction, 1922–1924, 1921–1932 NY Collection, JDC.

84. Circular appeal, 3/17/1921, Constantinople, ID: 238827, Folder: Turkey, Refugees and Emigrants, 1919–1921, 1919–1921 NY Collection, JDC.

85. ID: 352336, Folder: Turkey, Reconstruction, 1922–1924, 1921–1932 NY Collection, JDC.

86. For copies of Ottoman paperwork for the establishment of the *Caisse de Petits Prêts*, see Meclis-i İdare Imzaları, Constantinople, 11/17/1923, ID: 352296, Folder: Turkey, Reconstruction, 1922–1924, 1921–1932 NY Collection, JDC; Official Notice about legalization of Kassa, Constantinople, 11/17/1923, ID: 352293, Folder: Turkey, Reconstruction, 1922–1924, 1921–1932 NY Collection, JDC.

87. Exhibit A, American Joint Distribution Committee Reconstruction Department, 11/17/1923, ID: 352292, Folder: Turkey, Reconstruction, 1922–1924, 1921–1932 NY Collection, JDC.

88. ID: 352336, Folder: Turkey, Reconstruction, 1922–1924, 1921–1932 NY Collection, JDC.

89. Summary of Transactions of Caisse de Petits Prêts de Constantinople during the month of June, 1923, ID: 352373, Folder: Turkey, Reconstruction, 1922–1924, 1921–1932 NY Collection, JDC.

90. Caisse de Petits Prêts de Constantinople, Loans granted from April 1923 to April 30, 1924, ID: 352392, Folder: Turkey, Reconstruction, 1922–1924, 1921–1932 NY Collection, JDC.

91. Application form, 11/23/1923, Constantinople, ID: 352301, Folder: Turkey, Reconstruction, 1922–1924, 1921–1932 NY Collection, JDC.

92. Nahum, *La grande guerre et la guerre gréco-turque*, 57–58.

93. Sarah Abrevaya Stein, *Extraterritorial Dreams: European Citizenship, Sephardi Jews, and the Ottoman Twentieth Century* (Chicago, 2016), passim.

94. Nahum, *La grande guerre et la guerre gréco-turque*, 59.

95. Elías Arditti, *Izmir, París, Buenos Aires: Odisea de un Inmigrante* (Buenos Aires, 1993), 34, 54–55.
96. "Donos de Meksiko," *La Amerika*, 11/23/1917, 3.
97. Nahum, *La grande guerre et la guerre gréco-turque*, 73.
98. Ibid., 83.
99. Ibid., 88.
100. Quoted in Umut Özsu, "Fabricating Fidelity: Nation-Building, International Law, and the Greek-Turkish Population Exchange," *Leiden Journal of International Law* 24 (2011), 841.
101. Nahum, *La grande guerre et la guerre gréco-turque*, 40–41.
102. This is explored in ch. 5.
103. Soner Çağaptay, *Islam, Secularism, and Nationalism in Modern Turkey: Who is a Turk?* (London, 2006), 73.
104. "Djigantesko Movimiento de Emigrasion," *El Tiempo*, 3/12/1920, 5–6.
105. "La Emigrasion Djudia," *El Tiempo*, 8/27/2920, 3; "Emigrantes Israelitas de Ismirna," 6/11/1920, *El Tiempo*, 3.
106. "Buro de Informasion por la Amerika," *El Tiempo*, 1/2/1920, 6; "Para la Amerika," *El Tiempo*, 4/13/1920, 7; "American Steamship Agency," *El Tiempo*, 2/3/1920, 7; "Konstantinople-Marseya-Amerika del Sur," *El Tiempo*, 6/4/1920, 7; "Cunard Line," *El Tiempo*, 6/15/1920, 8; "Bueno Novedad por los Emigrantes," *El Tiempo*, 8/31/1920, 9.
107. *Buletino del Ospital Nasional Israelita "Or-Ahayim,"* (Constantinople, 1923), 6, 66, 74.
108. "Le comité italien d'assistance aux emigrants juifs," April–June 1923, *HaMenora*, 70.
109. On the foundation of the Italian Jewish Community in Constantinople, see Luca Zuccolo, "Gli italiani all'estero: Il caso ottomano," *Diacronie: Studi de Storia Contemporanea* 5, no. 1 (2011); Nora Şeni and Sophie Le Tarnec, *Les Camondo ou l'éclipse d'une fortune* (Paris, 1997).
110. Charles W. Fowle to Alfred Abrevaya, New York, 12/3/1919, ID: 238679, folder: Turkey, Transmission of Funds, 1919–1921, NY Collection, JDC.
111. "Rabbi Haim Nahum en New York," *La Amerika*, 11/11/1921, 1.
112. Leon Benezra to Haim Nahum, Cárdenas, Cuba, 6/1/1919, HM2/9073.4, CAHJP.
113. Fresco to Haim Nahum, New Brunswick, NJ, 4/21/1919, HM2/9073.4, CAHJP.
114. Simon Levy to Haim Nahum, New York, 1919, HM2/9073.4, CAHJP; Dr. L. Halphon on behalf of Salvador Cohen to Haim Nahum, Buenos Aires, 6/11/1919, HM2/9073.4, CAHJP.
115. D. Roffe to Haim Nahum, Tampico, Mexico, 5/14/1919, HM2/9073.4,

CAHJP; Jacobo Elnecave to Haim Nahum, Veracruz, Mexico, 5/24/1919, HM2/9073.4, CAHJP; Rev. Dr. Pereira Mendes on behalf of Paloma Cohen to Haim Nahum, New York City, 7/25/1919, HM2/9073.4, CAHJP; Ovadia Nathan to Haim Nahum, San Francisco, 6/11/1918, HM2/9073.4, CAHJP; Leon Benezra to Haim Nahum, Piraeus, 12/13/1918, HM2/9073.4, CAHJP; Raphael Aboressi to Haim Nahum, 1/21/1918, Bordeaux, France, HM2/9073.4, CAHJP.

116. "Lista de Nuestros Adjentes," *La Amerika*, 4/16/1920, 3.
117. "Bushka a Sus Ermanos," *La Amerika*, 2/7/1919, 5.
118. "Por la Imigrasion en Kuba," *La Amerika*, 9/9/1921, 2.
119. "Ley de Imigrasion Kontinua," *La Luz*, 4/23/1922, 4.
120. "La Ley sovre la Imigrasion," *La Luz*, 1/1/1922, 2.
121. "Los Sefaradim en Ardjentina," *La Luz*, 9/24/1922, 3.
122. "Por la Imigrasion en Kuba," *La Amerika*, 9/9/1921, 2.
123. "El Progreso en Meksiko," *La Amerika*, 8/19/1921, 4.
124. "Por la Imigrasion en Meksiko," *La Amerika*, 8/26/1921, 3.
125. "Oportunidad por Alkilar Buena Kaza con Renta Barata," *La Amerika*, 2/24/1922, 1.
126. Camila Pastor, *The Mexican Mahjar: Transnational Maronites, Jews, and Arabs under the French Mandate* (Austin, 2017), 60, 70–71.
127. Shelomo Meyuhas, "La Imigrasion de Nuestros Ermanos en Meksiko por Shelomo Mehuyas," *La Amerika*, 8/29/1919, 2.
128. 2/6/1920, DH.SN.THR, dosya: 86, gömlek: 34, BOA.
129. Ico Assael, 9/1/1919, New York Passenger Lists, 1820–1957, Year: 1919; Serial: T715; Roll: T715_2673; Line: 5; Page: 21, NARA.
130. "Un Viaje Fatal por Uriel Ben Veniste," *La Amerika*, 10/10/1919, 6.
131. Libby Garland, *After They Closed the Gates: Jewish Illegal Immigration to the United States, 1921–1965* (Chicago, 2014), 107.
132. "Munchas Imigrantes Parten a Meksiko," *La Amerika*, 8/18/1922, 1.
133. "Mexico i los Djidios," *La Luz*, 6/18/1922, 4.
134. Corinne A. Krause, "Mexico—Another Promised Land? A Review of Projects for Jewish Colonization in Mexico, 1881–1925," *American Jewish Historical Quarterly* 61, no. 4 (June 1972), 337–338; "El Plano Rotenberg por Kolonizasion Djudia en Meksiko," *La Amerika*, 8/11/1922, 1.
135. Krause, "Mexico—Another Promised Land?" 338–339; "Los Djudios de Ingletiera Favorezan Imigrasion en Meksiko," *La Amerika*, 6/20/1922, 2; "Imigrasion Djudia en Meksiko," *La Luz*, 6/18/1922, 1.
136. "Un Magnífico Edificio Cedido por un Extranjero para Hospital de Maternidad," *Excelsior*, 4/14/1922, 8.
137. "Hermoso Rasgo de un Prominente Miembro de la Colonia Otomana," *El Universal*, 2/22/1917, 3.

138. Mauricio Assael to Álvaro Obregón, 4/21/1922, Mexico City, Collection: Obregon-Calles, 805-A-120, AGN.

139. Personal Secretary to Mauricio Assael, 5/11/1922, Ibid.

140. Pablo Piccato, *City of Suspects: Crimes in Mexico City, 1900–1931* (Durham, 2001); Pablo Piccato, *The Tyranny of Opinion: Honor in the Construction of the Mexican Public Sphere* (Durham, 2010); Devi Mays, "'I Killed Her Because I Loved Her Too Much': Gender and Violence in the 20th Century Sephardi Diaspora," *Mashriq and Mahjar* 2, no. 1 (2014), 14–15; Pastor, *The Mexican Mahjar*, 83.

141. Adriana Brodsky, *Sephardi, Jewish, Argentine: Community and National Identity* (Bloomington, 2016), ch. 2 passim; Lily Pearl Balloffet, "From the Pampa to the Mashriq: Arab-Argentine Philanthropy Networks," *Mashriq & Mahjar* 4, no. 1 (2017), 4–5, 17; Steven Hyland, Jr., *More Argentine than You: Arabic-Speaking Immigrants in Argentina* (Albuquerque, 2017), 179.

142. "Antes de Tres Meses Será un Hecho la Creación del 'Hospital de Maternidad,'" *Excelsior*, 4/16/1922, 3.

143. "Assael y Cori Sara," 1909, #59, México, Distrito Federal, Registro Civil, Nacimientos, 1861–1934. Digital images. Archivo Estatal de Distrito Federal. Courtesy of the Academia Mexicana de Genealogia y Heraldica, p. 27.

144. Ibid.

145. Patrice Elizabeth Olsen, "Revolution in the City Streets: Changing Nomenclature, Changing Form, and the Revision of Public Memory," in *The Eagle and the Virgin: Nation and Cultural Revolution in Mexico, 1920–1940*, ed. Mary Kay Vaughan and Stephen E. Lewis (Durham: 2006), 123; Fondo Ayuntamiento, Gobierno del Distrito Federal, seccion: Secretaria General, subseccion: Rastros y mercados, vol. 3989, exp. 199, AHDF; Fondo Ayuntamiento, Gobierno del Distrito Federal, seccion: Secretaria General, subseccion: Rastros y mercados, vol. 3989, exp. 194, AHDF.

146. 5/7/1917, AHDF.

147. Fondo Ayuntamiento, Gobierno del Distrito Federal, seccion: Secretaria General, subseccion: Rastros y mercados, vol. 3989, exp. 212, AHDF.

148. Ibid.

149. Pastor, *The Mexican Mahjar*, 91.

150. "El Conocido Turco Miguel David Ha Cometido Estafas Considerable en el Puerto Jaroche," *El Democrata*, 7/5/1919, 7; "Notas de N. Laredo, Otra Contrabandista como Muchos," *Evolución*, 9/9/1917, 4; "Un Contrabandista Pidió Ámparo," *Excelsior*, 3/9/1920, 9.

151. "Una Cuadrilla de Turcos Ladrones," *El Democrata*, 4/22/1919, 7.

152. TSJDF, sección: siglo XX, serie: archivo historico, caja: 1691, folio: 303067, AGN.

153. "Viajeros," *El Universal*, 12/11/1920, 3.

154. "Casa Alberto Misrachi," *El Universal*, 11/23/1922, 6; Alberto Misrachi, HF,

Fondo: Ayuntamiento, Gobierno del Distrito Federal, seccion: gobernacion, nacionalizacion de extranjeros, vol. 1171, exp 24; Alberto Misrachi, Naturalization, DGG, Grecia, 2/361.10708, caja: 111, exp. 8, AGN.

155. Israel Assael, naturalización, September 10, 1907, Fondo Ayuntamiento, Gobierno del Distrito Federal, sección: certificaciones. Vol. 512, exp. 590, AHDF.

156. "$20,000 Fueron Robados a un Joyero Turco," *Excelsior*, 4/9/1919, 1.

157. "Cuantioso Despojo a un Árabe," *El Democrata*, 4/9/1919, 1.

158. "Pasearon un Cadaver por las Avenidas de Chapultepec," *La Epoca*, 4/27/1919, 5.

159. "Se Suicido el Joyero Turco Isidro Assael?" *Excelsior*, 4/13/1919, 1, 6, 8.

160. "Isidoro Assael No Fue Asesinado: Se Suicidó," *El Democrata*, 4/15/1919, 2; "Mucho Se Duda de que Assael Se Suicidara," *Excelsior*, 4/15/1919, 1; "Logicamente No Se Puede Sostener la Teoría del Homicidio de Isidoro Assael," *El Democrata*, 4/17/1919, 5; "Detalles de un Crimen," *Evolución*, 4/20/1919, 1.

161. "Las Deducciones Hechas por un Diario sobre la Muerte del Joyero Señor Isidro Assael," *Excelsior*, 4/17/1919, 10.

162. "Parece que Se Va Hacienda la Luz en el Asunto Assael," *Excelsior*, 4/22/1919, 3.

163. "La Muerte de Assael es Misterioso," *La Prensa*, 4/23/1919, 7

164. "No Han Aprehendido a los Asesinos del Joyero Isidro Asael," *Excelsior*, 6/10/1919, 1.

165. "Matansa de un Riko Turkino en Meksiko," *La Amerika*, 5/9/1919, 2.

166. Devin E. Naar, "Turkinos beyond the Empire: Ottoman Jews in America, 1893 to 1924," *Jewish Quarterly Review* 105, no. 2 (Spring 2015), 179.

167. Reill, *The Fiume Crisis*.

Chapter 4: "They Are Entirely Equal to the Spanish"

1. Death Reports in State Department Decimal File, 1910 to 1962; NAI Number: 302021;RG 59; Box: 3781; Box Description: 1910–1929 Mexico Ha – Lo, NARA.

2. Sara Halfon de Lahana, intestate case, 1926, folio: 344547, caja: 1902, serie: archivo historico, sección: siglo XX, TSJDF, AGN.

3. Sara Halfon de Lahana, intestate case, 1926, folio: 344547, caja: 1902, serie: archivo historico, sección: siglo XX, TSJDF, AGN; Scarlatt Tottu, personnel file, 18–11–2, SRE; 1927, gömlek: 3, dosya: 212, HR.İM, BOA; 6/14/1927, gömlek: 66, dosya: 219, HR.İM, BOA.

4. Salomon Lahana, RE, Estados Unidos, Caja 91, Tarjeta 66, AGN; Salomon Lahana Halfon, Naturalization, 31–12–66, SRE.

5. Fanny Lahana, RE, Estados Unidos, Caja 91, Tarjeta 64, AGN.

6. Simon Lahana to the American Consulate in Ambos Camarines, 11/30/1914, HM2/9073.2, CAHJP.

7. Jack Fitz Halfon, Naturalización, 1933, 2/361.11719, exp. 19, caja 121, Turquía, DGG, AGN.

8. Salomon Lahana Halfon, Naturalization, 31–12–66, SRE.

9. "Wills for Probate," *New York Times*, 5/27/1926, 29.

10. New York Passenger Lists, 1820–1957, Year: 1926; Arrival; Serial: T715; Roll: T715_3854; Line: 13; Page: 23, NARA.

11. Simon Lahana, RE, Apatridas, Caja 2, tarjeta 72, AGN.

12. John Torpey, *The Invention of the Passport: Surveillance, Citizenship, and the State* (Cambridge, 2000), 1, 111.

13. Tara Zahra, "The 'Minority Problem' and National Classification in the French and Czechoslovak Borderlands," *Contemporary European History* 17, no. 2 (May 2008), 140.

14. The Levis' later cards in the Registro de Extranjeros indicate that they were from Salonica and held Greek nationality, which I suspect was to evade restrictions on Turkish nationals post-1927. See Elvira Levy, tarjeta: 219, caja: 2, serie: Griegos, DM, AGN; Margot Levy, tarjeta: 1, caja: 3, serie: Griegos, DM, AGN; Rafael Levy, tarjeta: 3, caja: 3, serie: Griegos, DM, AGN.

15. Başvekalet, Fon no: 30 18 1 1, Yer No: 6.35.16, dosya: 102–3, sayı: 1976, BCA.

16. Elvira Levi de Cohen, interview by Monika Unikel, 1/27/1988, AAUJH.

17. Carole Fink, *Defending the Rights of Others; The Great Powers, the Jews, and International Minority Protection, 1878–1938* (New York, 2004), xvi.

18. Zahra, "Minority Problem," 138.

19. Laura Robson, *States of Separation: Transfer, Partition, and the Making of the Modern Middle East* (Oakland, 2017), 28–29.

20. Lerna Ekmekçioğlu, *Recovering Armenia: The Limits of Belonging in Post-Genocide Turkey* (Stanford, 2016), 94.

21. Yeşim Bayar, "In Pursuit of Homogeneity: The Lausanne Conference, Minorities and the Turkish Nation," *Nationalities Papers* 42, no. 1 (2014), 114.

22. Zahra, "Minority Problem," 145.

23. Bayar, "In Pursuit of Homogeneity," 115.

24. Treaty of Peace with Turkey Signed at Lausanne, July 24, 1923, in *The Treaties of Peace 1919–1923*, Vol. II (New York, 1924).

25. Fink, *Defending the Rights of Others*, passim.

26. Bayar, "In Pursuit of Homogeneity," 109.

27. Lerna Ekmekçioğlu, "Republic of Paradox: The League of Nations Minority Protection Regime and the New Turkey's Step-Citizens," *International Journal of Middle East Studies* 46 (2014), 666.

28. Umut Özsu, "Fabricating Fidelity: Nation-Building, International Law, and the Greek-Turkish Population Exchange," *Leiden Journal of International Law* 24 (2011), 831.

29. Ekmekçioğlu, *Recovering Armenia*, 7–8; Nur Bilge Criss, *Istanbul under Allied Occupation* (Leiden, 1999), 47–48.

30. Robson, *States of Separation*, 30.

31. Renée Hirschon, "Consequences of the Lausanne Convention: An Overview," in *Crossing the Aegean: An Appraisal of the 1923 Compulsory Population Exchange between Greece and Turkey*, ed. Renée Hirschon (New York, 2003), 14–15; Marc David Baer, *The Dönme: Jewish Converts, Muslim Revolutionaries, and Secular Turks* (Stanford, 2010), 141–154. For more on the population exchange, see Bruce Clark, *Twice a Stranger: The Mass Expulsions that Forged Modern Greece and Turkey* (Cambridge, 2006).

32. Özsu, "Fabricating Fidelity," 827–828.

33. Türkiye Büyük Millet Meclisi, Gizli Celse Zabıtları, 2 Mart 1339 (1923), 8; accessed online 12/13/2019.

34. Benjamin Bidjerano to AIU headquarters, 3/28/1923, microfilm at CAJHP-HM3/694, AIU Turquie XCVI E 1125.02, CAHJP.

35. Conorte Canneti, 8/30/1923, HM3/693, AIU Turquie XCIV E 1110.04a, CAHJP.

36. 1/18/1923, Dosya no: 94-14, Sira no: 20, Dosya Gömleği: 45, Kutu Numarası: 6, Fon no: 30 18 1 2, Başvekalet, BCA.

37. Ayhan Aktar, "Homogenising the Nation, Turkifying the Economy: The Turkish Experience of Population Exchange Reconsidered," in *Crossing the Aegean: An Appraisal of the 1923 Compulsory Population Exchange between Greece and Turkey*, ed. Renée Hirschon (New York, 2003), 91–93.

38. Soner Çağaptay, *Islam, Secularism, and Nationalism in Modern Turkey: Who Is a Turk?* (London, 2006), 15; Ahmet İçduygu and Özlem Kaygusuz, "The Politics of Citizenship by Drawing Borders: Foreign Policy and the Construction of National Citizenship Identity in Turkey," *Middle Eastern Studies* 40, no. 6 (Nov. 2004), 40.

39. Howard Lee Eissenstat, "The Limits of Imagination: Debating the Nation and Constructing the State in Early Turkish Nationalism" (PhD diss., 2007), 231.

40. Çağaptay, *Islam, Secularism, and Nationalism*, 15.

41. Ahmet İçduygu, Yılmaz Çolak, and Nalan Soyarık, "What Is the Matter with Citizenship? A Turkish Debate," *Middle Eastern Studies* 35, no. 4 (Oct. 1999), 195.

42. For a detailed analysis of protégé status and extraterritoriality among Ottoman-born Jews during and after the Ottoman Empire, and how European states sought to deal with their complicated status, see Sarah Abrevaya Stein, *Extraterritorial Dreams: European Citizenship, Sephardi Jews, and the Ottoman Twentieth Century* (Chicago, 2016).

43. 2/28/1922, dosya: 2–1, Yer Numarası: 4.50.17, Fon no: 30 18 1 2, Başvekalet, BCA; Salvador Sumany to AIU headquarters, 8/14/1923, TU-200/Turquie LXXXIX E 1044, AIU.

44. Vitali Haim Yabis, 6/29/1923, sayı: 2799, Dosya: 2–13, Yer No: 7.35.2, Fon

no: 30 18 1 1, Başvekalet, BCA; Isak Anfratati, 9/29/1923, Sayı: 2798, Dosya: 2–12, Yer No: 7.35.1, Fon no: 30 18 1 1, Başvekalet, BCA; Yasef Levi, 10/1/1924, Dosya no:1–136, Sira no: 6, Dosya Gömleği: 47, Kutu Numarası: 11, Fon no: 30 18 1 2, Başvekalet, BCA.

45. Subsecretary of the SRE to the Secretary of Gobernación, Mexico City, 11/6/1926, DDG, SRE, Turquia, 2/360(496)-1, caja: 14, exp. 12, AGN.

46. Zahra, "Minority Problem," 138–139.

47. Treaty of Peace with Turkey Signed at Lausanne.

48. Ibid.

49. Correspondence with Stacy Fahrenthold.

50. Lauren Banko, *The Invention of Palestinian Citizenship, 1918–1947* (Edinburgh, 2018), 78, 81–82, 85–86.

51. Stacy D. Fahrenthold, *Between the Ottomans and the Entente: The First World War in the Syrian and Lebanese Diaspora, 1908–1925* (New York, 2019), 155–157, 163.

52. Camila Pastor, *The Mexican Mahjar: Transnational Maronites, Jews, and Arabs under the French Mandate* (Austin, 2017), 73–74.

53. Tacuba de Morelos, D.F., 12/16/1926, DDG, SRE, Turquia, 2/360(496)-1, caja: 14, exp. 12, AGN.

54. Governor of San Luís Potosí to the Secretary of Gobernación, San Luís Potosí, 12/6/1926, DDG, SRE, Turquia, 2/360(496)-1, caja: 14, exp. 12, AGN.

55. Irapuato, Guanajuato, 12/11/1926, DDG, SRE, Turquia, 2/360(496)-1, caja: 14, exp. 12, AGN.

56. San Pedro, Coah., 1/5/1927, DDG, SRE, Turquia, 2/360(496)-1, caja: 14, exp. 12, AGN.

57. "Relaciones de Extranjeros Residentes en el Municipio de la Capital del Estado de S.L. Potosí en el Mes de Diciembre de 1926," DDG, SRE, Turquia, 2/360(496)-1, caja: 14, exp. 12, AGN.

58. Xicohtencatl, Tlaxcala, 12/15/1926, DDG, SRE, Turquia, 2/360(496)-1, caja: 14, exp. 12, AGN.

59. Angel Castillo Lanz to the Secretary of Gobernación, 7 Feb. 1927, DDG, SRE, Turquia, 2/360(496)-1, caja: 14, exp. 12, AGN.

60. Iguala, Guerrero, 12/20/1926, DDG, SRE, Turquia, 2/360(496)-1, caja: 14, exp. 12, AGN; Niltepec, Oaxaca, 1 June 1927, DDG, SRE, Turquia, 2/360(496)-1, caja: 14, exp. 12, AGN.

61. Secretary of Saltillo to the Secretary of Gobernacíon, Saltillo, Coahuila, 12/14/1926, DDG, SRE, Turquia, 2/360(496)-1, caja: 14, exp. 12, AGN.

62. León, Guanajuato, 12/13/1926, DDG, SRE, Turquia, 2/360(496)-1, caja: 14, exp. 12, AGN.

63. Acámbaro, 12/13/1926, DDG, SRE, Turquia, 2/360(496)-1, caja: 14, exp. 12, AGN.

64. Censo General de los Subditos Turcos Residentes en el Municipio de Veracruz, DDG, SRE, Turquia, 2/360(496)-1, caja: 14, exp. 12, AGN.

65. Consulado de Mexico en Constantinopla, 1923, 27–12–34, SRE; 3/30/1924, gömlek: 22, dosya: 101, HR.İM, BOA.

66. Tratado de Amistad entre México y Turquía, 1927, III-183–2, SRE.

67. Scarlatt Tottu to Adnan Bey, 4/20/1924, dosya: 103, gömlek: 11, HR.İM, BOA.

68. Scarlatt Tottu, personnel file, 18–11–2, SRE.

69. Ibid.

70. Pastor, *The Mexican Mahjar*, 80, 86.

71. For more on Spanish philo-sephardism, see Michael Alpert, "Dr. Angel Pulido and Philo-Sephardism in Spain," *Jewish Historical Studies* 40 (2005); Maria Antonia del Bravo, "Angel Pulido y el Sefardismo Internacional," *Hispania Sacra* 45, no. 92 (1993); Isabelle Rohr, "'Spaniards of the Jewish Type': Philosephardism in the Service of Imperialism in Early Twentieth-Century Spanish Morocco," *Journal of Spanish Cultural Studies* 12, no. 1 (Mar. 2011); Michal Friedman, "Reconquering 'Sepharad': Hispanism and Proto-Fascism in Giménez Caballero's Sephardist Crusade," *Journal of Spanish Cultural Studies* 12, no. 1 (Mar. 2011).

72. Türkiye Büyük Milliyet Meclisi, Gizli Celse Zabıtları, 3 Nisan 1340 (1924), 429–430.

73. Çağaptay, *Islam, Secularism, and Nationalism*, 25.

74. Nissim Sarfati to AIU headquarters, 12/4/1923, TU-06/Turquie II C 8.02f, AIU. He enclosed a French translation of an undated *Halk* article in his report.

75. Jacob Panigel to AIU headquarters, 6/20/1923, HM3/91, AIU Turquie IC 4.1c, CAHJP.

76. David Fresco, 11/6/1923, TU-06/ Turquie II C 8.09 b, AIU.

77. Letter from Tire to AIU headquarters, 2/7/1924, HM3/694, AIU Turquie XCVI E 1126.1, CAHJP.

78. David Fresco, 11/6/1923, TU-06/ Turquie II C 8.09 b, AIU.

79. Nathan Sissa, interview by Monika Unikel, 4/17/1989, AAUJH.

80. David Benveniste Fresco, 11/6/1923, TU-06/ Turquie II C 8.09 b, AIU; Benjamin Bidjerano, 9/3/1924, microfilm at CAJHP- HM3/693, AIU Turquie XCIV E 1110.3, CAHJP; Benjamin Bidjerano, 9/15/1925, microfilm at CAJHP-HM3/693, AIU Turquie XCIV E 1110.3, CAJHP. For parallel pressures on the Greek Orthodox community of Istanbul to increase Turkish education in their schools, see Alexis Alexandris, *The Greek Minority of Istanbul and Greek-Turkish Relations, 1918–1974* (Athens, 1992), 134–135. On Sephardi Jews in Salonica adopting Greek, see Eyal Ginio, "'Learning the Beautiful Language of Homer': Judeo-Spanish-Speaking Jews and the Greek Language and Culture between the Wars," *Jewish History* 16, no. 3 (2002), 245.

81. "Türkiye Cumhuriyeti Istanbul Vilayeti Maarif Müdüriyeti, Aded 12329," 2 Nisan 1340, and "Türkiye Cumhuriyeti Istanbul Vilayeti Maarif Müdüriyeti, Aded 557," 21 Haziran 1340, in TU-06/Turquie II C 8.08, AIU.

82. "La Prensa Turka Demanda la Ekspulsion delos Djudios," *La Vara*, 1/30/1925, 1.

83. "La Revolusion Turka i los Djudios," *El Tiempo*, 12/23/1925, 5. For a discussion of the Greek Orthodox community's debates over the relinquishing of minority rights, see Alexandris, *The Greek Minority*, 135–139.

84. *Mahkeme-yi Temyiz-i Hukuk Dairesi Riyaset-i Celilesine Salomon Elnekave-Madam Estrea Davasına dair Temyiz-i Cevap Layihasıdır* (Istanbul, 1927).

85. For an in-depth discussion of the Turkish press's creation and inflation of this affair, see Rıfat Bali, *Bir Türkleştirme Serüveni: Cumhuriyet Yıllarında Türkiye Yahudileri, 1923–1945* (Istanbul, 1999), 77–83.

86. Bali has parts of this article transliterated into Latin characters. Ibid, 78. For *El Tiempo*'s article, see "Violente Atako dela Prensa Turka contra el Elemento Djudio de Turkia," 2/19/1926, *El Tiempo*, 3–6.

87. Nejmeddine Sadik, 2/26/1926, *Akşam* in TU-06/Turquie II C 8.03h, AIU.

88. For reports on Bejarano's visit to Vali Suleyman Samy Bey, see "Le Grand-Rabbin chez vali," 2/21/1926, Stamboul, in TU-06/Turquie II C 8.03h, AIU.

89. "La délégation juive a Angora," 3/2/1923, *La République*; "La démarche juive à Angora," 2/24/1926, Stamboul, in TU-06/Turquie II C 8.03h, AIU.

90. "Une dépêche de la communauté juive d'Andrinople," 3/2/1926, *La République*, in TU-06/Turquie II C 8.03h, AIU.

91. "A la direction du journal "La République,"" 2/26/1926, *La République*, in TU-06/Turquie II C 8.03h, AIU.

92. "Les juifs de Cadikeuy," 2/26/1926, *La République*, in TU-06/Turquie II C 8.03h, AIU.

93. "Une protestation au nom de vingt mille juifs," 2/24/1926, Stamboul, in TU-06/Turquie II C 8.03h, AIU.

94. Philon Fresco to AIU headquarters, 2/24/1926, TU-06/Turquie II C 8.03h, AIU.

95. "Dans les écoles juives," 2/25/1926, *La République*, in TU-06/Turquie II C 8.03h, AIU.

96. "Revue de la presse, la question juive, du Milliet," 3/2/1926, *La République*, in TU-06/Turquie II C 8.03h, AIU.

97. Shelomo Saadi Halevy, "La Situasion de los Djudios de Turkia," *La Vara*, 9/17/1926, 1.

98. "Why the Sephardim Should Consider Mexico." *La Luz*, 2/1/1922, 1. It seems likely that the term "our friend" was not merely rhetorical, given the description of Albert Avigdor as a B'nai B'rith member, and the active role that Albert J. Torres, the editor of *La Luz*, took in various Sephardic community organizations. For more on Torres and *La Luz*, see Ben-Ur, "Ladino Press," 30–31.

99. Margalit Bejarano has echoed Avigdor's sentiments. See Margalit Bejarano, "The Sephardic Communities of Latin America: A Puzzle of Subethnic Fragments," in *Contemporary Sephardic Identity in the Americas: An Interdisciplinary Approach*, ed. Margalit Bejarano and Edna Aizenberg (Syracuse, 2012), 3–4.

100. Albert Avigdor, "Porke los Sefaradim Deven Pensar en Meksiko," *La Luz*, 2/2/1922, 1.

101. Lore Diana Kuehnert, "Pernicious Foreigners and Contested Compatriots: Mexican Newspaper Debates over Immigration, Emigration, and Repatriation, 1928–1936" (PhD diss., 2002), 16.

102. Sergio DellaPergola, "'Sephardic and Oriental' Jews in Israel and Western Countries: Migration, Social Change, and Identification," *Studies in Contemporary Jewry* 22 (2007); Sergio DellaPergola, "Hierarchic Levels of Subethnicity: Near Eastern Jews in the U.S., France, and Mexico," *Sociological Papers* 5, no. 2 (1996).

103. Joseph M. Papo, *Sephardim in Twentieth Century America: In Search of Unity* (San Jose, 1987), 27–28.

104. David Tacher, 7/7/1923, NYPL, 1820–1957, Year: 1923, Line: 12, Page: 224, Roll: T715_3325, Serial: T715, NARA.

105. Devin Naar, "Between 'New Greece' and the 'New World': Salonikan Jewish Immigration to America," *Journal of the Hellenic Diaspora* 35, no. 2 (Fall 2009), 67. For more on undocumented Eastern European Jewish immigration to the United States from Cuba, see Libby Garland, *After They Closed the Gates: Jewish Illegal Immigration to the United States, 1921–1965* (Chicago, 2014), 94.

106. Scarlatt Tottu, Personal File, 18-11-2, SRE.

107. Roberto Barokas, "A la Atansion de Los ke Pensan Imigrar en Amerika," *La Vara*, 8/1/1924, 7.

108. Libby Garland, "Not-Quite-Closed Gates: Jewish Alien Smuggling in the Post-Quota Years," *American Jewish History* 98, no. 3 (September 2008).

109. B'nai B'rith Mexican Bureau, Minutes of the Joint Committee, 7/20/1927, SC 1188, AJA.

110. Martin Zielonka, 1921, SC-5345, AJA.

111. Quoted in Garland, "Not-Quite-Closed Gates," 216.

112. Isaac Penhas, interview by Maty Sommer, 4/10/1989, AAUJH.

113. Daniela Gleizer, "Judíos Sefardíes: De España a México a través del Imperio Otomano," in *La Ciudad Cosmopolita de los Inmigrantes*, ed. Carlos Martínez Assad (Mexico Gobierno de la Ciudad de México), 2010. Such phenomena were not exclusive to Mexico; Marquesa Macadar notes similar expressions among Ladino-speaking Sephardi migrants in Uruguay. See Marquesa Macadar, "Sephardic Diaspora: A Case Study in Latin America" (PhD diss., 2009).

114. Rosalynda Pérez de Cohen, Simonette Levy de Behar, and Sophie Bejarano de Goldberg, *Sefarad de Ayer, Oy i Manyana: Presencia Sefardí en México* (Mexico City, 2010), 98.

115. Aviva Ben-Ur, "Where Diasporas Met: Sephardic and Ashkenazic Jews in the City" (PhD diss., 1998), 55; Papo, *Sephardim in Twentieth Century America*, 46–47.

116. Papo, *Sephardim in Twentieth Century America*, xiv; Aviva Ben-Ur, "In Search of the American Ladino Press: A Bibliographical Survey, 1910–1948," *Studies in Bibliography and Booklore* 21 (2001), 11.

117. "Kurso Gratis de la Lingua Kastiyana," *La Vara*, 8/29/1924, 11. For more, see Aviva Ben-Ur, *Sephardic Jews in America: A Diasporic History* (New York, 2009), 81–107.

118. Marcos Reinah, Roll: 1786972, Draft Board: 168, Registration Location: New York County, New York, World War I Draft Registration Cards, 1917–1918, NARA.

119. Daniel Montekio, Roll: 1786819, Draft Board: 157, Registration Location: New York County, New York, World War I Draft Registration Cards, 1917–1918, NARA; Foundational charter of La Fraternidad, 2/25/1929, accessed at http://www.jap.org.mx/diriap/index.php?iap=0052.

120. Moreno Chicurel, 1927, 2/361.2459, exp. 38, caja: 27, serie: Turquía, DGG, AGN.

121. Rose Marie Cadranel, Consular Report of Birth Abroad, 1923, Decimal Files, compiled 1910 – 1949, File Number: 131, Series Box Number: 362, Series MLR Number: A1 3001, Series ARC ID: 2555709, RG: 59, General Records of the Department of State, 1763 – 2002, NARA; Sarah Cadranel, Consular Report of Birth Abroad, 1925, File Number: 131, Series Box Number: 362, Series MLR Number: A1 3001, Series ARC ID: 2555709, Decimal Files, compiled 1910 - 1949; RG: 59, General Records of the Department of State, 1763 – 2002, NARA. By 1930, this particular family had relocated to Los Angeles, where the father opened a clothing store and where the eldest daughter, at age 16, trimmed hats for a living. See 1930 United States Federal Census, Year: 1930; Census Place: Los Angeles, CA; Roll: 150; Page: 7B; Enumeration District: 471; Image: 289.0; FHL microfilm: 2339885, NARA.

122. Cadranel de Eskenazi, Belina, 1922, folio: 312231, caja: 1740, serie: archivo historico, sección: siglo XX, TSJDF, AGN.

123. Max Eskenazi, 3/24/1923, Manifests of Statistical and Some Nonstatistical Alien Arrivals at Laredo, Texas, May 1903 - April 1955, Serial: A3437; Roll: 79, RG: 85, NARA; Balina Eskinaze, 7/17/1924, Manifests of Statistical and Some Nonstatistical Alien Arrivals at Laredo, Texas, May 1903 - April 1955, Serial: A3431, Roll: 91, RG: 85, NARA.

124. Belina, José, and Victoria Eskenazi, 1930 Mexican Census, Year: 1930; Census Place: Puebla, Puebla, Puebla; FHL Number: 1507859; Page: 132, accessed on Ancestry.com.

125. Pastor, *The Mexican Mahjar*, 44; Liz Hamui de Halabe, *Identidad Colectiva: Rasgos Culturales de los Inmigrantes Judeo-Alepinos* (Mexico City, 1997), 114.

126. "Sefardi Matado kon Grande Krueldad," *La Vara*, 3/20/1925, 1.

127. "El Matador de Moshe Alfassa," *La Vara*, 3/27/1925, 1. Unfortunately, this article, which should continue onto a following page, does not, leaving the reader unsure of the outcome.

128. Pablo Yankelevich, *¿Deseables o Inconvenientes? Las Fronteras de la Extranjería en el México Posrevolucionario* (Mexico, 2011), 99–109. For more on deportations of former Ottomans from the United States, see Chris Gratien and Emily K. Pope-Ojeda, "Ottoman Migrants, U.S. Deportation Law, and Statelessness during the Interwar Era," *Mashriq & Mahjar* 5, no. 2 (2018).

129. Marcos Reinah, Expulsión, 1924, 30–17–25, SRE.

130. Marcos Reinah, Expulsión, 1931, 2/362.2(18)-32, exp. 3, caja: 10, serie: Turquía, DGG, AGN.

131. Marcos Reinah, US draft card, New York; Roll: 1786972, Draft Board: 168, Registration Location: New York County, World War I Draft Registration Cards, 1917–1918, NARA.

132. "Names of New Yorkers who have Failed to Respond to the Draft," *The New York Times*, 10/29/1917, 8.

133. Shelomo Meyuhas, "Nuestros Djudios de Meksiko," *La Amerika*, 9/28/1917, 4.

134. Marcos Reinah Capsuto, 1936–1942, Naturalización, 27–19–27, SRE.

135. Albert Couriel, NYPL, 1820–1957, Year: 1914, Line: 24, Page: 3, Roll: T715_2353, Serial: T715, NARA.

136. For Couriel as Spanish, see Alberto Couriel, NYPL, 1820–1957, Year: 1917, Line: 12, Page: 96, Roll: T715_2541, Serial: T715, NARA; for Couriel as Greek from Salonica, see: Alberto Couriel, NYPL, 1820–1957, Year: 1918, Line: 16, Page: 121, Roll: T715_2568, Serial: T715, NARA; Alberto Couriel, NYPL, 1820–1957, Year: 1919, Line: 6, Page: 6, Roll: T715_2632, Serial: T715, NARA; Alberto Couriel, NYPL, 1820–1957, Year: 1920, Line: 1, Page: 85, Roll: T715_2756, Serial: T715, NARA; Alberto Couriel, NYPL, 1820–1957, Year: 1921, Line: 1, Page: 151, Roll: T715_3049, Serial: T715, NARA; Alberto Couriel, Manifests of Statistical and Some Nonstatistical Alien Arrivals at Laredo, Texas, May 1903 - April 1955, Roll: 76, Serial: A3437, RG: 85, NARA; for Couriel as Greek nationality and French race: Alberto Couriel, Manifests of Statistical and Some Nonstatistical Alien Arrivals at Laredo, Texas, May 1903 - April 1955, Roll: 76, Serial: A3437, RG: 85, NARA.

137. Marcos Reinah, Expulsión, 1924, 30–17–25, SRE.

138. Corinne Krause, "Mexico—Another Promised Land? A Review of Projects for Jewish Colonization in Mexico: 1881–1925," *American Jewish Historical Quarterly* 61, no. 4 (June 1972), 337–340.

139. Hamui de Halabe, *Identidad Colectiva*, 113–114.

140. Interview with Vitali Meshoulam by Monika Unikel. 1/16/1989, AAUHJ.

141. Pérez de Cohen, Levy de Behar, and Bejarano de Goldberg, *Sefarad de Ayer, Oy i Manyana*, 278, 283.

142. B'nai B'rith Mexican Bureau, Minutes of the Joint Committee, 7/20/1927, SC-1186, AJA.

143. Protección a Sirio Libaneses, 1926, 18-19-236, SRE.

144. "Sobre dispenciones presidenciales para evitar que entren extranjeros ilegalmente al país," 1923, 38-9-65, SRE.

145. Sara Halfon de Lahana, intestate case, folio: 344547, caja: 1902, sección: siglo XX, serie: archivo historico, TSJDF, AGN.

146. Victor Cohen, Naturalización, 1926, 2/361-1216, DGG, AGN.

147. Elias Sevy, naturalización, 1924, exp. 273, vol. 1172, sec.: gobernación, nacionalización de extranjeros, Fondo: Ayuntamiento, AHDF.

148. Lázaro Carillo, Naturalización, 1925, 2/361.180, exp. 5, caja 4, serie: Turquía, DGG, AGN; David Jesurum, Naturalización, 1925, 2/361.114, exp. 45, caja 2, serie: Turquía, DGG, AGN.

149. Samuel Cuenca, Naturalización, 1926, 2/361.1077, exp. 12, caja: 14, serie: Turquía, DGG, AGN.

150. Jacobo Levy, Naturalizacíon, 1926, 2/361.948, exp. 67, caja 12, serie: Turquía, DGG, AGN.

151. David Saul, Naturalización, 1926, 2/361.1313, exp. 39, caja 15, serie: Turquía, DGG, AGN.

152. Elias Bemaras, Naturalización, 1927, 2/361.2405, exp. 73, caja 26, serie: Turquía, DGG, AGN; Samuel Cuenca, Naturalización, 1926, 2/361.1077, exp. 12, caja: 14, serie: Turquía, DGG, AGN.

153. 2/367(22)4, exp. 28, caja 3, DGG, AGN.

154. Quoted from Carlos Antaramián, *Del Ararat al Popocatéptl: Los Armenios en México* (Mexico City, 2011), 71.

155. See Jacobo Levy, Naturalizacíon, 1926, 2/361.948, exp. 67, caja 12, serie: Turquía, DGG, AGN; Gabriel Yermia, Naturalización, 1926, 2/361.729, exp. 8, caja 10, serie: Turquía, DGG, AGN.

156. Alejandro Samuel Nyssen, Naturalización, 1926, 2/361.1033, exp. 48, caja 13, serie: Turquía, DGG, AGN; David Nyssen, Naturalización, 1926, 2/361.1029, exp. 44, caja 13, serie: Turquía, DGG, AGN.

157. Mauricio Benveniste, Naturalización, 1925, 2/361.280, exp. 49, caja 4, serie: Turquía, DGG, AGN.

158. See interviews of Sálomon Levy, Jaime Mitrani, Yoshúa Cancino Zambrano, AAUHJ.

159. Rafael Jassan, Reconocimiento de Hijo, 1924, folio: 337606, caja: 1891, sección: siglo XX, serie: archivo historico, TSJDF, AGN; Rafael Jassan, Reconocimiento de Hijo, 1924, folio: 337607, caja: 1891, sección: siglo XX, serie: archivo historico, TSJDF, AGN; Rafael Jassan, Zapateria, 10/1919, exp. 5692, vol. 3047, subsección: licencias en general, sec.: justicia, Fondo Ayuntamiento, AHDF.

160. Interview of Sálomon Levy, AAUHJ.

161. Jack Mizrahi, death announcement, Entry 205, Box Number: 1257, Box Description: 1930–1939 Mexico K – Mi, Records of the Department of State; RG: 59, NARA.

162. David Nyssen, Naturalización, 1926, 2/361.1029, exp. 44, caja 13, serie: Turquía, DGG, AGN.

163. Mordo Babany vs. María Luisa Guajardo, 1926, folio: 370115, caja: 2033, sección: siglo XX, serie: archivo historico, TSJDF, AGN; Mauricio Assael vs. Ramino Mena, 1926, folio: 363364, caja: 2000, sección: siglo XX, serie: archivo historico, TSJDF, AGN.

164. Kuehnert, "Pernicious Foreigners," 100, 122–125.

165. Comite Anti-Chino, 1926, 15-28-22, SRE; Liga Nacional Pro-Raza, 2/362.1(6–1)1, exp. 1, caja 14, DGG, AGN; La Delegación China pide protección, 2/367(6)1, exp. 26, caja 1, DGG, AGN.

166. Samuel Ochoa, "La Plaga Hebráica y las Funestas Consecuencias que de Ella Se Derivan para el País," *El Viajante*, 5, 27–28, Mexico- Near Print, Geography, AJA.

167. Díaz, Delgado y García, 11/5 (Israelitas), AGN.

168. *Diario Oficial*, 7/15/1927, quoted in Theresa Alfaro-Velcamp, *So Far from Allah, So Close to Mexico: Middle Eastern Immigrants in Modern Mexico* (Austin, 2007), 102–103.

169. Antaramián, *Del Ararat al Popocatéptl*, 66.

170. Restricciones a la Inmigración de Turcos, 1927, 21-26-51, SRE.

171. Restricciones a la Inmigración, 12/6/1929, 2.360(29)34, exp. 70, caja 9, DGG, AGN.

Chapter 5: The Sephardi Connection

1. "Dance Idol Dethroned," *Los Angeles Times*, 6/1/1928, 1.
2. "Mexican Scandal," *Manchester Guardian*, 6/4/1928, 12.
3. "Mexico Holds Actress as Aid to Gen. Alvarez," *Washington Post*, 6/2/1928, 3.
4. "Dance Idol Dethroned."
5. "Involve Chicago Man in Mexican Smuggler Ring," *Chicago Daily Tribune*, 6/5/1928, 19.
6. Colin M. MacLachlan and William H. Beezley, *El Gran Pueblo: A History of Greater Mexico*, 3rd ed. (Upper Saddle River, 2004), 298–300.
7. "Maria Conesa Breezes In," *Los Angeles Times*, 2/8/1930, A16.
8. Dirección General de Policia del Distrito Federal, 6/16/1928, DDG, 2/362.2(29)112, AGN.
9. See George J. Sánchez, *Becoming Mexican American: Ethnicity, Culture, and Identity in Chicano Los Angeles, 1900–1945* (Oxford, 1993), 209–226; Camille Guerin-Gonzales, *Mexican Workers and American Dreams: Immigration, Repatriation, and*

California Farm Labor, 1900–1939 (New Brunswick, 1994), 77–110; Francisco E. Balderrama and Raymond Rodríguez, *Decade of Betrayal: Mexican Repatriation in the 1930s* (Albuquerque, 2006).

10. Willem van Schendel, "Spaces of Engagement: How Borderlands, Illicit Flows, and Territorial States Interlock," in *Illicit Flows and Criminal Things: States, Borders, and the Other Side of Globalization*, ed. Willem van Schendel and Itty Abraham (Bloomington, 2005), 41.

11. Eduardo Sáenz Rovner, *The Cuban Connection: Drug Trafficking, Smuggling, and Gambling in Cuba from the 1920s to the Revolution* (Chapel Hill, 2008), 2, 12.

12. Itty Abraham and Willem van Schendel, "Introduction: The Making of Illicitness," in *Illicit Flows and Criminal Things: States, Borders, and the Other Side of Globalization*, ed. Willem van Schendel and Itty Abraham (Bloomington, 2005), 23.

13. Albert Cazés, 35-5-13, SRE.

14. Delay was a common tactic that Turkish authorities also employed toward American efforts to deport Turkish nationals. See Chris Gratien and Emily K. Pope-Ojeda, "Ottoman Migrants, U.S. Deportation Law, and Statelessness during the Interwar Era" *Mashriq & Mahjar* 5, no. 2 (2018), 142.

15. Geoffrey Lewis, *The Turkish Language Reform: A Catastrophic Success* (Oxford, 1999).

16. Senem Aslan, "'Citizen, Speak Turkish!': A Nation in the Making," *Nationalism and Ethnic Politics* 13, no. 2 (2007), 250–251.

17. Türkmenoğlu Zeynel Besim, "Türkiye'de Türkçe," *Hizmet*, 2/22/1928, quoted in Aslan, "'Citizen, Speak Turkish!,'" 256.

18. Aslan, "'Citizen, Speak Turkish!,'" 256.

19. Nissim M. Benezra, *Une Enfance juive à Istanbul (1911–1929)* (Istanbul, 1996), 116.

20. Marcy Brink-Danan, "Dangerous Cosmopolitanism: Erasing Difference in Istanbul," *Anthropology Quarterly* 84, no. 2 (2011), 445–446; Lerna Ekmekçioğlu, *Recovering Armenia: The Limits of Belonging in Post-Genocide Turkey* (Stanford, 2016), 116; Leyla Navaro, "Türkiye'de Yahudi Olmak," *Radikal*, 1/22/2009.

21. Elie Nathan to AIU headquarters, 1934, TU-06/ Turquie II C 8.03 1, AIU.

22. Soner Çağaptay, "Race, Assimilation, and Kemalism: Turkish Nationalism and the Minorities in the 1930s," *Middle Eastern Studies* 40, no. 3 (May 2004), 96.

23. Abraham Benveniste to AIU headquarters, 9/22/1927, TU-06/Turquie II C 8.02 G, AIU.

24. J. M. Landau, *Tekinalp, Turkish Patriot, 1883–1961* (Istanbul, 1984), 1–7.

25. Munis Tekinalp, *Tekinalp ve Türkleştirme*, transliterated by Yıldız Akpolat (Erzurum, 2005), 57.

26. Çağaptay, "Race, Assimilation, and Kemalism," 94.

27. Cemil Koçak, "Ayın Karanlık Yüzü: Tek-Parti Döneminde Gayri

Müslim Azınlıklar Aleyhinde Açılan Türklüğü Tahkir Davaları," *Tarih ve Toplum Yeni Yaklaşımlar* 1 (Mar., 2005), 148.

28. Koçak, "Ayın Karanlık Yüzü," 153.

29. Rıfat N. Bali, *Bir Türkleştirme Serüveni: Cumhuriyet Yıllarında Türkiye Yahudileri, 1923–1945* (Istanbul, 1999), 527–528; Koçak, "Ayın Karanlık Yüzü," 153–162.

30. Although the Republican Archives retain copies of decisions to prosecute these individuals, and these decisions make note that cases are attached, they are not. I know the names of some individuals prosecuted, the region in which they were prosecuted, and occasionally additional information like profession, nationality, or place of origin, but I do not know what precisely constituted their "insults." Cemil Koçak lists the records for 554 such cases. Koçak, "Ayın Karanlık Yüzü," 163–165.

31. For Manisa, see Avram Alaluf, 1932, Dosya no: 30, Sira no: 3, Dosya Gömleği: 245, Kutu Numarası: 39, Fon no: 30 10 0 0, Başvekalet, BCA; for Çanakkale, see Avram, 1932, Dosya no: 30, Sira no: 8, Dosya Gömleği: 245, Kutu Numarası: 39, Fon no: 30 10 0 0, Başvekalet, BCA; for Bursa, see Şimoyel oğlu Nesim, 11/10/1927, dosya: 30503, Yer No: 34.198.17, Fon no: 30 10 0 0, Başvekalet, BCA; for Uzunköprü, see Hayım karısı Ester, 11/15/1927, dosya: 30505, Yer No: 34.198.19, Fon no: 30 10 0 0, Başvekalet, BCA.

32. For cases not brought to prosecution, see Avram, 1935, Dosya no: 30, Sira no: 18, Dosya Gömleği: 259, Kutu Numarası: 41, Fon no: 30 10 0 0, Başvekalet, BCA; Istanbul'da Yasef, 1937, Dosya no: 30, Sira no: 1, Dosya Gömleği: 276, Kutu Numarası: 43, Fon no: 30 10 0 0, Başvekalet, BCA; Roben Leon, Avram Piha, Yako Mayo, 1936, Dosya no: 30, Sira no: 17, Dosya Gömleği: 270, Kutu Numarası: 42, Fon no: 30 10 0 0, Başvekalet, BCA.

33. Isak Efendi, 1929, Dosya no: 30, Sira no: 19, Dosya Gömleği: 209, Kutu Numarası: 36, Fon no: 30 10 0 0, Başvekalet, BCA.

34. Jozef oğlu Ravah, 1930, Dosya no: 30, Sira no: 14, Dosya Gömleği: 217, Kutu Numarası: 36, Fon no: 30 10 0 0, Başvekalet, BCA.

35. Kamhi, 1926, Dosya no: 31024, Sira no: 18, Dosya Gömleği: 179, Kutu Numarası: 32, Fon no: 30 10 0 0, Başvekalet, BCA.

36. See Dosya no: 30, Sira no: 11, Dosya Gömleği: 240, Kutu Numarası: 39, Fon no: 30 10 0 0, Başvekalet, BCA; the 1930 case brought in Izmir against Jozef and his wife Matilda, Dosya no: 30, Sira no: 6, Dosya Gömleği: 220, Kutu Numarası: 37, Fon no: 30 10 0 0, Başvekalet, BCA; the 1930 case in Istanbul brought against Moiz, the son of Mordahay, and Ester, the daughter of Hayim, Dosya no: 30, Sira no: 10, Dosya Gömleği: 221, Kutu Numarası: 37, Fon no: 30 10 0 0, Başvekalet, BCA; the 1932 case in Tekirdag against Salomon and his wife Sunbul, Dosya no: 30, Sira no: 19, Dosya Gömleği: 245, Kutu Numarası: 39, Fon no: 30 10 0 0, Başvekalet, BCA.

37. "El Pretentido Antisemitismo en Turquia," *La Boz de Oriente*, September 1935, 6.

38. "La Ceremonia en la Synagoga de Galata," *La Boz de Oriente*, October 1935, 13–14.

39. See Tekin Alp, "Türk Kültur Birliğinin Düsturları," *La Boz de Oriente*, 7/26/1934, 1; "Los Insidentes de la Trakya, el Antisemitismo No Es un Produkto Turko," *La Boz de Oriente*, 7/26/1934, 2–3; "El Rejimen Republikano en Turkia, del 1923 al 1934," *La Boz de Oriente*, 11/11/1934, 1–2; "La Turquisacion de las Minoridades en Turquia," *La Boz de Oriente*, 1/20/1935, 1; "Las Grandes Ovras de Ataturk y las Minoridades," *La Boz de Oriente*, 2/1/1935, 1; Moiz dal Mediko, "Cual Deve Ser la Lengua del Judio Turco," *La Boz de Oriente*, March 1935, 9. For an analysis of the *Trakya Olayları*, see Rıfat N. Bali, *1934 Trakya Olayları* (Istanbul, 2012); Hatice Bayraktar, "The Anti-Jewish Pogrom in Eastern Thrace in 1934: New Evidence for the Responsibility of the Turkish Government," *Patterns of Prejudice* 40, no. 2 (2006); Avner Levy, "1934 Trakya Yahudileri Olayı: Alınamayan Ders," *Tarih ve Toplum* 151 (Jul. 1994).

40. "La Turkia y los Judios," *La Boz de Oriente*, 2/1/1935, 2–3.

41. Leo Strauss, "Persecution and the Art of Writing," *Social Research* 82, no. 1 (2015), 82.

42. See Menahem Balli, 1930–1931, VII(N)-195–6, SRE.

43. Çagaptay, "Citizenship Policies," 605–608.

44. Haim Vitale Rovero Abuaf, who arrived in Mexico in 1924, traveled with a *hüviyet cüzdanı* [identity card] rather than with a passport. Haim Vitale Rovero Abuaf, Naturalización, 1924, 2/361.10732, exp. 32, caja 111, serie: Turquía, DGG, AGN.

45. Such as 152 people in November, 1929, Dosya no: 2–191, Sira no: 9, Dosya Gömleği: 56, Kutu Numarası: 6, Fon no: 30 18 1 2, Başvekalet, BCA; 158 individuals in February of 1935, Dosya no: 2–404, Sira no: 4, Dosya Gömleği: 10, Kutu Numarası: 51m Fon no: 30 18 1 2, Başvekalet, BCA; and numerous others.

46. 9/14/1932, Dosya no: 2–328, Sira no: 14, Dosya Gömleği: 61, Kutu Numarası: 31, Fon no: 30 18 1 2, Başvekalet, BCA.

47. 2/21/1934, Dosya No: 2–377, Sira no: 8, Dosya Gömleği: 9, Kutu Numarası: 42, Fon no: 30 18 1 2, Başvekalet, BCA.

48. For Merkado, see Hayim oğlu Merkado Kohen, 2/5/1930, Dosya no: 2–206, Sira no: 19, Dosya Gömleği: 6, Kutu Numarası: 8, Fon no: 30 18 1 2, Başvekalet, BCA; for Nelli Kohen, see 9/3/1930, Dosya no: 2–231, Sira no: 5, Dosya Gömleği: 60, Kutu Numarası: 13, Fon no: 30 18 1 2, Başvekalet, BCA; for Victoria, see Isak Arditi kızı Victoria, 2/18/1931, Dosya no: 2–245, Sira no: 4, Dosya Gömleği: 12, Kutu Numarası: 18, Fon no: 30 18 1 2, Başvekalet, BCA.

49. Meir Behmoiras to AIU headquarters, 8/13/1920, TU-15/Turquie V E 78, AIU.

50. Lina Behmoiras to AIU headquarters, 3/19/1928, TU-15/Turquie V E 77, AIU.

51. 1934, III-297–12, SRE.

52. Ibid.

53. Turcos Naturalizados, 1946, L-E-1125, SRE.

54. Legación de Turquie to the Secretary of the Mexican Foreign Ministry, 10/18/1934, expediente III-297–12, SRE.

55. Mehmet Munir, 11/29/1934, Dosya no: 400, Sira no: 28, Dosya Gömleği: 802, Kutu Numarası: 267, Fon no: 30 10 0 0, BCA.

56. 1934, III-297–12, SRE.

57. "Un Contrabandista Pidió Ámparo," 3/9/1920, *Excelsior*, 9; "Contrabanda de Sedas en Equipajes de los Árabes," 1922–1923, 19–20–30, SRE; Theresa Alfaro-Velcamp, *So Far from Allah, So Close to Mexico: Middle Eastern Immigrants in Modern Mexico* (Austin, 2007), 33–39.

58. Interview with Sálomon Levy, by Monika Unikel, 1/4/1989, AAUJH.

59. Jews of all stripes were heavily involved in the textile trade. See Adam Mendelsohn, *The Rag Race: How Jews Sewed Their Way to Success in America and the British Empire* (New York, 2014).

60. "War Declared on Smugglers," *Los Angeles Times*, 6/18/1928, 12.

61. Camila Pastor, *The Mexican Mahjar: Transnational Maronites, Jews, and Arabs under the French Mandate* (Austin, 2017), 79–80, 91; Andrew Arsan, *Interlopers of Empire: The Lebanese Diaspora in Colonial French West Africa* (London, 2014), 85.

62. Pablo Yankelevich, "Extranjeros Indeseables en México (1911–1940): Una Aproximación Cuantitativa a la Aplicación del Artículo 33 Constitucional," *Historia Mexicana* 53, no. 3 (Jan.–Mar. 2004), 737–738.

63. Alberto Salem to Plutarco Elías Calles, Guatemala City, 10/15/1928, 2/362.2(29)112, DDG, AGN.

64. Abraham Alberto Salem, Naturalización, 1931, 2/361.5467, exp. 67, caja: 58, Grecia, DDG, AGN.

65. Pablo Piccato, *The Tyranny of Opinion: Honor in the Construction of the Mexican Public Sphere* (Durham, 2010), ch. 5.

66. Restrictions on immigration, 12/6/1929, 2.360(29)34, exp. 70, caja 9, DGG, AGN.

67. Ibid.; Aristide Zolberg, *A Nation by Design: Immigration Policy in the Fashioning of America* (Cambridge, 2006), 11, 224.

68. Expulsion of Communists, 1929, 2/362.2(29)-162, exp. 16, caja: 21, DGG, AGN.

69. Letter from Unión Revolucionaria de Mexicanos Naturalizados protesting letter in *La Patria*, 1933, 2.360(29)8139, exp 10, caja 11, DGG, AGN.

70. Comité Permanente Pro-México de Afuera, 1933, 2/360(29)8141, exp: 12, caja:11, serie: Israel, AGN.

71. Cámara Nacional de Comercio, Industría y Minería, 1933, 2/360(11)8045, exp. 48, caja 3, DGG, AGN.

72. Alicia Gojman de Backal, *Camisas, Escudos y Desfiles Militares: Los Dorados y el Antisemitismo en México (1934–1940)* (Mexico City, 2000), 154–167.

73. Campaña Nacionalista de Labor, 1930, 2/361.4899, exp. 99, caja 52, DGG, AGN.

74. Liga Nacional Anti-China, 1930, exp. 215, registro 5036, 14834, Collection: Pascual Ortíz Rubio, AGN.

75. Cámara Israelita de Industría y Comercio, queja contra Unión de Comerciantes Mexicanos de Fresnillo, 1936, 2/360(28)17737, exp: 54, caja: 8, serie: Israel, DGG, AGN.

76. Liga de Defensa Nacional, 1931, 2/360(29)56, exp. 44, caja 10, DGG, AGN.

77. Comerciantes en Pequeño del Mercado La Lagunilla, 1930, 121–A-I-1, Collection: Álvaro Obregón-Plutarco Elías Calles, AGN.

78. Formation of Comité Nacionalista, Aguascalientes, 1931, 2/360(1)1, exp. 1, caja: 1, DGG, AGN.

79. Cámara Nacional de Comercio in Iguala, Gro., 1932, 2/360(9)8037, exp. 35, Caja 3, DGG, AGN; Asociación Regional de Comerciantes e Industriales Mexicanos, 1932, 507/10, Collection: Abelardo L. Rodríguez, AGN.

80. Campaña Nacionalista del Edo. de Puebla, 1931, 2/360(18)5, exp. 18, caja 4, DGG, AGN.

81. Liga Defensa de Propietarios de Zapaterías, Peleterías, y Similares, DF, 1931, 2/360(29)67, exp. 27, caja 10, DGG, AGN. The Syrio-Lebanese, in particular, were alleged to frequently burn their establishments to collect insurance money. See the 1931 expulsion case against Saad and Gaber in Rosita, Coahuila, 2/362.2(3)28, exp. 27, caja 2, DGG, AGN.

82. Gojman de Backal, *Camisas, Escudos y Desfiles Militares*, 163–166.

83. "El Hitlerismo en Mexico," *La Boz de Oriente*, September 1935, 8; "En Mexico," *La Boz de Oriente*, November 1935, 9.

84. Comité Pro-Raza, 1934, 181/11, Collection: Abelardo Rodríguez, AGN; Comité Pro-Raza, 1933–1935, 521.6/6, Collection: Lázaro Cárdenas del Río, AGN. Gojman de Backal notes that the Comité Pro-Raza was the most closely aligned with contemporary European fascist groups of any organization in Mexico. See Gojman de Backal, *Camisas, Escudos y Desfiles Militares*, 165.

85. Alberto Farji to SRE, 1/20/1934, III-119–3, SRE; Alberto Farji pide garantías, 2/27/1934, 2/367(496)/10031, DGG, AGN; Alberto Farji, complaint, 1934, 2/367(21)-1, exp. 33, caja 7, serie: Turquía, DGG, AGN.

86. Mexico- Near Print, Geography, AJA. For more on the Café Bojor, see interview with Jaime Mitrani, by Anita Viskin, 12/14/1988, AAUHJ.

87. Asociación Israelita de Aboneros, 1930, 2/360(29)50, exp: 35, caja: 10, DGG, AGN; Asociación de Comerciantes Israelitas en Pequeño, 1930, 2/360(29)52, exp: 29, caja: 10, DGG, AGN.

88. Circular 23, Box 3, Boletinos y Circulares, 1931–1950, CDICA, Mexico City, Mexico.

89. *Directorio Comercial, Industrial, y Profesional*, 1932, Mexico- Near Print, Geography, AJA.

90. Max King vs. Jack Penhas, 1934, Exp. 43, no. 16, Fondo: Cámara Israelita de Arbitrajes en Tramite, 1930–1935, CDICA.

91. Cámara Israelita de Industría y Comercio, queja contra Unión Comerciantes Mexicanos de Fresnillo, 1936, 2/360(28)17737, exp: 54, caja: 8, DGG, AGN; Cámara Israelita de Industría y Comercio, 1936, 2/360(13)22223, exp: 50, caja: 4, DGG, AGN; Cámara Israelita de Industría y Comercio, pide garantías, 1932, 2/367(26)14, exp. 16, caja 4, DGG, AGN; Cámara Israelita de Industría y Comercio, queja, 1931, 2/360(22)6, exp: 11, caja: 6, DGG, AGN.

92. Cámara Israelita de Industría y Comercio, presidential telegrams, 1933, 181/8–1, Collection: Abelardo Rodríguez, AGN.

93. Extranjeros en general, 1932, exp. 40, Caja: 320, Dir. Gral. de Investigaciones Políticas y Sociales (IPS), AGN.

94. Report on Expulsion of Foreigners, 1934, 2/360(29)8143, exp 14, caja 11, DGG, AGN.

95. Elias Grayeb y Hnos, Expulsión, 1928, 2/362.2(26)42, exp. 21, caja 14, DGG, AGN.

96. Manual Mina, Expulsión, 1930, 2/362.2(29)234, exp. 2, caja 23, DGG, AGN.

97. Conference on the White Slave Trade, Vienna, 1909, 7-7-138, SRE.

98. 4/6/1930, IV-169–17, SRE.

99. Informa que diez muchachas han sido embarcadas destinadas a la trata de blancos, April, 1930, IV-144–83, SRE.

100. Naar, Lili, inmigración, June–July 1930, IV-144–84, SRE. Much of the literature on transnational sex trafficking in Latin America involves Argentina. See Donna L. Guy, *Sex and Danger in Buenos Aires: Prostitution, Family, and Nation in Argentina* (Lincoln, 1990), esp. 17–23, 120–129; Sandra McGee Deutsch, *Crossing Borders, Claiming a Nation: A History of Argentine Jewish Women, 1880–1955* (Durham, 2010), 105–147; Isabel Vincent, *Bodies and Souls: The Tragic Plight of Three Jewish Women Forced into Prostitution in the Americas* (New York, 2006); Edward J. Bristow, *Prostitution and Prejudice: The Jewish Fight against White Slavery, 1870–1939* (London, 1983).

101. "Hijas de la chingada" would be colloquially translated into English as something approximating "fucking whores." Victor N. Pessah, Naturalización, 1926, 2/361.1401, exp. 28, caja 16, serie: Turquía, DGG, AGN; Victor Pessa, folio: 404694, caja: 2212, sección: siglo XX, serie: archivo historico, TSJDF, AGN.

102. Expulsion to Cuba, 1929, 2/362.2(29)-144, exp. 27, caja: 20, DGG, AGN.

103. Ex. 14, caja 11, 2/360(29)8143, DGG, AGN.

104. Daniela Gleizer, *El Exilio Incómodo: México y los Refugiados Judíos, 1933–1945* (Mexico City, 2011), 67.

105. Circular confidencial, num. 250, 10/17/1933, 2/360(29)8144, exp. 15, caja 11, DGG, AGN. See Prohibiciones y restricciones establecidas en material migratoria, 8/11/1934, III-2334–12, Departamento Diplomatico, SRE.

106. Jose Behar Motola, tarjeta 89, Caja 2, serie: Cubanos, RE, DM, AGN; Jose Benezra, tarjeta 111, Caja 2, serie: Cubanos, RE, DM, AGN; Moises Behar, tarjeta 81, Caja 1, serie: Turcos, RE, DM, AGN; Fortuna Motola Bejar, tarjeta 206, Caja 2, serie: Turcos, RE, DM, AGN; Victor Esquinazi Hasday, tarjeta 29, Caja 2, serie: Griegos, RE, DM, AGN; Matilde Esquenazi Mitrani, tarjeta 27, Caja 2, serie: Griegos, RE, DM, AGN; Sabeto Lilo, tarjeta 18, Caja 3, serie: Griegos, RE, DM, AGN; Isaac Mitrani, tarjeta 107, Caja 3, serie: Griegos, RE, DM, AGN; Raquel Mitrani de Esquinazi, tarjeta 113, Caja 3, serie: Griegos, RE, DM, AGN; Rebeca Mitrani, tarjeta 115, Caja 3, serie: Griegos, RE, DM, AGN.

107. Pepo Saltiel Griego, 1924, exp. 251, vol. 1172, sec.: gobernación, nacionalización de extranjeros, Fondo: Ayuntamiento, AHDF; Elias Sevy Turco, 1924, exp. 252, vol. 1172, sec.: gobernación, nacionalización de extranjeros, Fondo: Ayuntamiento, AHDF; Peppo Saltiel, Naturalización, 1931, 2/361.5997, exp. 96, caja: 63, serie: Grecia, DGG, AGN; Elias Sevy, Naturalización, 1929, 2/361.3552, exp. 52, caja: 39, serie: Grecia, DGG, AGN.

108. See Aron Rodrigue, "Jewish Enlightenment and Nationalism in the Ottoman Balkans: Barukh Mitrani in Edirne in the Second Half of the Nineteenth Century," *Princeton Papers: Interdisciplinary Journal of Middle Eastern Studies* 12 (2005).

109. My thanks to Ipek Yosmaoğlu for this observation.

110. Roberto Becherano Ditrani, tarjeta 69, caja: 1, serie: Griegos, RE, DM, AGN; Susana Becherano Ditrani, tarjeta 71, caja: 1, serie: Griegos, RE, DM, AGN; Ezra Behar, tarjeta 76, caja: 1, serie: Griegos, RE, DM, AGN; Isidoro Behar, tarjeta 77, caja: 1, serie: Griegos, RE, DM, AGN; Samuel Moscatel, tarjeta 133, caja: 1, serie: Griegos, RE, DM, AGN.

111. Libby Garland, *After They Closed the Gates: Jewish Illegal Immigration to the United States, 1921–1965* (Chicago, 2014), 106–107.

112. Vitali Meshoulam, interview by Monika Unikel, 1/16/1989, AAUHJ.

113. Inmigración de los señores Jacobo, Rahamin y Meshulam Cohen, 1929, IV-158–69, SRE.

114. Rahamin y Meshulam Cohen, sus inmigraciones, 1929, IV-155–114, SRE.

115. Julia Phillips Cohen, "Oriental by Design: Ottoman Jews, Imperial Style, and the Performance of Heritage," *American Historical Review* 119, no. 2 (April, 2014).

116. See interviews with Sálomon Levy, by Monika Unikel, 1/4/1989 and Jaime Mitrani by Anita Viskin, 12/14/1988, AAUJH. For allegations that Jews and Armenians sold fake Oriental carpets, see "À travers Paris—Israël contre Israël," *Le Matin*, 5/22/1899. My thanks to Julia Phillips Cohen for this reference.

117. Alfaro-Velcamp, *So Far from Allah*, 133–138; Jacob Norris, "Exporting the Holy Land: Artisans and Merchant Migrants in Ottoman-Era Bethlehem," *Mashriq & Mahjar* 2 (2013), passim.

118. Carlos Antaramián, *Del Ararat al Popocatéptl: Los Armenios en México* (Mexico City, 2011), 55.

119. See Cámara Israelita de Industría y Comercio de México, "Directorio Comercial, Industrial, y Professional," Mexico- Near Print, Geography, AJA.

120. Sálomon Levy, interview by Monika Unikel, AAUJH.

121. Similarly, when Isaac Capon was away from Mexico in 1930, his wife Mathilde took over his business concerns. See Saul Carasso y Concepción Gómez de Carasso vs. Manuel Calderon de la Barca, 1930, folio: 451549, caja: 2383, sección: siglo XX, serie: archivo historico, TSJDF, AGN.

122. Mauricio Assael, 7/8/1927, Manifests of Statistical and Some Nonstatistical Alien Arrivals at Laredo, Texas, May 1903–April 1955, Serial: A3437, Roll: 99, RG: 85, NARA.

123. Herman Schwab vs. Mauricio Assael, 1928, folio: 395862, caja: 2173, sección: siglo XX, serie: archivo historico, TSJDF, AGN; Mauricio Assael, Liquidación judicial, 1928, folio: 399455, caja: 2192, sección: siglo XX, serie: archivo historico, TSJDF, AGN; Max Weinberg vs. Mauricio Assael, 1928, folio: 403304, caja: 2207, sección: siglo XX, serie: archivo historico, TSJDF, AGN.

124. Mauricio Assael, 8/20/1931, NYPL, 1820–1957, Year: 1931, Line: 1, Page: 149, Roll: T715_5019, Serial: T715, NARA; Sálomon Ninio, passport renewal, 06/1933, Paris, IV-668–9, SRE; Sálomon Ninio, passport renewal, 6/8/1933, Paris, IV-640–9, SRE.

125. Manuel Modiano, 4/25/1928, NYPL, 1820–1957, Year: 1928, Page: 29, Line: 24, Roll: T715_4253, Serial: T715, NARA. For Modiano's naturalization petition, see 18–17–15, SRE; for his traveling, see Manuel Modiano, 6/9/1926, NYPL, 1820–1957, Year: 1926, Line: 10, Page: 23, Roll: T715_3865, Serial: T715, NARA; Manuel Modiano, 1/17/1928, Nonstatistical Manifests and Statistical Index Cards of Aliens Arriving at Laredo, Texas, May 1903 - November 1929, Roll: 64, Serial: A3379, RG: 85, NARA; Manuel Modiano, 4/25/1928, NYPL, 1820–1957, Year: 1928, Line: 24, Page: 29, Roll: T715_4253, Serial: T715, NARA; Manuel Modiano, 6/8/1929, Nonstatistical Manifests and Statistical Index Cards of Aliens Arriving at Laredo, Texas, May 1903 - November 1929, Roll: 64, Serial: A3379, RG: 85, NARA; Manuel Modiano, 8/20/1929, NYPL, 1820–1957, Year: 1929, Line: 30, Page: 39, Roll: T715_4561, Serial: T715, NARA; Manuel Modiano, 11/1931, Texas Passenger Lists, 1896–1957, Manifests of Aliens Granted Temporary Admission at Laredo, Texas, December 1, 1929 - April 8, 1955, Roll: 11, Serial: M1772, RG: 85, NARA.

126. Records for Leon Alazraki and Mario Naar, 1/20/1931, NYPL, 1820–1957, Year: 1931, Line: 1, Page: 21, Roll: T715_4902, Serial: T715, NARA.

127. Alazraki, Moise, Permiso de Inmigración, 1932, IV-409–43, SRE; Moïse Alazraki, tarjeta de identificacíon, 1/1933, IV-641–44, SRE.

128. Moïse Alazraki, 9/6/1932, NYPL, 1820–1957, Year: 1932, Line: 2, Page: 27, Roll: T715_5220, Serial: T715, NARA; Moïse Alazraki, 2/15/1933, NYPL, 1820–1957, Year: 1933, Line: 2, Page: 30, Roll: T715_5293, Serial: T715, NARA; Records

for Moïse Alazraki and Salomon Cohen, 9/19/1933, NYPL, 1820–1957, Year: 1933, Line: 1, Page: 40, Roll: T715_5392, Serial: T715, NARA; Moïse Alazraki, 3/27/1935, NYPL, 1820–1957, Year: 1935, Line: 2, Page: 1, Roll: T715_5623, Serial: T715, NARA; Moise Alazraki, 5/30/1935, Alphabetical Manifests of Non-Mexican Aliens Granted Temporary Admission at Laredo, Texas, December 1, 1929 - April 8, 1955, Roll: 1, Serial: M1771, RG: 85, NARA; Records for Moise Alazraki, Regina Margonato de Alazraki, and Samuel Alazraki, 12/24/1936, NYPL, 1820–1957, Year: 1936, Line: 9, Page: 73, Roll: T715_5916, Serial: T715, NARA; Moise Alazraki, 7/5/1938, Alphabetical Manifests of Non-Mexican Aliens Granted Temporary Admission at Laredo, Texas, December 1, 1929 - April 8, 1955, Roll: 1, Serial: M1771, RG: 85, NARA.

129. See Records for Saul and Concepción Carasso, 4/30/1932, Texas Passenger Lists, 1866–1959, Page: 1, Roll: 30, NARA; Saul Carasso, 8/2/1933, NYPL, 1820–1957, Year: 1933, Line: 19, Page: 30, Roll: T715_5364, Serial: T715, NARA; Saul Carasso, 12/12/1933, NYPL, 1820–1957,Year: 1933, Line: 14, Page: 221, Roll: T715_5426, Serial: T715, NARA; Saul Carasso, 2/5/1935, NYPL, 1820–1957, Year: 1935, Line: 25, Page: 172, Roll: T715_5604, Serial: T715, NARA; Saul Carasso, 5/19/1936, NYPL, 1820–1957, Year: 1936, Line: 1, Page: 146, Roll: T715_5804, Serial: T715, NARA; Isaac Capon, 1/31/1931, Texas Passenger Lists, 1896–1959, Page: 79, Roll: 29, NARA; Isaac Capon, 3/22/1932, NYPL, 1820–1957, Year: 1932, Line: 1, Page: 165, Roll: T715_5128, Serial: T715, NARA; Isaac Capon, 7/13/1932, NYPL, 1820–1957, Year: 1932, Line: 1, Page: 13, Roll: T715_5186, Serial: T715, NARA.

130. 3/30/1933, IV-427-64, SRE.

131. Elnecave is listed as the reference on the cards of Isaac Mizrahi, tarjetas 189 and 193, caja: 2, serie: Turcos, RE, DM, AGN; and Maria N. Harabon de Mizrahi, tarjeta 42, caja: 2, serie: Turcos, RE, DM, AGN, both from Guatemala. For Simon Lahana's reentry information, see tarjeta: 74, caja: 2, serie: Apatridas, RE, DM, AGN. For additional connections to Guatemala, see Alberto Benroudi, inmigración, 10/31/1929, IV-157-87, SRE.

132. For connections between Cuba and Colombia, see Jacobo Yaffe, Naturalización, 1928, 2/361.2670, exp. 65, caja 29, serie: Turquía, DGG, AGN; Records for Salomon, Kadijn, and Victoria Behar, Julia Mitrani de Levi, and Barzilay and Zimon Levy, 9/4/1928, New Orleans Passenger Lists, 1820–1945, T905_125; for connections between Mexico and Argentina, see Jacobo (Jacques) Tarragan, 5/26/1929, NYPL, 1820–1957, Year: 1929, Line: 9, Page: 143, Roll: T715_4499, Serial: T715, NARA; and Enrique L. Botton and Rosi Cohen de Botton, 3/22/1931, NYPL, 1820–1957, Year: 1931, Line: 3, Page: 208, Roll: T715_4929, Serial: T715, AGN.

133. Confidencial: Prohibiciones y restricciones establecidas en material migratoria, 8/11/1934, III-2334-12, Departamento Diplomatico, SRE.

134. Pastor, *The Mexican Mahjar*, 146–150.

Chapter 6: Forge Your Own Passport

1. Mexico City, 10/16/1946, Fresco Personnel File, 31–15-8, SRE.

2. José Gorostiza to the Director of the Archivo General, Mexico City, 10/10/1946, Mauricio Fresco Personnel File, 31–15-8, SRE.

3. Mexico City, 10/16/1946, Fresco Personnel File, 31–15-8, SRE.

4. Birth of Mauricio Fresco, 381, registered 9/9/1926, Registro Civil del Estado de Yucatán, México. Courtesy of the Academía Mexicana de Genealogía y Heraldica, accessed via Ancestry.com, 2/11/2016.

5. Mauricio D. Fresco, Naturalización, DDG, SRE, Turquia, 2/361.3899, caja 42, exp. 97, AGN.

6. Ibid.; Viviane Wayne, *Inshallah: In Pursuit of My Father's Youth* (Santa Barbara, 2002), 17.

7. The Oficial Mayor of the SRE to the Oficial Mayor of the *Secretaria de Gobernación*, 12/28/1929, Mexico City, in Mauricio D. Fresco, Naturalización, DDG, SRE, Turquia, 2/361.3899, caja 42, exp. 97, AGN.

8. "How British Engineers Saved a Chinese Railway," *China Weekly Review*, 11/14/1931, 406.

9. *Jueves de Excelsior*, Mexico City, 12/10/1936, reprinted in "Fresco Gets Credit for Penning Latest Tome on City," Fresco Personnel File, SRE.

10. SRE IV-341–13.

11. For more on Chinese migrants in Mexico, see Robert Chao Romero, *The Chinese in Mexico, 1882–1940* (Tucson, 2010); Julia María Schiavone Camacho, *Chinese Mexicans: Transpacific Migration and the Search for a Homeland, 1910–1960* (Chapel Hill, 2012); José Jorge Gómez Izquierdo, *El Movimiento Antichino en México (1871–1934): Problemas del Racismo y del Nacionalismo durante la Revolución Mexicana* (Mexico City, 1992); Grace Peña Delgado, *Making the Chinese Mexican: Global Migration, Localism, and Exclusion in the U.S.-Mexico Borderlands* (Stanford, 2012); Elliott Young, *Alien Nation: Chinese Migration in the Americas from the Coolie Era through World War II* (Chapel Hill, 2014), 197–247. For Chinese Mexicans after the 1931 pogroms, see Fredy González, *Paisanos Chinos: Transpacific Politics among Chinese Immigrants in Mexico* (Berkeley, 2017).

12. "Consular Information," *The North-China Herald*, 5/24/1933, 306.

13. "To Visit Hongkong: Ex-President of Mexico Coming, Mr. A. Rodriguez on Tour," *South China Morning Post*, 9/18/1935, 10.

14. "Issued by Consul Official Here," Fresco Personnel File, 31–15-8, SRE.

15. Mauricio Fresco to the Consul of Mexico in Yokohama, 6/29/1933. Ibid.

16. Mauricio Fresco, "Trade between Mexico and China," *Chinese Economic Journal* 16 (1935), 300.

17. Ibid., 301.

18. Mauricio Fresco [writing as G. E. Miller], *Shanghai, The Paradise of Adventurers* (New York. 1937).

19. Ibid., 16.

20. "Fresco Book on Sha'i Aims to 'Reveal' Bad Conditions, Characters," *Shanghai Evening Post and Mercury*, 6/3/1937, in Fresco Personnel File, 31–15–8, SRE.

21. "Fresco Gets Credit for Penning Latest Tome on City," Fresco Personnel File, 31–15–8, SRE.

22. Hugo Restall, "From 'Hunting Opium and Other Scents' to '400 Million Customers,'" *Wall Street Journal*, 3/6/2009.

23. 704/166, Collection: Cárdenas, AGN.

24. Sarah Abrevaya Stein, *Extraterritorial Dreams: European Citizenship, Sephardi Jews, and the Ottoman Twentieth Century* (Chicago, 2016), 73–75.

25. Dona Dionisia Pallaci y Levy de Benbasat, naturalización, 1942, 31–9–28, SRE; Sem Oscar Fua, naturalización, 1925, DDG, 2/361–281, AGN; Miguel Palacci, Visa Issue, 5/27/1919, M1085, Investigative Reports of the Bureau of Investigation, 1908–1922, series: Old German Files, 1909–21, case number: 362282, roll: 797, NARA; "El Centro de Paris," *El Universal*, 8/14/1920, 8; "Los que Viajan," *El Universal*, 11/28/1919, 8.

26. Mauricio D. Fresco, Naturalization, DDG, SRE, Turquia, 2/361.3899, caja 42, exp. 97, AGN.

27. Roberto Sovrado, Naturalization. DDG, SRE, Turquia, 2/361.2013, caja 22, exp. 68, AGN.

28. "How British Engineers Saved a Chinese Railway," 406.

29. Interview with Leon Gattegno, AAUHJ.

30. Luís Geller, *Alberto Misrachi, Galerista: Una Vida Dedicada a Promover el Arte de México* (Mexico City, 1998), 24–25.

31. Fresco Personnel File, 31–15–8, SRE.

32. Juan Manuel Alvarez del Castillo to the SRE, Departamento Consular, Lisbon, 1/31/1942, Fresco Personnel File, 31–15–8, SRE.

33. Mauricio Fresco Papers, Library of Congress.

34. Mauricio Fresco, "Prefacio," in Atticus, *El Milagro Griego* (Mexico City, 1942), 5–7.

35. Mauricio Fresco, *Yo He Estado en Paris con los Alemanes* (Mexico City, 1944), 3.

36. Ibid, 11.

37. Ibid., 19–20.

38. Ibid., 20.

39. Friedrich E. Schuler, *Mexico between Hitler and Roosevelt: Mexican Foreign Relations in the Age of Lázaro Cárdenas, 1934–1940* (Albuquerque, 1998), 140–141.

40. Fresco, *Yo He Estado en Paris*, 18–19.

41. Ibid., 27.

42. José Papo, *En attendant l'aurore: Activité de la communauté séphardite de Paris pendant l'occupation 1940–1945* (Paris, 1945), 32; Corry Guttstadt, *Turkey, the Jews, and the Holocaust* (Cambridge, 2013), 186–187.

43. Guttstadt, *Turkey, the Jews, and the Holocaust*, 188–189.

44. Stein, *Extraterritorial Dreams*, 123.

45. Papo, *En attendant l'aurore*, 36.

46. Guttstadt, *Turkey, the Jews, and the Holocaust*, 189–211. For comparisons with Turkish Jews in Germany, see Marc David Baer, "Turk and Jew in Berlin: The First Turkish Migration to Germany," *Comparative Studies in Society and History* 55, no. 2 (2013).

47. Papo, *En attendant l'aurore*, 47.

48. Gitta Amipaz-Silber, *Sephardi Jews in Occupied France: Under the Tyrant's Heel, 1940–1944* (Jerusalem, 1995), 52–53, 61–63.

49. Fresco, *Yo He Estado en Paris*, 20.

50. Roberto Sovrado, naturalización, 1927, exp. 68, caja 22, Turquia, 2/361.2013, SRE, DGG, AGN.

51. Friedrich E. Schuler, *Mexico Between Hitler and Roosevelt* (Albuquerque, 1998), 52; III-140-40, SRE. In 1933, many Jewish communities throughout the world used boycotts as a means of protesting anti-Semitic Nazi policies. On March 31, 1933, a group of Turkish, Polish, and German Jews in Turkey organized a protest in Taksim and a boycott of German goods. See Başvekalet, Fon no: 30 10 0 0, Kutu Numarası: 110, Dosya Gömleği: 734, Sira no: 7, Dosya no: 94C, BCA; Daniela Gleizer, *El Exilio Incómodo: México y los Refugiados Judíos, 1933–1945* (Mexico City, 2011), 87–89, 90–96.

52. Gleizer, *El Exilio Incómodo*, 121–127, 140–141.

53. Emphasis in original. Report on the proposal to attract and encourage Jewish immigration to Mexico, 7/14/1937, Collection: Cárdenas, 711/516, AGN.

54. Daniela Gleizer, "Gilberto Bosques y el Consulado de México en Marsella (1940–1942)," *Estudios de Historia Moderna y Contemporánea de México* 49 (2015), 59, 67.

55. Daniela Gleizer, "International Rescue of Academics, Intellectuals and Artists from Nazism During the Second World War: The Experience of Mexico," in *European and Latin American Social Scientists as Refugees, Émigrés and Return-Migrants*, ed. Ludger Pries and Pablo Yankelevich (Cham, 2019), 183.

56. Ibid., 182.

57. Gleizer, "Gilberto Bosques," 67–70.

58. Ibid., 60.

59. Guy Benveniste, *From Paris to Berkeley: A Memoir* (Berkeley, 2010), 50, 67–68.

60. III-2439-3, SRE.

61. Gaston Gerassy, tarjeta 73, Caja 2, serie: Griegos, RE, DM, AGN; Michel

Gerassy, tarjeta 75, Caja 2, serie: Griegos, RE, DM, AGN; on "economic" versus "political" refugees, see Gleizer, *El Exilio Incómodo*, passim; Daniela Gleizer, "La Politica Mexicana frente a la Recepción de Refugiados Judíos (1934–1942)," in *México, País Refugio: La Experiencia de los Exilios en el Siglo XX*, ed. Pablo Yankelevich (Mexico City, 2002), 125.

62. Michel Gerassy to Mexican Legation in Paris, October 3, 1944, III-717–23, SRE.

63. Mauricio Fresco to Michel Gerassy, 10/10/1944, III-717–23, SRE; "Plans Legation Opening," *New York Times*, 8/24/1944, 5.

64. Ríos Zertuche to Michel Gerassy, 10/2/1944, III-717–23, SRE; Laure Gerassi, tarjeta 74, Caja 2, serie: Griegos, RE, DM, AGN.

65. Wayne, *Inshallah*, 35.

66. Fresco, *Paris*, 29.

67. Fresco, *Paris*, 29–30; Gleizer, "Gilberto Bosques," 60.

68. Antonio Berna Salido, *Somos: Homenaje de los Republicanos Españoles a las Representaciones Diplomatica y Consular de México en Francia* (Mexico City, 1944).

69. Mauricio Fresco, *La Emigración Republicana Española: Una Victoria de México* (Mexico City, 1950), 9.

70. Fresco, *La Emigración Republicana Española*, 10. For more on Spanish intellectuals in Mexico, see Sebastian Faber, *Exile and Cultural Hegemony: Spanish Intellectuals in Mexico, 1939–1975* (Nashville, 2002).

71. Fresco, *La Emigración Republicana Española*, 20.

72. Ibid., 20. The perception of shared hispanism was an ideology promulgated among the early Republican refugees to Mexico and by certain Mexican politicians, including Cárdenas. See Patricia W. Fagen, *Exiles and Citizens: Spanish Republicans in Mexico* (Austin, 1973), 144–153.

73. Mario Ojeda Revah, *Mexico and the Spanish Civil War: Political Repercussions for the Republican Cause* (Brighton, 2015), 194.

74. Revah, *Mexico and the Spanish Civil War*, 182.

75. Gad Nassi, *Jewish Journalism and Printing Houses in the Ottoman Empire and Modern Turkey* (Istanbul, 2001), 35; Mauricio Fresco to Abraham Galanté, 4/26/1949, published in *Sephardi Lives: A Documentary History, 1700–1950*, ed. Julia Phillips Cohen and Sarah Abrevaya Stein (Stanford, 2014), 379–380.

76. Mauricio Fresco to Abraham Galanté, 4/26/1949, published in *Sephardi Lives*, 379–380.

77. "Argentina Contestará el Libro Azul," *La Prensa*, 2/22/1946, 1.

78. Fresco [writing as Miller], *Shanghai, The Paradise of Adventurers*, 44, 46–47, 65–71.

79. Ibid., 63.

80. Wayne, *Inshallah*, 17.

81. Allyson Hobbs, *A Chosen Exile: A History of Racial Passing in American Life* (Cambridge, 2014), 5.

82. Ibid., 8.

83. Karl Jacoby, *The Strange Career of William Ellis: The Texas Slave Who Became a Mexican Millionaire* (New York, 2016), xx, 99.

84. Ibid., 99.

85. Mauricio Fresco, *Synthèse du conflit du pétrole au Mexique* (Bordeaux, 1938); Fresco, *La Emigración Republicana Española*.

86. Exam of Mauricio Fresco, 10/27/1939, Paris, Fresco Personnel File, 31–15–8, SRE.

87. Mauricio Fresco, *Un Mundo Curioso* (Mexico City, 1962), 1.

88. Wayne, *Inshallah*, 17.

89. Hobbs, *A Chosen Exile*, 6.

90. Anne-Marie Fresco Lynette, Bautismos 1933–1947, Nuestra Señora de Lourdes, Centro, Distrito Federal, Mexico, accessed via Ancestry.com on 2/11/2016.

91. Wayne, *Inshallah*, 127–130.

92. Devin Naar, "Between 'New Greece' and the 'New World': Salonikan Jewish Immigration to America," *Journal of the Hellenic Diaspora* 35, no. 2 (Fall 2009), 76.

Conclusion

1. Ovadia Nathan, 3/30/1912, Year: 1912, Arrival: New York; Microfilm: T715, Roll: 1829, Line: 4, Page: 220, NARA.

2. Ovadia Nathan, 7/24/1912, 1908–1935 Border Entries; Roll: T-5500, Library and Archives Canada, accessed via Ancestry.com, 4/25/2012; "Peddler is Arrested," *Duluth News Tribune*, 11/15/1912, 7; Hasia R. Diner, *Roads Taken: The Great Jewish Migrations to the New World and the Peddlers Who Forged the Way* (New Haven, 2015), 84–85.

3. Ovadia Nathan, Payrolls- Southern Pacific Divisions, California State Railroad Museum Library, Sacramento, California; Ovadia Nathan, World War I Draft Registration Cards, 1917–1918, San Francisco County, CA; Roll: 1543844; Draft Board: 1, NARA; Ovadia Nathan, Conscription matter, FBI case file, Old German Files, Ovidia [sic] Nathan, #8000–253176, NARA.

4. "Position Wanted," *San Francisco Chronicle*, 10/23/1919.

5. Year: 1920; Census Place: Petaluma, Sonoma, California; Roll: T625_151; Page: 6B; Enumeration District: 146; *Buyers' Guide of San Francisco* (San Francisco, 1921), 1125.

6. Ovadia Nathan to Hahambaşı, 6/11/1918, HM2/9073.4, CAHJP.

7. Ovadia Nathan marriage with Mary Menier Clark, Entry 3001, Series Box Number: 519; File Number: 133, Series ARC ID: 2555709, Series MLR Number: A1, Marriage Reports in State Department Decimal Files, 1910–1949; RG: 59, General Records of the Department of State, 1763 – 2002, NARA.

8. Archivo General del Registro del Estado de Tamaulipas, México. Courtesy of the Academía Mexicana de Genealogía y Heráldica, pp. 137–138.

9. "Left on Wedding Day," *El Paso Herald Post*, 4/20/1933, 2.

10. Ovadia Nathan, tarjeta: 37, caja: 120, serie: Estadounidenses, RE, DM, AGN.

11. Esther Belleli, tarjeta: 86, caja: 1, serie: Griegos, RE, DM, AGN; Moises Belleli, tarjeta: 87, caja: 1, serie: Griegos, RE, DM, AGN.

12. Year: 1930; Census Place: Laredo, Webb, Texas; Roll: 2407; Page: 10A; Enumeration District: 0014; FHL microfilm: 2342141. From United States of America, Bureau of the Census, *Fifteenth Census of the United States, 1930* (Washington, DC: 1930).

13. Julia Phillips Cohen, "The East as a Career: Far Away Moses and Company in the Marketplace of Empires," *Jewish Social Studies* 21, no. 2 (Winter 2015); Julia Phillips Cohen, "Oriental by Design: Ottoman Jews, Imperial Style, and the Performance of Heritage," *American Historical Review* 119, no. 2 (April, 2014).

14. *Worley's Jacksonville (Texas) City Directory, 1930* (Dallas, 1930), 291; Ovadia Nathan, in *El Paso City Directory 1934* (El Paso, 1934), 734.

15. "Around the Town with the Gadder," *El Paso Herald Post*, 12/15/1933, 15.

16. Ovadia Nathan, Texas Death Certificates, 1903–1982, Texas Department of State Health Services, Austin, Texas.

17. Norman Goldberg, *Chicago Tribune*, Nov. 25, 2016; Ovadia Nathan, Applications for Headstones for U.S. Military Veterans, 1925–1940, RG 99, Microfilm publication M1916, ARC ID: 596118, NARA.

18. Donna Gabaccia, *Italy's Many Diasporas* (London, 2000), 11.

19. Elliott Young, *Alien Nation: Chinese Migration in the Americas from the Coolie Era through World War II* (Chapel Hill, 2014), 5.

20. Elaine Carey, *Women Drug Traffickers: Mules, Bosses, and Organized Crime* (Albuquerque, 2014), 14.

21. Young, *Alien Nation*, 1–2.

22. Diner.

23. Jenna Weissman Joselet, *The Wonders of America: Reinventing Jewish Culture, 1880–1950* (New York: 1994), 5; Andrew R. Heinze, *Adapting to Abundance: Jewish Immigrants, Mass Consumtpion, and the Search for American Identity* (New York: 1990), Chap. 4.

24. Robert A. Orsi, *The Madonna of 115th Street: Faith and Community in Italian Harlem, 1880–1950*, 3rd Ed. (New Haven, 2010), xxxviii.

25. Mauricio Fresco to Abraham Galanté, 4/26/1949, in *Sephardi Lives: A Documentary History, 1700–1950*, ed. Julia Phillips Cohen and Sarah Abrevaya Stein (Stanford, 2014), 379–380.

WORKS CITED

Archives

Akten, Haus-, Hof- und Staatsarchiv, Vienna, Austria (HHSA)
Alliance Israélite Universelle, Paris, France (AIU)
American Jewish Archives, Cincinnati, United States (AJA)
Archivo de Amigos de la Universidad Hebrea de Jerusalén, Mexico City, Mexico (AAUHJ)
Archivo Estatal de Distrito Federal, Mexico City, Mexico
Archivo General de la Nación, Mexico City, Mexico (AGN)
Archivo General del Registro del Estado- Tamaulipas, Tamaulipas, México
Archivo Histórico del Distrito Federal, Mexico City, Mexico (AHDF)
Archivo Histórico Genaro Estrada, Secretaría de Relaciones Exteriores, Mexico City, Mexico (SRE)
Başbakanlık Cumhuriyet Arşivi, Ankara, Turkey (BCA)
Başbakanlık Osmanlı Arşivi, Istanbul, Turkey (BOA)
California State Railroad Museum Library, Sacramento, California
Central Archives for the History of the Jewish People, Jerusalem, Israel (CAHJP)
Centro de Documentación e Investigación de la Comunidad Ashkenazí de México, Mexico City, Mexico (CDICA)
Joint Distribution Committee Archive, New York City (JDC)
Library and Archives Canada, Ottawa, Canada
Library of Congress, Washington, DC, United States
National Archives and Records Administration, Silver Springs, Maryland (NARA)
Texas Department of State Health Services, Austin, Texas

Published Primary Sources

Aciman, André. *Out of Egypt: A Memoir*. New York: Picador, 1994.
Aray, Suat. *Bir Galatasaraylının Hatıraları*. Izmir: TCDD Basımevi, 1959.
Arditti, Elías. *Izmir, París, Buenos Aires: Odisea de un Inmigrante*. Buenos Aires: n.p., 1993.
Benezra, Nissim M. *Une Enfance juive à Istanbul (1911–1929)*. Istanbul: Isis Press, 1996.
Ben Ghiat, Alexandre. *La Haggadah de Ben Ghiat*. Izmir: El Meseret, 1919.
———. *Livro-Jurnal de la Gerra Djeneral*. Izmir: El Meseret, 1919.
Benveniste, Guy. *From Paris to Berkeley: A Memoir*. Berkeley: Les Éditions de Montrose, 2010.
Berna Salido, Antonio. *Somos: Homenaje de los Republicanos Españoles a las Representaciones Diplomática y Consular de México en Francia*. Mexico City: Publicaciones Somos, 1944.
Bilgen-Reinart, Üstün. *Porcelain Moon and Pomegranates: A Woman's Trek through Turkey*. Toronto: Dundurn Press, 2007.
Buletino del Ospital Nasional Israelita "Or-Ahayim." Constantinople: Fratelli Haim, 1923.
Buyers' Guide of San Francisco. San Francisco: n.p., 1921.
Cohen, Julia Phillips, and Sarah Abrevaya Stein, eds. *Sephardi Lives: A Documentary History, 1700–1950*. Stanford: Stanford University Press, 2014.
Commission centrale de secours aux israélites ottomans éprouvés de la guerre. Constantinople: Imprimerie F. Loeffler, 1917.
Eli, Nissim Shem-Tov. *Haggadah dela Gerra por Dia de Pesah*. Constantinople: Sosieta Anonima de Papeteria i de Imprimeria, 1919.
El Paso City Directory, 1934. El Paso: Hudspeth Directory Co., 1934.
Estrugo, José M. *Los Sefardíes*. Havana: Editorial Lex, 1958.
Fresco, Mauricio. *La Emigración Republicana Española: Una Victoria de México*. Mexico City: Editores Asociados, 1950.
———. *Un Mundo Curioso*. Mexico City: Editores Asociados, 1962.
———. "Prefacio." In Atticus. *El Milagro Griego*. Mexico City: Editora Mexicana, 1942.
———. *Synthèse du conflit de pétrole au Mexique*. Bordeaux: Imprimerie Delmas, 1938.
———. "Trade between Mexico and China." *Chinese Economic Journal* 16 (1935): 300–301.
———. *Yo He Estado en Paris con los Alemanes*. Mexico City: M. Fresco, 1944.
———. [writing as G. E. Miller]. *Shanghai, The Paradise of Adventurers*. New York: Orsay Publishing House, 1937.

Galanti, Avram. *Vatandaş: Türkçe Konuş! Yahud Türkçe'nin Ta'mîmi Meselesi, Tarihî, İçtimâî, Siyasî Tedkik*. Istanbul: Hüsn-i Tabîat Matbaası, 1928.

Guéron, A. *Journal du Siège d'Andrinople, 30 octobre 1912–26 mars 1913*. Istanbul: Isis Press, 2002.

Haker, Erol. *From Istanbul to Jerusalem: The Itinerary of a Young Turkish Jew*. Istanbul: Isis Press, 2003.

Johnson, Clarence Richard, ed. *Constantinople To-Day, or The Pathfinder Survey of Constantinople, a Study in Oriental Social Life*. New York: Macmillan, 1922.

Karmona, Elia. *Haggadah dela Gerra Djeneral*. Constantinople: Imprimeria del Djugeton, 1920.

———. *Komo Nasio Elia Karmona: Komo Se Ingrandisio i Komo Se Izo Direktor del "Djugeton."* Istanbul: n.p., 1926.

———. *El Mayoral Djudio*. Constantinople: Imprimeria Arditi, 1910.

———. *La Novia Aguna: Romanso Nasional Djudia*. Constantinople: Djugeton Press, 5682.

Laskaridhis, Catherine. *Quinze mille jours à Constantinople ma patrie*. Athens: n.p., 1987.

Mahkeme-yi Temyiz-i Hukuk Dairesi Riyaset-i Celilesine Salomon Elnekave- Madam Estrea Davasına dair Temyiz-i Cevap Layihasıdır. Istanbul: Cumhuriyet Matbaası, 1927.

Miller, G. E. *See* Fresco, Mauricio.

Morin, Edgar. *Vidal et les siens*. Paris: Seuil, 1989.

Nahum, Henri. *La grande guerre et la guerre gréco-turque vues par les instituteurs de l'Alliance Israélite Universelle d'Izmir*. Istanbul: Isis Press, 2003.

Nalpas, Joseph. *Annuaire des commerçants de Smyrne et de l'Anatolie*. Smyrne: Imprimerie Journal de Smyrne, 1894.

Navon, A.H. *Joseph Pérez: Juifs de Ghetto*. Paris: Calmann-Lévy, 1925.

Papo, José. *En attendant l'aurore: Activité de la communauté Séphardite de Paris pendant l'occupation 1940–1945*. Paris: n.p., 1945.

Reports Received by the Joint Distribution Committee of Funds for Jewish War Sufferers. New York: Press of Clarence S. Nathan, 1916.

Saserdote, Ben Yitzhak. *Refael i Miriam: Novela de la Vida de los Djudios del Oriente*. Constantinople: Imprimeria Aboav i Kohen, 1910.

Sason, N. *Silabario en Turko-Espanyol*. Istanbul: Isak Gabai, 1905.

Schemonti, Joseph A. *États des Ottomans au Méxique: Devoirs de l'Empire à leur Égard, Remèdes*. Constantinople: Moderne Imp. Francaise, 1909.

Tekinalp, Munis. *Tekinalp ve Türkleştirme*. Transliterated by Yıldız Akpolat. Erzurum: Fenomen Yayıncılık, 2005.

The Treaties of Peace 1919–1923, Vol. II. New York: Carnegie Endowment for International Peace, 1924.

Türkiye Büyük Millet Meclisi, Gizli Celse Zabıtları. Secret court records of the Turkish Parliament, accessible at http://www.tbmm.gov.tr/kutuphane/tutanak_sorgu.html. Last accessed 12/13/2019.

United States of America, Bureau of the Census. *Fifteenth Census of the United States, 1930*. Washington, DC: NARA, 1930.

Wayne, Viviane. *Inshallah: In Pursuit of My Father's Youth*. Santa Barbara: Fithian Press, 2002.

Worley's Jacksonville (Texas) City Directory, 1930. Dallas: John F. Worley Directory Co., 1930.

Yaliz, T. *El Insendio del 17–18 Agosto 1917*. Salonika: n.p., 1919.

Periodicals

L'Akcham (Istanbul)
The American Israelite (Cincinnati)
La Amerika (New York City)
La Boz del Pueblo (New York City)
La Boz de Oriente (Istanbul)
Chicago Daily Tribune (Chicago)
China Weekly Review (Shanghai)
Correspondence d'Orient (Paris)
El Democrata (Mexico City)
El Diario (Mexico City)
Diario del Hogar (Mexico City)
Duluth News Tribune (Duluth)
El Paso Herald Post (El Paso)
La Epoca (Mexico City)
La Epoka (Salonica)
Evolución (Laredo)
Excelsior (Mexico City)
HaMenora (Istanbul)
El Imparcial (Mexico City)
Al-Jawater (Mexico City)
La Jeune Turquie (Paris)
Journal d'Orient (Istanbul)
Jueves de Excelsior (Mexico City)
Los Angeles Times (Los Angeles)
La Luz (New York City)
The Manchester Guardian (Manchester)
Le Matin (Paris)
El Meseret (Izmir)

The Mexican Herald (Mexico City)
El Mundo (Havana)
The New York Times (New York City)
The North China Herald (Shanghai)
El País (Mexico City)
La Prensa (San Antonio)
La Opinión (Veracruz)
Radikal (Istanbul)
La République (Istanbul)
San Francisco Chronicle (San Francisco)
South China Morning Post (Hong Kong)
El Tiempo (Istanbul)
El Universal (Mexico City)
La Vara (New York)
El Viajante (Monterrey)
The Wall Street Journal (New York City)
The Washington Post (Washington, DC)

Secondary Sources

Abraham, Itty, and Willem van Schendel. "The Making of Illicitness." In *Illicit Flows and Criminal Things: States, Borders, and the Other Side of Globalization.* Ed. Willem van Schendel and Itty Abraham, 1–37. Bloomington: Indiana University Press, 2005.

Adatto, Albert. "Sephardim and the Seattle Sephardic Community." MA thesis, University of Washington, 1939.

Ahmad, Feroz. "War and Society under the Young Turks, 1908–1918." *Review (Fernand Braudel Center)* 11, no. 2 (Spring, 1988): 265–286.

Akarlı, Engin Deniz. "Ottoman Attitudes Towards Lebanese Emigration, 1885–1910." In *The Lebanese in the World: A Century of Emigration.* Ed. Albert Hourani and Nadim Shehadi, 109–138. London: I.B. Tauris, 1992.

Akın, Yiğit. *When the War Came Home: The Ottomans' Great War and the Devastation of an Empire.* Stanford: Stanford University Press, 2018.

Aktar, Ayhan. "Homogenising the Nation, Turkifying the Economy: The Turkish Experience of the Population Exchange Reconsidered." In *Crossing the Aegean: An Appraisal of the 1923 Compulsory Population Exchange between Greece and Turkey.* Ed. Renée Hirschon, 79–96. New York: Berghahn Books, 2003.

Alexandris, Alexis. *The Greek Minority of Istanbul and Greek-Turkish Relations, 1918–1974.* Athens: Centre for Asia Minor Studies, 1992.

Alfaro-Velcamp, Theresa. *So Far from Allah, So Close to Mexico: Middle Eastern Immigrants in Modern Mexico*. Austin: University of Texas Press, 2007.

Almanza Huesca, Beatriz A. "La Entrada de los Ejércitos Revolucionarios a la Ciudad de México (1913–1915)." *Revista Mexicana de Sociología* 56, no. 3 (Jul.–Sep. 1994): 151–172.

Alonso, Ana María. "Conforming Disconformity: 'Mestizaje,' Hybridity, and the Aesthetics of Mexican Nationalism." *Cultural Anthropology* 19, no. 4 (Nov. 2004): 459–490.

Alpert, Michael. "Dr. Angel Pulido and Philo-Sephardism in Spain," *Jewish Historical Studies* 40 (2005): 105–119.

Amipaz-Silber, Gitta. *Sephardi Jews in Occupied France: Under the Tyrant's Heel, 1940–1944*. Jerusalem: Rubin Mass Ltd., 1995.

Antaramián, Carlos. *Del Ararat al Popocatéptl: Los Armenios en México*. Mexico City: SEDEREC, 2011.

———. "La Merced, Mercado y Refugio, El Caso Armenio," *ISTOR* IX, no. 36 (Spring, 2009): 106–130.

Arsan, Andrew. "Failing to Stem the Tide: Lebanese Migration to French West Africa and the Competing Prerogatives of the Imperial State." *Comparative Studies in Society and History* 53 (2011): 450–478.

———. *Interlopers of Empire: The Lebanese Diaspora in Colonial French West Africa*. London: Hurst, 2014.

Aslan, Senem. "'Citizen, Speak Turkish!': A Nation in the Making." *Nationalism and Ethnic Politics* 13, no. 2 (2007): 245–272.

Aviles-Galán, Miguel Angel. "Measuring Skulls: Race and Science in Vicente Riva Palacio's *México a través de los siglos*." *Bulletin of Latin American Research* 29, no. 1 (2010): 85–102.

Aydıngün, İsmail, and Esra Dardağan. "Rethinking the Jewish Communal Apartment in the Ottoman Communal Building," *Middle Eastern Studies* 42, no. 2 (March, 2006): 319–334.

Baer, Marc David. *The Dönme: Jewish Converts, Muslim Revolutionaries, and Secular Turks*. Stanford: Stanford University Press, 2010.

———. "Turk and Jew in Berlin: The First Turkish Migration to Germany." *Comparative Studies in Society and History* 55, no. 2 (2013): 330–355.

Balderrama, Francisco E., and Raymond Rodríguez. *Decade of Betrayal: Mexican Repatriation in the 1930s*. Albuquerque: University of New Mexico Press, 2006.

Bali, Rıfat N. *1934 Trakya Olayları*. Istanbul: Libra Kitap, 2012.

———. *Bir Türkleştirme Serüveni: Cumhuriyet Yıllarında Türkiye Yahudileri, 1923–1945*. Istanbul: Iletişim, 1999.

Balloffet, Lily Pearl. "From the Pampa to the Mashriq: Arab-Argentina Philanthropy Networks." *Mashriq & Mahjar* 4, no. 1 (2017): 4–28.

Banko, Lauren. *The Invention of Palestinian Citizenship, 1918–1947.* Edinburgh: Edinburgh University Press, 2018.

Bayar, Yeşim. "In Pursuit of Homogeneity: The Lausanne Conference, Minorities and the Turkish Nation." *Nationalities Papers* 42, no. 1 (2014): 108–125.

———. "The Trajectory of Nation-Building through Language Policies: The Case of Turkey during the Early Republican Period (1920–1938)." *Nations and Nationalism* 17, no. 1 (2011): 108–128.

Bayraktar, Hatice. "The Anti-Jewish Pogrom in Eastern Thrace in 1934: New Evidence for the Responsibility of the Turkish Government." *Patterns of Prejudice* 40, no. 2 (2006): 95–111.

Beezley, William H. *Judas at the Jockey Club and Other Episodes of Porfirian Mexico.* Lincoln: University of Nebraska Press, 1987.

Beezley, William H., and Linda A. Curcio-Nagy. "Introduction." In *Latin American Popular Culture: An Introduction.* Ed. William H. Beezley and Linda A. Curcio-Nagy, xii-xxi. New York: Rowman and Littlefield, 2000.

Bejarano, Margalit. "Constitutional Documents of Two Sephardic Communities in Latin America (Argentina and Cuba)." *Jewish Political Studies Review* 8, no. 3/4 (Fall 1996): 127–148.

———. "From All Their Habitations: Sephardic Jews in Cuba." *Judaism* 51, no. 1 (Winter 2002): 96–108.

———. "The Sephardic Communities of Latin America: A Puzzle of Subethnic Fragments." In *Contemporary Sephardic Identity in the Americas: An Interdisciplinary Approach.* Ed. Margalit Bejarano and Edna Aizenberg, 3–30. Syracuse: Syracuse University Press, 2012.

Benbassa, Esther. *Haim Nahum: A Sephardic Chief Rabbi in Politics, 1892–1923.* Translated by Miriam Kochan. Tuscaloosa: University of Alabama Press, 1995.

Benbassa, Esther, and Aron Rodrigue. *Sephardi Jewry: A History of the Judeo-Spanish Community, 14th-20th Centuries.* Berkeley: University of California Press, 2000.

Ben-Naeh, Yaron. "Moshko the Jew and His Gay Friends: Same-Sex Sexual Relations in Ottoman Jewish Society," *Journal of Early Modern History* 9, no. 1–2 (2005): 79–108.

———. "The Zionist Struggle as Reflected in the Jewish Press in Istanbul in the Aftermath of the Young Turk Revolution, 1908–1918." In *Late Ottoman Palestine: The Period of Young Turk Rule; Studies in Honor of Prof. Haim Gerber.* Ed. Yuval Ben-Bassat and Eyal Ginio, 241–257. London: I.B. Tauris, 2011.

Ben-Ur, Aviva. "Identity Imperative: Ottoman Jews in Wartime and Interwar Britain." *Immigrants and Minorities: Historical Studies in Ethnicity, Migration, and Diaspora* (2014): 1–31.

———. "In Search of the American Ladino Press: A Bibliographical Survey, 1910–1948." *Studies in Bibliography and Booklore* 21 (2001): 11–51.

———. *Sephardic Jews in America: A Diasporic History*. New York: New York University Press, 2009.

———. "Where Diasporas Met: Sephardic and Ashkenazic Jews in the City," PhD diss., Brandeis University, 1998.

Benveniste, Annie. *Le Bosphore à la Roquette: La communauté judéo-espagnole à Paris (1914–1940)*. Paris: Éditions L'Harmattan, 1989.

———. "The Judeo-Spanish Community in Paris." In *From Iberia to Diaspora: Studies in Sephardic History and Culture*. Ed. Norman A. Stillman and Yedida K. Stillman, 168–175. Leiden: Brill, 1999.

Blumi, Isa. *Ottoman Refugees, 1878–1939*. London: Bloomsbury, 2013.

Bokser de Liwerant, Judit. *Imágenes de un Encuentro: La Presencia Judía en México durante la Primera Mitad del Siglo XX*. Mexico City: UNAM, 1992.

Borovaya, Olga. *Modern Ladino Culture: Press, Belles Lettres, and Theater in the Late Ottoman Empire*. Bloomington: Indiana University Press, 2012.

Brink-Danan, Marcy. "Dangerous Cosmopolitanism: Erasing Difference in Istanbul." *Anthropology Quarterly* 84, no. 2 (2011): 439–474.

Brinkmann, Tobias. "From Immigrants to Supranational Transmigrants and Refugees: Jewish Migrants in New York and Berlin before and after the Great War." *Comparative Studies of South Asia, Africa, and the Middle East* 30, no. 1 (2010): 47–57.

Bristow, Edward. *Prostitution and Prejudice: The Jewish Fight against White Slavery, 1870–1939*. London: Schocken Books, 1983.

Brodsky, Adriana. *Sephardi, Jewish, Argentine: Community and National Identity*. Bloomington: Indiana University Press, 2016.

Brown, Jonathan C. "Foreign and Native-Born Workers in Porfirian Mexico." *The American Historical Review* 98, no. 3 (Jun. 1993): 786–818.

Brubaker, Rogers. "Migration, Membership, and the Modern Nation-State: Internal and External Dimensions of the Politics of Belonging." *Journal of Interdisciplinary History* XLI, no. 1 (Summer, 2010): 61–78.

Buchenau, Jürgen. "Small Numbers, Great Impact: Mexico and Its Immigrants, 1821–1973." *Journal of American Ethnic History* 20, no. 3 (Spring, 2001): 23–49.

Çağaptay, Soner. "Citizenship Policies in Interwar Turkey." *Nations and Nationalism* 9, no. 9 (2003): 601–619.

———. *Islam, Secularism, and Nationalism in Modern Turkey: Who is a Turk?* London: Routledge, 2006.

———. "Race, Assimilation, and Kemalism: Turkish Nationalism and the Minorities in the 1930s." *Middle Eastern Studies* 40, no. 3 (May 2004): 86–101.

Campos, Michelle U. *Ottoman Brothers: Muslims, Christians, and Jews in Early Twentieth-Century Palestine*. Stanford: Stanford University Press, 2011.

Carey, Elaine. *Women Drug Traffickers: Mules, Bosses, and Organized Crime.* Albuquerque: University of New Mexico Press, 2014.
Caron, Vicky. *Between France and Germany: The Jews of Alsace-Lorraine, 1871–1918.* Stanford: Stanford University Press, 1988.
Castiglione, Frank. "'Levantine' Dragomans in Nineteenth Century Istanbul: The Pisanis, the British, and Issues of Subjecthood." *Osmanlı Araştırmaları / The Journal of Ottoman Studies* 44 (2014): 169–195.
Cernea, Ruth Fredman. *Almost Englishmen: Baghdadi Jews in British Burma.* Lanham: Lexington Books, 2007.
Cherem, Bella. "La Integración de los Judíos Alepinos en la Historia de México." In *Los Judíos de Alepo en México.* Ed. Liz Hamui de Halabe and Fredy Charabati, 125–148. Mexico City: Magüen David, 1989.
Clark, Bruce. *Twice a Stranger: The Mass Expulsions that Forged Modern Greece and Turkey.* Cambridge: Harvard University Press, 2006.
Clifford, James. *Routes: Travels and Translation in the Late Twentieth Century.* Cambridge: Harvard University Press, 1997.
Cohen, Julia Phillips. *Becoming Ottomans: Sephardi Jews and Imperial Citizenship in the Modern Era.* Oxford: Oxford University Press, 2014.
———. "Between Civic and Islamic Ottomanism: Jewish Imperial Citizenship in the Hamidian Era." *International Journal of Middle East Studies* 44 (2012): 237–255.
———. "The East as a Career: Far Away Moses and Company in the Marketplace of Empires." *Jewish Social Studies* 21, no. 2 (Winter 2015): 35–77.
———. "Oriental by Design: Ottoman Jews, Imperial Style, and the Performance of Heritage." *American Historical Review* 119, no. 2 (April, 2014): 364–398.
Cohen, Julia Phillips, and Sarah Abrevaya Stein, "Sephardic Scholarly Worlds: Toward a Novel Geography of Modern Jewish History." *Jewish Quarterly Review* 100, no. 3 (Summer 2010): 349–384.
Criss, Nur Bilge. *Istanbul under Allied Occupation.* Leiden: Brill, 1999.
Danon, Dina. "Francos." In *Encyclopedia of Jews in the Islamic World.* Ed. Norman Stillman. Leiden: Brill, 2010. Consulted online on 8/29/2019 at https://referenceworks-brillonline-com.proxy.lib.umich.edu/entries/encyclopedia-of-jews-in-the-islamic-world/francos-SIM_000671?s.num=0&s.f.s2_parent=s.f.book.encyclopedia-of-jews-in-the-islamic-world&s.q=francos
Deal, Roger A. "War Refugees and Violence in Hamidian Istanbul." *Middle Eastern Studies* 49, no. 2 (2013): 179–190.
de Certeau, Michel. *The Practice of Everyday Life.* Berkeley: University of California Press, 1984.
Del Bravo, María Antonia. "Angel Pulido y el Sefardismo Internacional," *Hispania Sacra* 45, no. 92 (1993): 739–762.

Delgado, Manuel. "Marca y Territorio: Sobre la Hipervisibilidad de los Inmigrantes en los Espacios Públicos Urbanos." In *La Inmigración en la Sociedad Española.* Ed. Joaquín García Roca and Joan Lacomba Vázquez, 351–362. Barcelona: Ediciones Bellaterra, 2008.

DellaPergola, Sergio. "Hierarchic Levels of Subethnicity: Near Eastern Jews in the U.S., France, and Mexico." *Sociological Papers* 5, no. 2 (1996): 1–42.

———. "'Sephardic and Oriental' Jews in Israel and Western Countries: Migration, Social Change, and Identification." *Studies in Contemporary Jewry* 22 (2007): 3–43.

Deringil, Selim. "'They Live in a State of Nomadism and Savagery': The Late Ottoman Empire and the Post-Colonial Debate." *Comparative Studies in Society and History* 45, no. 2 (Apr. 2003): 311–342.

———. *The Well-Protected Domains: Ideology and the Legitimation of Power in the Ottoman Empire 1876–1909.* 2nd ed. London: I.B. Tauris, 2011.

Deutsch, Sandra McGee. *Crossing Borders, Claiming a Nation: A History of Argentine Jewish Women, 1880–1955.* Durham: Duke University Press, 2010.

Diner, Hasia R. *Roads Taken: The Great Jewish Migration to the New World and the Peddlers Who Forged the Way.* New Haven: Yale University Press, 2015.

Eissenstat, Howard Lee. "The Limits of Imagination: Debating the Nation and Constructing the State in Early Turkish Nationalism," PhD diss., UCLA, 2007.

Ekmekçioğlu, Lerna. *Recovering Armenia: The Limits of Belonging in Post-Genocide Turkey.* Stanford: Stanford University Press, 2016.

———. "Republic of Paradox: The League of Nations Minority Protection Regime and the New Turkey's Step-Citizens," *International Journal of Middle East Studies* 46 (2014): 657–679.

Elmaleh, Abraham. *Le Professeur Abraham Galante: Sa vie et ses oeuvres.* Istanbul: Kâğıt ve Basım İşleri, 1947.

El-Rouayheb, Khaled. *Before Homosexuality in the Arab-Islamic World, 1500–1800.* Chicago: University of Chicago Press, 2005.

Erickson, Edward J. *Defeat in Detail: The Ottoman Army in the Balkans, 1912–1913.* Westport, CT: Praeger, 2003.

———. "From Kirkilisse to the Great Offensive Turkish Operational Encirclement Planning, 1912–22." *Middle Eastern Studies* 40, no. 1 (Jan. 2004): 45–64.

Faber, Sebastian. *Exile and Cultural Hegemony: Spanish Intellectuals in Mexico, 1939–1975.* Nashville: Vanderbilt University Press, 2002.

Fagen, Patricia W. *Exiles and Citizens: Spanish Republicans in Mexico.* Austin: University of Texas Press, 1973.

Fahmy, Ziad. "Jurisdictional Borderlands: Extraterritoriality and 'Legal Chameleons' in Precolonial Alexandria, 1840–1870." *Comparative Studies in Society and History* 55, no. 2 (2013): 305–329.

Fahrenthold, Stacy D. *Between the Ottomans and the Entente: The First World War in the Syrian and Lebanese Diaspora, 1908–1925*. New York: Oxford University Press, 2019.

———. "Former Ottomans in the Ranks: Pro-Entente Military Recruitment among Syrians in the Americas, 1916–1918." *Journal of Global History* 11, no. 1 (March 2016): 88–112.

Fermaglich, Kirsten. *A Rosenberg by Any Other Name: A History of Jewish Name Changing in America*. New York: New York University Press, 2018.

Fink, Carole. *Defending the Rights of Others: The Great Powers, the Jews, and International Minority Protection, 1878–1938*. New York: Cambridge University Press, 2004.

Fleming, K. E. *Greece: A Jewish History*. Princeton: Princeton University Press, 2008.

Foran, John. "Race, Class, and Gender in the Making of the Mexican Revolution." *International Review of Sociology* 6, no. 1 (March, 1996): 139–156.

Frankel, Jonathan. *The Damascus Affair: Ritual Murder, Politics, and the Jews in 1840*. Cambridge: Cambridge University Press, 1997.

Freeze, ChaeRan Y. *Jewish Marriage and Divorce in Imperial Russia*. Hanover, NH: Brandeis University Press, 2002.

Friedman, Michal. "Reconquering 'Sepharad': Hispanism and Proto-Fascism in Giménez Caballero's Sephardist Crusade," *Journal of Spanish Cultural Studies* 12, no. 1 (Mar. 2011): 35–60.

Frierson, Elizabeth Brown. "Gender, Consumption, and Patriotism: The Emergence of an Ottoman Public Sphere." In *Public Islam and the Common Good*. Ed. Armando Salvatore and Dale F. Eickelman, 99–128. Leiden: Brill, 2006.

Gabaccia, Donna R. "Is Everywhere Nowhere? Nomads, Nations, and the Immigrant Paradigm of United States History." *Journal of American History* 86, no. 3 (Dec. 1999): 1115–1134.

———. *Italy's Many Diasporas*. London: University College London, 2000.

Garland, Libby. *After They Closed the Gates: Jewish Illegal Immigration to the United States, 1921–1965*. Chicago: University of Chicago Press, 2014.

———. "Not-Quite-Closed Gates: Jewish Alien Smuggling in the Post-Quota Years." *American Jewish History* 98, no. 3 (September 2008): 197–224.

Geller, Luís. *Alberto Misrachi, Galerista: Una Vida Dedicada a Promover el Arte de México*. Mexico City: Editorial Sylvia Misrachi, 1998.

Ghobrial, John-Paul A. "The Secret Life of Elias of Babylon and the Uses of Global Microhistory." *Past & Present* 222, no. 1 (Feb. 2014): 51–93.

Ginio, Eyal. "'Learning the Beautiful Language of Homer': Judeo-Spanish Speaking Jews and the Greek Language and Culture between the Wars." *Jewish History* 16, no. 2 (2002): 235–262.

———. "Mobilizing the Ottoman Nation during the Balkan Wars (1912–1913): Awakening the Ottoman Dream." *War in History* 12, no. 2 (2005): 156–177.

Gleizer, Daniela. "De la Apertura al Cierre de Puertas: La Inmigración Judía en México durante las Primeras Décadas del Siglo XX." *Historia Mexicana* 60, no. 2 (Oct.–Dec. 2010): 1175–1227.

———. *El Exilio Incómodo: México y los Refugiados Judíos, 1933–1945*. Mexico City: Centro de Estudios Históricos, 2011.

———. "Gilberto Bosques y el Consulado de México en Marsella (1940–1942)." *Estudios de Historia Moderna y Contemporánea de México* 49 (2015): 54–76.

———. "International Rescue of Academics, Intellectuals and Artists from Nazism During the Second World War: The Experience of Mexico." In *European and Latin American Social Scientists as Refugees, Émigrés and Return-Migrants*. Ed. Ludger Pries and Pablo Yankelevich, 181–203. Cham: Palgrave Macmillan, 2019.

———. "Judíos Sefardíes: De España a México a través del Imperio Otomano." In *La Ciudad Cosmopolita de los Inmigrantes*. Ed. Carlos Martínez Assad, 9–39. Mexico: Gobierno de la Ciudad de México, 2010.

———. "La Politica Mexicana frente a la Recepción de Refugiados Judíos (1934–1942). In *Mexico, País Refugio: La experiencia de los exilios en el siglo XX*. Ed. Pablo Yankelevich, 119–138. Mexico City: Conaculta, 2002.

Göçek, Fatma Müge. "The Decline of the Ottoman Empire and the Emergence of Greek, Armenian, Turkish, and Arab Nationalisms." In *Social Constructions of Nationalism in the Middle East*, ed. Fatma Müge Göçek, 15–83. Albany: State University of New York Press, 2002.

Gojman de Backal, Alicia. *Camisas, Escudos y Desfiles Militares: Los Dorados y el Antisemitismo en México (1934–1940)*. Mexico City: Fondo de Cultura Económica, 2000.

———. *Jacobo Granat: Una Vida de Contradicciones entre la Comunidad y el Cine*. Mexico City: Comunidad Ashkenazí de México, 2012.

Goldstein, Eric L. "Contesting the Categories: Jews and Government Racial Classification in the United States." *Jewish History* 19, no. 1 (2005): 79–107.

———. *The Price of Whiteness: Jews, Race, and American Identity*. Princeton: Princeton University Press, 2006.

Gómez Izquierdo, José Jorge. *El Movimiento Antichino en México (1871–1934): Problemas del Racismo y del Nacionalismo durante la Revolución Mexicana*. Mexico City: Instituto Nacional de Antropología e Historia, 1992.

González, Fredy. *Paisanos Chinos: Transpacific Politics among Chinese Immigrants in Mexico*. Berkeley: University of California Press, 2017.

Gonzalez, Michael J. "Imagining Mexico in 1910: Visions of the *Patria* in the Centennial Celebration in Mexico City." *Journal of Latin American Studies* 39, no. 3 (Aug. 2007): 495–533.

Gratien, Chris, and Emily K. Pope-Ojeda. "Ottoman Migrants, U.S. Deportation

Law, and Statelessness during the Interwar Era." *Mashriq & Mahjar* 5, no. 2 (2018): 125–158.

Gualtieri, Sarah. *Between Arab and White: Race and Ethnicity in the Early Syrian American Diaspora.* Berkeley: University of California Press, 2009.

———. "Gendering the Chain Migration Thesis: Women and Syrian Transatlantic Migration, 1878–1924." *Comparative Studies of South Asia, Africa, and the Middle East* 24, no. 1 (2004): 67–78.

Guerin-Gonzales, Camille. *Mexican Workers and American Dreams: Immigration, Repatriation, and California Farm Labor, 1900–1939.* New Brunswick: Rutgers University Press, 1994.

Gutman, David. "Agents of Mobility: Migrant Smuggling Networks, Transhemispheric Migration, and Time-Space Compression in Ottoman Anatolia, 1888–1908." *InterDisciplines* 1 (2012): 48–84.

———. "Armenian Migration to North and South America, State Power, and Local Politics in the Late Ottoman Empire." *Comparative Studies of South Asia, Africa, and the Middle East* 34, no. 1 (2014): 176–190.

———. "Migrants, Revolutionaries, and Spies: Surveillance, Politics, and Ottoman Identity in the United States." In *Living in the Ottoman Realm: Empire and Identity, 13th–20th Centuries.* Ed. Christine Isom-Verhaaren and Kent E. Schull, 284–296. Bloomington: Indiana University Press, 2016.

Guttstadt, Corry. *Turkey, the Jews, and the Holocaust.* Cambridge: Cambridge University Press, 2013.

Guy, Donna L. *Sex and Danger in Buenos Aires: Prostitution, Family, and Nation in Argentina.* Lincoln: University of Nebraska Press, 1990.

Hamui de Halabe, Liz. *Identidad Colectiva: Rasgos Culturales de los Inmigrantes Judeo-Alepinos en México.* Mexico City: JGH Editores, 1997.

———. *Transformaciones en la Religiosidad de los Judíos en México: Tradición, Ortodoxia y Fundamentalismo en la Modernidad Tardía.* Mexico City: Grupo Noriega Editores, 2005.

Hamui de Halabe, Liz, and Fredy Charabati. *Los Judíos de Alepo en México.* Mexico City: Magúen David, 1989.

Hanley, Will. *Identifying with Nationality: Europeans, Ottomans, and Egyptians in Alexandria.* New York: Columbia University Press, 2017.

Harel, Yaron. "The Rise and Fall of the Jewish Consuls in Aleppo." *Turcica* 38 (2006): 233–250.

Havassy, Rivka. "Con el Tiempo y Progreso (With Time and Progress): The Sephardi Cantigas at the Dawn of the Twentieth Century." *European Judaism* 44, no. 1 (Spring 2011): 121–135.

Heinze, Andrew R. *Adapting to Abundance: Jewish Immigrants, Mass Consumption, and the Search for American Identity.* New York: Columbia University Press, 1990.

Hernández, José Angel. "From Conquest to Colonization: Indios and Colonization Policies after Mexican Independence." *Mexican Studies/Estudios Mexicanos* 26, no. 2 (Summer 2010): 291–322.

Hirschon, Renée. "Consequences of the Lausanne Convention: An Overview." In *Crossing the Aegean: An Appraisal of the 1923 Compulsory Population Exchange between Turkey and Greece*. Ed. Renée Hirschon, 13–22. New York: Berghahn Books, 2003.

Hobbs, Allyson. *A Chosen Exile: A History of Racial Passing in American Life*. Cambridge: Harvard University Press, 2014.

Hyland, Jr., Steven. *More Argentine than You: Arabic-Speaking Immigrants in Argentina*. Albuquerque: University of New Mexico Press, 2017.

İçduygu, Ahmet, Yılmaz Çolak, and Nalan Soyarık. "What Is the Matter with Citizenship? A Turkish Debate." *Middle Eastern Studies* 35, no. 4 (Oct. 1999): 187–208.

İçduygu, Ahmet, and Özlem Kaygusuz. "The Politics of Citizenship by Drawing Borders: Foreign Policy and the Construction of National Citizenship Identity in Turkey." *Middle Eastern Studies* 40, no. 6 (Nov. 2004): 26–50.

İpek, Nedim, and K. Tuncer Çağlayan. "The Emigration from the Ottoman Empire to America." In *Turkish Migration to the United States: From Ottoman Times to the Present*. Ed. A. Deniz Balgamış and Kemal H. Karpat, 29–45. Madison: University of Wisconsin Press, 2008.

Isyar, Bora. "The Origins of Turkish Republican Citizenship: The Birth of Race." *Nations and Nationalism* 11, no. 3 (2005): 343–360.

Jacoby, Karl. *The Strange Career of William Ellis: The Texas Slave Who Became a Mexican Millionaire*. New York: Norton, 2016.

Joselit, Jenna Weissman. *The Wonders of America: Reinventing Jewish Culture, 1880–1950*. New York: Hill and Wang, 1994.

Kalderon, Albert E. *Abraham Galanté: A Biography*. New York: Sepher-Hermon Press, 1983.

Karpat, Kemal. "The Ottoman Emigration to America, 1860–1914." *International Journal of Middle East Studies* 17 (May 1985): 175–209.

———. *The Politicization of Islam: Reconstructing Identity, State, Faith, and Community in the Late Ottoman State*. New York: Oxford University Press, 2001.

Kasaba, Reşat. "Dreams of Empire, Dreams of Nation." In *Empire to Nation: Historical Perspectives on the Making of the Modern World*. Ed. Joseph W. Esherick, Hasan Kayalı, and Eric Van Young, 198–225. Lanham, MD: Rowman and Littlefield Publishers, 2006.

Kayalı, Hasan. *Arabs and Young Turks: Ottomanism, Arabism, and Islamism in the Ottoman Empire, 1908–1918*. Berkeley: University of California Press, 1997.

Kerem, Yitzchak. "The Migration of Rhodean Jews to Africa, 1900–1914." *Jewish Affairs* 61, no. 3 (Sept. 2006): 18–21.

Khater, Akram Fouad. *Inventing Home: Emigration, Gender, and the Middle Class in Lebanon, 1870–1920*. Berkeley: University of California Press, 2001.
King, Charles. *Midnight at the Pera Palace: The Birth of Modern Istanbul*. New York: Norton, 2014.
Klich, Ignacio. "Argentine-Ottoman Relations and Their Impact on Immigrants from the Middle East: A History of Unfulfilled Expectations, 1910–1915." *The Americas* 50, no. 2 (Oct. 1993): 177–205.
Klich, Ignacio, and Jeffrey Lesser. "'Turco' Immigrants in Latin America." *The Americas* 53, no. 1 (July 1996): 1–14.
Kobrin, Rebecca. *Jewish Bialystok and Its Diaspora*. Bloomington: Indiana University Press, 2010.
Koçak, Cemil. "Ayın Karanlık Yüzü: Tek-Parti Döneminde Gayri Müslim Azınlıklar Aleyhinde Açılan Türklüğü Tahkir Davaları." *Tarih ve Toplum Yeni Yaklaşımlar* 1 (March, 2005): 147–208.
Köroğlu, Erol. *Ottoman Propaganda and Turkish Identity: Literature in Turkey during World War I*. London: Taurus Academic Studies, 2007.
Krause, Corinne. *Los Judíos en México: Una Historia con Énfasis Especial en el Periodo de 1857 a 1930*. Mexico: Universidad Iberoamericana, 1987.
———. "Mexico—Another Promised Land? A Review of Projects for Jewish Colonization in Mexico: 1881–1925." *American Jewish Historical Quarterly* 61, no. 4 (June 1972): 325–341.
Kreiser, Klaus. "Turban and Türban: 'Divider between Belief and Unbelief.' A Political History of Modern Turkish Costume." *European Review* 13, no. 3 (2005): 447–458.
Kuehnert, Lore Diana. "Pernicious Foreigners and Contested Compatriots: Mexican Newspaper Debates over Immigration, Emigration, and Repatriation, 1928–1936." PhD diss., University of California, Riverside, 2002.
Landau, J. M. *Tekinalp, Turkish Patriot, 1883–1961*. Istanbul: Nederlands Historisch-Archaeologisch Instituut, 1984.
Lear, John. "Mexico City: Space and Class in the Porfirian Capital, 1884–1910." *Journal of Urban History* 22 (1996): 454–490.
Lee, Erika. "Enforcing the Borders: Chinese Exclusion along the U.S. Borders with Canada and Mexico, 1882–1924." *Journal of American History* 89, no. 1 (Jun. 2002): 54–86.
Lehmann, Matthias B. *Emissaries from the Holy Land: The Sephardic Diaspora and the Practice of Pan-Judaism in the Eighteenth Century*. Stanford: Stanford University Press, 2014.
———. "Rethinking Sephardi Identity: Jews and Other Jews in Ottoman Palestine." *Jewish Social Studies* 15, no. 1 (Fall, 2008): 81–109.
Lesser, Jeffrey. "(Re)Creating Ethnicity: Middle Eastern Immigration to Brazil." *The Americas* 53, no. 1 (July 1996): 45–65.

Levi, Avner. "1934 Trakya Yahudileri Olayı: Alınamayan Ders." *Tarih ve Toplum* 151 (Jul. 1994): 10–17.

———. "The Jewish Press in Turkey." In *Jewish Journalism and Printing Houses in the Ottoman Empire and Modern Turkey*. Ed. Gad Nassi, 13–27. Istanbul: Isis Press, 2001.

Levy, Avigdor. "Introduction." In *The Jews of the Ottoman Empire*. Ed. Avigdor Levy, 1–149. Princeton, N.J.: The Darwin Press, 1994.

———. "The Siege of Edirne (1912–1913) as Seen by a Jewish Eyewitness: Social, Political, and Cultural Perspectives." In *Jews, Turks, Ottomans: A Shared History, Fifteenth Through the Twentieth Century*. Ed. Avigdor Levy, 153–193. Syracuse, NY: Syracuse University Press, 2002.

Lewis, Geoffrey. *The Turkish Language Reform: A Catastrophic Success*. Oxford: Oxford University Press, 1999.

Lohr, Eric. *Russian Citizenship: From Empire to Soviet Union*. Cambridge: Harvard University Press, 2012.

Lomnitz, Claudio. "Anti-Semitism and the Ideology of the Mexican Revolution." *Representations* 110, no. 1 (Spring 2010): 1–28.

Macadar, Marquesa. "Sephardic Diaspora: A Case Study in Latin America." PhD diss., Indiana University, 2009.

MacLachlan, Colin M., and William H. Beezley. *El Gran Pueblo: A History of Greater Mexico*, 3rd Ed. Upper Saddle River: Prentice Hall, 2004.

Malinovich, Nadia. *French and Jewish: Culture and the Politics of Identity in Early Twentieth-Century France*. Oxford: The Littman Library of Jewish Civilization, 2008.

Manela, Erez. *The Wilsonian Moment: Self-Determination and the International Origins of Anticolonial Nationalism*. Oxford: Oxford University Press, 2007.

Marglin, Jessica. "The Two Lives of Mas'ud Amoyal: Pseudo-Algerians in Morocco, 1830–1912." *International Journal of Middle East Studies* 44, no. 4 (Nov. 2012): 651–670.

Massad, Joseph A. *Desiring Arabs*. Chicago: University of Chicago Press, 2007.

Mays, Devi. "'I Killed Her Because I Loved Her Too Much': Gender and Violence in the 20th Century Sephardi Diaspora." *Mashriq and Mahjar* 2, no. 1 (2014): 4–28.

———. "Recounting the Past, Shaping the Future: Ladino Literary Responses to World War War." In *World War I and the Jews*. Ed. Marsha Rozenblit and Jonathan Karp, 201–221. New York: Berghahn Books, 2017.

Mazower, Mark. *Salonika: City of Ghosts*. New York: Vintage Books, 2004.

McCaa, Robert. "Missing Millions: The Demographic Costs of the Mexican Revolution." *Mexican Studies/Estudios Mexicanos* 19, no. 2 (Summer, 2003): 367–400.

McKeown, Adam M. *Melancholy Order: Asian Migration and the Globalization of Borders*. New York: Columbia University Press, 2008.

Mendelsohn, Adam. *The Rag Race: How Jews Sewed Their Way to Success in America and the British Empire*. New York: New York University Press, 2014.

Meron, Orly C. *Jewish Entrepreneurship in Salonica, 1912–1940: An Ethnic Economy in Transition*. Brighton: Sussex Academic Press, 2011.

Molho, Rena. "The Jewish Community of Salonika and Its Incorporation into the Greek State, 1912–1919." *Middle Eastern Studies* 24, no. 4 (Oct. 1988): 391–403.

———. "Popular Antisemitism and State Policy in Salonika during the City's Annexation to Greece." *Jewish Social Studies* 50, no. 3/4 (Summer 1988–Autumn 1993): 253–264.

Monsiváis, Carlos. "Notas sobre Cultura Popular en México." *Latin American Perspectives* 5, no. 1 (1978): 98–118.

Morson, Gary Saul. *Narrative and Freedom: The Shadows of Time*. New Haven: Yale University Press, 2007.

Naar, Devin. "Between 'New Greece' and the 'New World': Salonikan Jewish Immigration to America." *Journal of the Hellenic Diaspora* 35, no. 2 (Fall 2009): 45–89.

———. "From the 'Jerusalem of the Balkans' to the 'Goldene Medina': Jewish Immigration from Salonika to the United States." *American Jewish History* 93, no. 2 (Dec. 2007): 435–473.

———. "A Guidebook for Sephardi Immigrants." https://jewishstudies.washington.edu/sephardic-studies/a-guide-for-sephardic-immigrants. Accessed 9/10/2019.

———. "Turkinos beyond the Empire: Ottoman Jews in America, 1893 to 1924." *Jewish Quarterly Review* 105, no. 2 (Spring 2015): 174–205.

Nail, Thomas. *The Figure of the Migrant*. Stanford: Stanford University Press, 2015.

Najar, José D. "The Privileges of Positivist Whiteness: The Syrian-Lebanese of São Paulo, Brazil (1888–1939)." PhD diss., Indiana University, 2012.

Najmabadi, Afsaneh. *Women with Moustaches and Men without Beards: Gender and Sexual Anxieties of Iranian Modernity*. Berkeley: University of California Press, 2005.

Nassi, Gad. *Jewish Journalism and Printing Houses in the Ottoman Empire and Modern Turkey*. Istanbul: Isis Press, 2001.

Needell, Jeffrey D. *A Tropical Belle Epoque: Elite Culture and Society in Turn-of-the-Century Rio de Janeiro*. Cambridge: Cambridge University Press, 1987.

Neuberger, Mary C. *Balkan Smoke: Tobacco and the Making of Modern Bulgaria*. Ithaca: Cornell University Press, 2013.

Neyzi, Leyla. "Trauma, Narrative and Silence: The Military Journal of a Jewish 'Soldier' in Turkey during the Greco-Turkish War." *Turcica* 35 (April 2003): 291–313.

Norris, Jacob. "Exporting the Holy Land: Artisans and Merchant Migrants in Ottoman-Era Bethlehem." *Mashriq & Mahjar* 2 (2013): 14–40.

Odman, Aslı. "Meksika'daki Osmanlı Saat Kulesi." *Toplumsal Tarih* 167 (Nov. 2007): 44–51.

Ojeda Revah, Mario. *Mexico and the Spanish Civil War: Political Repercussions for the Republican Cause*. Brighton: Sussex Academic Press, 2015.

Olsen, Patrice Elizabeth. "Revolution in the City Streets: Changing Nomenclature, Changing Form, and the Revision of Public Memory." In *The Eagle and the Virgin: Nation and Cultural Revolution in Mexico, 1920–1940*. Ed. Mary Kay Vaughan and Stephen E. Lewis, 119–134. Durham: Duke University Press, 2006.

Ong, Aihwa. *Flexible Citizenship: The Cultural Logics of Transnationality*. Durham: Duke University Press, 1999.

Orlove, Benjamin, and Arnold J. Bauer. "Giving Importance to Imports." In *The Allure of the Foreign: Imported Goods in Postcolonial Latin America*. Ed. Benjamin Orlove, 1–30. Ann Arbor: University of Michigan Press, 1997.

Orsi, Robert A. *The Madonna of 115th Street: Faith and Community in Italian Harlem, 1880–1950*, 3rd ed. New Haven: Yale University Press, 2010.

Özsu, Umut. "Fabricating Fidelity: Nation-Building, International Law, and the Greek-Turkish Population Exchange." *Leiden Journal of International Law* 24 (2011): 823–847.

Papo, Eliezer. *Ve-hitalta le-vinkha ba-yom ha-hu: Paradyot Sefaradiyot-Yehudiyot 'al ha-Hagadah shel Pesah*, Vols. I and II. Jerusalem: Ben Zvi Institute, 2012.

Papo, Joseph M. *Sephardim in Twentieth Century America: In Search of Unity*. San Jose: Pele Yoetz Books, 1987.

Pastor, Camila. *The Mexican Mahjar: Transnational Maronites, Jews, and Arabs under the French Mandate*. Austin: University of Texas Press, 2017.

Peña Delgado, Grace. *Making the Chinese Mexican: Global Migration, Localism, and Exclusion in the U.S.-Mexico Borderlands*. Stanford: Stanford University Press, 2012.

Pérez de Cohen, Rosalynda, Simonette Levy de Behar, and Sophie Bejarano de Goldberg. *Sefarad de Ayer, Oy i Manyana: Presencia Sefardí en México*. Mexico City: n.p., 2010.

Piccato, Pablo. *City of Suspects: Crime in Mexico City, 1900–1931*. Durham: Duke University Press, 2001.

———. *The Tyranny of Opinion: Honor in the Construction of the Mexican Public Sphere*. Durham: Duke University Press, 2010.

Pilcher, Jeffrey M. "Many Chefs in the National Kitchen: Cookbooks and Identity in Nineteenth-Century Mexico." In *Latin American Popular Culture*. Ed.

William H. Beezley and Linda A. Curcio-Nagy, 123–137. New York: Rowman and Littlefield, 2000.

Pollard, Lisa. *Nurturing the Nation: The Family Politics of Modernizing, Colonizing, and Liberating Egypt, 1905–1923*. Berkeley: University of California Press, 2005.

Portes, Alejandro, Luis Eduardo Guarnizo, and William J. Haller. "Transnational Entrepreneurs: An Alternative Form of Immigrant Economic Adaptation." *American Sociological Review* 67, no. 2 (Apr. 2002): 278–298.

Powell, T. G. "Mexican Intellectuals and the Indian Question, 1876–1911." *The Hispanic American Historical Review* 48, no. 1 (Feb. 1968): 19–36.

Qafisheh, Mutaz M. "The International Law Foundations of Palestinian Nationality: A Legal Examination of Palestinian Nationality under the British Rule." PhD diss., Université de Genève, 2007.

Quataert, Donald. *The Ottoman Empire, 1700–1922*. Cambridge: Cambridge University Press, 2005.

Razek, Rana. "Trails and Fences: Syrian Migration Networks and Immigration Restriction, 1885–1911." *Amerasia Journal* 44, no. 1 (2018): 105–126.

Reill, Dominique. *The Fiume Crisis: Surviving in the Wake of the Habsburg Empire*. Cambridge: Harvard University Press, forthcoming.

Robson, Laura. *States of Separation: Transfer, Partition, and the Making of the Modern Middle East*. Oakland: University of California Press, 2017.

Rodrigue, Aron. *French Jews, Turkish Jews: The Alliance Israélite Universelle and the Politics of Jewish Schooling in Turkey, 1860–1925*. Bloomington: Indiana University Press, 1990.

———. "Jewish Enlightenment and Nationalism in the Ottoman Balkans: Barukh Mitrani in Edirne in the Second Half of the Nineteenth Century." *Princeton Papers: Interdisciplinary Journal of Middle Eastern Studies* 12 (2005): 127–143.

———. "Jewish Society and Schooling in a Thracian Town: The Alliance Israélite Universelle in Demotica, 1897–1924." *Jewish Social Studies* 45, no. 3/4 (Summer–Autumn 1983): 263–286.

Rohr, Isabelle. "'Spaniards of the Jewish Type': Philosephardism in the Service of Imperialism in Early Twentieth-Century Spanish Morocco." *Journal of Spanish Cultural Studies* 12, no. 1 (Mar. 2011): 61–75.

Romero, Robert Chao. *The Chinese in Mexico, 1882–1940*. Tucson: University of Arizona Press, 2010.

Rosenberg, Clifford. *Policing Paris: The Origins of Immigration Control between the Wars*. Ithaca: Cornell University Press, 2006.

Sáenz Rovner, Eduardo. *The Cuban Connection: Drug Trafficking, Smuggling, and Gambling in Cuba from the 1920s to the Revolution*. Chapel Hill: University of North Carolina Press, 2008.

Sánchez, George J. *Becoming Mexican American: Ethnicity, Culture, and Identity in Chicano Los Angeles, 1900–1945*. Oxford: Oxford University Press, 1993.

Schiavone Camacho, Julia María. *Chinese Mexicans: Transpacific Migration and the Search for a Homeland, 1910–1960*. Chapel Hill: University of North Carolina Press, 2012.

Schuler, Friedrich E. *Mexico between Hitler and Roosevelt: Mexican Foreign Relations in the Age of Lázaro Cárdenas, 1934–1940*. Albuquerque: University of New Mexico Press, 1998.

Schuster, Paulette Kershenovich. *The Syrian Jewish Community in Mexico City in a Comparative Context: Between a Rock and a Hard Place*. Saarbrücken: Lambert Academic Publishing, 2012.

Şeni, Nora, and Sophie Le Tarnec. *Les Camondo ou l'éclipse d'une fortune*. Paris: Acte Sud-Hébraica, 1997.

Smith, Marian L. "Race, Nationality, and Reality: I.N.S. Administration of Racial Provisions in U.S. Immigration and Nationality Law since 1898." *Prologue: Quarterly of the National Archives and Records Administration* 34, no. 2 (Summer 2002).

Stabb, Martin S. "Indigenism and Racism in Mexican Thought: 1857–1911." *Journal of Inter-American Studies* 1, no. 4 (Oct. 1959): 405–423.

Stein, Sarah Abrevaya. "Citizens of a Fictional Nation: Ottoman-Born Jews in France during the First World War." *Past & Present* 226 (2015): 227–254.

———. *Extraterritorial Dreams: European Citizenship, Sephardi Jews, and the Ottoman Twentieth Century*. Chicago: University of Chicago Press, 2016.

———. *Making Jews Modern: The Yiddish and Ladino Press in the Russian and Ottoman Empires*. Bloomington: Indiana University Press, 2004.

———. "Protected Persons? The Baghdadi Jewish Diaspora, the British State, and the Persistence of Empire." *American Historical Review* 116, no. 1 (Feb. 2011): 80–108.

Strauss, Leo. "Persecution and the Art of Writing." *Social Research* 82, no. 1 (2015): 79–97.

Tawil, Randa. "Racial Borderlines: Ameen Rihani, Mexico, and World War I." *Amerasia* 44, no. 1 (2018): 85–104.

Tenorio-Trillo, Mauricio. "1910 Mexico City: Space and Nation in the City of the Centenario." *Journal of Latin American Studies* 28, no. 1 (Feb. 1996): 75–104.

———. *I Speak of the City: Mexico at the Turn of the Twentieth Century*. Chicago: University of Chicago Press, 2012.

———. *Mexico at the World's Fairs: Crafting a Modern Nation*. Berkeley: University of California Press, 1996.

Toktaş, Şule, and Fatih Resul Kılınç. "Jewish Immigration to the American Continent." *The Journal of Migration Studies* 4, no. 1 (Jan.–June 2018): 30–64.

Topik, Steven C. "When Mexico Had the Blues: A Transatlantic Tale of Bonds, Bankers, and Nationalists, 1862–1910." *The American Historical Review* 105, no. 3 (Jun. 2000): 714–38.

Toprak, Zafer. "Nationalism and Economics in the Young Turk Era (1908–1918)." In *Industrialisation, Communication, et Rapports Sociaux en Turquie et en Mediterranée Orientale*. Ed. Jacques Thobie and Salgur Kançal, 259–266. Paris: L'Harmattan, 1991.

Torpey, John. *The Invention of the Passport: Surveillance, Citizenship, and the State*. Cambridge: Cambridge University Press, 2000.

Truzzi, Oswaldo M. S. "At the Right Place at the Right Time: Syrians and Lebanese in Brazil and the United States, a Comparative Approach." *Journal of American Ethnic History* 16, no. 2 (Winter 1997): 3–34.

Uluengin, Mehmet Bengü. "Secularizing Anatolia Tick by Tick: Clock Towers in the Ottoman Empire and the Turkish Republic." *International Journal of Middle East Studies* 42 (2010): 17–36.

Ülker, Erol. "Foreign Capital, Allied Occupation, and Class Politics in Istanbul: Constantinople Tramways and Electric Company." Paper presented at Middle East Studies Association, Washington, DC, November 2014.

Van Schendel, Willem. "Spaces of Engagement: How Borderlands, Illicit Flows, and Territorial States Interlock." In *Illicit Flows and Criminal Things: States, Borders, and the Other Side of Globalization*. Ed. Willem van Schendel and Itty Abraham, 38–68. Bloomington: Indiana University Press, 2005.

Vincent, Isabel. *Bodies and Souls: The Tragic Plight of Three Jewish Women Forced into Prostitution in the Americas*. New York: Harper Perennial Press, 2006.

Watenpaugh, Keith. "Between Communal Survival and National Aspiration: Armenian Genocide Refugees, the League of Nations, and the Practices of Interwar Humanitarianism." *Humanity* 5, no. 2 (Summer 2014): 159–181.

———. "The League of Nations' Rescue of Armenian Genocide Survivors and the Making of Modern Humanitarianism, 1920–1927." *American Historical Review* (Dec. 2010): 1315–1339.

Weiner, Richard. "Battle for Survival: Porfirian Views of the International Marketplace." *Journal of Latin American Studies* 32, no. 3 (Oct. 2000): 645–670.

Weis, Robert. "Immigrant Entrepreneurs, Bread, and Class Negotiation in Postrevolutionary Mexico City." *Mexican Studies/Estudios Mexicanos* 25, no. 1 (Winter 2009): 71–100.

Yankelevich, Pablo. *¿Deseables o Inconvenientes? Las Fronteras de la Extranjería en el México Posrevolucionario*. Mexico: Bonilla Artigas Editores, 2011.

———. "Explotadores, Truhanes, Agitadores y Negros: Deportaciones y Restricciones a Estadounidenses en el México Revolucionario." *Historia Mexicana* 57, no. 4 (Apr.–Jun. 2008): 1155–1199.

———. "Extranjeros Indeseables en México (1911–1940): Una Aproximación Cuantitativa a la Aplicación del Artículo 33 Constitucional." *Historia Mexicana* 53, no. 3 (Jan.–Mar. 2004): 693–744.

Yerasimos, Hélène and Stéphane. "Rêves et cauchemars d'une ville perdue." In *Istanbul, 1914–1923: Capitale d'un monde illusoire ou l'agonie des vieux empires*. Ed. Stéphane Yerasimos, 133–153. Paris: Éditions Autremont, 1992.

Yerasimos, Stéphane. "Jeunes et Vieux Turcs dans la tourmente." In *Istanbul, 1914–1923: Capitale d'un monde illusoire ou l'agonie des vieux empires*. Ed. Stéphane Yerasimos, 154–170. Paris: Éditions Autremont, 1992.

Young, Elliott. *Alien Nation: Chinese Migration in the Americas from the Coolie Era through World War II*. Chapel Hill: University of North Carolina Press, 2014.

Zahra, Tara. *The Great Departure: Mass Migration from Eastern Europe and the Making of the Free World*. New York: Norton, 2016.

———. "The 'Minority Problem' and National Classification in the French and Czechoslovak Borderlands." *Contemporary European History* 17, no. 2 (May 2008): 137–165.

Ze'evi, Dror. *Producing Desire: Changing Sexual Discourse in the Ottoman Middle East, 1500–1900*. Berkeley: University of California Press, 2006.

Zolberg, Aristide. *A Nation by Design: Immigration Policy in the Fashioning of America*. Cambridge: Harvard University Press, 2006.

Zuccolo, Luca. "Gli italiani all'estero: Il caso otomano." *Diacronie: Studi de Storia Contemporanea* 5, no. 1 (2011): 9–12.

Zürcher, Erik J. "Little Mehmet in the Desert: The Ottoman Soldier's Experience." In *Facing Armageddon: The First World War Experienced*. Ed. Hugh Cecil and Peter H. Liddle, 230–241. London: Leo Cooper, 1996.

———. "The Ottoman Conscription System in Theory and Practice." In *Arming the State: Military Conscription in the Middle East and Central Asia, 1775–1925*. Ed. Erik J. Zürcher. London: I.B. Tauris, 1999.

INDEX

abono. See peddling
Abuof, Isaac, 47–48
Agudat Bnai Israel, 109
Alazraki, Leon, 43, 46, 220, 257n104
Alazraki, Moïse, 210, 220
Aleppan Jews, 14
Al Ettehad, 77
Alfassa, Moshe, 167–68
Algranati, Isaac, 33
Alianza Monte Sinaí, 120
Al-Jawater, 81
Alliance Israélite Universelle (AIU): elevation of French culture and, 36; Jewish refugees and, 62; minority protections and, 156; Ottoman military service and, 64, 67; support of migration and, 36; waning power of, 113
Álvarez, José, 180–81
Anatolia, 28, 30, 58, 67, 103, 116, 122, 126, 146, 154. *See also* Ottoman Empire
anti-Semitism, 141, 186–87, 227
Antoinette, Marie, 39, 43, 79–80
Arditi, Victoria, 189
Argentina, 36, 76, 124
Armenia, 103, 113

Armenian genocide, 146
Armenians, 28, 189
Arriola, Angelina, 175
Asher, Maurice, 87
Ashkenazi Jews: as a distinct community, 13–14; illegal entry into the US and, 163–64; migration to Mexico and, 126–27; tension with Sephardi Jews and, 117–18
Asociación de Comerciantes Israelitas en Pequeños, 200
Asociación Israelita de Aboneros, 200
Asociación Regional de Comerciantes e Industriales Mexicanos, 199
Assael, Albert, 38–39, 43, 45
Assael, Eduardo, 228–29
Assael, Esther, 228–29
Assael, Isaco (Ico), 22–23, 30, 39, 45, 120, 126, 134–35
Assael, Israel (Isidoro), 39, 43, 134–36
Assael, Johanan (Juan), 39, 43, 78–79
Assael, Mauricio: bankruptcy and, 209; children of, 131; clothing of, 21–22, 41; conflict with Marie Antoinette and, 80; Enemy Trading List and, 83;

immigration of, 39; Mexican citizenship and, 43, 89–93, 127–28, 130, 210, 214; philanthropy and, 120, 127–30; store robbery and, 133
Assael, Sara, 229
Assael family, 23, 39, 43, 45–46, 50, 78–79
Association cultuelle oriental Israélite de Paris, 70
Averof (ship), 103
Avigdor, Albert, 159–61
Ávila-Camacho, Manuel, 227
Azicri, Salvador, 209–10

Babany, Mordo, 175
Balli, Menahem, 173, 188
bananas, 3
Barsimantov, David, 87
Beaulieu, Anatole Leroy, 185
Becherano family, 206–7
Behar, Isaac, 211
Behmoiras, Lina, 189
Bejarano, Haim, 114, 116
Belleli, Moises, 240–41
belonging, 8–10, 18–19, 23, 55, 99, 102, 129–34, 139, 182
Bemaras, Elias, 173
Benbassa, Esther, 13
Benbassat, Denise, 74
Beneviste, Isaac, 83, 91
Benezra, Nissim, 109
Ben Ghiat, Alexandre, 65–66, 105–8, 110–11, 113
Ben Ghiat, Moses, 31–33
Benuzillo, Jacques, 221–22
Benveniste, Guy, 228
Benveniste, Isaac, 43
Benveniste, Mauricio, 174
Bey, Rahmi, 106, 108
birth certificates: doctoring of, 54, 100; Fresco, Mauricio and, 215–16
B'nai B'rith: anti-Jewish agitation and, 200; *Caisse de Petits Prêts* and, 118–19;

financial assistance to migrants and, 122–23; integration of Jews into Mexico and, 163–64; Jewish colonies and, 171; members of, 160; migrant aid in Mexico and, 125
Bosques, Gilberto, 229–30, 233
Brinkmann, Tobias, 8
bureaucratic institutions: research and, 17; social identity and, 16

Cadranel, Mathilde, 166
Cadranel, Nissim, 166
Caisse de Petits Prêts, 118–19
Calles, Plutarco Elías, 171, 176, 180–81, 197
Cámara Israelita de Industría y Comerico de México (CIICM), 200–202, 208, 227
Cámara Nacional de Comerico, 197–99
Campaña Nacionalista de Labor, 198
Campaña Nacionalista del Estado de Puebla, 199
Canada, 239
capitulation agreements, 28–29, 37, 49, 59, 105, 143
Capon, Isaac, 42–43, 45–46, 75–76, 85, 95, 120, 125, 164, 171, 214
Capon, Mathilde, 120, 214
Carasso, Saul, 42–43, 45, 120, 228
Cárdenas, Lázaro, 200, 220, 227
Carillo, Lárazo, 173
Carranza, Venustiano, 72, 74, 90, 97, 169
Casino Árabe, 81
Casino Turco, 51, 81
Castro, Salomon, 43
Cazés, Albert, 182–83, 191–92
Central Powers, 81
Central Reconstruction Committee of Constantinople, 116–17
Centro Mercantil de Pieles y Calzados, 199
Chevet Ahim, 77
Chicorel, Moreno, 165
citizenship: changing of nationality and,

28, 210; defining, 23; meaning of, 244; and nationality, 146; Ottoman, 28
Clark, Mary Menier, 240
class, 13, 63–64, 194–95
Cloak List, 83, 85
clothing: clothes-switching and, 21–23; fez, 21, 23, 111; importing of to Mexico, 135–36
Cohen, Benjamin, 173
Cohen, Julia Phillips, 208
Cohen, Moises, 207
Cohen, Santiago, 210
Cohen, Sara, 194
Cohen, Victor, 172
colonia otomana, 93, 128
Colombia, 48
Comerciantes en Pequeño Mercado La Amerika Lagunilla, 198
Comité Anti-Chino, 176
Comité Central Israelita, 227
Comité Nacionalista, 198
Comité Patriótico Otomano, 50–51
Comité Permanente Pro-México de Afuera, 197
Comité Pro-Raza, 200
Comité Pro Refugiados, 227
Committee of Union and Progress (CUP), 58–59
Conesa, María, 180–81
Constantinople: Allied blockade of the Dardanelles and, 105; Allied forces administration of, 102–7, 110; cost of living and, 112–13; foreign aid and, 113–18; Jewish refugees and, 62, 114–15, 118; Jewish subgroups in, 113–17; outbreaks of disease and, 115. *See also* Istanbul
Corkidhi, Benjamin, 85–86, 92
Corri, Rachel, 21–22, 39, 41, 209
Couriel, Alberto, 169–70
Couriel, Jacques, 87–88, 169–70
Couriel, Julia, 169
Cristero Rebellion, 180

Cuba, 29, 54, 77, 124, 141
Cuenca, Samuel, 173
Cumhuriyet, 157, 187

de la Huerta, Adolfo, 169
DellaPergola, Sergio, 162
denaturalization, 121, 187–92
Departamento Confidencial, 202
d'Espèrey, Franchet, 102
diaspora, 5–7, 15, 47, 123–24, 160, 168, 244–45
Díaz, Porfirio, 24, 40–41, 55, 71, 94, 256n95
Disease Act, 42
dissimulation, 24
Dışişleri Bakanlığı (ministry of foreign affairs), 17
Drancy internment camp, 225

Effendi, Isak, 186
El Democrata, 134–35
El Djugeton, 107
El Excelsior, 231
El Gráfico, 203
El Hijo de Ahuizote, 72
Elkus, Abram, 84
El Meseret, 31–33, 35, 64, 67–68, 105
Elnecave, Jacobo, 212
Elnecave brothers, 83–85
Elnekave, Estrea, 156
Elnekave, Salomon, 156
El Sábado Secreto, 38
El Tiempo: estate claimants and, 138–39; Jewish patriotism and, 157–58; Ottoman war effort and, 56–57, 70; post war emigration and, 122; prisoners of war and, 66; publisher of, 1; religious minorities and, 155; shuttering of, 187; WWI press censorship and, 105
El Universal, 128, 203
Emergency Quota Act (1921), 124, 153, 161

Emergency Refugee Committee, 171
emigration, 5, 26–29, 66–69, 122
Enemy Trading List, 83, 86
Entente Powers, 81–83, 103, 108, 110–11
Ergas, Alberto, 167–68
Eskenazi, Belinda Cadranel de, 166
Esteva, Gonzalo, 48–49
Estrada, Genaro, 179, 222
Estrugo, José, 70–71
États des Ottomans au Méxique (Schemonti), 24–26
Evian Conference, 227
Excelsior, 127–30, 134–35
extraterritoriality, 37, 219–20

Fais, Rafael, 163
Farias, Roberto, 163
Farji, Alberto, 199–200
fascism, 192
Federation of Russian Jews, 115
Fehmi, Hasan, 154
Fermaglich, Kirsten, 250n4
Fisher, Edgar J., 104
food, 3
Ford, Henry, 200
Forge Your Own Passport (Fresco), 2
France: connections to Mexico and, 208–12; Jews and the military, 69–71; migration to, 36–38; Nazi occupation of Paris and, 223–25; Sephardi presence in, 38, 211; travel restrictions for Turkish subjects and, 90–91; Treaty of Lausanne and, 148
Francophilia, 9, 15, 40–41, 45–46, 69–70, 131, 133–34, 208–9
Fresco, David, 1, 155, 187, 216. See also *El Tiempo*
Fresco, Mauricio: birth certificate request and, 215–16; Chinese migrants in Mexico and, 218–19; cultivating nativeness and, 233; diplomatic examination and, 233–34; exploitation of humanity and, 231–32, 246; family of, 236; importance of his false documentation and, 232–33; Jewishness and, 224–25; Mexico's importance and, 223–24; multilingualism and, 222–23; Nazi occupation of Paris and, 223–25; racial passing and, 234–35; recounting of his life and, 1–2, 231; Sephardi networks and, 217, 220–22, 227, 235–36; *Un Mundo Curioso*, 234
Fresco, Philon, 158
Freymann, Enrique, 225, 234
Fua brothers, 220–21

Gabai, Clement, 42
Galanté, Abraham, 1, 29, 231
Galatasaray Lycée, 103
gender, 7, 195
Gerassy, Gaston, 229
Gerassy, Michel, 229
Germany, 77, 81
Gojman, Alicia, 197–98
González, María Luisa, 174
Granat, Jacobo, 75
Grayeb brothers, 202–3
Great Powers, 99, 105, 110, 142
Greece, 68, 104, 111–12, 120–21, 144–45
Guéron, Angèle, 61

Habif, Marcos E., 47–48
Haggadah dela Gerra Djeneral (Karmona), 107
Haggadah dela Gerra por Dia de Pesah (Shem-Tov 'Eli), 107
Hahambaşı, 77
Hakki, İbrahim, 49
Halfon, Joseph, 78
Halfon, Sara. *See* Lahana, Sara Halfon Fiss de
Halk, 154
Hamui, Liz, 14
Habsburgs, 27

Hellenic High Commissaire, 112
Helú, José, 81
Herrerías, Lucrecia, 174
Hirsch, Baron de, 40
homosexuality, 47, 259n127
Huerta, Victoriano, 72
hypermobility. *See* mobility/hypermobility

immigrants: ability to transform and, 23–24; Americanizing of names and, 23; desirability of, 22–24; race and, 9; terminology and, 5. *See also* migrants
immigration restrictions: Canada and, 239; flouting of, 16, 54, 272n154; Mexico and, 16, 41, 88, 171–72, 176, 178–79, 196–97, 206–7, 212–13, 245; United States and, 34–35, 42, 124, 126–27, 140, 153, 161, 163
improvisation, 24
Istanbul, 69, 102, 104, 114, 118, 145, 157. *See also* Constantinople
Izmir, 111–12, 120–21

Jassan, Jack, 175
Jewish cemeteries: Greek soldiers destroying of, 111; importance of, 75–76; Karataş and, 106, 116, 119; Monte Sinaí, 40, 75–76, 95, 136, 138
Jewish Chronicles, 158
Jewish Colonization Association (JCA), 36
Jewish communities: boycotts of German businesses and, 227; commitment to Mexico and, 95; distinctness of, 13–14; migration and, 11; Sephardi Jews and, 52; Syrian Jews and, 51
Jewishness, 9, 13, 224–25, 235–36, 245
Jewish Relief Society of Mexico, 45
Jews: access to travel documentation and, 126; anti-Semitism and, 141, 186–87, 227; appeals to foreign powers and, 119–20; castigation of, 43; confiscation of Jewish property and, 142; in the French army, 69–71; Greek forces treatment of, 111; interethnic cooperation and, 75–76; marriage to Mexican citizens and, 174; migration to Mexico and, 170–71; military conscription and, 63–68; minority rights in Turkey and, 156–57; Nazi occupation of Paris and, 225–26; patriotism and, 57, 71, 95, 151–52, 157, 159; positivism and, 41; prominence of Italian Jews and, 123; as refugees and, 11, 59, 62, 69, 93–94, 104, 112–21, 227–30; Syrian, 47, 51; Turkish citizenship and, 146–47; Turkish language and, 184–85; Turkish nationality and, 150; WWI and, 62. *See also* Ottoman Empire; religious minorities; Sephardi Jews
Johnson-Reed Act, 124, 153, 161
Joint Distribution Committee (JDC), 113–18, 120, 123

Kapitulo, Gabriel, 34
Karmona, Elia, 29, 107–8
Kemal, Mustafa, 21, 102, 104, 109–10
King, Max, 201
Kohen, Albert, 231
Kohen, Merkado, 189
Kohen, Nelli, 189
Kuehnert, Lore Diana, 176
Kuridistan, 104

La Amerika: connecting the Sephardi diaspora and, 124; Jewish associations in Mexico and, 75–76; Mexico and, 126; migration and, 34–35, 61; Russian Jewish refugees and, 115
La Boz de Oriente, 186–87
La Boz de Türkiye, 231
La Cristiada, 180
La Cucaracha (song), 3
Ladino (language). *See* language

Ladino publications: bureaucracy and, 29; defense of Jews' multiple loyalties and, 95–96; draft dodging and, 68; immigration and, 31–32, 124; importance of, 30; Mexican Revolution and, 72; Mexico and, 31, 33, 126; migration and, 2–3, 33–34; networks and, 13; reach of, 35; regulation of Ottoman subjects abroad and, 77; reporting on bad actors and, 7; Russian Jewish refugees and, 115; Zionism and, 109. See also *El Tiempo*

La Epoka, 31–32

La Fraternidad, 165, 171, 221

La Haggadah de Ben Ghiat (Ben Ghiat), 107

Lahana, Isaac, 173

Lahana, Sara Halfon Fiss de, 138–40, 151

Lahana, Simon, 78, 138–40, 212

La Liga Nacional Pro-Raza, 176

La Luz, 159–60

Landau, Jacob, 202

language: AIU and, 36; Ladino publications and, 35; multilingualism and, 240; Ottoman Empire and, 26, 52, 59; Sephardi Jews and, 9, 160–61, 164, 217, 222–23; similarities between Ladino and Spanish and, 3, 231; Turkey and, 184–85, 187

La Novia Aguna (The Grasswidow Bride), 29

La Opinión, 73

La Raza Cósmica, 152

La République, 158, 187

Las Damas de Buena Voluntad, 171

La Vara, 163, 167–68

Law of Military Obligation (1914), 64

League of Nations, 115

Lebanese Chamber of Commerce, 193–94

Lehmann, Matthias, 5–6

Letayf, Antonio, 44

Levi, Elvira, 142, 159

Levi, Margot, 141–42

Levi, Rafael, 141–42

Levy, Abraham, 100, 137

Levy, Fanny, 98, 100, 137

Levy, Sáloman, 52–55, 87–88, 169, 175, 208

Levy, Sara, 74–75, 85

Ley de Migración (1909), 41

Liga de Defensa Nacional, 198

Liga Defensa de Propietarios de Zapaterías, 199

Liga Pro Cultura Alemana, 224

Madero, Francisco I., 71–72, 75

Manela, Erez, 108

marijuana, 3

Maronite Christians, 14–15

marriage: Aleppan Jews and, 14; migrants marrying locals and, 44, 174–75, 178, 218, 224; migration and, 7; transnational family ties and, 166–67; Treaty of Lausanne and, 147; Turkish legal system and, 156; validity of, 79, 138–40

masculinity, 129–30

mass consumption market, 44. See also peddling

Matalon, Esther, 39

Maya, Alberto, 173

Mazal, Harry, 86

Mazal, Ruben, 173

Mechulam, Roberto, 83

Megali Idea (Big Idea), 104

Mehmed VI, 108

Mendeli Yiddish theater group, 116

Meshullam, Joseph, 106

Mexican constitution: anti-church provisions and, 180; Article 33 of, 72, 94; citizenship laws and, 72; constitution of 1857, 72; constitution of 1917, 72, 94, 181

Mexican Jewish Colonization Association, 127
Mexican secretariat of foreign relations (SRE), 17, 49–50, 97, 178–79, 182–83, 203, 215
Mexico: anti-Chinese boycott and, 218–19; anti-foreigner rhetoric in, 72–75, 81, 94, 176–77, 192, 196–205, 212–13, 243, 256n95; anti-Jewish attitudes and, 227, 230; centenary of independence and, 50–51; Circular 250 and, 204–5, 212–13; clothing imports and, 135–36; commerce with Turkey and, 151; as a desired destination for Sephardi Jews, 159–62, 165; diplomatic relations with Turkey and, 182–83; encouragement of immigration and, 162, 176; exploitation of Mexican workers and, 202–3; expulsion from, 169–70, 175, 192–95, 202–4; falsified travel documents and, 172; Francophilia and, 15, 40–41, 45–46, 131, 133–34, 208–9; immigrant entrepreneurs and, 43–44; immigrants and, 22; immigration restrictions and, 16, 41, 88, 171–72, 176, 178–79, 190–91, 196–97, 206–7, 212–13, 245; import of contraband and, 180–81; Jewish colonization and, 40, 171; Ladino publications and, 31, 33, 126; *Maximato* period and, 203–4; Mexican identity and, 223–24; Mexican Revolution and, 3, 71–72; migrants and the legal system of, 47, 138–40; migration to, 38–39, 42, 52, 125, 151–52; migration to as a waypoint to the US, 162–64; monitoring of foreign nationals and, 206; naturalization and, 43, 127–30, 172, 174, 178, 197, 216, 220, 226; Ottoman diplomatic relations and, 25, 48–50, 150, 178; Ottoman expatriates in, 25, 48; *Pax Porfiriana* and, 24; peddling and, 44, 132; pernicious foreigners and, 168–70, 180–81, 192–95, 200, 203–4; pogroms in, 199; public order and, 131–32; refugees and, 227–30; repatriation of immigrants and, 194–95; smuggling and, 133, 196, 204; Treaty of Lausanne and, 147–53; whitening of its population and, 52, 175, 256n95. *See also* Mexican constitution

Meyuhas, Shelomo, 125–26
migrants: Chinese, 172, 174, 176, 198–200, 218; coercive networks and, 7, 47–48; economic, 227; family reunification and, 207–8; peddling and, 44; as a permanent status, 8; postwar chaos and, 99–102; race and, 152; states and, 246; terminology and, 5; Ukrainian Jewish, 116. *See also* immigrants
migration: Age of Migration and, 10–11; chain, 30; community and, 11; forced, 37, 144–45; to France, 36; Ladino publications and, 31–35; opportunity and, 2; Ottoman Empire's restrictions on, 28; technology and, 2; terminology and, 5; WWI and, 4, 56
millet, 54, 77
Milliyet, 158
Mina, Manuel, 203
Misrachi, Alberto, 134, 222
Misrachi, Amelia, 222
Mitrani, Rebecca, 16, 205–6, 214
Mizrahi, Jack, 175
mobility/hypermobility, 2, 4–6, 12–14, 181, 236, 242, 244
Modiano, Manuel, 210
Montekio, Daniel, 165
Monte Sinaí Jewish cemetery, 40
Morin, Edgar, 37
Muhtars, 54

Munir, Mehmet, 190–91
music, 3
Muslims, 26, 58–59

Naar, Devin, 236
Nabon, Albert, 111
Nahum, Haim, 56–58, 66, 77–78, 109, 122–23, 240
Nail, Thomas, 5, 7
Nathan, Ovadia, 239–42
National Chamber of Commerce, 194
nationalism, 57–58, 65, 109, 176, 261n9
nationalities: and citizenship, 146; establishment of classifications and, 4, 141, 143; Italo-Turkish War and, 37; Russo-Turkish War of 1877-1878 and, 37; Sephardi migrants and, 166, 217; states preferences and, 2; Treaty of Lausanne and, 148
nation-building, 4–6, 8, 17, 20, 153
naturalization: Assael, Mauricio and, 89–93; Fresco, Mauricio and, 216; Mexico and, 127, 172, 197, 226; Ottoman subjects and, 28–29; United States and, 139, 240; Yermia Valanci, Gabriel and, 100
Nazis, 223–26, 228, 231
Near East Relief Fund, 113
networks: Jewish communities and, 13–14; Ladino publications and, 13; mobility and, 6–7; patronage, 167, 192, 194, 196, 217, 220–22, 235–36. *See also* transnational networks
New York Times, 104, 140, 169
Nur, Rıza, 145, 159
Nyssen, Alejandro, 174
Nyssen, David, 175

Obregón, Álvaro, 127, 129, 169, 176
Odabachian family, 208
Or-Ahayim Jewish National Hospital, 62
Oriental Jewish Federation of America, 84

Ottoman Empire: Balkan Wars and, 56–64, 66–67, 93–94; certificates of travel and, 69; changing demographics of, 58; diplomatic mission in Mexico and, 25, 48–50, 150, 178; dissolution of, 15–16; emigration of its subjects and, 26–29, 68–69; equality and religious minorities in, 26; exit permits and, 54; financial opportunities in, 29–30; Jews and war efforts and, 57–60, 63–68, 93–96; nationalism and, 57–59, 65; Ottomanism and, 25–26; passports and, 27–28; regulation of subjects abroad and, 76–77, 81, 84–85; religious minorities and, 51–53, 58–59, 63–64, 94; Tanzimat reforms of 1839 and, 26–27; Treaty of Mudros and, 102–3, 110; Treaty of Sèvres and, 103–4, 111; Turco-Italian War and, 37, 53, 55, 67; universal military conscription and, 63–65; wars and, 55, 58–61; WWI and, 64–65, 102–3; Young Turk Revolution and, 24–26, 49, 51, 53. *See also* Anatolia; Ladino publications; Republic of Turkey; Sephardi Jews; Thrace

Palacci, Dionisia, 85
Palacci, Miguel, 85–86, 220
Palestine, 148
Papo, José, 226
Paris. *See* France
Paris Peace Conference, 99, 103, 142–43
Pasha, Enver, 108
Pasha, Talaat, 108
passports: falsification of, 231–32, 244–45; French, 125–26; Nazis and, 231; sharing of, 36; states use of, 2, 27–28; WWI and, 4, 69; Yermia Valanci, Gabriel and, 97–98
Pastor, Camila, 9
Pax Porfiriana, 24

peddling, 44, 132, 175, 243–44
Penhas, Jack, 201–2
perniciousness, 72–73, 94, 168–70, 192, 195, 200–201, 243
Pesqueria, Fernando, 183
Pessah, Victor, 203–4
philanthropy, 113–18, 120, 122–23, 127–30
Plan of Guadalupe (1913), 72, 90, 92
polygamy, 34–35
positivism, 25, 41, 50
prisoners of war, 66
protégé status, 37, 60, 117, 119–20, 220, 236

race: establishment of classifications and, 4; immigration restrictions and, 124, 212–13; Jewish immigrants to the US and, 270n137; migrants and, 9, 152; migration to Mexico and, 41, 175; perniciousness and, 195; racial determinism and, 41; racial passing and, 232–33, 235; racial refugees and, 227–28; scientific racism and, 232; states preferences and, 2; Treaty of Lausanne and, 147–48
racial passing. *See* Fresco, Mauricio; race
Rechid, Mustapha, 48
refugees, 11, 58–62, 69, 104, 112–21, 213, 217, 221, 227–30, 233
Reill, Dominique, 99
Reinah, Marcos, 76, 165, 168–71, 175
religion, 4, 14–15, 180, 213
religious minorities: denaturalization of, 188–89; economic dominance of, 59; minority protection and, 142–46, 156, 177; Ottoman Empire and, 26, 51–53, 58–59, 63–64, 94
remittances, 29, 44, 196
Republic of Turkey: castigation of Jews and, 43, 153–55, 157–58; citizenship and nationality in, 146, 155, 172–73, 177, 182, 187, 191; commerce with Mexico and, 151; confiscation of minority owned property and, 142, 154; cost of living and, 112–13; denaturalization and, 121, 187–92, 226; diplomatic relations with Mexico, 183–84; formation of, 102–5; hostilities with Greece and, 111–12, 120–21; Jewish minority rights and, 156–59, 177; minority emigration and, 145–46, 153–55; nationalism and, 109–10; nationality of former Ottoman subjects and, 147–53; protecting Turkishness and, 186–87; relocation of Greek Orthodox residents and, 144–46; Turkification and, 59, 146, 153–55, 158–59, 181–82, 184–87, 213. *See also* Ottoman Empire
Revah, Josef, 186
Rieur, Jacques, 113
Rihani, Ameen, 81
Rivas Puigcever, Francisco, 38
Rıza, Ahmed, 25
Robson, Laura, 144
Rockefeller Foundation, 115
Rodrigue, Aron, 13
Rodríguez, Abelardo, 190, 200, 202
Roffe, Israel, 83
Roffe, Nissim, 86–87
Rozanes, Nissim, 38, 71
Russian Empire, 26–27
Russo, Judith, 63
Russo, Nissim, 109
Russo-Turkish War of 1877-1878, 37

Sacal, Theofilo, 75
Salem, Abraham, 194–95
Salem, Albert, 42
Salmen, Kasem, 133
Saltiel, Peppo, 206
Salvo, A.B., 85
Sánchez, Juan, 91
San Francisco Chronicle, 240

Saul, David, 173
Schemonti, Joseph A., 24–26, 48, 51
Schmill, Miguel Vidal, 75
Secretaría de Relaciones Exteriores (secretariat of foreign relations). *See* Mexican secretariat of foreign relations (SRE)
self-fashioning, 24, 40
Sephardi Jews: assimilation and, 124–25, 185, 227; belonging and, 8–10, 134–35; changing identities and, 86–89, 95–96, 232–33; commonalities with Mexicans and, 160–61; conflicting loyalties and, 55, 69–71, 95–96; deaths and foreign legal systems, 78–79; as a distinct community, 13–15, 47, 52; economic status in Mexico and, 175–77; effect of Ottoman wars on, 60–62, 67, 93–94, 123–24; the Enemy Trading List and, 83–86; entrepreneurial success and, 43–44; familial networks and, 30; family disapprobation and, 47–48; formation of support organizations in Mexico and, 200–202; French passports and, 125–26; historical records and, 17; *Megali Idea* and, 104; Mexican Revolution and, 71–75; Mexico as a desired destination, 159–62, 165; migration and opportunity and, 2; migration to France and, 37–38; migration to Mexico and, 38–39, 42, 52, 125, 145, 152–53, 170–71; migration to Mexico as a waypoint to the US, 162–64; mobility and, 5–6, 236; Nahum, Haim and, 77–78; naturalization as Americans and, 166; naturalization as Mexicans and, 43, 172–74, 178; obstacles to mobility and, 181–82, 205–7, 209–13; patronage networks and, 167, 192, 194, 196, 217, 220–22, 235–36; performing French identity and, 208–12;

perniciousness and, 168–70, 201; policing structures and, 167–68; as prisoners of war, 66; smuggling and, 193; tensions with Ashkenazi Jews and, 117–18; transnational networks and, 23, 40, 167, 216, 243–44; United States treatment of, 70–71, 164. *See also* immigrants; Jews; migrants; Ottoman Empire
Sevy, Elias, 206
Shanghai, The Paradise of Adventurers (Fresco), 219–20
Shem-Tov 'Eli, Nissim, 107–8
smuggling, 133, 192–93
Sobrado (Sovrado), Roberto, 220–21, 226–27
Sociedad de Beneficencia Alianza Monte Sinaí, 75–76, 89, 125
Société de Bienfaisance Israélite de Marseilles, 68
Soriano, Henri, 158
Spanish (language). *See* language
Spanish and Portuguese Sisterhood, 165
Spanish Civil War, 229–30
SRE. *See* Mexican secretariat of foreign relations (SRE)
states, 2, 4, 43, 50–51, 242–44, 246. *See also* nation-building
Stein, Sarah Abrevaya, 119
Syria-Mount Lebanon League of Liberation, 81
Syrians, 87
Syrio-Lebanese Christian Ottomans, 51

Tacher, David, 163
Taranto, Isaac, 109
Taranto, Jacques, 36
Tekinalp, Munis, 185, 187
Tello, Manuel, 218, 221
Tenorio-Trillo, Maurico, 98
Thrace, 30, 60–62, 67–69, 103, 112, 126, 145, 206. *See also* Ottoman Empire
Tottu, Scarlatt, 139, 150–51, 163, 172
Trakya Olayları, 187

transnational networks: the Enemy Trading List and, 83, 86; familial ties and, 166–67, 207; financial, 46, 171; Fresco, Mauricio and, 216–17, 220–22; Mexican anti-foreigner sentiment and, 73, 209–12; nation-building projects and, 5; Nazis persecution of Jews and, 227; Sephardi migrants and, 23, 243–44. *See also* networks

Treaty of Lausanne, 141–53, 156, 158–59, 177

Treaty of Mudros, 102–3, 110

Treaty of Sèvres, 103–5, 111

turcos, 9–10, 73, 132–33, 150, 170, 195

turkino, 34, 135–36

Turkish Grand National Assembly, 104

Turkish Hearths Organization *(Türk Ocakları)*, 59

Türk Yurdu. See Committee of Union and Progress (CUP)

Unión de Industriales y Comerciantes de La Amerika Cuidad de León, 199

Unión Israelita Chevet Ahim, 163

Unión Nacionalista Mexicana Pro-Raza y Salud Pública, 198

Unión Revolucionaria de Mexicanos Naturalizados, 197

United States: immigration restrictions and, 34–35, 42, 124, 126–27, 140, 153, 161, 163; marginalization of Sephardi migrants and, 164; migration to, 32; military personnel in Constantinople and, 106; Ottoman subjects and military service and, 81–82; representation of Ottoman subjects abroad and, 77, 81, 84–85; treatment of Sephardi Jews and, 70–71

Un Mundo Curioso (Fresco), 234

Vasconcelos, José, 152

Villa, Pancho, 72–74, 84

visas, 2, 4, 27, 227, 229

Vittel internment camp, 228

Weinberg, Max, 209

Weis, Robert, 44

Wilson, Woodrow, 72

women: denaturalization and, 189; exploitation of, 132, 175, 195–96, 203; as laborers and businesswomen, 10, 249n30; marriage and, 7, 218; *Maximato* period and, 203; Ottoman wars and, 78; patriotism among Turkish, 56–57; philanthropy and, 127–31; Sephardi-Mexican relations and, 174–75

World War I: Cloak List and, 83, 85; displacement of Jews and, 62; Enemy Trading List and, 83, 86; loyalties of Ottoman subjects and, 80–83; migration and, 56, 69; national self-determination and, 99, 108; Ottoman Empire and, 55, 58, 64–65; the passport age and, 4; press censorship and, 105; religious minorities and, 64

xenophobia, 172, 203

Yaffe, Jacobo, 211–12

Yermia Valanci, Gabriel, 97–102, 137

Yo He Estado en Paris con los Alemanes (Fresco), 223–24

Young, Elliott, 242–43

Young Men's Hebrew Association social club, 75

Zahra, Tara, 141, 143

Zapata, Emiliano, 71–72, 74

Zapatistas, 73, 84

Zielonka, Martin, 40, 163

Zionism, 94, 109–10

Stanford Studies in Jewish History and Culture
David Biale and Sarah Abrevaya Stein, Editors

This series features novel approaches to examining the Jewish past in the form of innovative work that brings the field into productive dialogue with the newest scholarly concepts and methods. Open to a range of disiplinary and interdisciplinary approaches from history to cultural studies, this series publishes exceptional scholarship balanced by an accessible tone, illustrating histories of difference and addressing issues of current urgency. Books in this list push the boundaries of Jewish Studies and speak compellingly to a wide audience of scholars and students.

For a complete listing of titles in this series, visit the Stanford University Press website, www.sup.org.

Clémence Boulouque, *Another Modernity: Elia Benamozegh's Jewish Universalism*
2020

Dalia Kandiyoti, *The Converso's Return: Conversion and Sephardi History in Contemporary Literature and Culture*
2020

Marc Volovici, *German as a Jewish Problem: The Language Politics of Jewish Nationalism*
2020

Dina Danon, *The Jews of Ottoman Izmir: A Modern History*
2019

Omri Asscher, *Reading Israel, Reading America: The Politics of Translation Between Jews*
2019

The authorized representative in the EU for product safety and compliance is:
Mare Nostrum Group
B.V Doelen 72
4831 GR Breda
The Netherlands

www.ingramcontent.com/pod-product-compliance
Lightning Source LLC
Chambersburg PA
CBHW031753220426
43662CB00007B/391